INDIGENOUS CELEBRITY

INDIGENOUS CELEBRITY
ENTANGLEMENTS WITH FAME

Edited by Jennifer Adese and Robert Alexander Innes

UNIVERSITY OF MANITOBA PRESS

Indigenous Celebrity: Entanglements with Fame

25 24 23 22 21 1 2 3 4 5

University of Manitoba Press
Winnipeg, Manitoba, Canada
Treaty 1 Territory
uofmpress.ca

Cataloguing data available from Library and Archives Canada
ISBN 978-0-88755-906-8 (PAPER)
ISBN 978-0-88755-922-8 (PDF)
ISBN 978-0-88755-921-1 (EPUB)
ISBN 978-0-88755-923-5 (BOUND)

Cover image by Steven Paul Judd, *Two Loves* (2015)
Cover Design by David Drummond
Interior design by Jess Koroscil

Printed in Canada

This book has been published with the help of a grant from the Federation for the Humanities and Social Sciences, through the Awards to Scholarly Publications Program, using funds provided by the Social Sciences and Humanities Research Council of Canada.

The University of Manitoba Press acknowledges the financial support for its publication program provided by the Government of Canada through the Canada Book Fund, the Canada Council for the Arts, the Manitoba Department of Sport, Culture, and Heritage, the Manitoba Arts Council, and the Manitoba Book Publishing Tax Credit.

Funded by the Government of Canada | Canada

CONTENTS

INTRODUCTION

Indigeneity, Celebrity, and Fame: Accounting for Colonialism

Jennifer Adese and Robert Alexander Innes

In late 2016, Canadian literary celebrity Joseph Boyden came under intense scrutiny regarding his identity claims by both Indigenous and mainstream news media; in some cases, journalists seemed to think that his status as part of the broader Canadian literary scene meant that Boyden was immune to critical questioning. A number of journalists derided questions raised about his identity claims, suggesting that they were little more than petty attacks.[1] Indigenous news outlet Aboriginal Peoples Television Network, on the other hand, and journalist Jorge Barrera in particular, published investigative pieces digging into Boyden's identity claims. They also examined accusations of plagiarism launched against Boyden in the wake of his being "opened up" to critical public scrutiny.[2] It became clear, at the outset, that a number of individuals had begun to take note of the shifting character of Boyden's claims and of the disturbing similarity between his work and that of the late Anishinaabe author Ron Geyshick. Yet many people hesitated to raise their concerns publicly. Why did it seem to some that Boyden was off-limits? Why did some hesitate to consider—or avoid discussing altogether—the accusations made against him? *Something* undergirded this reluctance and at the same time stoked fierce counter critiques intended to preserve Boyden and his legacy.

It is this something that the authors of this volume are interested in. In the context of this volume, that something is *celebrity* and the power, influence, and recognition that come with being construed as an "Indigenous celebrity." Boyden's status as an Indigenous-identified and -identifying literary celebrity, and the social, cultural, economic, and other forms of capitalism that came with his Indigeneity and celebrity status, cast a dark shadow over those concerned about what they framed as inconsistencies in his public narrativization of his Indigenous identity. To many, Boyden was "too big to fail" in that as the darling of the Canadian literary scene—and *the* voice on Indigenous issues in media in the early part of the 2010s—he was above reproach. At a key juncture in the history of Canada, that of intensive global attention to the legacies of its residential school system, Boyden emerged as a kind of "great hope"—a self-identifying Métis person in the ways that John Ralston Saul likens as a go-between of Indigenous and Canadian—that reached out and promised a bridge between two seemingly disparate worlds.[3] Eric Andrew-Gee writes that, "in an age of reconciliation, this mixed background was an asset: Boyden came to be seen as a 'shining bridge,' as one Indigenous scholar called him, able to mediate between white and Indigenous, at a time when the task seemed more urgent than ever."[4] Boyden's purported mixedness was a healing salve for the gaping wounds ripped open by Canada's long overdue reckoning with its devastatingly violent residential school system.

As Toni Bruce and Christopher Hallinan write in their book chapter on Aboriginal Australian runner Cathy Freeman, who won a gold medal in track and field for her victory in the 400-metre race at the 2000 Sydney Olympic Games, when unable to avoid confronting their horrific treatment of Indigenous people, settler colonial nations such as Australia tend to seek out symbols of national reconciliation.[5] Much like how Canadian literary circles, the media, and the government positioned Boyden as a beacon of reconciliation, Freeman's athletic accomplishments and indeed her very visage were upheld to demonstrate "powerfully and visually . . . the joining of two key parts of Australia's psyche: the first inhabitants and the white settlers/invaders."[6] Even after the 1994 Commonwealth Games, as Freeman began to speak more publicly about the discrimination that she had faced, white Australians constructed her as a symbol of national reconciliation: first, when she was selected to light the Olympic flame at the opening ceremony of the 2000 Summer Olympic Games in Sydney; second, following her win in the

400-metre race, when during her victory lap she "carried both the Australian and [the] Aboriginal flags—a true symbol of reconciliation and pride of her Aboriginal cultural heritage."[7]

Although Freeman was depicted in the media as reluctant to use her new-found celebrity to speak on "political causes," she nevertheless soundly critiqued Australian Prime Minister John Howard's refusal to issue a formal apology to Aboriginal people, in particular the stolen generations apprehended from their families under government policy.[8] In the case of Freeman, however, the intense public attention that accompanied her impressive win, and actively perpetuated the image of her as an icon of reconciliation, led her to gradually withdraw from the spotlight.[9] Whereas she appeared to reject attempts to make her into an Indigenous "reconciliation celebrity," Boyden, in contrast, leaned into the attention that his literary celebrity garnered, undertaking speaking engagements, appearing on panels and in/on the news, and writing op-eds, all on the subject of reconciliation. His words repeatedly reinforced the promise that, despite the horrific violence that Canada had perpetrated on Indigenous children, the country might yet arrive at a place of unity with Indigenous people: "We are at that crossroads in our country, the one where we face the decision of whether we strive for true reconciliation or whether we remain a country in denial. There is no more room for the politics of divisiveness. Now is the time where we must all come together as a nation not to just accept but begin to reconcile with what is our darkest stain."[10] So, again, whereas Freeman was placed in the role of reconciliation celebrity and took steps to remove herself from it, Boyden actively worked to take on such a role in the public consciousness, without any evidence, unlike Freeman, that he had actually experienced any racism or other oppression as a result of his supposed Indigeneity.

In spite of this lack of demonstrable lived experience, Boyden became what Elizabeth DiEmanuele calls a "Post-TRC Indigenous celebrity," defined as "a figure in constant negotiation between 'legitimizing' their position for the public, demonstrating their political utility, and modeling what a nation-to-nation relationship could look like. The Indigenous celebrity-diplomat is Canada's educator who resists oppression but who also compromises to make space for an Indigenous future in a settler-landscape that has done everything to suppress it."[11] For some, Boyden's name became synonymous with reconciliation, but it was this very thing—his willingness and comfort in speaking and advocating on behalf of Indigenous people writ large—that also came to open Boyden up to critique, ultimately leading to his retreat from the public eye. Keen observers began to notice that, across his interventions in conversations on reconciliation, he inconsistently narrated his identity as an Indigenous person and his connections to Indigenous communities. At times, he invoked Indigeneity broadly, while at other times he referred to specific nodes of Indigenous national identity: Métis, Mi'kmaq, Ojibway, and Nipmuc, what Barrera termed a "shape-shifting" identity.[12] According to writer Rebeka Tabobondung of Wasauksing First Nation, when she asked Boyden which Indigenous nation he was from, he told her "Wasauksing First Nation"—yet no one in the community could confirm that he was, in fact, from there.[13] To be sure, media outlets initially (and generally) focused far more on his identity claims than they did on the accusations of plagiarism that Boyden faced. In the ways that celebrity scandals function—even on the seemingly small scale of Canadian literary celebrity and of Indigenous celebrity—the details of his private life and questions about his character were far more titillating to the public than the work that he had (or had not) done. Although many Indigenous people took to social media to decry his shifting identity claims and to question whether Boyden was exploiting those claims, many of his celebrity friends spoke out on his behalf, and the tide was relatively slow to turn toward questioning him, his claims, and by extension his integrity. When it did turn, however, it was profound, and in spite of a number of attempts by Boyden to address critiques, he began to shrink from public life.[14]

Some of this retreat from public life is framed as voluntary. In an interview with Candy Palmater of CBC Radio, Boyden states that "I've become too much of a go-to guy. I should be allowing those with deeper roots in their communities to speak for their communities. . . . Others need to speak and I do apologize for taking too much of the airtime. . . . It's time to jump off that train and pull back a bit."[15] Here Boyden also acknowledges the enticing lure of celebrity, noting that his "ego has gotten a little too big."[16] He has since largely disappeared from the media landscape, and what has remained in the wake of this incident are complex questions about the nature of Indigenous relations to the notions of celebrity and fame. What also remains is that it matters greatly whether those positioned as Indigenous celebrities, marked for public consumption by all audiences, *are* in fact Indigenous and whether they are *recognized* by other Indigenous people *as* Indigenous people.

Conversations on Boyden intensified with the revelation that neither he nor the late great-uncle—"Injun Joe"—whom he used as a touchpoint for authenticity was an Indigenous person. This led us, as the editors of this volume, to question the manner and mode in which we elevate Indigenous people—or, in this case, those who claim to be Indigenous but carry with them often murky backstories about their connections to Indigenous communities. This raises a number of questions. What are the implications of Indigenous involvement with celebrity culture? How have Indigenous people become taken up and, at times, consumed by celebrity? What is the role of the non-Indigenous public in the celebrification of Indigenous people (or those who are effectively marketed and who market themselves as bona fide Indigenous people)?[17] What are the responsibilities of Indigenous celebrities to the communities that they come from and purport to represent? Are there innately Indigenous conceptualizations of celebrity, and if so how do Indigenous understandings of "well knownness," fame, and/or celebrity differ from mainstream and/or "whitespread" conceptualizations of celebrity? Finally, how have racism, colonization, and the global circulation of discourses of celebrity affected Indigenous people and communities the world over? The chapters in this volume explore these questions and the complexities of Indigenous people's relationships with celebrity and fame in past, present, and ongoing contexts, identifying commonalities, tensions, and possibilities. The multidisciplinary contributions to this volume thus explore the inherent complexities of Indigenous people's relationships with celebrity and fame on a global scale.

Celebrity Studies: Theories and Approaches

In order to work through some of the tensions, limits, and possibilities wrought by Indigenous people's entanglements with celebrity culture, and to reclaim discourses of well knownness from the at times narrow cast of celebrity, it is worth discussing, at least in brief, some of the central tenets of celebrity studies. Etymologically, the word *celebrity* arises from "the Latin *celebritas* for 'multitude' or 'fame' and *celeber* meaning *'frequented,' 'populous,' or 'famous'*)," and it "originally meant not a person but a condition—as the *Oxford English Dictionary* says, 'the condition of being much talked about.'"[18] As the term expanded, it began to be used to speak to the condition of a person—a particularly well-known person. Over the centuries, various technologies would enable the global reach of certain figures and produce diffuse articulations and expressions of well knownness.

Some of the earliest scholars writing on the subject of celebrity, such as Daniel Boorstin, argued that the "Graphic Revolution" of the nineteenth century as the prime reason that "the slow, the 'natural,' way of becoming well known" was displaced by processes in which fame is actively manufactured.[19] Whereas prior to the Graphic Revolution history and time were the determinants of a person's well knownness, Boorstin argued that "we (the television watchers, the movie goers, radio listeners, and newspaper and magazine readers) and our servants (the television, movie, and radio producers, newspaper and magazine editors, and ad writers) can so quickly and so effectively give a man 'fame.'"[20] With the Graphic Revolution came a shift in which well knownness could be actively sought, performed, and maintained via media networks, and to Boorstin this meant that well knownness as a "hallmark of greatness" came to mean one's ability to get into the news and stay there.[21]

In the decades since the publication of Boorstin's book, the study of celebrity has exploded, with scholars agreeing or disagreeing with and building upon his initial take. Richard Dyer is largely credited with introducing celebrity studies as a discrete field of study in 1977.[22] However, it was through the late 1970s and into the 1980s, with the rise of globalization, that some of the earliest and most sustained attention paid to studying celebrity emerged—and came in the form of studies on celebrity impacts on marketing and advertising. Scholars working in this area turned their attention to studying the possibilities (and problems) of celebrity advertisements for public audiences.[23] Since then, the field has continued to expand, becoming incredibly diffuse, and in recent years much of the research on celebrity has been focused on its social, cultural, and political implications, alongside the impacts of new technological forms on the accumulation of attention capital and new processes of celebrity making.

One of the leading theorists in the field today, Chris Rojek, draws our attention to the ways that mass communication, print, analog, and more recently digital media have enabled the rapid accumulation of what he calls "attention capital," which confers celebrity.[24] For Rojek, how attention capital is garnered in effect allows us to identify three kinds of celebrity formation: ascribed, achieved, and celetoids.[25] Ascribed celebrity is attention capital given to those who, for example, are seen as "hereditary titled individuals," such as members of royal families born into, and with, recognition.[26] Achieved celebrity, in contrast, "derives from recognized talents and accomplishments."[27] The third kind of celebrity that Rojek identifies are celetoids, whom he defines as "individuals who attain intense bursts of fame. The term is an amalgamation of 'celebrity' and 'tabloid.'"[28] For Rojek, the celetoid signals the central role of media in contributing to the accumulation of attention capital, but he also highlights the precarity of celebrity as conferred through media.[29] Celetoids who accumulate attention capital in "intense bursts" might (or might not) continue to flare, but principally they are manufactured, in Graeme Turner's view, to satisfy public demand for more celebrities. Turner writes that "the accelerated commodity life cycle of the celetoid has emerged as an effective industrial solution to the problem of satisfying demand."[30]

By their nature, then, celetoids are disposable forms of celebrity, never intended to occupy public view for very long. In the years since Rojek and Turner first grappled with the emergence of a "new kind" of celebrity (flagging the advent of reality television), other advances in media have continued to open up avenues available to people for the accumulation of celebrity capital. Theresa Senft, drawing on Michael Goldhaber's 2009 work on the existence of an "attention economy," argues that new media move us from being passive consumers to active producers of "attention." Rather than looking at the accumulation of attention capital as a thing, she argues, we should more concretely consider *how* technological shifts have refashioned the manner in which attention capital is accumulated and by whom. As Senft argues, the hyper-intensification of social media produces a landscape wherein *anyone* could (presumably) become a star. The arrival of new technologies has hailed the formation of "micro-celebrity," in which such "stars accumulate capital because they get attention; they accumulate capital because they have managed to *turn themselves from citizens to corporations*, vis-à-vis the proprietary organization of the attention of others."[31] As ever more people cultivate their online personas and attract attention from people whom they know—and those whom they do not—they garner "follows" on blogs and other social media sites. In turn, they emerge as smaller-scale celebrities—micro-celebrities.

Alice Marwick summarizes micro-celebrity, noting that celebrity has "traditionally been viewed as something someone is, based on how well known he or she is; micro-celebrity, by contrast, is something someone does."[32] It therefore speaks to "a state of being famous to a niche group of people, but it is also a behavior: the presentation of oneself as a celebrity regardless of who is paying attention."[33] In the context of micro-celebrity, "there are two ways of achieving internet fame—by consciously arranging the self to achieve recognition, or by being ascribed fame by others due to one's accomplishments."[34] Micro-celebrities therefore owe their existence to their cultivation of public personas that attract "follows," "likes," and "shares." As one iteration of the celetoids whom Rojek discusses, micro-celebrities in the digital landscape emerge across sites not traditionally associated with celebrity making—home-making, interior designing, organization consulting, meme making, travel blogging, et cetera. The advent of digital technologies and social media in particular has provided new avenues for the accumulation of attention capital and led to a refashioning of celebrity. The conversation and public discourse on celebrity has therefore become incredibly diffuse.[35] What remains fairly consistent since Boorstin wrote his book, however, is that scholars generally support the view that celebrity is a manufactured process, that it is contingent on the accumulation of attention capital, and therefore that it is inextricably tied to capitalism itself.

Kerry Ferris writes that, "as celebrity studies establishes itself in the academy, it has begun to develop in both comprehensiveness and complexity, with a variety of sub-areas and different theoretical and methodological approaches."[36] This is undoubtedly true. The field itself is far too expansive for us to discuss at length here. It is also outside our scope for this chapter in that one of the critical arguments that we are advancing here is that, even in current iterations, celebrity studies has been unable to offer a sufficiently and necessarily nuanced understanding of Indigenous people's encounters with celebrity. Although such theories are important for situating the myriad ways that celebrity has been conceptualized, expressed, acquired, achieved, ascribed, and so on, left unaccounted for in the majority of these accounts is how Indigenous people navigate celebrity and the accumulation of attention capital within a landscape of racism and global processes of colonization.

"Mainstream" theorizing on celebrity has suffered from a lack of concerted engagement with questions of race and racism even though processes of celebrity making are inseparable from race and racism. This has led a number of Black scholars to forge new pathways to contemplate the implications of race and racism for Black celebrities.[37] Black celebrity studies has challenged scholars to think of how racism and racialized sexism inform access to, and performances of, celebrity but also to recognize appropriations of Blackness within the industries associated with celebrity and the significant contributions of Black celebrities—their ability "to shape important political and social debates alongside the limitations placed on them through media discourse."[38] This sits in contrast to Boorstin and Rojek, and to some extent Senft, whose work assumes a kind of "neutral subject," eliding the ways that celebrity is constructed through the lenses of racism, colonialism, and racialized sexism. Neither achieved nor ascribed celebrity—or celetoid celebrity—is universal. Achieved celebrity has always been mediated by access: that is, the ability of those racialized as "non-white" to access the means to ascend to celebrity. As Sarah Jackson argues, "black celebrities are subject to incredibly limited conditions for inclusion and acceptance across time."[39] Race and racism are also implicated in ascribed celebrity. For example, royal weddings of the English monarchy are broadcast worldwide, and like the Royals (always capitalized) themselves they are ascribed a particular celebrity status. Meanwhile, "Nigerian princes" are the butts of many pejorative email scam-related jokes. Racism and discourses of civilization and savagery shape socio-historical processes in which such distinctions emerge. Celebrity itself is not a new development and in fact is "simply the extension of a long-standing condition" of elevating certain humans above others on the basis of perceptions of certain characteristics.[40] What we mean by this, then, is that not all heredity is viewed with equal admiration on the global stage; colonialism is the context in which particular forms of European ascribed celebrity have been circulated globally.

Recognition accorded to members of royal families on the basis of heredity is contingent on the embedded belief that particular kinds of human organization are superior to others. This is precisely why Robert Clarke puts forth that celebrity studies must also be attentive to the place of celebrities within "contemporary late capitalist cultures" that have been "profoundly influenced by the histories and legacies of European colonial imperialism."[41] Colonial regimes, he postulates, "benefited from the performance of the stars—the celebrated adventurers, explorers, missionaries, soldiers of fortune, scientists, artists, administrators, writers, and so on—whose lives and achievements served as endorsement for colonial exploits and as comforting cultural metonyms in domestic fantasies of superiority."[42] For Clarke, celebrity, or fame, itself has been an important commodity in the circulation of European colonial markets. Although the tendency of celebrity studies, cultural studies, and media studies has been to treat celebrity as a phenomenon apart from colonialism, Clarke instead crucially argues that celebrity, as fame, has "long been a significant commodity in the cultural and political economies of European colonial regimes."[43] In the contemporary context, "celebrity colonialism" appears to be most recognizable in instances in which celebrities are able to use their fame "in bizarre and disturbing ways to leverage public institutions in purportedly 'vulnerable' nations."[44] Here Clarke points to articles from 2006 in which it was reported that Brad Pitt and Angelina Jolie had effectively banned Namibian media from reporting on the birth of their child Shiloh. Clarke, drawing on the work of Adam Elkus, notes that "Western celebrity culture is implicated in contemporary neo-colonialism in Africa and elsewhere, despite the declarations of individual celebrities to the contrary."[45]

Although Clarke's analysis does not account for the racial dynamics at work between Pitt and Jolie's whiteness and the purported Blackness of Namibians,[46] his intervention is nevertheless vital. Rather than seeing his work as a valuable contribution to recognizing the limits of cultural studies and media studies, prominent scholars working in celebrity studies, such as Turner, have critiqued Clarke's intervention as a sideshow arising from a field of postcolonial literary studies with no meaningful investment "in the analysis of popular culture."[47] Turner argues that, though cultural studies and media studies represent the "heartland of celebrity studies . . . where academics already interested in popular culture and representation have readily applied themselves to the discussion of particular celebrities as texts," literary studies is ill equipped for the task of addressing celebrity in an appropriate manner.[48] Yet it is clear from Black scholars, and the Indigenous scholars in this volume, that cultural studies and media studies have failed to speak meaningfully to Black and Indigenous people's experiences with celebrity. To this end, then, irrespective of its disciplinary location and questions about the suitability of literary studies to speak to celebrity culture, Clarke's intervention stands: we cannot speak of celebrity without accounting for colonialism. The elevation of certain humans and some human characteristics above others within celebrity culture cannot be decoupled from centuries-old discourses of civility and savagery, of white superiority and Black and Indigenous inferiority, that have long established a foundation for deeply striated patterns of celebrity formation.

We must not, however, think of celebrity in a singular sense. Indigenous people have long been drawn into "whitestream" celebrity culture (to borrow from contributors Kim Anderson and Brendan Hokowhitu) and able to use the platform accorded to them to amplify the voices of their communities, to challenge discourses of civilization and savagery, and to resist colonization. Likewise, as Jackson notes with respect to African American celebrities, their "public location and crossover influence . . . allow them unique access to mainstream debates around race and nation and thus a level of agency to influence such debates rarely allowed [to] or achieved by other African Americans."[49] The work of Olivier Driessens resonates here; he argues that "we should not ignore the differences between individualistic and collectivisitic cultures, western and non-western societies, and their implications for the value and ways of achieving celebrity status therein."[50] Driessens advances the argument that it is far more fruitful for those studying celebrity to understand that there might be no such singular thing, that scholars should recognize that there is a patchwork of celebrity cultures (small and large), and that we should be attuned to specific socio-historical and -cultural processes in which they arise and exist. He also highlights a vital point raised by Jackson and the scholars within this volume: celebrity might look entirely different in the context of what he calls "collectivistic cultures," in which Indigenous people and Black people are not only *individual* public voices but also become, are seen as, and are expected to be voices for the *collective* communities from which they come. We will return to this shortly.

Indigenous Interventions: Celebrity Entanglements and Resistance

In recent years, a growing number of scholars have taken up examinations of Indigenous experiences with and conceptualizations of celebrity, attentive to dimensions of racism, colonialism, colonial nationalism, and Indigeneity.[51] Cecilia Morgan offers a historically situated analysis of "travellers through empire," Indigenous people who, she argues, crossed the Atlantic

Ocean to Europe as transatlantic celebrities. In an analysis that resonates with Coll Thrush's *Indigenous London: Native Travelers at the Heart of Empire*, she contends that Indigenous people existed in dual capacities: inside the market for colonial oddities, and outside the celebrity machine, arriving in Europe as agents of their own (Indigenous) selves and of their nations.[52] The drawing up of Indigenous people into early whitestream celebrity circuits was ultimately driven, however, by the desires of non-Indigenous people to view and interact with Indigenous people in ways that affirmed deeply ingrained racial stereotypes of Indigenous people as savages. Whereas Indigenous people were figured as savages, people of European descent, particularly those of Anglo-Saxon background, were imagined as "whites," as bearers of civilization, and as racially superior to inferior "red Indians."

Métis scholar Emma LaRocque writes that this "civ/sav dichotomy" is an "ideological container for the system construction of self-confirming 'evidence' that Natives were savages who 'inevitably' had to yield to the superior powers of civilization as carried forward by Euro-Canadian civilizers."[53] As some of the authors in this book discuss, Indigenous people the world over have thus been constructed through travellers' journals, creative fiction, and other forms of media as animalistic, constitutive of lesser humans, who would inevitably "die out" in the face of a superior civilization.[54] For example, Euro-Canadian tourists in the nineteenth century desired "authentic Indians"; they wished to absorb visually Indians before they disappeared with the purported inevitability of time, modernization, and civilization.[55] This is consistent with Morgan's analysis, wherein she argues that a desire for consuming Indianness ungirded the popularizing of select Indigenous people. An Indigenous person's ability to *achieve* celebrity among non-Indigenous people was largely mediated by one's confirmation of racial stereotypes of Indianness.

Morgan writes in detail of the cases of those she refers to as transatlantic celebrities, such as Gakiiwegwanebi (Peter Jones), Shahwundais (John Sunday), Kahgegagahbowh (George Copway), and Naaniibawikwe (Catherine Sutton). They were catapulted into transatlantic celebrity as a result of their roles as Mississauga people engaged in missionary and religious work amid a growing kind of global humanitarian celebrity culture.[56] The aforementioned Mississauga, Morgan contends, were important examples of the kind of "new" celebrity enabled by mass media. They were not necessarily propped up by wealthy aristocrats, as other Indigenous people in the past had been upon arrival in Europe; rather, she writes, "the medium of the British press, both missionary and secular," introduced them to ever-growing audiences.[57] The missionary movement, Morgan writes, used tactics of celebrity cultivation familiar to other forms of celebrity—such as theatrical celebrity—and engaged in "crafting and manipulation of images and reputations through prints, pamphlets, paintings, and material artifacts; the development of an obsession with bodies; the circulation of details of domestic or private matters which collapsed the distinction between private and public; and, finally, the cultivation of the notion of an achieved, rather than ascribed, celebrity."[58] Although she distinguishes between achieved and ascribed celebrity, she never fully situates her use of the latter.

We can fairly assume that by distinguishing between them Morgan draws from Rojek's work, as outlined above. Flagging such early characterizations of celebrity and fame hinges on the idea that an Indigenous person's well knownness was tied to his or her achievements and, to some extent, exceptionalism rather than an inherited well knownness drawn from his or her position as dominant in social hierarchies. Morgan argues that Peter Jones, in particular, "achieved the status of a religious *and* Indigenous celebrity."[59] In a sense, he *achieved* celebrity by his religious devotion, and in a departure from Rojek's definition he was *ascribed* celebrity by his existence as an Indigenous person and the British fascination with "Indians." In this sense, ascribed celebrity refers to something external to oneself, perhaps something that one does not even have control over; one is "made" by others and does not "earn" her or his celebrity. Taken in this way, then, Morgan's writing implies that Indigenous celebrity was derived from British fascination with Indigenous people as objects subjected to the British gaze. Widespread attention to various Indigenous people was premised on the projections of imperialists of "their own desires and fantasies onto Indigenous subjects."[60]

Morgan recoups space for people such as Jones to be seen by imperialists as "individuals with names and histories" and not just members of an exotic "dying race" through her acknowledgement that Indigenous people were not "helpless victims of colonial history" but used every opportunity available to them to challenge colonial policies that had detrimental impacts on them and other Indigenous people.[61] Here Morgan makes it clear that Indigenous entanglements with celebrity culture in Europe were not exclusively for the (white) "us" but arose from within a meaningful entrenchment in one's own existence as an Indigenous person. When Gakiiwegwanebi (Peter Jones) met with Queen Victoria, he presented her with a petition (opposing Francis Bond Head's plan to remove First Nations from southern Ontario to "Indian Territory" on Manitoulin Island) and a wampum belt, presumably one invoking the queen's obligations under the Treaty of Niagara of 1764. Gakiiwegwanebi thus used the doors opened by religious and Indigenous celebritization (written as such to reflect the process by which Indigenous people were constructed and represented as celebrities and people "of note") to advocate for his people. He thus engaged in celebrity culture not for the benefit of a (white) "us" but in direct opposition to the very tenets of white settler colonialism.

In addition to utilizing access granted by his celebrification, Gakiiwegwanebi rejected core tenets of celebrity culture, of making the private public, as he grew weary of the attention that he garnered when he appeared in traditional Mississauga clothing. He eventually refused "to wear anything other than his black suit, for, when 'clad in the garb of an Englishman,' he attracted 'little or no notice' when not making public appearances."[62] His refusal to put himself on display outside formal appearances, and his rejection of celebrity culture's hyperintensive desire to eliminate the private lives of celebrified people, are notable. Gakiiwegwanebi rejected attempts to market his Indigeneity and refused to sacrifice himself to the rapaciousness of celebrity and fame. Although it is difficult for us to gauge through Morgan's analysis whether his strategic dressing for public appearances played a role in the reception of his messages, it is likely that the fetishistic desire for Indigenous people as "Indian objects" detracted from the important activism that he, and others like him, undertook.

The fetishization of Indigenous "clothing, jewellery, hair, and gesture" under imperialism meant that the adoption of traditional clothing played an important role in facilitating Indigenous access to European publics (and thus the wider circulation of the causes or messages that Indigenous people shared on arrival in Europe), and the refusal to fulfill Euro-Western fantasies of Indigeneity produced a notable tension.[63] It reflected what Michelle Flood argues in "Intersectionality and Celebrity Culture": insofar as celebrity culture has afforded "wide platforms" that have given people "a persuasive potentiality that cannot be ignored," discourses in circulation "simultaneously become disciplining and emancipatory structures for marginalized groups."[64] Likewise, Karen Fox argues in her chapter in this volume, drawing on the work of Anna Haebich, the idea that Indigenous celebrities' embrace of the trappings of modernity (in this case clothing) signalled their assimilation into Euro-Western cultures and values obscures the complex relations at work. Indeed, in the case of Gakiiwegwanebi, like others, he came to insist on wearing "a form of male dress that had come to signify sober, industrious, respectable middle-class masculinity" that allowed him to shield himself from the prying eyes of celebrity culture.[65]

That a line was drawn and recognized between public objectification and "normalcy" of dress reflects a consideration of this tension. Gakiiwegwanebi's niece Naaniibawikwe (Catherine Sutton), as an additional example, condemned calls for her to appear in Mississauga clothing. She elected to wear an English dress for her meeting with the queen. Naaniibawikwe rebuked calls for her to wear "Indian dress," rhetorically postulating, after missionaries tried to "civilize the Indian, and make us like white people: and was I to go back and dress like pagan Indians, and come over here to shew myself?"[66] She faced particular pressure from the band council of her community to dress in accordance with English desires for "Indian costume." When pressed on why she "didn't fetch [her] Indian dress," she recounted that she told her band council that she refused, stating, "I had none, this was my dress; this is the way we dress. I tell them we are not pagan, that we try to be like white people—to be clean and decent, and do what we can to be like the civilized people."[67] Although to some her statements might sound "colonized," that Naaniibawikwe "bought in" to her own people's inferiority, it is also possible that her statements and her adoption of "white people" clothes comprised a profound rejection of the contradictory nature of white desires for Indianness. Although celebrity culture's fetishization of Indianness demanded that Indigenous people dress and therefore perform a particular celebritized ideal of Indianness, people such as Gakiiwegwanebi and Naaniibawikwe troubled and rejected this pressure. This, Morgan argues, is precisely because they travelled not to become celebrities but for distinct religious and political reasons. In particular, in their homelands, they were embroiled in struggles against colonization, gradual attempts to dismantle their collective cultures, concerted pushes by colonial governments to force them into individualistic capitalist regimes, and efforts to transform their lands from collectively held property to privately held property.

This echoes the aforementioned passage from Jackson regarding how access to whitestream celebrity culture enables celebrified African American people to influence public discourse and, with hope and by extension, the lived social and political realities of African American communities. Indigenous people likewise used the platforms offered by whitestream celebrity to attempt to speak back to colonizers, often at the highest registers possible. Since these early encounters, Indigenous people the world over have continued to amplify their voices via whitestream celebrity to address the experiences of their people under colonization and the ongoing struggle against the genocide of their nations. As much as whitestream celebrity culture has done for "global media conglomerates," it also "functions as a site in which meanings of affluence, visibility, accountability, value, talent and inequality are contested and struggled over."[68] This function marks it as particularly important for Indigenous people and other racialized people, generally denied access to decision making within nation-states because of race-based marginalization and oppression. Celebrity, then, is also a site of struggle, a site of contestation, and as Patrick McCurdy writes, we ought to distinguish that there are "celebrity *activist[s]*" and "*celebrity* activists." The former term refers to a person "loosely defined as an individual who gains a prominent or notorious status in new media as a result of his or her activism."[69] The latter term refers to "individuals who use their celebrity status to undertake activism."[70] In their study of Tūhoe Māori activist Tame Iti, Julie Cupples and Kevin Glynn situate Iti as a celebrity *activist* whose half-century of struggle against New Zealand's colonization of his people has propelled him, often in contentious ways, into whitestream media and celebrity culture.[71]

In contrast, as Glenn D'Cruz writes in the context of Adnyamathanha and Narungga footballer Adam Goodes, the attention paid to him allowed him "to contribute to national conversations about race and national identity in the public sphere."[72] Yet both Iti and Goodes—along with Freeman—faced critiques for actions that D'Cruz argues defied dominant culture's attempts to "neuter" them politically.[73] For D'Cruz, the "status of the black celebrity is dependent on both the endorsement of the dominant white culture, and the political neutering of the black celebrity."[74] This is particularly why "reconciliation" celebrities hold so much appeal; they navigate a delicate balance between maintaining the endorsement and support of dominant white culture and couching their political messages. Cupples and Glynn highlight a poignant truth with respect to Iti and non-Indigenous public reception of his activism. It was not until a documentary film was created that presented Iti as a "softer man" that the non-Indigenous public scaled back (somewhat) their vitriolic dislike of him.[75] Also at work here under the surface is what D'Cruz notes with respect to Goodes: endowed qualities of celebrities (heroism and athletic prowess in the context of sport) intersect with discourses of and ideas about masculinity. Discourses of masculinity circulate as well with respect to Iti and as reflected in Anderson and Hokowhitu's chapter in this volume. In contrast, Kahente Horn-Miller contends in her chapter with how celebrity culture is not only racialized with respect to Indigeneity but also deeply sexist. Masculinity and femininity are thus discourses that not only run through contemporary Indigenous encounters with whitestream celebrity but also resonate deeply with the experiences of Mississauga, as discussed earlier. Racialized and gendered assumptions also frame the terrain in which Indigenous people can see whitestream celebrity culture as a site for possibility.

In spite of this seemingly intractable bind, Indigenous people—as the chapters in this volume demonstrate—have myriad strategies for refusing and rejecting co-optation by whitestream celebrity culture. In the cases of Iti, Gakiiwegwanebi, Shahwundais, Kahgegagahbowh, Naaniibawikwe, and others such as kahntinetha Horn, Indigenous people consistently name the violence that they have experienced, never swaying from their commitment to use their platform to speak the truths of their peoples. In the case of Iti, Cupples and Glynn argue, his active refusal to have his *voice* co-opted, even as his *image* often was, helped to "shift public discourse around him."[76] There is a distinction between Iti and the others, however, in that he appears to fit into the framing of celebrity *activist*, whereas the others were well known for other reasons and in turn used the attention given to them to confront the oppression of their peoples. Truthfully, neither of McCurdy's framings seems to fit overly well in the context of Indigenous celebrities or celebrified Indigenous people. Whether they become well known for their activism or well known in a manner that enables them to promote political or social change, it remains that being born Indigenous persons in a world where hierarchies of human society have actively worked toward their destruction is itself a political act.[77] To be Indigenous and live under ongoing oppression is to be political.

At the same time, some have argued that, in addition to walking a political tightrope between "dominant white culture" and responsibilities as Indigenous people to Indigenous communities, celebrified Indigenous people are constrained in their activism. Rosemary Popoola, Matthew Egharevba, and Oluyemi Oyenike Fayomi, writing in the context of celebrity advocacy on women's rights in Nigeria, put forth that "celebrities only have the power to call the attention of the government to social problems confronting women. They do not have the legal and executive power to make meaningful changes. Most of the issues that they fight for have ended up producing administrative and legal decisions that end on the desk[s] of governors and heads of government across the country."[78] There is undoubtedly truth to this in that, inasmuch as celebrity activism can draw *attention* to matters of injustice, it alone cannot guarantee material change.

Beyond all of this, the dialectical tension between non-Indigenous publics and celebrified Indigenous people, there exists another reality. Although this book is intended for everyone to read and think about, the chapters are not concerned only with mapping Indigenous relations to whitestream celebrity and fame; nor are they overly concerned with battling whitestream celebrity culture's long-standing preoccupation with individualism. Lorraine York writes about the cultivation of what she terms "Indigenous publics in Canada," suggesting that Indigenous publics enable "alternative and overlapping celebrity phenomena [that] offer us a means of decentering existing assumptions about the individualistic nature of celebrity (even as individualistic modes of celebrity continue to circulate within those publics). Indeed, Indigenous media publics in Canada hold the potential to reconfigure celebrity as a collectivist achievement."[79] York appears to highlight Indigenous people's relationship with celebrity in order to figure out what it can offer to whitestream celebrity. She juxtaposes Indigenous celebrity with mainstream celebrity, suggesting that the collectivist nature of Indigenous celebrity engagement resists the troubling individualism of other expressions of celebrity.

It appears, then, that some of the academic writing on Indigenous celebrity is geared to making intelligible what the relationship means to an invisibilized white "us." There is no discussion in York's work, for example, of Black/African American celebrity and the way that people (e.g., Colin

Kaepernick, to offer a recent example) effectively use their celebrity status to draw attention to histories of injustice from a position rooted in a commitment to collective social justice.[80] So celebrified Indigenous people are *once again* essentialized—this time for hanging on to a sense of collectivism, of responsibility and reciprocity to community—and cast as agents to guide an (invisibilized white) "us" to decentre the individualism of contemporary celebrity culture. Yet, as the chapters herein demonstrate, though many celebrified Indigenous people draw from the attention capital given to them to narrativize oppression publicly, as Renée Mazinegiizhigoo-kwe Bédard's chapter and many others highlight, Indigenous people have their own conceptualizations of what it means to be well known and recognized within their respective nations, spheres of recognition, and Indigenous languages.

The chapters herein provide a comprehensive, Indigenous-centred engagement with celebrity and fame that foregrounds Indigenous perspectives and objectives. Although some of the authors reflect on particular people or communities concerned with the (white) "us," many more focus on what Indigeneity and celebrity might or might not mean for Indigenous peoples, communities, and nations. As mentioned, our intention here is not to provide a comprehensive historical account of all Indigenous entanglements with celebrity, nor is it to provide an in-depth theorization of cultural and media studies approaches to celebrity. Rather, our purposes are to highlight some of the prevailing points of overlap among Indigeneity, celebrity, and fame and to prod at some of the tensions. Each of the chapters elaborates on the often fraught relationships among these things. Some reject outright the juxtaposition of the terms "Indigenous," "celebrity," and "fame," whereas others position celebrity in multiple registers that see Indigenous people making diverse interventions in celebrity culture and practices of celebritization.

Where Is the "Indigenous" in Indigenous Celebrity?

As mentioned, the chapters in this volume examine, expand, and critique Indigenous entanglements with celebrity and fame while navigating the complexities of Indigenous recognition and well knownness. Each of the chapters engages with the impacts and implications of processes of celebritization and the tensions evoked therein when Indigenous ways of knowing, being, seeing, and living in the world collide with, or reject, celebrity. In

Chapter 1—"Mino-Waawiindaganeziwin: What Does Indigenous Celebrity Mean within Anishinaabeg Contexts?"—Renée Mazinegiizhigoo-kwe Bédard explains that Anishinaabeg have no word in their language for the modern concept of celebrity. Through an engagement with Anishinaabeg language, ideas, laws, and ethics, she examines the relationship between traditional Anishinaabeg ways of knowing and celebrity status in relation to teachings on leadership, authority, and responsibility to all our relations on Mother Earth. Bédard contextualizes this examination by considering how particular Anishinaabeg are accorded respect because they live in accordance with their traditional teachings as Anishinaabeg; they thus reflect the central importance of Anishinaabeg values in garnering respect from other Anishinaabeg. This, she notes, sits in stark contrast to the heavy emphasis on individualism at the root of Euro-Western celebrity culture.

The second chapter echoes Bédard's analysis in many ways. David Lakisa, Katerina Teaiwa, Daryl Adair, and Tracy Taylor present a profound analysis, originally published in the *International Journal of the History of Sport* in 2019 and revised here, derived from a series of ten interviews with retired Pasifika and Māori rugby players in Australia. Through talanoa, a research method that, according to the authors, is a "culturally appropriate and 'authentic' way for researchers to engage with Pasifika communities," they elucidate how the interviewees understand their place within semi-/professional rugby as rooted in communal Pasifika values that emphasize respect, love, humility, and reciprocity within and through kinship networks. The retired athletes, who migrated to Australia in or after 1969, highlight the significant role that mana played in shaping their lives as successful athletes. The authors observe that mana, a pan-Pacific concept "denoting spiritual power, integrity, or status or the acquisition of success and prestige by (and conferring on) an individual, group, or object in sport and other contemporary settings," is central to any conversation on Pasifika sport involvement. The authors write that "an object's or person's mana benefits others, and in this case the retired Pasifika pioneers are accorded great mana because of their revolutionary influence, respect, and power to perform in early Australian Rugby League competitions." They also note that, though "acquiring 'mana' or prestige for the collective benefit is considered commonplace and praiseworthy in Pasifika cultures, it can place enormous social, emotional, and economic pressures on young male Pasifika athletes." In particular, the authors flag how racism continued to affect the athletes, reflecting that the status associated with being an elite athlete was not enough to safeguard them from racism. In fact, some of the pressures discussed involved being tied to their Pasifikaness. The chapter introduces an important conversation on the intersection between Pasifika and Māori people, sports, and success and recognition. Although the authors do not explicitly invoke celebrity, we contend that sports celebrities (both mainstream and Indigenous) are important in our societies, and it is important for us to include a chapter that speaks to this. At the same time, its focus on Pasifika ways of knowing and understanding one's role within what we as editors have referred to at times as "celebrity culture" is reminiscent of Bédard's evocative challenge to thinking of celebrity only through the lens of mainstream (and whitestream) ideas of well knownness.

Kahente Horn-Miller's chapter, titled "My Mom, the 'Military Mohawk Princess': kahntinetha Horn through the Lens of Indigenous Female Celebrity," is resonant with the first two chapters in its attention to how her mother was effectively able to use the attention garnered by her engagement with mainstream celebrity to push back against a system that oppressed her people in her home community of Kahnawà:ke. Here celebrity culture's desire to elevate select individuals became a strong light that Horn used to shine on and challenge the impacts of collective oppression—upholding values core to Horn's existence as Kanien'kehá:ka. Horn-Miller writes that kahntinetha's legacy reflects the fact that Canada "didn't know what to make of her because she didn't match the stereotypes that most had been socialized to—she was Indigenous, beautiful, smart, vocal, and could throw a good punch." Her work as an Indigenous model in an "industry populated by whiteness" in the mid–late twentieth century saw kahntinetha made into "the Indian Princess of the Indigenous and Canadian imaginations." Through a series of interviews with family members, along with an analysis of photographs and short movies, Horn-Miller argues that, though kahntinetha was shaped externally by the multiple narrations of projected Indigenous feminine identity, she nevertheless "countered them with stories of her own making."

The fourth chapter, by Jonathan Hill and Virginia McLaurin, continues the book's focus on addressing the impacts on and implications for individual Indigenous people entangled with and ensnared by celebrity culture. They acknowledge the complexities facing Indigenous celebrities who also engage in activism related to the concerns of their people. In "Indigenous Activism and Celebrity: Negotiating Access, Expectation, and Obligation," the authors contend that Indigenous people as celebrities adopt activist roles for myriad reasons. Some Indigenous celebrities are driven, or even pressured, to speak on behalf of causes and concerns stemming from their own experiences as Indigenous people, from those of their home communities, or from those of other First Nations, while some actively seek to use their access to wider audiences to work on behalf of the struggles facing their nations (as with respect to kahntinetha Horn in Chapter 3). In their chapter, Hill and McLaurin draw from original ethnographic interviews with Indigenous celebrities directly involved in recent pipeline struggles. They discuss the relational complexities that Indigenous celebrity-activists manage in their celebrity and activism and address the impacts on Indigenous celebrities as they navigate through constellations of expectations, roles, and obligations among the audiences and communities that they engage.

In Chapter 5, "Rags-to-Riches and Other Fairytales: Indigenous Celebrity in Australia 1950–80," Karen Fox offers a critical overview of the rise of a number of Indigenous Australians on the celebrity circuit in the middle decades of the twentieth century. Fox contrasts this rise with a capacious examination of the repressive nature of Australian colonization of Indigenous lives and the subsequent civil and land rights resistances to such marginalization. In a line of analysis resonant with that of Hill and McLaurin, Fox ultimately argues that popular portrayals of Indigenous Australian celebrities often elided differences in their lives, experiences, and cultural backgrounds, drawing on a vision of Indigeneity differentiated only by tropes such as assimilated/traditional and authentic/inauthentic. Arguing that Indigenous celebrities were often placed under considerable pressure to represent both their people and—in the context of increased international criticism of racially restrictive societies—a positive view of Australian race relations, Fox also demonstrates the considerable strength and resilience of Indigenous celebrities who negotiated such pressures. She extends one of the thematic threads of the volume—the way in which Indigenous people navigate the affront to collectively held responsibilities posed by the enticing pull of individual forms of recognition.

Fox also highlights how Australia, as a settler colonial state, constructs nationalist fairytales with regard to Indigenous people. Kim Anderson and

Brendan Hokowhitu, in Chapter 6, speak to a different kind of fairytale, that of "gentleman versus savage." They utilize the framework of Indigenous masculinities to analyze the March 2012 boxing match between then Member of (Canadian) Parliament Justin Trudeau (now prime minister) and Patrick Brazeau, an Algonquin person and Canadian senator. Through reference to media coverage and Canadian public response to the match, Anderson and Hokowhitu note that the narrative of the event traded in well-worn stereotypical dichotomies of gentleman versus savage that, rather than being held up for scrutiny, were celebrated in Canadian media, by the public, and in the country's political landscape. By analyzing the discursive construction of white hetero masculinity, Anderson and Hokowhitu reveal that Brazeau was caught in an intractable representational bind: his loss echoes the continual subjugation of Indigenous people in everyday life; had he won, though, he would have been seen as enacting violence because of his status as an "ignoble savage." The chapter highlights the tensions that Indigenous people face when racist stereotypes are amplified through celebrity and the media's embrace and facilitation of them. Their discussion resonates with Horn-Miller's discussion of how her mother navigated the seemingly inescapable racist stereotypes of Indigenous women as Indian princesses.

Anderson and Hokowhitu's discussion of the resilience of stereotypes is echoed by Jenny Davis in Chapter 7. She contends with the figuration of Indigenous "last language speakers" as a subgenre of "'last' Indians." Davis makes a fascinating intervention into media representations of Indigenous language speakers, endangered languages, and Indigenous erasure. She extends Jean O'Brien's work on "firsting and lasting," in which "lasting"—in the case of the chapter by Davis—signals the practice of reporting on "'last' speakers of endangered [Indigenous] languages" as representative of a "centuries-old practice of creating famous Indians as a means of counting down the inevitable end of Indigenous people, assuming an unavoidable loss of culture, space, and eventually existence." Davis argues that such "superlative enumeration" overemphasizes language endangerment and linguistic decline while simultaneously de-emphasizing the ongoing emergence of new language speakers and efforts toward language reclamation.

In Chapter 8, "Celebrity in Absentia: Situating the Indigenous People of the Andaman and Nicobar Islands in the Indian Social Imaginary," Aadita Chaudhury examines the context for particular Indigenous groups within

India expected to contribute to national narratives that frame India as a model of multiculturalism. Chaudhury writes that India is home to countless ethnic groups, a trait often highlighted by the Indian state to promote national unity, models of multiculturalism, and tourism among its citizens and the world at large. Chaudhury argues that Indigenous peoples who inhabit the union territories of Andaman and Nicobar Islands occupy a special niche in the Indian state's image, essentially becoming "celebrities in absentia." Although Indigenous-inhabited areas are technically off limits to mainlanders, as dictated by Indian law, increasing settler presence in the area has meant a continued fascination with the Indigenous communities. Ultimately, Chaudhury argues, this near-celebrity status of the Indigenous Andamanese has been created with little, if any, input from them; the fame of the last of India's unadulterated Indigeneity of the Andaman Islands has been propelled to new heights through tourism campaigns, popular books, and movies set in the islands. The emphasis on "lasting" echoes Davis's discussion in the preceding chapter as Chaudhury's chapter also makes an important intervention in conversations on celebrity in that whitestream media are implicated in the treatment of the Indigenous people of Andaman and Nicobar Islands. Chaudhury also highlights the fact that the reproduction of Indigenous marginalization in and co-optation into nationalist narratives through celebritization is not exclusive to white settler colonial contexts and provides a moving analysis that enriches the volume. Through a line of analysis that also resonates with Fox's chapter, Chaudhury demonstrates how Indigenous people are strategically drawn into multiculturalist narratives—in this case rendered celebrities in absentia—to aid the Indian state in engaging in national branding and distinguishing itself on the international stage.

Christina Giacona's "Marvin Rainwater and 'The Pale Faced Indian': How Cover Songs Appropriated a Story of Cultural Appropriation" (Chapter 9) speaks to Davis's invocation of O'Brien's analysis of "lasting." Giacona demonstrates what happens not only when music celebrities appropriate and transform Indigenous music but also when notions of "loss" and the forecasted disappearance of Indigenous people are extended through music production and performance. In her critical analysis of the circulation of the song "The Pale Faced Indian" by Cherokee-descended singer-songwriter John Loudermilk, Giacona reveals that successive renditions gradually changed the lyrics from detailing the pain and trauma of forced assimilation. Unlike other songs at this time, she writes, the storyline depicted its Native American subjects not as "braves" or "warriors" but as a nation that had lost its identity through forced assimilation. Over time, however, successive rewrites and changes profoundly shifted its narrative. The release of one version in particular, in 1968, English pop singer Don Fardon's "(The Lament of the Cherokee Reservation Indian) Indian Reservation," not only changed the lyrics of the song but also retitled it. Giacona argues that this marked a turning point in which the song's original meaning and intent were obscured, and the song was turned into a lament for a purportedly extinct and lost people—resonating with Chaudhury's chapter and focus on the process of making celebrities in absentia.

In Chapter 10, "Collectivity as Indigenous Anti-Celebrity: Global Indigeneity and the Indigenous Rights Movement," Sheryl Lightfoot—through a powerful analysis of the global Indigenous rights movement as a form of Indigenous *anti*-celebrity—discusses how Indigenous global rights activists consciously eschew any individual attribution in favour of the collective Indigenous struggle. Framing rights struggles as anti-celebrity, Lightfoot argues that global Indigeneity is a supranational layer of Indigenous identity added to the already complex web of kinship, tribal, and national identities that Indigenous people maintain. She argues that it is not a *universalizing* force; rather, as a shared identity, it seeks *unified* action, grounded in a set of collectively held ideals and enacted through conscious and deliberate non-individualized political and strategic actions. The distinction between unified and universalizing is key to understanding the movement and the anti-celebrity ethos that it embodies, and it brings us back to the moving discussions in Chapters 1 and 2 of Indigenous worldviews and collective responsibility. Through an examination of the development of a sense of global Indigenous rights, Lightfoot argues that the global Indigenous rights movement deliberately aims to secure collectively the distinctiveness and singularity of individual Indigenous nations, cultures, and communities.

In the closing chapter of the book, w. C. Sy likewise poses an evocative challenge to celebrity with a moving, personalized reflection on the "unsettling" and "restlessness" of celebrity. It is a notable shift in the tone of the book and a departure from the preceding chapters that makes a profound set of closing statements. Sy moves through her piece from a place acknowledging various entanglements with celebrity: the celebritizing pull of the "reconciliation moment" (and thus narratives of reconciliation, happy multiplicity, and multiculturalism, as discussed in other chapters); as an outcropping of mass Indigenous social movements; and through the crushing weight of interpersonal encounters with celebritization. In a particularly poignant line, Sy writes that they "want to eschew the expected, to celebrate Indigenous celebrity: that is, to celebrate Indigenous celebrity as though Indigenous celebrated presence in settler public spaces is a great arrival." Sy engages with Anishinaabe thought and experience to tackle the innately troubling pulls of celebrity as an individual pressure and a social pressure, ultimately pushing for a space that "suspend[s] a celebration of Indigenous celebrity and not to be marked as a 'crab in a bucket' for doing so. I want to understand the why of my unsettled, restless mind and give testimony to my personal wounds from unknowing entanglements with those wanting to be celebrities." It is here, in stark terms, that readers are confronted with the palpable unsettling wrought by the upending of Indigenous lives and their recentring on individualism, capitalism, and celebritization. Sy's chapter is a thoughtful intervention that draws the collection to a powerful close.

As a number of the chapters show, Indigenous peoples have always had their own ways of bestowing respect, acknowledgement, admiration, and appreciation on members of their societies, and in many cases this has been tied to individual contributions to collective well-being. But "traditional forms of recognition" have come to exist alongside an entirely different way of conceptualizing human value and worth increasingly associated with capital. Each chapter demonstrates that the concepts of celebrity and fame are therefore not new to Indigenous people, and the fields of production that give rise to celebrity and fame—particularly film, music, art, literature, and sport—still cling to a desire for Indigeneity. Emma LaRocque writes that Indigenous peoples "are still being hounded and haunted by White North America's image machine."[81] In this sense, members of the public consume the images of Indigenous people and Indigenous celebrities insofar as they fit prefabricated expectations of Indigeneity that pose no challenge to celebrity, fame, and the norms of individualistic capitalism that they uphold. Star-making industries have been central architects of Indigenous dispossession, and thus celebrity and fame exist as extensions of individualism and capitalism imported into the lives of Indigenous people via global systems of colonization that have deeply affected and influenced them. As the chapters in this volume detail, this is manifested in the exploitation of Indigenous people as objects of entertainment, the entertainment industry's crafting of and relying on (and profiting from) racial stereotypes, and the manner in which an ethic of individual exceptionality and success has tried to supplant Indigenous intra- and intercommunal relationships rooted in collectivity.

To be sure, Indigenous people's entanglements with celebrity and fame have also been driven at times by their desire to see themselves publicly in fields generally associated with celebrity and fame. But as the chapters highlight, Indigenous people exercise agency in navigating celebrity and fame as they are presented to them. As Bédard points out in her chapter, with reference to the "core function of Anishinaabe mino-miikana bimaadizwin," they "prioritize collective survival over an individualistic and human-centric mindset." To this end, though Indigenous people might be drawn up by celebrity circuits and fame, those in such positions often use the wider public platforms that they gain to advocate on behalf of their people. As Hill and McLaurin note in their chapter, though there are challenges in doing so, and of course exceptions, the engagement of Indigenous people with celebrity and fame is one notable way in which they confront and challenge the white North American "image machine" that LaRocque identifies.

Taken together, these chapters give us an opportunity to think more expansively and critically about how Indigeneity, celebrity, and colonization intersect. Certainly, the book does not address all of the topics within Indigenous celebrity studies. There are many Indigenous peoples whose distinctive contexts and voices are not represented here. There are also Indigenous celebrity-making vehicles such as the Indigenous television and film industry, contemporary and even traditional music, and Indigenous awards shows that could be explored in greater depth. So too could recently emergent social media celebrities and academic celebrities. As more Indigenous people move into the realm of celebrity, scholars will need to pose questions about and examine critically the implications for Indigenous societies. This book is the first foray into this exciting new field of study.

NOTES

1 Konrad Yakabuski, "Attacks on Joseph Boyden's Identity Should Set Off Alarm Bells," *Globe and Mail*, 29 December 2016, https://www.theglobeandmail.com/opinion/attacks-on-joseph-boydens-identity-should-set-off-alarm-bells/article33444228 (accessed 21 February 2019); Stassa Edwards, "When Criticism Becomes Persecution," *Jezebel*, 10 January 2017, https://jezebel.com/when-criticism-becomes-persecution-1790803651 (accessed 21 February 2019); Maurice Switzer, "Opinion: Indigenous Cultural Police and Joseph Boyden," *Anishinabek News*, 5 September 2018, http://anishinabeknews.ca/2018/09/05/opinion-indigenous-cultural-police-and-joseph-boyden (accessed 21 February 2019).

2 Jorge Barrera, "Author Joseph Boyden's Shape-Shifting Indigenous Identity," Aboriginal Peoples Television Network (APTN), 23 December 2016, https://aptnnews.ca/2016/12/23/author-joseph-boydens-shape-shifting-indigenous-identity (accessed 21 February 2019); Jorge Barrera, "Similarities between Joseph Boyden Story and Ojibway Healer's Published Work Trigger Questions," Aboriginal Peoples Television Network (APTN), 22 February 2017, https://aptnnews.ca/2017/02/22/similarities-between-joseph-boyden-story-and-ojibway-healers-published-work-trigger-questions (accessed 21 February 2018).

3 John Ralston Saul, *A Fair Country: Telling Truths about Canada* (Toronto: Penguin, 2009).

4 Eric Andrew-Gee, "The Making of Joseph Boyden," *Globe and Mail*, 4 August 2017, https://www.theglobeandmail.com/arts/books-and-media/joseph-boyden/article35881215/ (accessed 15 January 2020).

5 Toni Bruce and Christopher Hallinan, "The Quest for Australian Identity," *Sport Stars: The Cultural Politics of Sporting Celebrity* 2, no. 3 (2001): 257–73.

6 Ibid., 257.

7 "Cathy Freeman," Australian Institute of Aboriginal and Torres Strait Islander Studies (AIATSIS), 22 May 2017, https://aiatsis.gov.au/explore/articles/cathy-freeman (accessed 15 January 2020).

8 Karina Marlow, "15 Years On, Cathy Freeman's Olympic Gold Still a Potent Symbol of Reconciliation," National Indigenous Television (NITV), 25 September 2015, https://www.sbs.com.au/nitv/article/2015/09/25/15-years-cathy-freemans-olympic-gold-still-potent-symbol-reconciliation (accessed 15 January 2020).

9 "I Ran Away from Games Fame, Says Cathy Freeman," *West Australian*, 19 May 2017, https://thewest.com.au/sport/i-ran-away-from-my-icon-status-says-cathy-freeman-ng-b88481683z (accessed 15 January 2020).

10 Joseph Boyden, "First Came Truth. Now Comes the Hard Part," *Maclean's*, 25 June 2015, https://www.macleans.ca/news/canada/first-came-truth-now-comes-the-hard-part/ (accessed 15 January 2020).

11 Elizabeth DiEmanuele, "Moving towards 'Pow Wow–Step': Constructions of 'the Indian' and A Tribe Called Red's Mobilization of Art as Resistance" (MA Thesis, McMaster University, 2015).

12 Barrera, "Author"; Barrera, "Similarities."

13 Andrew-Gee, "Making."

14 On 24 December 2016, Boyden tweeted his response to the APTN article: "My name is Joseph Boyden. I'm from mixed blood background of mostly Celtic heritage, but also Nipmuc roots from Dartmouth, Massachusetts on my father's side and Ojibwe roots from Nottawasaga Bay traced to the 1800s on my mother's side. There has been some confusion as to my Indigenous identity, and I am partly to blame. As I've delved into my heritage over the last twenty-five years, I've used the

term Metis in the past when referring to myself as a mixed blood person. I do not trace my roots to Red River, and I apologize to any Red River Metis I've upset. To the best of my knowledge, I've never referred to myself as Mi'kmaq but in some interviews in the past I assume my Nipmuc heritage was misheard as Mi'kmaq. My Uncle Erl, who died a number of years before I was born and referred to in a recent APTN interview regarding my heritage, did know his roots but chose to publicly outright deny them. This was common practice in the 1940s and 1950s." For the full response, see https://web.archive.org/web/20190227055232/https:/twitter.com/josephboyden/status/812798846438928384. The following January Boyden appeared on CBC Radio with his friend Candy Palmater to speak in defence of his identity claims, but he also claimed that he had "become a bit too big" in terms of taking space in media conversations on Indigenous issues. See Jessica Wong, "Joseph Boyden Sorry 'for Taking Too Much of the Airtime' on Indigenous Issues," CBC News, 11 January 2017, https://www.cbc.ca/news/entertainment/boyden-cbc-indigenous-roots-1.3931284 (accessed 15 January 2020). See also Joseph Boyden, "My Name Is Joseph Boyden," *Maclean's*, 2 August 2017, https://www.macleans.ca/news/canada/my-name-is-joseph-boyden/ (accessed 9 January 2019).

15 Quoted in Wong, "Joseph Boyden Sorry."

16 Ibid.

17 Olivier Driessens distinguishes between two oft-used terms, "celebritization" and "celebrification." The former refers to "the societal and cultural changes implied by celebrity. Celebrification, in contrast, comprises the changes at the individual level, or, more precisely, the process by which ordinary people or public figures are transformed into celebrities." Olivier Driessens, "The Celebritization of Society and Culture: Understanding the Structural Dynamics of Celebrity Culture," *International Journal of Cultural Studies* 16, no. 6 (2013): 643. For further explanation, see the full article.

18 "Celebrity," in *Merriam-Webster* dictionary, https://www.merriam-webster.com/dictionary/celebrity (accessed 23 July 2017).

19 Daniel J. Boorstin, *The Image: A Guide to Pseudo-Events in America* (1961; reprinted, New York: Vintage, 2012), 46.

20 Ibid., 57.

21 Ibid., 47.

22 Sharon Marcus, *The Drama of Celebrity* (Princeton, NJ: Princeton University Press, 2019).

23 Michael E. Jones, "Celebrity Endorsements: A Case for Alarm and Concern for the Future," *New England Law Review* 15, no. 3 (1979): 521–44; Charles Atkin and Martin Block, "Effectiveness of Celebrity Endorsers," *Journal of Advertising Research* 23, no. 1 (1983): 57–61; Michael A. Kamins, "Celebrity and Noncelebrity Advertising in a Two-Sided Context," *Journal of Advertising Research* 29, no. 3 (1989): 34–42; Grant McCracken, "Who Is the Celebrity Endorser? Cultural Foundations of the Endorsement Process," *Journal of Consumer Research* 16, no. 3 (1989): 310–21; Roobina Ohanian, "Construction and Validation of a Scale to Measure Celebrity Endorsers' Perceived Expertise, Trustworthiness, and Attractiveness," *Journal of Advertising* 19, no. 3 (1990): 39–52; Roobina Ohanian, "The Impact of Celebrity Spokespersons' Perceived Image on Consumers' Intention to Purchase," *Journal of Advertising Research* 31, no. 1 (1991): 46–54.

24 Chris Rojek, "Celebrity," in *The Wiley-Blackwell Encyclopedia of Consumption and Consumer Studies*, ed. Daniel Thomas Cook and J. Michael Ryan (New York: Wiley-Blackwell, 2015), 1–3.

25 Chris Rojek, "Celebrity and Celetoid," in *The Blackwell Encyclopedia of Sociology*, 15 February 2007, https://doi.org/10.1002/9781405165518.wbeosc013 (accessed 23 June 2017).

26 Ibid.

27 Ibid.

28 Ibid.

29 Ibid.

30 Graeme Turner, "The Mass Production of Celebrity: 'Celetoids,' Reality TV and the 'Demotic Turn,'" *International Journal of Cultural Studies* 9, no. 2 (2006): 156.

31 Theresa M. Senft, "Microcelebrity and the Branded Self," in *A Companion to New Media Dynamics*, ed. John Hartley, Jean Burgess, and Axel Bruns (New York: Wiley-Blackwell, 2013), 346; see also Theresa M. Senft, *Camgirls: Celebrity and Community in the Age of Social Networks* (New York: Peter Lang, 2008).

32 Alice E. Marwick, *Status Update: Celebrity, Publicity, and Branding in the Social Media Age* (New Haven, CT: Yale University Press, 2013), 114.

33 Ibid.

34 Ibid.

35 Kerry O. Ferris, "The Next Big Thing: Local Celebrity," *Society* 47, no. 5 (2010): 392.

36 Ibid.

37 See Franklin E. Frazier, *Black Bourgeoisie* (New York: Free Press, 1957); Ed Guerrero, "The Black Man on Our Screens and the Empty Space in Representation," *Callaloo* 18, no. 2 (1995): 395–400; John Milton Hoberman, *Darwin's Athletes: How Sport Has Damaged Black America and Preserved the Myth of Race* (Boston: Houghton Mifflin Harcourt, 1997); Jennifer L. Knight, Traci A. Giuliano, and Monica G. Sanchez-Ross, "Famous or Infamous? The Influence of Celebrity Status and Race on Perceptions of Responsibility for Rape," *Basic and Applied Social Psychology* 23, no. 3 (2001): 183–90; Andrew M. Kaye, *The Pussycat of Prizefighting: Tiger Flowers and the Politics of Black Celebrity* (Atlanta: University of Georgia Press, 2007); Caroline A. Streeter, "Faking the Funk? Mariah Carey, Alicia Keys and (Hybrid) Black Celebrity," in *Black Cultural Traffic: Crossroads in Global Performance and Popular Culture*, ed. Harry J. Elam Jr. and Kennell Jackson (Ann Arbor: University of Michigan Press, 2005), 185–207; Kwakiutl L. Dreher, *Dancing on the White Page: Black Women Entertainers Writing Autobiography* (Albany: SUNY Press, 2008); William Fitzhugh Brundage, ed., *Beyond Blackface: African Americans and the Creation of American Popular Culture, 1890–1930* (Chapel Hill: University of North Carolina Press, 2011); Ellis Cashmore, *Beyond Black: Celebrity and Race in Obama's America* (London: A&C Black, 2012); Caroline A. Streeter, *Tragic No More: Mixed-Race Women and the Nexus of Sex and Celebrity* (Boston: University of Massachusetts Press, 2012); Sarah J. Jackson, *Black Celebrity, Racial Politics, and the Press: Framing Dissent* (New York: Routledge, 2014); Andre Nicholson, "The Classification of Black Celebrity Women in Cyberspace," in *Black Women and Popular Culture: The Conversation Continues*, ed. Adria Y. Goldman et al. (Lanham, MD: Lexington Books, 2014), 273–90; Emilie Raymond, *Stars for Freedom: Hollywood, Black Celebrities, and the Civil Rights Movement* (Seattle: University of Washington Press, 2015); Nicole R. Fleetwood, *On Racial Icons: Blackness and the Public Imagination* (New Brunswick, NJ: Rutgers University Press, 2015); John A. Hodgson, *Richard Potter: America's First Black Celebrity* (Charlottesville: University of Virginia Press, 2018); Spring-Serenity Duvall and Nicole Heckemeyer, "#BlackLivesMatter: Black Celebrity Hashtag Activism and the Discursive Formation of a Social Movement," *Celebrity Studies* 9, no. 3 (2018): 391–408; and Carrie Teresa, *Looking at the Stars: Black Celebrity Journalism in Jim Crow America* (Lincoln: University of Nebraska Press, 2019).

38 Jackson, *Black Celebrity*, 5; see also Raymond, *Stars for Freedom*, xiii.

39 Jackson, 1.

40 Turner, "Mass Production."

41 Robert G.H. Clarke, *Celebrity Colonialism: Fame, Power and Representation in Colonial and Postcolonial Cultures* (Cambridge, UK: Cambridge University Press, 2009), 1.

42 Ibid., 2.

43 Ibid.

44 Ibid. See also Zine Magubane, "The (Product) Red Man's Burden: Charity, Celebrity, and the Contradictions of Coevalness," *Journal of Pan African Studies* 2, no. 6 (2008): 1–25; and Ilan Kapoor, *Celebrity Humanitarianism: The Ideology of Global Charity* (Abingdon: Routledge, 2013).

45 Clarke, *Celebrity Colonialism*, 2; see also Magubane, "Red Man's Burden"; Kapoor, "Celebrity Humanitarianism."

46 See Cashmore, *Beyond Black*; and Jackson, *Black Celebrity*.

47 Graeme Turner, "Approaching Celebrity Studies," *Celebrity Studies* 1, no. 1 (2010): 12.

48 Ibid.

49 Jackson, *Black Celebrity*, 5.

50 Driessens, "Celebritization," 643.

51 See John Ramsland and Christopher Mooney, *Remembering Aboriginal Heroes: Struggle, Identity and the Media* (Melbourne: Brolga Publishing, 2006); Julie Cupples and Kevin Glynn, "The Celebritization of Indigenous Activism: Tame Iti as Media Figure," *International Journal of Cultural Studies* 22, no. 6 (2019): 770–87; James E. Cunningham, "The Nammys versus the Grammys: Celebrity, Technology, and the Creation of an Indigenous Music Recording Industry in North America," *World of Music* 49, no. 1 (2007): 155–70; Andrew S. King, "Just Relations: Indigenous Families in Australian Lifestyle Media," *Australian Journal of Communication* 36, no. 2 (2009): 17–33; Cecilia Morgan, "Missionaries and Celebrity within the Transatlantic World: The Ojibwa of Upper Canada, 1830–1860," in *Celebrity Colonialism: Fame, Power and Representation in Colonial and Postcolonial Cultures*, ed. R.G.H. Clarke (Cambridge, UK: Cambridge University Press, 2009), 15–36; Roshaya Rodness, "Thomas King's National Literary Celebrity and the Cultural Ambassadorship of a Native Canadian Writer," *Canadian Literature* 220 (2014): 55–72; Catherine Bishop and Richard White, "Explorer Memory and Aboriginal Celebrity," in *Indigenous Intermediaries: New Perspectives on Exploration Archives*, ed. Shino Konishi, Maria Nugent, and Tiffany Shellam (Canberra: ANU Press, 2015), 31–66; Joy S. Kasson, *Buffalo Bill's Wild West: Celebrity, Memory, and Popular History* (New York: Hill and Wang, 2015); Lorraine York, "Celebrity and the Cultivation of Indigenous Publics in Canada," in *Celebrity Cultures in Canada*, ed. Katja Lee and Lorraine York (Waterloo, ON: Wilfrid Laurier University Press, 2016), 93–110; and Glenn D'Cruz, "Breaking Bad: The Booing of Adam Goodes and the Politics of the Black Sports Celebrity in Australia," *Celebrity Studies* 9, no. 1 (2018): 131–38.

52 Cecilia Morgan, *Travellers through Empire: Indigenous Voyages from Early Canada* (Montreal and Kingston: McGill-Queen's University Press, 2017), 79.

53 Emma LaRocque, *When the Other Is Me: Native Resistance Discourse, 1850–1990* (Winnipeg: University of Manitoba Press, 2011), 37.

54 Ibid., 38; see also Robert F. Berkhofer, *The White Man's Indian: Images of the American Indian, from Columbus to the Present* (New York: Vintage, 1979); Deborah Doxtator, *Fluffs and Feathers: An Exhibit on the Symbols of Indianness: A Resource Guide* (Brantford, ON: Woodland Cultural Centre, 1992); Daniel Francis, *The Imaginary Indian: The Image of the Indian in Canadian Culture* (1992; reprinted, Vancouver: Arsenal Pulp Press, 2004); Shari M. Huhndorf, *Going*

Native: Indians in the American Cultural Imagination (Ithaca, NY: Cornell University Press, 2001); Paige Raibmon, *Authentic Indians: Episodes of Encounter from the Late-Nineteenth-Century Northwest Coast* (Durham, NC: Duke University Press, 2005); and Jennifer Adese, "Colluding with the Enemy? Nationalism and Depictions of 'Aboriginality' in Canadian Olympic Moments," *American Indian Quarterly* 36, no. 4 (2012): 479–502.

55 Francis, *The Imaginary Indian*.

56 Morgan, *Travellers through Empire*, 79.

57 Ibid., 58. For a discussion of the role of racial stereotypes in English receptions of Indigenous travellers, see also Coll Thrush, *Indigenous London: Native Travelers at the Heart of Empire* (New Haven: Yale University Press, 2016).

58 Ibid., 79–80.

59 Ibid., 80.

60 Ibid., 85.

61 Ibid., 59.

62 Ibid., 89.

63 Ibid., 24.

64 Michelle Flood, "Intersectionality and Celebrity Culture," *Women's Studies in Communication* 42, no. 4 (2019): 422.

65 Morgan, *Travellers through Empire*, 89.

66 Quoted in ibid., 92.

67 Ibid.

68 Cupples and Glynn, "Celebritization," 771.

69 Patrick McCurdy, "Conceptualizing Celebrity Activists: The Case of Tamsin Omond," *Celebrity Studies* 4 (2013): 311.

70 Ibid.

71 Cupples and Glynn, "Celebritization."

72 D'Cruz, "Breaking Bad," 134.

73 Ibid.

74 Ibid.

75 Cupples and Glynn, "Celebritization," 782.

76 Ibid., 781–82.

77 Gerald R. Alfred and Wilbert H. Ahern, *Heeding the Voices of Our Ancestors: Kahnawake Mohawk Politics and the Rise of Native Nationalism* (Toronto: Oxford University Press, 1995), 1.

78 Rosemary Popoola, Matthew Egharevba, and Oluyemi Oyenike Fayomi, "Celebrity Advocacy and Women's Rights in Nigeria," *Journal of Asian and African Studies* 56, no. 1 (2020): 11.

79 York, "Celebrity," 95.

80 Duvall and Heckemeyer, "#BlackLivesMatter."

81 LaRocque, *When the Other Is Me*, 22.

CHAPTER 1

Mino-Waawiindaganeziwin: What Does Indigenous Celebrity Mean within Anishinaabeg Contexts?

Renée E. Mazinegiizhigoo-kwe Bédard

As I understand it, as an Anishinaabe-kwe (Anishinaabe woman), mewenzhaa (in the long ago), Gizhew-Manidoo (the Creator, the Great Spirit, the Great Mystery, the One Who Loves Us Unconditionally) created everything in the cosmos, and last to be created were human beings. Anishinaabeg scholar Darren Courchene (Sagkeeng First Nation) offers that the first human being was described as "*Ani niisayi'ii naabe owe akiing* (a human was lowered onto the earth)" or Anishinaabe.[1] The Anishinaabeg are Indigenous to Mishi-mikinaak-o-minis (Turtle Island), or North America, specifically present-day Canada and the United States of America. Our Anishinaabeg culture, spirituality, governance system, and dialects are connected to our relationships with Anishinaabe-akiing (Anishinaabeg Territory), which surrounds the Great Lakes of Turtle Island (including Lake Superior, Lake Huron, Lake Ontario, Lake Erie, and Lake Michigan). Our ancestors have dwelled on these lands for thousands of years and countless generations.

Also, as I understand it, Anishinaabemowin (Anishinaabeg language) was first bestowed on the Anishinaabeg[2] peoples by Gizhew-Manidoo. We refer to Anishinaabemowin as Gizhew-Manidoo-omiigiwewinan (the Creator's original gifts). Gizhew-Manidoo gave each of these original human beings izhinikaazowin (a name), odoodemiwin (a clan), odi-nawemaaginiwin (a family), and Anishinaabemowin (language) before placing them on the earth. With Anishinaabemowin, these original human beings were able to communicate with each other in a way that is gichitawaa (sacred, spiritual) and in keeping with the Gizhew-Manidoo-omiigiwewinan, along with the Ogichi-inaakonigewin (the Great Binding Law) that governs how all things in the universe should exist in harmony and balance. But Anishinaabemowin also carries much more than simple communication. Anishinaabemowin words contain a paradigm connected by memory to identity, space, time, and place. In this way, words guide our miikana bimaadiziwin (life path) as human beings, as Anishinaabeg.

Within these contexts, the word mino-waawiindaganeziwin[3] offers a glimpse of the Anishinaabeg paradigm. Mino-waawiindaganeziwin describes the character of a person of worth, esteem, respect, fame, or renown. In Anishinaabeg cultural contexts, it is not a word used by people to describe themselves. Instead, such a description is bestowed on an individual only by someone else in the community. An individual who is mino-waawiindaganeziwin is recognized for leadership, talents, expertise, or gifts that contribute to the vitality of Anishinaabeg culture, community, and nationhood; conversely, the person might be recognized for the lack of those qualities. The word has a double meaning for either the best or the worst qualities of character that a person can exhibit within the community. In this word, we find a concept full of nuanced meanings combining ideas of identity and culture. When the word mino-waawiindaganeziwin is used, it echoes the traditions of our Anishinaabeg ancestors, merging what we now call history, spirituality, geography, and governance to talk about a nation's relationship with Anishinaabe-akiing. From an Anishinaabeg perspective, mino-waawiindaganeziwin is that trace of our relationships with people and places and evidence of a nation connected by memory to a distinctive cultural worldview. Indigenous peoples' languages on Mishi-mikinaak-o-minis are the oldest sets of records and teachers for how to live as human beings on this continent. Among Anishinaabeg, language records our collective presence and memories as shaped by the place in which it originates. Replacing Anishinaabemowin words with English words colonizes the Anishinaabeg paradigm, erasing its primacy and rendering culture invisible.

In this chapter, I contrast the Anishinaabeg word mino-waawiindaganeziwin with the terms "Indigenous celebrity," "celebrity," and Western notions of "celebrity status." My purpose here is to assert that the use of Anishinaabeg words instead of English words is about the survival of our unique Anishinaabeg cultural identity and our system of knowledge. The use of Anishinaabeg words is a fundamental part of this chapter and includes inserting Anishinaabeg words into the text to fulfill my responsibility as an Anishinaabe-kwe. In the Anishinaabeg way, I also include these words to acknowledge Anishinaabemowin as an original gift from Gizhew-Manidoo.

Anishinaabemowin is prioritized throughout this chapter because the colonizers' languages—specifically English and French—are void of the necessary Anishinaabeg contexts required to interpret, orient, and navigate the world as Anishinaabeg. Using an English word such as *celebrity*, even if attached to the word *Indigenous*, can inadvertently or intentionally make invisible the Anishinaabeg worldview. Furthermore, the term "Indigenous" becomes a way to group specific nations and cultures together as if they are all the same, for the sake of convenience or out of ignorance. My intention in this chapter is to assert that the use of the term "mino-waawiindaganeziwin" speaks to an Anishinaabeg paradigm that must be prioritized and not replaced by terms such as "Indigenous celebrity" or "celebrity" because they erode Anishinaabeg sovereignty, identity, and traditional knowledge.

The English words *Indigenous celebrity*, *celebrity*, and *celebrity status* have replaced traditional Anishinaabemowin words such as mino-waawiindaganeziwin once used regularly. However, the language of the colonizers saturates our lives and often works to control the public narratives regarding the construction of our identities as Indigenous peoples. Today the dominant non-Indigenous society idolizes celebrity culture and celebrity status. Indigenous celebrities become an invention of a Euro–North American obsession with controlling and marketing Indigenous imagery through the lens of colonization.

Scholar Elvin Lim warns that celebrity culture has saturated Euro–North American society at all points, not just in the arts and entertainment industries, but also in areas of government, faith, academics, and sport, to name a few. Lim notes that celebrity status is a dangerous trend rooted in the fact that

> celebrities have name recognition. They are easy on the eyes. And they pretend really well. . . . It is no wonder that good actors make great politicians. Like actors, politicians use image consultants to change how they look; their words are crafted by somebody else; they have publicists for image (or damage) control. And so mimesis occurs alike in art and in politics. Because both the actor and the politician revel in the attention that comes with being on stage, Plato did not think it wise that actors should have a political role in the republic. . . . Our politicians and our citizens today worship at the altar of make-believe (politicians make, and citizens believe) images.[4]

Similarly, writer Tim Willard recognizes that the rise of celebrity status in Western society has resulted in a level of moral deficiency that he says threatens to destabilize North American society. He challenges the dangers to a society that glorifies celebrity and "envision[s] *celebrity* as a means to influence people. Even though influence exists as an inherent by-product of leadership, it is not something to be pursued and possessed as a kind of currency. Leaders must be wary of falling into the trap of thinking that in order to possess and 'leverage' influence you must build your personal celebrity. This is the great lie."[5] Both Lim and Willard recognize that Euro–North American culture has elevated celebrities to roles of leadership and influencers of culture and society at large. The musician Bono says that "being a celebrity is a currency that should be used to bring change."[6] He speaks a truism of Euro–North American culture. He voices a dictum in which culture has become a servant to celebrity and opportunistic individuals who pursue and leverage status as a way to expand individual agency, power, and worship. That might be a truism of non-Indigenous society, but that statement has never been a dictum of Anishinaabeg culture.

Instead, Anishinaabeg peoples hold the esteem and elevation of individuals under strict cultural codes, which differ from nation to nation. Our Anishinaabeg language contains many words in which cultural codes are embedded in teachings that accompany them. Here I seek to highlight the word mino-waawiindaganeziwin (esteemed person, renowned individual, famous person) along with cultural teachings that accompany the use of this term. Prioritizing the word is a method of generating Anishinaabeg identity through a combination of emotional and intellectual knowledges within the kinetics of our land-based worldviews as Anishinaabeg people of Mishimikinaak-o-minis. Within this Anishinaabemowin word, we are offered agency to generate meanings of how Anishinaabeg live through the ways that we think, live, and respond to our ecosystems. By writing this chapter, I seek to demonstrate that the nature of knowledge within Anishinaabemowin is under threat when replaced by the English term "celebrity" and how mino-waawiindaganeziwin is an important theoretical anchor for living life within an Anishinaabeg worldview. I contend that using the word mino-waawiindaganeziwin offers a different set of intellectual practices than the ones privileged in the term "celebrity." It follows a different set of theories of how knowledge is constructed, generated, and communicated to the world. Ultimately, my aim in this chapter is to reveal how Western concepts of celebrity are incommensurable with mino-waawiindaganeziwin.

We should not stop using our Anishinaabeg ways of knowing or risk perpetuating our own colonization by replacing Anishinaabeg words with English words. Reclaiming and using mino-waawiindaganeziwin instead of the term "celebrity" is an important step toward decolonization and resistance. I do this because, as Courchene warns, what language am I communicating in right now? English. I was told once that, if we cannot say the Anishinaabemowin word for any naturally occurring object or phenomenon, then we cannot claim it to be ours, and that aspect of our world will be lost to us forever.[7] If we allow the world to keep naming and labelling us as Anishinaabeg peoples, then we are allowing it to claim us, own us, and dictate how we exist as human beings.

Embodying Mino-Waawiindaganeziwin

Using Anishinaabeg language to describe leaders, role models, and people whom we look up to is critical to maintaining an Anishinaabeg worldview or identity. When I hear the word *celebrity* attached to the names of Anishinaabeg and other Indigenous leaders, Elders, actors, musicians, painters, activists, and so on, I admit that it makes me a bit uncomfortable because in Western culture that word has certain cultural and historically negative contexts as well as layered meanings that do not mesh ethically with Anishinaabeg cultural ways of knowing. The English word *celebrity* causes me to recall the dark history of Hollywood "Indian" stereotypes, exploitation, and oshki-danabiwin (colonization).[8] It is a difficult fit for describing any Anishinaabeg person or any Indigenous people of Mishi-mikinaak-o-minis because it exists within the cultural contexts of European societies and is a tool of colonization. Furthermore, it is a foreign concept that has no equivalent within the epistemological or axiological context of the Anishinaabeg peoples of Mishi-mikinaak-o-minis. We have no teachings that go with the origin, meaning, or use of the term. The English language has been used for the express purpose of colonizing and indoctrinating Anishinaabeg peoples and erasing our knowledge systems.

The Anishinaabeg never elevated individuals in the same way that mainstream Euro–North American culture celebrates individuals such as Donald Trump, Kim Kardashian, Justin Bieber, Pope Francis, Justin Trudeau, the Dalai Lama, and many others. Instead, Indigenous peoples across Turtle Island remember and recognize our prominent political leaders, such as Tecumseh (Shawnee); actor Adam Beach (Saulteaux,[9] Dog Creek First Nation); musician Robbie Robertson (Cayuga and Mohawk, Six Nations of the Grand River First Nation), lead guitarist and songwriter for the rock group The Band, as well as singer and socio-political activist Buffy Sainte-Marie (Plains Cree, Piapot Plains Cree First Nation); and visual artists such as Daphne Odjig (Anishinaabeg, Wikwemikong Unceded First Nation), to name just a few. Many of these individuals have been described as Indigenous celebrities by mainstream society. Moreover, they are people whose names are repeated within our communities until they have become part of the collective knowledge of Indigenous peoples of Turtle Island.

I choose to describe strategically some Anishinaabeg leaders and people who are well known as celebrities (local or otherwise), through the use of the word mino-waawiindaganeziwin, so that they are rooted in Anishinaabeg contexts. As an Anishinaabe-kwe, I admired Anishinaabeg painters Norval Morrisseau (Sandy Point First Nation) and Daphne Odjig (Wikwemikong Unceded First Nation), after whom I modelled my painting style. As an academic, I am drawn to emulate Anishinaabeg scholars Winona LaDuke (White Earth First Nation), Leanne Betasamosake Simpson (Alderville First Nation), Louise Erdrich (Turtle Mountain First Nation), and Basil Johnston (Parry Island First Nation). There are also Anishinaabeg Gchi-aya'aag (Anishinaabeg Elders)[10] who are my cultural role models, including Anishinaabe-kwewag Gchi-aya'aag (Women Elders). Anishinaabeg Elders

Edna Manitowabi and Shirley Ida Williams, both from Wikwemikong Unceded First Nation, have influenced me greatly with their teachings on culture and language. These individuals fit the Anishinaabeg concept of mino-waawiindaganeziwinan[11] because their names have been spoken over and over by the community with admiration, esteem, and respect. They have become known as leaders within the collective consciousness of Indigenous communities across Turtle Island.

Anishinaabeg communities measure whether these celebrities, as community members, are allowed to inhabit positions such as mino-waawiindaganeziwin within their nations. This means that they can be a celebrity in mainstream culture but are or are not a mino-waawiindaganeziwin based on community accreditation. For many generations, Anishinaabeg communities have raised or lowered individuals as leaders based on communal acceptance. In this way, Anishinaabeg communities validate or offer communally sanctioned credentials to individuals who seek to act as positive representatives and contributing leaders within their communities. A credentialled individual has to be of good moral standing, maintain healthy relationships with the community, and uphold cultural obligations or responsibilities as set out by the people. Being communally accredited is provisional and subject to scrutiny, criticism, or disavowment by the community based on the rectitude of the individual.

Within Anishinaabeg society, an upstanding human being is required to embody Anishinaabe mino-bimaadiziwin (living the good life or good way as a human being) and respect the Anishinaabe-inaakonigewinan (natural laws). Anishinaabeg Elder Sherry Niizhoosake Copenace (Onigaming First Nation) offers that "Anishinaabe are taught to be dedicating themselves to be aware [of] and caring to everything within and around you, at every moment and in daily life."[12] Supporting this, Anishinaabeg-Métis scholar and lawyer Mikinaakikwe Aimée Craft adds that the "Anishinaabe way of life is centered on relationships, and responsibilities are associated to each of those relationships. These relationships give rise to rights, obligations and responsibilities. Rights, obligations and responsibilities are exercised both individually and collectively by the Anishinaabe."[13] There are expectations that all Anishinaabeg will recognize and uphold their particular place in Creation, follow the rules of Creation in order to maintain harmony and peace, not put themselves above others, and respect other beings' responsibilities in Creation.

As mino-waawiindaganeziwinan, socially recognized and approved by their communities, it is their responsibility to use their status for the betterment of the people, to represent their people ethically, and to walk that ethical path of Anishinaabe mino-miikana bimaadiziwin (the good path of life as a human being).

> *Maamidonendaman baanimaa gwayak*
> *e-bimaadiziyan ohomaa akiikang.*
> *Mii baanimaa ge-waabamaj Gzhe-Mnidoo.*
>
> Remember that you should live a straight life on this earth.
> So then you will see the Great Spirit.[14]

The core function of Anishinaabe mino-miikana bimaadiziwin is to prioritize collective survival over an individualistic and human-centric mindset. The Euro–North American understanding of celebrity does not harmonize with this worldview because it prioritizes individualism over communal well-being.

Compared with celebrity status based on individualism, self-glorification, and personal benefits, the sensibility of a mino-waawiindaganeziwin is required to be devoted to communal relationality and accountability to the entire Anishinaabeg community. The status of the mino-waawiindaganeziwin is dependent on communal recognition and permission to represent a particular nation or community. Undertaking the work is premised on continued permission and approval of past or present conduct. What makes celebrity status satisfactory in Anishinaabeg communities is that people such as Morrisseau, Robertson, Beach, and Sainte-Marie are also community members culturally credentialled by the wider Indigenous community across Turtle Island. In their own ways and by their own means, their celebrity status benefits the entire Indigenous community rather than compromises, colonizes, or erases the cultural integrity of Indigenous peoples.

Reclaiming the Mino-Waawiindaganeziwinan

In contemporary contexts, using language as the mode of delivery for cultural identity and preservation requires a radical stance against the hyper-extractivist society that has pillaged and selected those parts of Anishinaabeg culture—or any Indigenous culture—as more palatable to mainstream society. For too long, our identities have been easily co-opted to fit within an inclusive narrative of a multicultural society. Because language is a tool of creation, invention, and imagination, it represents a method of radical transformation and evolution. As an Anishinaabe-kwe, I am not interested in inclusion or compatibility of Indigeneity with celebrity culture. In fact, I warn against it! I am interested in unapologetic declarations of our differences. Within our own words are the road maps to enact revolution, reclamation, and resurgence of our land-based identities.

According to Simpson, "the process of speaking Nishnaabemowin, then, inherently communicates certain values and philosophies that are important to Nishnaabeg being. Breaking down words into the 'little words' they are composed of often reveals a deeper conceptual—yet widely held—meaning."[15] I have been taught by Anishinaabeg linguist and Elder Shirley Ida Williams that words have their own stories encoded into their components that reveal deeper meanings. Breaking down a word into what Simpson calls "little words," or smaller parts, reveals the dimensions of the intellectual information accumulated within that word over generations of being passed down from person to person. Such knowledge is referred to as gikendaasowin (synthesis knowledge, teachings, personal knowledge/understanding passed down from generation to generation). All of this resides in the "little words" embedded in the word mino-waawiindaganeziwin.

Mino- refers to something or someone that is good, nice, or well.[16] Mino- tells us that the community has deemed the individual esteemed, respected, and worthy of being remembered because she or he has lived up to communal and cultural standards of what it means to embody Anishinaabeg. To describe someone or something as good is not taken lightly and denotes rectitude.

Waawiindan translates into "explain it, keep telling about it."[17] Next I looked at the word waawiinjigaazo, which means "s/he is talked about repeatedly, 'they' keep talking about him."[18] Then I examined the word wiindan, and it concerns naming something or someone. Wiindan translates into "name it, mention its name, give it a name."[19]

Finally, -win, at the end of waawiindaganeziwin, is used to refer to "a way it is done."[20] -Win also represents a state of being, living, doing, relating, and understanding. I understand -win as a choice to "carry," "act," or "represent" one's self in a particular way. With this in mind, waawiindaganeziwin holds teachings and expresses life through a person's actions. It tells us about the character of the individual. In this way, the use of Anishinaabemowin is strategic and intentional.

Anishinaabemowin is our source of identity formation, and it is a critical tool for the survival of our people and our identities as Anishinaabeg. Breaking down the "little words" here might appear to be just a device to help readers better understand the contexts of these words, but for me it is a strategy of resistance and reclamation of identity. As Anishinaabeg Elder Joe Auginaush asserts, "we're not losing our language, our language is losing us."[21] Over the years, I have felt saddened and sometimes jealous that others possessed the language, and I couldn't hold a simple conversation because my family did not speak Ojibwe for fear of not passing in mainstream society. Similarly, Courchene states that

> I must say that I was proud and envious, then and now, about the ability of friends and strangers to speak with efficiency and fluency. I asked my mother why we do not speak our language anytime and anywhere we felt like it, just like the cultural groups we observed during our time at the mall. My mother's response is the reason I am writing this. She said, "*We have been taught that our language is useless. We have been taught that our language is wrong. We have been taught to be ashamed of ourselves. Many [Anishinaabe-Ojibweg] have come to believe that this is true.*"[22]

Oshki-danabiwin (colonization) has taken so much from us that my act of resistance is to prioritize the language and teach myself, and share what I have learned, so that the worldview encoded in the language is restored to its prominence within our communities. Elder Shirley Ida Williams once said that Anishinaabemowin is the "Creator's language," and if we want to be, be heard, and be recognized by the rest of Creation as Anishinaabeg then we have to reclaim our language, because it is the gift bestowed on us by Gizhew-Manidoo.

Anishinaabeg Language's Relationship to Identity Formation

Ts'its'tsi'nako, Thought-Woman
Is sitting in her room
And whatever she thinks about appears
Thought-Woman, the spider,
Named things and
as she *named* them
they appeared.[23]

As Original Man traveled the Earth . . . [he] talked with the animals. He *named* them as he went.[24]

Thoughts transformed into words or names constitute the basis of identity formation or acknowledgement of established identity. Laguna Pueblo writer Leslie Marmon Silko (Laguna Pueblo Reservation) and Anishinaabe Elder Bawdwaywidun Edward Benton-Banai (Odawazawguh i gunning or Lac Courte Oreilles Reservation) explain in these epigraphs that words and names contain potent energies that create our epistemologies or sense of reality concerning the cosmos. Anishinaabemowin is "our original way of speaking which allows us to process and express our thoughts. It is our way of communicating with Creation, with Spirit, and with one another."[25] Moreover, Anishinaabemowin articulates a system of axiological values concerning how we live and relate to each other. In this way, language is the primary vehicle of communication through which we relate to Creation and are recognized by Creation. Language carries the ethical parameters for human conduct with our indinawemaaganag[26] or relatives in Creation (e.g., humans, animals, fish, plants, celestial beings, earth beings, and so on) as well as the responsibilities that humans must uphold in those relations.

Anishinaabemowin and specific dialects developed over thousands of years of existing in specific regions, and they reflect the relationships that human beings formed with their environments. Words embody compacts, covenants, or treaties between human beings and clans of animals, birds, plants, celestial bodies, water, rocks, and so on. The landscape responds best with those Anishinaabeg who speak Anishinaabemowin to Creation and are appropriately named to use the language given to the Anishinaabeg by

Gizhew-Manidoo (the Creator), the Spirit of Nanaboozho (the Trickster), and other Spirit Beings.[27] Therefore, attaching the word *celebrity* to an Anishinaabeg person or any Indigenous person results in cognitive dissonance and discord; Creation does not recognize that foreign language in relation to those who are Anishinaabeg. Anishinaabemowin articulates specific understandings of temporal-spatial relationality, ethics, and spirituality.

To replace Anishinaabeg words with non-Anishinaabeg words alters the sense of reality and relationality with Creation. In 1984, Marie Battiste (Mi'kmaq, Potlo'tek First Nation) referred to this phenomenon of replacing Indigenous intellectual traditions with Euro-Canadian intellectual traditions as "cognitive assimilation and cultural imperialism."[28] A couple of years later she called it "cognitive imperialism."[29] In her book *Dancing on Our Turtle's Back*, Simpson also uses the term "cognitive imperialism" to demonstrate the process of disempowerment that occurs when Anishinaabeg peoples use the colonizer's language rather than their own Anishinaabeg language. Simpson believes that there is empowerment in using our Anishinaabeg intellectual traditions embedded in the language because it "reveals a deeper conceptual . . . meaning."[30] She adds that "learning through the language" provides those who are not fluent in it with a window through which to experience the complexities and depth of our culture."[31] Simpson contends that decolonization can occur only through the use of our own intellectual traditions. She borrows Audre Lorde's words, saying that using European words such as *celebrity* is using "the master's tools," which she thinks is not a culturally effective strategy of resistance for Anishinaabeg peoples. According to Simpson, when Anishinaabeg peoples are convinced or tricked not to utilize their knowledge systems, it fosters cognitive imperialism, which is "insidious and infectious" and "[aims] at convincing us that we are weak and defeated people, and that there [is] no point in resisting or resurging."[32] She insists that we need to decolonize our minds of the "web of colonial traps" to find the pre-settler consciousness and resist by using "our own tools, strategies, values, processes, and intellect."[33] Yellowknives Dene scholar Glen Coulthard (Denendeh, Northwest Territories) adds that Indigenous intellectual traditions provide Indigenous peoples with mechanisms for "a radical alternative to the structural and psycho-affective facets of colonial domination."[34]

Without our Anishinaabeg language, our cultures break down, our ties to each other become fractured, and our relationships with nature, the

Great Spirit, and the order of all things become broken. Without the use of Anishinaabemowin, the Anishinaabeg cease to exist as a people and a living culture, which in Western civilization has led to the creation of stereotypes and misrepresentations. Mino-waawiindaganeziwin occupies a specific space and idiom within the culture, so it is necessary for cultural integrity to acknowledge its existence and place in Creation. So what is the impact of attaching a Western word such as *celebrity* to Anishinaabeg people and identity? Can or should the word even appear alongside the words describing Anishinaabeg people?

For direction on the appropriateness of connecting European words to Indigenous identities, I look to Robert Bunge, a Lakota Sioux, and Blackfoot (Kainai) Elder Leroy Little Bear (Blood Indian First Nation) for guidance within Indigenous contexts. Bunge ventures that "language is a spiritual experience. [Our Indigenous language] is not only the language of the sweat lodge, but is an everyday sacred way of perceiving and expressing these perceptions. The universe of discourse of the dominant European tongues is that of an impersonal, inanimate, mechanistic and amoral state of affairs while the universe of discourse of Lakota and other [Indigenous] languages is one of a personal, animate and moral state of being."[35] Bunge advocates that Indigenous languages are essential to Indigenous identities and one's sense of self: "A people who lose their language and their view of the universe expressed by that language, can no longer survive as a people, although they can survive as rootless individuals."[36] He believes that Indigenous languages ground our sense of being in what Anishinaabeg call Anishinaabe inaadiziwin, meaning "our original values and our original way of living our life and being Anishinaabe in the fullest sense."[37] In other words, the language that we use as Anishinaabeg people contains cultural protocols on how to be Anishinaabeg, whereas European languages only teach one how to think and act European or Euro–North American.

The Anishinaabeg worldview encapsulated within Anishinaabeg language "comprises the values and traditions of a community as well as the social and political formation of a group of people who define themselves as unique."[38] The 1996 Royal Commission on Aboriginal Peoples of Canada (RCAP) indicates that language is essential to Indigenous identity: "Language is the principal instrument by which culture is transmitted from one generation to another, by which members of a culture communicate meaning and make sense of their shared experience. Because language defines the world and experience in cultural terms, it literally shapes our way of perceiving—our world view."[39] RCAP supports Bunge's claim that language is crucial to a healthy integrated Indigenous identity. Bunge points out that "language is not just another thing we do as humans—it is *the thing* we do. It is a total environment; we live in language as a fish lives in water. It is the audible and visible manifestation of the soul of a people."[40] In this way, language enables human beings to navigate and find meaning in the world. Roger Spielmann offers that "a person from any tradition should be able to look to their own intuition about language in order to get a grasp of the issue."[41] What Bunge, RCAP, and Spielmann are referring to here is how cultural axiology is embedded in language.

Therefore, to connect European and Anishinaabeg language is morally problematic and leads to a phenomenon that Elder Little Bear calls "jagged worldviews colliding."[42] He explains that, because of the ongoing process of colonization, Indigenous and European worldviews, including desires and values, continuously collide, overlap, and compete for social, political, and cultural control.[43] Elder Little Bear believes that adoption of the cultures and languages of the colonizers has left Indigenous people with a fragmented consciousness, a random jigsaw puzzle of competing views of the world.[44] In his opinion, "no one has a pure worldview that is 100 percent Indigenous or Eurocentric; rather, everyone has an integrated mind, a fluxing and ambidextrous consciousness, a precolonized consciousness that flows into a colonized consciousness and back again. It is this clash of worldviews that is at the heart of many current difficulties with effective means of social control in postcolonial North America. It is also this clash that suppresses diversity in choices and denies Aboriginal people harmony in their daily lives."[45] I seek to determine whether there is embedded meaning in the Euro–North American word *celebrity* that can connect to Anishinaabe-gikendaasowin (knowledge) and Anishinaabe-inendamowin (worldview). I recognize that the Euro–North American word *celebrity* has already been attached to Indigeneity, and I recognize that it has begun to replace traditional words and teachings. Which teachings can the Euro–North American definitions of the word *celebrity* provide to help us understand and judge if the word can resonate with Anishinaabeg cultural beliefs?

What Is a Celebrity?

How smooth must be the language of the whites, when they can make right look like wrong, and wrong like right.
—Black Hawk, Sauk, early 1800s[46]

There are multiple variations in the meaning of and the context for the word *celebrity* in European languages. As Lakota and American Indian Movement activists Russell Means and Bayard Johnson note, Old World languages are "combinations of older languages and are traceable to the same few mother tongues."[47] The English-based *Oxford Dictionary* defines the word *celebrity* as "[a] famous person, especially in entertainment or sport. . . . The state of being well known."[48] The dictionary notes that the word originates from "Late Middle English (in the sense [of] 'solemn ceremony')" and "from Old French celebrite or Latin celebritas, from celeber, celebr- 'frequented or honoured.'"[49] *Merriam-Webster* offers a similar definition: "the state of being celebrated. Fame. The actress lived a life of celebrity."[50] In terms of etymology, *Merriam-Webster* offers a similar explanation of origins but has a few more details than the *Oxford Dictionary*: "Middle English *celebrite*, 'fame, renown,' borrowed from Middle French & Latin; Middle French *celebrité*, borrowed from Latin *celebritāt-*, *celebritās* 'busy or crowded conditions, reputation, fame,' from *celebr-*, *celeber* 'much used, frequented, widely known, famed' + *-itāt-*, *-itās* -ity."[51] In summary, the core characteristics of these definitions reveal a person who is celebrated, honoured, well known, or famous and a person who is living a celebrity lifestyle. These definitions form a basis of understanding European ontology related to the concept of celebrity.

Celebrity in Euro–North American cultures arises from past and present heroes, leaders, and cultural icons. In cultures across Europe and North America, heroes appear to come from all walks of life, including gods, goddesses, prophets, martyrs, politicians, warriors, athletes, doctors, inventors, authors, activists, spiritual leaders, artists, musicians, and cultural innovators. Books, poems, songs, plays, photographs, paintings, and films document the achievements of these individuals and have resulted in celebrity culture, including fame, social status, worship, and lifestyle. Currently, the nature and function of celebrity status in Euro-American-Canadian cultures are socially constructed phenomena that accentuate a mostly inauthentic human persona or what Daniel Boorstin calls a "pseudo-event." Boorstin explains that it is something or someone that is noteworthy and celebrated because of the ambiguous nature of its identity or nature, not grounded in reality. He uses words such as *produced*, *contrivance*, *concealment*, and *packaged* to provide a context for understanding the unreal nature of pseudo-events. Boorstin explains that "the celebrity is a person who is well-known for their well-knownness."[52] He offers that celebrity is "fabricated on purpose to satisfy our exaggerated expectations of human greatness."[53] Theorist Graeme Turner adds that, "while heroic figures are distinguished by their achievements or by 'the great simple virtues of their character,' celebrities are differentiated 'mainly by trivia of personality.'"[54] According to Boorstin, the ranks of celebrity comprise those "skilled in the marginal differentiation of their personalities."[55] Turner also notes that fame is a phenomenon manufactured and nurtured, not necessarily gained through the achievement of great deeds, but today it is most often obtained by differentiating personalities from competitors.[56] Echoing this view, scholar Larry Leslie asks, "is it now possible for anyone, or everyone, to become a celebrity? Are we living proof that pop artist Andy Warhol was prophetic years ago when he said that one day everyone in the world will be famous for 15 minutes?"[57] Turner and Leslie are warning that anyone can become famous, not for esteem but for notoriety.

Boorstin's and Turner's definitions of celebrity point out how the inauthentic image of the celebrity in North America and Europe has resulted from and contributed to ontological and axiological deficits. Turner explains that the evolution of celebrity in Western cultures reflects a "more disinterested and less moralistic proposition," and the "phenomenon of celebrity reflects an ontological shift"[58] away from core values saying that fake personalities are unethical and unhealthy.[59] He explores how celebrity culture results from the degradation of core ontological beliefs that have supported community well-being. Cultural meanings are now negotiated and organized in ways that result in "a net cultural loss—customarily, a loss of community as human relations attenuate and fragment under the pressure of contemporary political and social conditions. As a result of such conditions, the argument goes, there is an affective deficit in modern life. Some of our closest social relations seem to be in decline: the nuclear family, the extended family and the withdrawal of the family unit from the wider suburban community . . . are among the symptoms we might name."[60] Turner illustrates how the rise of celebrity culture coincides with the weakening of social relationships and the loss of community-mindedness in Western cultures across Europe and North America.

Additionally, Chris Rojek explains that a new pseudo–community dynamic has evolved in Western cultures that he describes as "parasocial interactions," which exist over distances between the celebrity and the follower, who are strangers to each other.[61] Turner explains that "among our compensations for the loss of community is an avid attention to the figure of the celebrity and a greater investment in our relations with specific versions of this figure."[62] Turner's and Rojek's critiques of the history of celebrity culture paint a picture of a degenerative disease with symptoms of moral deficit and the diminishing value of family and community in favour of a cult of individual personalities. Dan Brockington points out that modern celebrity is materialistic and tends to connect with community only from personal motivation: "Celebrity describes sustained public appearances that are materially beneficial."[63] Moreover, Turner and Rojek reveal that celebrity culture is divorced from those moral imperatives that prioritize communal ties and responsibilities.

Graeme Turner and Rojek suggest that celebrity is divorced from moral imperatives. As such, it has been used strategically to facilitate political policies of acculturation and colonization of Anishinaabeg peoples. Celebrity status helps to subvert and suppress Indigeneity and replace it with the fabricated status of "celebrity Indian,"[64] evident in the history of "Indians" in the films recorded by anthropologists and the industry of Hollywood movies. The documentary film *Reel Injun* (2009), directed by Neil Diamond, Catherine Bainbridge, and Jeremiah Hayes, offers an insightful and entertaining look at the rise of "Indigenous celebrity" in the film industry spanning over a century.[65] Anishinaabe film critic Jessie Wente (Serpent River First Nation) states in the documentary that "Native Americans were among the first subjects [recorded on film]. Thomas Edison shot silents [i.e., silent films] about Native Americans [the first recorded images]. This is in the late 1800s. Thomas Edison unveiled his kinetoscope in Times Square and it was a penny-machine that played the Laguna Pueblo's ceremonies and dances, and those were the very first moving images. There were more than a hundred silents made involving Native Americans as very much a part of American history, which of course was still very much ongoing at the time that cinema was being born." Early anthropological films tried to present "Indians" as a dying race and a near-mythological people who required documentation before they disappeared. In *Reel Injun*, Jim Jarmush notes that North American culture "wanted to perpetuate the idea that these people are now mythological. They don't even really exist. They are like the dinosaurs." Wente also notes that early Hollywood movies projected "Indians" because of the "romance of the tragedy. Greek, Roman tragedy." According to scholar Daniel Francis, the "Hollywood Indian" is the first "Indian" to be seen as a "celebrity" in Western society.[66] Unfortunately, the "celebrity Indian"[67] emerged as a closed form that traps all Indigenous peoples of Turtle Island within a false reality that haunts us to this day.

Francis notes that Hollywood films of the 1900s were aimed to "amuse, not to edify: they used Indians for their entertainment value . . . [which] reduced the complexity of Native cultures to a few familiar stereotypes. North Americans were force-fed images of painted, tomahawk-wielding warriors in feather headdresses mounted on horseback."[68] Movies were one of the most important instruments in the creation of the "celebrity Indian" and created to steer narratives of colonization and civilization. The movies, Francis says,

> invariably situate Indians in the past, usually on the western frontier. The result is that Indians in the movies seem marginal to modern life. Sympathetic regret or retrospective outrage are the feelings these movies seem most likely to evoke. In a sense, Indian movies have never really been about Indians at all. They have been about White concerns: White guilt, White fear, White insecurity. The persistent popularity of Performing Indians—whether in the Wild West Show or in the movies—suggests that these forms of entertainment respond to a deep anxiety that non-Natives have about our place in North America, and a deep need to legitimate our presence here. Some movies have dealt with this anxiety by dehumanizing Indians, turning them into savage monsters, or drunken buffoons, who have to be eradicated before civilization can take root. Other movies have romanticized Indians for their wisdom and natural virtue.[69]

"Movie Indians" in the film industry were rarely played by Indigenous actors, which created a dangerous mechanism of abuse and violation. The real celebrities behind the onscreen characters were predominantly white or mixed-race actors.[70] The fantasy of playing "Indian" became ingrained in the narratives of the film industry; therefore, it is not surprising that this became a reality in North American society with celebrity figures such as Grey Owl, Iron Eyes Cody, and Chief Buffalo Child Long Lance, to name just a few.[71] For these reasons, the word *celebrity* carries a great deal of historical and cultural baggage as an instrument of erasure, exploitation, and extinguishment.

Theorists such as Boorstin, Turner, Rojek, Leslie, and Brockington argue that the moral deficiencies in the word reveal a concept that is highly individualistic and materialistic, highlights behaviour that restricts and minimizes community interaction, presents false identities, and is highly competitive. These characteristics are a problem from Anishinaabeg ontological and axiological positions. Too many of the attributes of celebrity fail to resonate ethically within Anishinaabeg culture, and I recognize immediately that the meanings of this word and the contexts of its use can be very dangerous for Anishinaabeg people because the word does not reiterate our intellectual traditions encapsulated in the word mino-waawiindaganeziwin. Anishinaabeg words speak the truth of what the person represents, and that is a powerful site of agency for our people that gets lost when replaced by English words.

With these definitions and this history in mind, I look at the words *Indigenous*, *celebrity*, and mino-waawiindaganeziwin, and I recognize the great divide in understanding our roles as human beings in the cosmos. Why do those of European heritage see the world so differently? Why do these cultural ways of knowing seek to extinguish Anishinaabeg ways of being and living? I recognize that often this is done in ignorance, but it is done nonetheless. Therefore, the only tool to prevent it—or at least to resist it—is to assert our own words and names. To forget, to ignore, or to replace our own words is to lose what makes us Anishinaabeg. Lakota activists Means and Johnson recognize the dangers that come from the colonization and loss of Indigenous languages. They state that, "if you've forgotten the names of the clouds, you've lost your way."[72]

Concluding Thoughts

In this chapter, I have written about the power of language and how our radical departure from seeking inclusion within the term "celebrity" is our point of revolution and the resurgence of our identities outside the mechanism that perpetuates colonization for the benefit of Euro–North American mainstream society. As Simpson states, "standing at the foot of a map of loss is clarity."[73] Rather than perpetuating loss through colonization and divesting our power as Anishinaabeg people, prioritizing the word mino-waawiindaganeziwin over the word *celebrity* occupies a space of empowerment outside mechanisms of colonization. Mino-waawiindaganeziwin creates the space for our stories and for us to become the stories. It creates the space to put Anishinaabeg intelligence at the centre (not at the margin) and to use its energy to drive the new narrative. Using Anishinaabemowin offers us a glimpse of Anishinaabeg brilliance, including our ethics, values, theories, methodologies, stories, and cosmologies, all enmeshed in ancestral intelligence and rooted in the continued occupation of our traditional territories, the source sites of the language. The use of words such as mino-waawiindaganeziwin manifests an alternative Anishinaabeg reality separate from the colonial reality. This mission propels my writing, and it is my purpose to reawaken other Anishinaabeg and other Indigenous peoples also to take it up as their mission of resurgence, reclamation, and revolution.

NOTES

1 Darren Courchene, "Language *as the* Root of Ojibwe Knowledge," *Geez Magazine*, Fall 2015, 26, http://www.academia.edu/30414319/Language_as_the_root_of_Ojibwe_knowledge (accessed 20 October 2018).

2 "Anishinaabeg" is an umbrella term for those "nations" rooted in the same linguistic dialect, cultural teachings, and intellectual traditions. Those who use the term to describe themselves as Anishinaabe (meaning human being) are composed of the following "nations": Anishiniwag (Oji-Cree), Ojibweg, Odaawaag, Bodéwadmik, Odishkwaamagiig (Nipissing), Misizaagiwininiwag (Mississaugas), Omàmiwininiwak (Algonquin), and Leni Lenape (Delaware). The Anishinaabeg inhabit the Great Lakes region in both Canada and the United States. In Anishinaabemowin (Anishinaabeg language), the word Anishinaabeg means the original human beings. See Edward Benton-Banai, *The Mishomis Book: The Voice of the Ojibway* (Minneapolis: University of Minnesota Press, 1988), 2–5; also see "anishinaabe" in *The Ojibway People's Dictionary*, https://ojibwe.lib.umn.edu/main-entry/anishinaabe-na (accessed 3 November 2017).

3 The spelling of mino-waawiindaganeziwin was taken from the online dictionary *Translate Ojibwe*. See "waawiindaganeziwin+an," in *Translate Ojibwe*, http://www.translateojibwe.com/en/dictionary-english-ojibwe/celebrity (accessed 30 October 2017).

4 Elvin Lim, "Why Celebrities Do Not Leaders Make," *OUPBlog: Oxford University Press's Academic Insights for the Thinking World*, 24 May 2011, 2071, https://blog.oup.com/2011/05/celebrity-politicians/ (accessed 1 November 2019).

5 Tim Willard, "The Big Difference between the Celebrity Leader and the Devoted Leader," *Church Leaders*, 12 December 2014, https://churchleaders.com/pastors/pastor-articles/244313-big-difference-celebrity-leader-devoted-leader.html (accessed 30 October 2017).

6 Quoted in Cosmus Butunyi, "Bono: Celebrity Is a Currency to Be Used to Bring about Change," *East African*, 12 April 2010, http://www.theeastafrican.co.ke/magazine/Bono-Celebrity-is-a-currency-to-be-used-to-bring-about-change/434746-897132-idv6dj/index.html (accessed 28 October 2017).

7 Courchene, "Language," 26.

8 Ibid.

9 Saulteaux are the Western Ojibwe or Plains Ojibwe. They are recognized as belonging to the cultural family of Anishinaabe peoples. *Saulteaux* is the French word for "people of the rapids."

10 The spelling of gchi-aya'aag comes from Michael McNally, *Honoring Elders: Aging, Authority, and Ojibwe Religion* (New York: Columbia University Press, 2009), 1.

11 In this context, I am referring to more than one person. Mino-waawiidaganeziwin is singular, and mino-waawiidaganeziwinan is plural.

12 Aimée Craft, "Anishinaabe Nibi Inaakonigewin Report: Reflecting the Water Laws Research Gathering Conducted with Anishinaabe Elders," 2014, 8, http://create-h2o.ca/pages/annual_conference/presentations/2014/ANI_Gathering_Report_-_June24.pdf (accessed 28 November 2017).

13 Ibid., 16.

14 Roger Spielmann, *"You're So Fat!" Exploring Ojibwe Discourse* (Toronto: University of Toronto Press, 1998), 158.

15 Leanne Betasamosake Simpson, *Dancing on Our Turtle's Back: Stories of Nishnaabeg Re-Creation, Resurgence and a New Emergence* (Winnipeg: Arbeiter Ring Publications, 2011), 49.

16 See "mino," in *The Ojibway People's Dictionary*, https://ojibwe.lib.umn.edu/main-entry/mino-pv-lex (accessed 14 October 2018).

17 See "waawiindan," in *The Ojibway People's Dictionary*, https://ojibwe.lib.umn.edu/main-entry/waawiindan-vti (accessed 29 November 2017).

18 See "waawiinjigaazo," in *The Ojibway People's Dictionary*, https://ojibwe.lib.umn.edu/main-entry/waawiinjigaazo-vai (accessed 29 November 2017).

19 See "wiindan," in *The Ojibway People's Dictionary*, https://ojibwe.lib.umn.edu/main-entry/wiindan-vti (accessed 17 September 2020).

20 Seven Generations Education Institute, "The Seven Grandfather Teachings, The Seven Teachings," http://www.7generations.org/?page_id=2396 (accessed 29 November 2017).

21 Courchene, "Language," 26.

22 Ibid.

23 Leslie Marmon Silko, *Ceremony* (New York: Penguin Books, 1977), 1; emphasis added.

24 Benton-Banai, *The Mishomis Book*, 7; emphasis added.

25 Seven Generations Education Institute, "Mino-Bimaadiziwin, Principles," http://www.7generations.org/?page_id=104 (accessed 29 November 2017).

26 See Mary Siisip Geniusz, *Plants Have So Much to Give Us, All We Have to Do Is Ask: Anishinaabe Botanical Teachings* (Minneapolis: University of Minnesota Press, 2015), 336; McNally, *Honoring Elders*, 46; and "indinawemaaganag," in *The Ojibway People's Dictionary*, http://ojibwe.lib.umn.edu/main-entry/inawemaagan-na (accessed 27 November 2017).

27 Benton-Banai, *The Mishomis Book*, 5–7.

28 Marie Battiste, "Micmac Literacy and Cognitive Assimilation: A Paper Presented to the Mokakit Indian Education Research Association 1984 International Conference London, Ontario," 26 July 1984, https://files.eric.ed.gov/fulltext/ED267957.pdf (accessed 29 November 2017).

29 Marie Battiste, "Micmac Literacy and Cognitive Assimilation," in *Indian Education in Canada: The Legacy*, ed. Jean Barman, Yvonne Hébert, and Don McCaskill (Vancouver: UBC Press, 1986), 23.

30 Simpson, *Dancing on Our Turtle's Back*, 49.

31 Ibid.

32 Ibid., 14.

33 Ibid., 24, 32.

34 Glen S. Coulthard, "Subjects of Empire: Indigenous Peoples and the 'Politics of Recognition' in Canada," *Contemporary Political Theory* 6, no. 4 (2007): 456.

35 Robert Bunge, "Language: The Psyche of a People," in *Our Languages, Our Survival*, ed. Freda Ahenakew and Shirley Fredeen (Vermillion: University of South Dakota, 1987), 17.

36 Ibid., 19.

37 Seven Generations Education Institute, "Mino-Bimaadiziwin, Principles."

38 Spielmann, *"You're So Fat!"*, 55.

39 Canada, Royal Commission on Aboriginal Peoples, *Gathering Strength*, vol. 3 of *Report of the Royal Commission on Aboriginal Peoples* (Ottawa: Canada Communications Group, 1996), 563.

40 Bunge, "Language," 13; emphasis added.

41 Spielmann, *"You're So Fat!"*, 54.

42 Leroy Little Bear, "Jagged Worldviews Colliding," in *Reclaiming Indigenous Voice and Vision*, ed. Marie Battiste (Vancouver: UBC Press, 2000), 77.

43 Ibid., 84–85.

44 Ibid.

45 Ibid., 85.

46 Quoted in Russell Means and Bayard Johnson, *If You've Forgotten the Names of the Clouds, You've Lost Your Way: An Introduction to American Indian Thought and Philosophy* (Porcupine, SD: Treaty Publications, 2012), 3.

47 Ibid.

48 See "celebrity," in *Oxford Dictionaries*, https://en.oxforddictionaries.com/definition/celebrity (accessed 3 October 2017).

49 Ibid.

50 See "celebrity," in *Merriam-Webster*, https://www.merriam-webster.com/dictionary/celebrity (accessed 3 October 2017).

51 Ibid.

52 Daniel Boorstin, *The Image: A Guide to Pseudo-Events in America* (New York: Vintage, 1961); Graeme Turner, *Understanding Celebrity* (London: SAGE, 2013), 58.

53 Boorstin, *The Image*, 65.

54 Turner, *Understanding Celebrity*, 5.

55 Boorstin, *The Image*, 65.

56 Turner, *Understanding Celebrity*, 5–6.

57 Larry Z. Leslie, *Celebrity in the 21st Century: A Reference Handbook* (Santa Barbara, CA: ABC-CLIO, 2011), 20.

58 Turner, *Understanding Celebrity*, 5, 6.

59 Ibid., 6.

60 Ibid.

61 Chris Rojek, *Fame Attack: The Inflation of Celebrity and Its Consequences* (New York: Bloomsbury Academic, 2012), 52.

62 Turner, *Understanding Celebrity*, 6.

63 Dan Brockington, *Celebrity Advocacy and International Development* (London: Routledge, 2014), xxi.

64 Daniel Francis, *The Imaginary Indian: The Image of the Indian in Canadian Culture* (Vancouver: Arsenal Pulp Press, 1992), 109.

65 *Reel Injun*, dir. Neil Diamond et al., Lorber Films, 2010 (DVD).

66 Francis, *The Imaginary Indian*, 105–11.

67 Ibid., 107.

68 Ibid., 105–7.

69 Ibid., 107.

70 Ibid., 105; *Reel Injun*.

71 None of these individuals was actually Indigenous and made up false identities to pass as Indigenous.

72 Means and Johnson, *If You've Forgotten the Names of the Clouds*, 5.

73 Leanne Betasamosake Simpson, *As We Have Always Done: Indigenous Freedom through Radical Resistance* (Minneapolis: University of Minnesota Press, 2017), 15.

CHAPTER 2

Empowering Voices from the Past: The Playing Experiences of Retired Pasifika Rugby League Athletes in Australia

David Lakisa, Katerina Teaiwa, Daryl Adair, and Tracy Taylor

Leading Pacific scholar Epeli Hau'ofa offers a widely accepted reconceptualization of the Pacific in his influential essay "Our Sea of Islands."[1] He argues that Pacific Islanders are connected rather than separated by the sea, and he views the ocean as a highway long traversed by Pacific ancestors. His was a call for greater "Pacific empowerment," both economically and geographically, for Pasifika people to shake off views of belittlement, boundedness, and smallness in resistance to histories of imperialism and neocolonialism by "establishing new resource bases and expanded networks for circulation."[2] In the context of Pasifika (Pacific Islander and Māori) athletes, in this chapter we assert that there is much to be (re)learned about Australian Rugby League history by giving primacy to empowered voices of "Pasifika pioneers"—retired professional players in Australia's National Rugby League (NRL). What follows is an exploration of empowering voices and lived experiences of ten retired male Pasifika rugby league players in Australia. We explore the complex pathways of Pasifika labour migration, the mixed experiences of social inclusion, and the navigation of cultural identity in the league. This research adds scholastic value by giving a Pasifika voice, interpretation, and perspective,[3] largely unaddressed in popular histories of the Australian Rugby League.

As the lead author, I [David Lakisa] have had the privilege of speaking with and learning from selected Pasifika pioneers. My goal is to give voice to these men via the Pasifika cultural practice of talanoa (to converse), a process that also enables insights into their families. In terms of research with Pasifika athletes, I was able to gain access to these footballers from a particular perspective, that of the "cultural insider." I am a New Zealand–born Polynesian (Samoan) man who migrated to Australia in the late 1980s with previous experience as a former rugby league administrator in the NRL—specifically in the area of coaching and development. This research experience left me feeling humbled and awed by their significant contributions, sacrifices, and resilience, both on and off the playing field.

In October 2013, I was welcomed into the modest home of a retired Polynesian rugby league player in the outskirts of Sydney. The tall, broad-shouldered, and soft-spoken Samoan, now in his mid-sixties, migrated to Australia in 1970 after being recruited into the (then) New South Wales Rugby Football League (NSWRFL) competition. As I made my way across the living room of his humble two-bedroom unit, which had minimal furnishings, I instinctively lowered myself below his eye level and said politely "tulou" (excuse me) as a mark of humility and respect consistent with the etiquette of talanoa. As I sat on the couch, I glanced around the room expecting to see precious rugby league memorabilia or artifacts that resembled Pasifika cultures, such as kava bowls or traditional fine mats. To my surprise, there was none. Instead, only a few family photographs were spread around the tidy room, with a recliner nestled squarely in front of an old television set. So, before any discussion of the rugby league, the next thirty minutes of shared dialogue or talanoa were spent exchanging customary Pasifika greetings. In this case, that involved acknowledging one another's aiga (family) and aganu'u (village), shared experiences of migration to Australia, religious backgrounds, and the opportunity to build rapport by switching comfortably between Samoan and English.

Our shared dialogue became more than casual conversation; our talanoa was deep, intimate, and often emotional, which allowed us to bond quickly, as though we had known each other a long time. The gentleman spoke with a calm yet authoritative tone as he reminisced about memorable, and not so memorable, football pastimes. He included narratives about recruitment, former teams, teammates, coaches, playing tours, and, importantly, his family's and extended family's migration to Australia in 1970. This initial conversation reaffirmed to me the importance of being attuned to Pasifika cultural sensibilities in rapport building and the effect that it has on generating authentic voices for Pasifika people.

Pasifika Migration to Australia

Pasifika labour migration to Australian shores dates back to the exploitative practice of "blackbirding." South Sea Islanders, known colloquially as "the kanakas" and hailing from the Solomon Islands, Vanuatu, and several other Pacific Islands, were often forcibly brought to Queensland to work in the sugar cane industry as very poorly paid indentured labourers.[4] This process began as early as 1863 and eventually involved as many as 62,000 migrants. When Australia became a federated nation, restrictive residential and migration policies, notably the Pacific Islanders Labourers Act 1901, had negative impacts on the South Sea Islander community.[5] Against the odds, these people had established themselves with family and property, but their forced repatriation was consistent with the racially exclusive "white Australia policy" of Australian governments. The gradual dismantling of racially selective immigration policies, from the end of the Second World War to the early 1970s, provided unexpected and welcome opportunities for global migration to Australia, which obviously included the Pacific Islands and Oceania regions.[6] The flow of Pasifika migrants since the late twentieth century has been significant in fact; a recent report by the Australian Bureau of Statistics indicates that 1.4 percent of the national population self-describe as Pasifika by way of ancestry,[7] with the majority having migrated via New Zealand.[8]

Geopolitically, Pasifika communities in Australia are ethnically diverse in terms of culture, custom, language, and relation across what are known as the Melanesian, Micronesian, and Polynesian regions of Oceania.[9] Pasifika population groups are fast growing and youthful, with the largest Pasifika communities residing in Australia identifying as Māori, Samoan, Tongan, Fijian, and Cook Islanders.[10] However, household studies reveal a bleak picture socio-economically, and in Australia Pasifika peoples have lower life expectancy rates than the national average, and they experience problems of access to government benefits and educational opportunities depending on their citizenship status.[11] Pasifika families have a higher number of dependants compared with national averages and generally reside in the low socio-economic regions of the largest capital cities—Sydney, Brisbane, and Melbourne.[12]

The "Pasifika Turn" in the Australian Rugby League

Compared with just two decades ago, Pasifika identities are much more visible in Australian sport and popular culture.[13] This is especially so in the sport of rugby, with the NRL being one of the largest sport competitions in Australia. Māori contributions to rugby began as early as the late nineteenth century.[14] In 1908, an "All Māori" New Zealand rugby league team played a series of touring matches in New South Wales and Queensland.[15] The arrival of what was described locally as a "flamboyant"[16] and "mysterious"[17] team quickly captured the Australian public's interest; the visit also played a role in helping the NSWRFL to establish itself financially.[18] Furthermore, the inaugural All Māori tour presented an opportunity for the visitors to play in the NSWRFL. Peter Moko was the first in 1909, followed by Glen Pakere, Brownie Paki, and Ted Pickrang in 1910, 1923, and 1930, respectively,[19] becoming Pasifika pioneers in Australian Rugby League competitions. In the wake of changing migration laws, a small number of Pasifika players based in New Zealand plied their trade in Sydney-based rugby league clubs during the 1970s and 1980s[20] and participated in a local competition in Melbourne.[21] It was not until the 1990s that a steady influx of players of Pasifika descent, mainly New Zealand–born, turned into a substantial cohort in what was then the Australian Rugby League.[22] This growth was the result, in part, of the adoption of professionalism for rugby codes (union and league) in the mid-1990s.[23] This meant that rugby offered a genuine career opportunity for talented players. For latent athletic talent from Pacific Islands, this contributed to outward migratory patterns to various rugby-playing, developed countries.[24] Today there is substantial Pasifika recruitment, participation, and movement across professional (and semi-professional) rugby competitions across Australia,[25] New Zealand,[26] Oceania,[27] Europe, and Japan.[28]

Numerically and proportionally, the most significant Pasifika representation is in the NRL, the Australasian-based, premier rugby league competition. Pasifika participation in the NRL was reportedly 9 percent when the league, as it stands today, was formed in 1998.[29] A decade later it had grown to 12 percent.[30] Today it stands at an extraordinary 46 percent of contracted players.[31] These growing rates of participation are also reflected at the level of international competition. At the 2013 Rugby League World Cup tournament, approximately 46 percent of participating players were of Pasifika descent. Additionally, teams from New Zealand (since 2008), Papua New Guinea (since 2014), and Fiji (since 2020) compete in the NRL second-tier competitions in New South Wales and Queensland. In all cases, Pasifika footballers are "on the move," migrating from the (developing) Global South to countries in the (developed) Global North, circulating their football prowess across larger, wealthier regions of the world.[32] This means that now there are very few rugby contests without Pasifika representation.[33]

The "Pasifika turn" or influence of Pasifika in the Australian Rugby League has understandably attracted research attention to Pasifika cultures and experiences, especially in terms of complexities of upward mobility and labour migration for Pasifika footballers in Australia.[34] Previous research shows that Pasifika NRL player motivations are represented by family-, faith-, and culture-based forms of attachment.[35] However, these motivations and priorities are often misunderstood by non-Pasifika coaching staff because of their lack of knowledge of common Pasifika values and customs, such as respect, spirituality, service, and reciprocity, or their insensitivity toward those cultural attributes.[36] In any case, for (semi-)professional Pasifika footballers, retelling their experiences of navigating and coping with the successes and pressures of playing rugby in Australia is attached to the pan-Pacific concept of mana, denoting spiritual power, integrity, or status or the acquisition of success and prestige by (and conferring on) an individual, group, or object in sport and other contemporary settings.[37]

Mana is critical in any discussion of Pasifika achievements and movements in sport.[38] Essentially, an object's or person's mana benefits others, and in this case retired Pasifika pioneers are accorded great mana because of their revolutionary influence, respect, and power to perform in early Australian Rugby League competitions. Conversely, in light of today's burgeoning NRL rates of participation, Katerina Teaiwa points to niu (new) mana, referring to the application of mana in a contemporary diasporic context. She argues that, for Pasifika footballers, increased media exposure and high expectations placed on self and others "dramatically increase the pressures on athletes . . . to be responsible for not just their own, but everyone's image, everyone's hopes, and everyone's mana."[39] So, though acquiring mana or prestige for the collective benefit is considered commonplace and praiseworthy in Pasifika cultures,[40] it can place enormous social, emotional, and economic pressures on young male Pasifika athletes.[41] This further highlights the complex context of intersecting and regularly negotiated socio-cultural, geopolitical, and economic goals for Pasifika communities,[42] in this case past and present Pasifika footballers.

Positioning Talanoa in Rugby League Histories

The talanoa method is a culturally appropriate and "authentic" way for researchers to engage with Pasifika communities, for it literally speaks to Pasifika sensibilities and traditions of communication.[43] Talanoa has been applied widely in Pacific research methodology,[44] not only because the qualitative process derives from oral, dialogic cultural practice, but also because talanoa is essentially concerned with strengthening relationships and respectful communications.[45] The "fluid" and "nimble" conversations that characterize talanoa differ in structure and tone from formal and semi-structured interviews or quantitative surveys commonly associated with Western research methods. In other words, talanoa is more than just informal, open-ended conversation; it is infused with marked emotional and cultural Pasifika sensibilities.[46] This lends itself to "a personal encounter" in which "people story their issues, their realities and aspirations,"[47] and creates and nurtures socio-spatial ties or connections.[48]

Talanoa, as with any research approach, has its limitations. First, a major drawback in the use of talanoa is the assumption that the researcher is well versed in the relevant facets of Pasifika culture. Although there are commonalities among Pasifika cultures, there are also differences; they are diverse in ethnicities, customs, languages, and relations across what are known as the Melanesian, Micronesian, and Polynesian regions of Oceania.[49] In short, researchers need to be prepared for such diversity through nuanced dialogues and varied cultural and kinship competencies,[50] in this case acknowledging and sharing one's family, faith, or cultural connections. Second, and along the lines of cultural competency and cultural appropriation, talanoa is dependent on building rapport. It is particularly important that researchers are appropriately attuned to ethnic markers concerned with Pasifika values of respect, sense of community, and service—whether they are of Pasifika or non-Pasifika heritage.[51] If the initial relationship-building phase is poor, then it will most likely lead to negative, underwhelming, inauthentic, and untrustworthy conversations.[52] In terms of talanoa, formal and informal arrangements necessitate different cultural approaches.[53] For example, talanoa with someone of the opposite gender, family members, the sick or elderly, chiefs/nobles, or religious leaders might warrant different customary approaches, such as a formal invitation to sit together on the ground, a kava ceremony, religious rites or ceremonies, prayers, or gift giving and receiving. These engagements, on the face of it, are a "simpler" process for a "cultural insider" or someone of Pasifika heritage already familiar with some or all of the cultural norms. For a non-Pasifika researcher, there is a steeper hill to climb. However, there are sometimes complexities that confront the Pasifika researcher more than someone from outside that cultural domain, such as respecting one's elders by not asking too many questions. In other words, as part of Pasifika hierarchical social systems, younger people are expected to defer to their elders. Another example is experiencing initial hesitation and refusal by certain interviewees for fear of being exploited, especially if they are unknown to the researcher. Whatever the background of the researcher, all approaches to talanoa require culturally appropriate respect, appreciation, and reciprocity.

The positioning of talanoa in Australian sport histories, consistent with postcolonial approaches, aligns with the call for Indigenous interpretations of Pasifika history and knowledge.[54] This means extending Pasifika ways of knowing or modes of "Pacific enquiry" beyond Eurocentric assumptions and approaches that currently dominate the academy.[55] For example, the long-standing practice of European framing of Pacific Islanders as underdeveloped, drawing geopolitical boundaries in their ocean,[56] and seeing islanders as bounded by the smallness of their landscapes in comparison to the immensity of their waterways. Like Hau'ofa,[57] Teaiwa challenges this framing of Oceania "motivated by a sense of concern that geopolitical powers such as Australia and the United States need to be as interested in what they can learn from the Pacific as in what they can gain from dominating it."[58] In the Australian context, including studies of professional sport, empirical studies of Pasifika communities have typically drawn on perspectives from New Zealand, the Pacific Islands, or the United States,[59] with little engagement with Pasifika research models and theories such as the Fonofale model,[60] Vanua research framework,[61] and Kaupapa Māori research methodology.[62] These modes of Pacific enquiry are commonly used in the areas of health, education, and social science, but they are not present in sport and leisure management research. Pasifika research in Australia, especially the talanoa method, has not fundamentally shaped the approaches of researchers, whether they are from within or outside Pasifika communities. That said, talanoa is the most appropriate method for this research because of the cultural knowledge, experiences, and sensibilities of the primary researcher and the ten interviewees.

The Talanoa Sessions

A sample group of retired Pasifika players was drawn from Australian Rugby League histories and literature. From this search, twenty-one men were identified and eighteen approached, with ten responding and agreeing to participate. These ten retired Pasifika players satisfied three major criteria. First, they migrated to Australia (1960 or later) to ply their trade contractually in professional or semi-professional rugby league competitions. Second, by way of residency, they now call Australia home. Third, through personal communication with the researcher, they self-identified as Pacific Islander and/or Māori. The age range of the participants was from thirty-eight to sixty-nine. Ten participants were adequate for the purposes of this qualitative study, noting the limited number of retired Pasifika footballers who fit the selection criteria.

My previous employment as the Pacific Islander coaching and development officer for the New South Wales Rugby League (2007–11) provided me with unique access to and familiarity with eight of the ten participants, and I used a third-party agreement via a referral system for participants whom I did not know. Ethical approval by the University of Technology Sydney Human Ethics Committee was also granted prior to any talanoa session. Pseudonyms were used for participants to maintain their privacy. Talanoa schedules were made flexible with dates, times, and venues convenient to the participants (see Table 1). This resulted in nine interviews conducted in New South Wales and one in Queensland.

Table 1: Overview of the Talanoa Sessions

Pseudonym	Ethnicity	Location of Interview	Year of Retirement
Semi	Fijian	Leagues Club	1974
Tomasi	Fijian	Home	1974
Mataio	Samoan	Home	1977
Henare	Māori and Samoan	Home	1987
Tama	Māori	Workplace	1997
Viliame	Fijian	Home	2000
Mosese	Fijian	Home	2000
Peni	Fijian	Home	2001
Tevita	Tongan	Home	2005
Mikaele	Samoan	Workplace	2013

The purpose of the talanoa sessions was to help empower past and, to a lesser extent, rethink present Pasifika voices in sport-related labour migration and sport career experiences in rugby league competitions. The challenges and obstacles of Pasifika players' individual journeys help us to better understand them, their cultures, their communities, and their sport clubs. Each talanoa session was recorded, transcribed, and coded for themes and sub-themes using the data analysis software NVivo. Four key overarching themes emerged from the collective data: (1) family obligations, including upward mobility and migration experiences; (2) attitudes toward Pasifika race and identity; (3) the influence of mateship; and (4) politics surrounding (un)equal salaries. The following sections outline each theme and the stories represented within it. Occasional links to contemporary Pasifika footballer trends and experiences are included to provide contrast and further highlight the complexities of the lived experiences of retired Pasifika athletes.

Pasifika Pioneer Voices

Family Obligations

In all cases, the interviewees placed collective achievements above their own, indicating family or whanau (Māori), aiga (Samoan), or famili (Tongan) as the most influential and motivating factor in their participation in Australian Rugby League competitions. Peni, a respondent of Fijian descent, described his first-grade debut as "the proudest moment of my career," humbly declaring that "running out onto the field and to look up and see my parents sitting there and smiling at me, yeah, that was number one. Just to acknowledge them and for them to nod back, yeah, that was special." Viliame also attributed his football achievements to parental sacrifices, recounting with a determined expression on his face that "my parents worked hard to give us the better life. I've always seen my father and mom work hard, so being a professional footballer wasn't working hard. It afforded me the luxury to help my family and my parents and my sisters, and then later it gave me the opportunity to look after my kids."

The critical decision to accept or reject semi-/professional playing contracts was heavily influenced by family or kinship networks. Most of the former players interviewed were reluctant to sign initial contract offers until they had consulted with their family members. Henare, who vividly recalled his staunch Māori mother instructing him, "no, you're going [to Australia]," admitted that her "tough love" approach was motivated not merely by financial reward but also the chance for him to branch out and experience life outside New Zealand. He added that "I eventually went, and I ended up staying" despite at one stage wanting to quit, partly because of homesickness, but mainly because of the physical demands of training, especially compared with New Zealand clubs. Mataio also admitted being on the verge of quitting because of the tough training regime of his new Australian team, but he "stuck it out," partly to avoid any ridicule from extended family for failing to make it in Australia. Viliame, who signed an overseas contract, also heeded his late father's advice: "Your word is your bond. I don't want you to waste that opportunity." The retired Fijian reflected that "it was never about me, the money, or the fame and stuff like that. I could have gone to other clubs for more money, but in those days I felt loyal." The retired players all discussed how they were motivated by collective or familial benefits rather than individual gain, as is customary in Pasifika cultures.[63] This aspiration was underpinned by shared values, such as respect, love, humility, and reciprocity within and throughout kinship networks.[64]

Despite the enormous pressure to "provide off and perform on" the rugby playing field, on the whole the retired players clearly voiced a willingness and strong sense of obligation to provide financial support for immediate and often extended family members. This support had influenced their motivation to become paid footballers. However, they expressed various perspectives on the limits to their collective responsibilities. For example, Mosese remarked that, "especially with immediate family, you help them out here and there. Then it gets to a point where you just say no because enough is enough," even comparing his gift-giving efforts to a "money tap that I had to turn off, you know, like a human ATM [automatic teller machine]." When questioned about whether foreign remittances caused problems, Henare, who migrated to Australia from New Zealand, noted casually that "it did in a way, but I never said anything. If they wanted x amount, then no problem. But, if they wasted the money, then I stopped giving it to them." Being taken advantage of financially by a family member seemed to be a common experience with most of the players. Peni, a player raised with traditional Fijian values, freely conceded that "it's just the way we're brought up, I guess, big family and stuff, and you just got to help out where you can, especially if you played first grade or NRL or whatever." However, Mosese was particularly critical: "Lending money to so-called family and going into business with them was one of the biggest mistakes in my career. The hardest thing was the influences around me, peer pressure."

Two of the retired players noted that their parents placed no expectation or overt pressure on them for financial aid. Yet they still chose to provide monetary support to them. Peni framed his thoughts this way: "I felt like I owed them heaps (a lot) for my upbringing. I got to look after them. I've got to repay them for getting me to where I was. They didn't really say much, but I felt it was my honour to look after them financially."

Peni spent his first match payment cheque on a new fridge for his mother, simply because that was what "she needed." Henare shared a similar experience: "Mom didn't expect it [remittances], but I sent money anyway." Interestingly, Tevita offered his personal view of gift-giving attitudes between Pasifika and non-Pasifika teammates: "We Polynesians are way more giving. That's the difference; we give, and that's part of our culture. We give, where Palagis [non-Samoan or -Tongan], when they marry, and when they move out, it's just them. Their moms and dads are to the side." Like other global sport migrant communities that share a strong sense of collective responsibility[65] by providing shared support, for example African and European migrants in professional football leagues,[66] Tevita felt obligated financially and culturally—such as with funerals, birthdays, and weddings—even after he had retired from professional rugby league play. His attitude toward giving was shaped by his financial stability, owing to a career spanning ten years in the professional era and a successful transition out of the sport in post-retirement. He said that, "compared to my siblings, mom and dad always expected me to put in more. I'm giving more now than when I was playing."

In summary, family obligations and a culture of respect and reciprocity underpinned the playing experiences of those interviewed. The consequent behaviours and actions ranged from motivationally positive to pressures and burdens since individual and family attitudes toward gift giving and providing collective support for kinship networks vary, depending on individual preference, financial stability, and how mana is accorded through an individual's kinship ties.

Pasifika Identity

A recurrent theme among the interviewees was the importance of connectedness to one's cultural identity. In the context of sport, discovering or rediscovering one's ethnocultural identity can cause athletes to "weave" or "negotiate" their identities across private and public domains.[67] Yet, to these retired footballers, culture was not only important but also "sacred." As Viliame noted, "you don't just shove it and put it in a corner somewhere." He also proudly declared the lifelong advice that his parents gave to him: "Never forget where you're from or who you are." Henare described his cultural pride this way: "I was so proud of where I've come from." However, he also experienced racialized assumptions or profiling based on physical appearance, such as skin colour. As Henare noted, "a lot of them thought I was Aborigine. I said, 'I'm Polynesian,' and they said, 'what's that?'" In fact, opposing players would intentionally call him "a Koori [Indigenous Australian from the NSW region] . . . to try to get you upset and put you off your game. But it didn't bother me because I knew they didn't even know what a Polynesian was." All ten retired players mentioned that racialized assumptions were a regular occurrence during their playing careers. Tomasi, of Fijian descent, said that "everyone thought I was Māori because I was black." He recalled amusingly that "I was asked if I was Cuban." Viliame, also of Fijian descent, added that "they [non-Pasifika] automatically thought that I was Māori because I said I came from New Zealand." In another instance, Mataio, of Samoan descent, was even selected for and participated in an Aboriginal representative side simply because "I was black." Despite not discounting their ethnicity and cultural roots, Tomasi and Mosese felt somewhat undeterred when their "Pasifikaness" went undetected. When asked why they did not disclose their correct ethnicity to anyone, for example during media interviews, Tomasi merely replied that "no one asked me before." Mosese simply accepted his status as a minority in the game, saying in a laid-back manner that, "when I came through [the playing grades] there were hardly any Fijians, but I didn't really feel socially isolated because that's how it was." Yet other retired players made conscious efforts to correct or avoid mistaken identities. As Viliame stated, "I would stop them and say, 'I'm actually Fijian.' I never ever just went 'yeah, yeah.' I always made sure." Henare said that "they didn't know what a friggin' Polynesian was back then, so I set a goal to let them know exactly what a Polynesian is and how good we are and everything else."

The narratives of these interviewees reveal complex negotiations and perceptions between players' views of themselves and wider public ignorance of or indifference toward their cultural backgrounds. In other words, opposing players, teammates, the Australian media, and rugby league fans either did not know that these players were Pasifika or chose not to acknowledge it. The exceptions arose from perceptions and appearances or the status of being "coloured" or "not coloured enough," more so than Pasifika, and this could attract racism, bigotry, and prejudice. Racial profiling and stereotyping of

Pasifika athletes in Australian sport can result in ambivalence about Pasifika ethnic identities.[68] Or, as Kristen McGavin describes it, "being Nesian" or Pacific Islander in Australia is authenticated and negotiated through certain behaviours and perceptions of self and others.[69]

Racial Vilification

Various perspectives were expressed as interviewees recounted how they were subject to intense incidents of racial abuse and vilification, particularly those who retired in the 1970s–90s. Despite being a member of a prestigious and revered rugby league club, Semi reflected on his harsh treatment by some fans: "People would call me black this and black that. I was even spat on as I ran out onto the field. They yelled out 'go back, you coconuts! Go back to Fiji.'" Many of the retired players disclosed that racist remarks were directed toward them at almost every game, and Mosese remembered being called a "f'n n*****." In response, he, among others, developed "thick skin," showing tremendous courage and resilience. As Henare responded, "I copped[70] so much I didn't want to retaliate. I set myself a goal with all the racist things I copped. I didn't want to give the Polynesians a bad name by revenge. I'm not going to give in." Tevita, among others, was more casual about and even tolerant of abuse from opposing players, concluding that racial tirades were "just part of the game" and used solely as a form of game-play intimidation. Mosese added that "you just handle it. The guys on the field, they don't really mean it." Mataio affirmed that "all the racist stuff didn't bother me. I just loved playing the game." As Tevita put it, "all that racist stuff is water off a duck's back." Viliame offered a more forgiving and stoic approach, admitting that he simply put up with the offensive and racist comments "because of how I was grounded" in his parents' advice "to always treat people with respect." Tama, heavily involved in the coaching and development of predominantly Pasifika athletes, expressed stern disapproval of some rugby league coaching staff and club administrators who made blatant racist comments about players, such as "there's too many coconuts in that team" or "look at those black $#%@."

Interestingly, Henare and Mikaele observed that racial slurs were "not just from white people. You get abuse from Kiwis, Māoris, or other [Pacific] Island folk as well." In terms of labels used to describe each other's connectedness to culture, Tama, who migrated to Australia from New Zealand in the early

1990s and maintained a strong sense of his Māori identity throughout his life, referred to some other Polynesians in the lower grades (division teams) as "already Aussie." This referred to people who assimilated into Australian "mainstream" culture and were now disconnected from their cultural roots.

There is a sad irony on the rugby league playing field that treating others with respect, or being revered among the playing group, seems to have meant that Pasifika players accepted racist taunts. This approach still exists in rugby league competitions. Although there have been a small number of formal complaints about on-field racial vilification in the NRL of Indigenous Australian and Pasifika footballers, specifically in the past decade,[71] implicit forms of racism or racist talk have also come to the fore in Australian Rugby League media. For example, segments of popular football talk shows have mocked the broken English of Pacific Island–born players and the mispronunciations of Pasifika footballers' names. In other instances, rugby league commentators have blamed poor on-field performances on "bro culture,"[72] referring to players who become too complacent because of the closeness and unity between Pacific Islanders and Māori. Another commentator described Pasifika players as using a "coconut style" of football[73]—referring to the freestyle and laid-back nature of Pacific Islanders. Although these representations have been passed off as light entertainment, and despite some Pasifika players offering anglicized versions of their names for the sake of convenience,[74] these occurrences of casual racism have been labelled "offensive" and "disrespectful" by Pasifika and non-Pasifika viewers alike.[75] In spite of the present challenges within Australian Rugby League circles, and particularly within the media, important here are the remarkable strength, resilience, and tolerance of retired players who experienced racial abuse and vilification. The tone of the interviews quickly changed from largely sobriety to excitement when the conversation shifted to off-field camaraderie and lasting friendships with teammates.

Mateship

Broadly speaking, the term "mateship" refers to the rich and valued Antipodean version of male fraternity throughout Australian white settler history.[76] In the context of Australian Rugby League histories, retired Pasifika players interviewed agreed that throughout their playing careers they forged lifelong friendships with Pasifika and non-Pasifika teammates. When asked about his fondest memories of the sport, Tomasi said, with a reminiscent smile, that "it was all about my mates," and Mataio recounted happily that "we [teammates] always stuck together." Tevita, who migrated to Australia with his family at a young age, said that he did not feel socially excluded mainly because he had built such a strong rapport with many of his non-Pasifika teammates coming up through the junior playing ranks, specifically under fifteen years and older. He also stressed the tight camaraderie and sense of security that he felt when his Pasifika teammates got together. Tevita put it this way: "It's just the way we are because we just click together. We understand each other's jokes, and that's why we laugh, because we laugh at each other. You can't do that with the palagis [whites] until you get to play first grade all the time. Then you can sort of migrate with the boys, but when they first came together it's just automatically go with your own kind until you get to know the boys more, and you [start] clicking, but you still hang with your own kind."

The research findings highlighted a tendency for Pasifika players to gravitate initially to other Pasifika players until there was a level of trust and comfort with non-Pasifika teammates and coaches.[77] For example, Mikaele remarked that, "when the [Pasifika] boys get together, we have a lot of fun and joke around. Some of the other [non-Pasifika] boys come in and say, 'oh, the "brothers" are together again.'" Lameko Panapa and Murray Phillips also suggest that, where there is a dominant non-Pasifika environment, ethnic differences among players can be overridden in favour of forging new identities and shared experiences.[78] A prime example is the experience of Mataio, appointed captain despite being the only Pasifika player on the team. He made deliberate decisions to ensure that mateship or team unity was paramount, regardless of cultural background, by regularly organizing team functions and ensuring that "after every game we went back to the league's club to mingle. We didn't go anywhere else." Mataio spoke about his approach this way: "They all looked up to me because I said, 'wherever I go, we all go together. We never go individually. When I leave, we all leave, so we ha[ve] no problems. Then you can do what you want after that.'"

His experience highlights that mateship can extend beyond cultural differences. The other nine retired players shared similar experiences. Each reminisced about specific teammates by recalling their nicknames, cultural backgrounds, occupations, and personalities. Semi, Tomasi, Viliame, and

Mikaele spoke fondly about reunions with past teams and teammates or the deaths of former teammates, coaches, and family members. These accounts of the value and place of mateship by retired Pasifika footballers characterized connectedness and strong patterns of social cohesion among peer groups in the rugby league.[79] This held true even when Pasifika players were selected to play for an Australian representative team, or their Queensland or New South Wales state team, instead of their cultural heritage–based team. Tama suggested using mateship as a way of determining a player's country of eligibility and still maintaining one's cultural identity or Māori dom, specifically referring to some New Zealand–born players selected to play for Australia: "You're always going to be Kiwi, you're just happening to play for Australia. . . . They're playing with their mates."

The Politics of Unequal Salaries

Since the game turned professional in 1995, the NRL became a full-time career option for rugby league athletes and, in this case, male Pasifika footballers. One player described the significant increase in his salary, happily leaving a "team meeting with heavy pockets" of cash. Another retired player slowly nodded in contemplation, saying that "it was great money at that time." However, that was not always the case. Many of the retired Pasifika players interviewed shared poignant views of exploitation and "being underpaid," especially compared with their non-Pasifika teammates. "Polys [Polynesians] just get 'used' massively. Palagis are always going to get more money than you. Maybe because they talk more, and they ask more questions, but we don't ask the questions. We probably want to say more, but we can't. It's like we're too shy, or we just can't say it."

This view was echoed by Henare, who, despite playing in the pre-professional era, said that "they're [non-Pasifika] always going to take advantage of us [Pasifika]. That's how I'm always going to look at it. It's starting to change now because we're [Pasifika] getting the top money," referring to current high-profile Pasifika players. At the time, Henare signed a minimal playing contract and blamed self-ignorance and the lack of financial literacy for what he perceived to be failed contract negotiations. As the season progressed, he unexpectedly found himself comparing his contract with those of his non-Pasifika teammates. He had a moment of revelation about his potential greater earning capacity: "Hang on, some of these blokes are getting paid more than me! Then someone suggested I should get an accountant, so I did." He thought that doing so helped him to make smarter financial decisions moving forward. In a similar way, Mosese reflected on his perceived poor financial management, conceding that "I lacked guidance or a mentor." Yet, when comparing today's playing cohort, who receive a minimum annual salary of approximately $100,000 Australian, Tevita defended strongly their sense of entitlement or earning capacity: "Kids deserve everything they can get today. You can't really compare us with today's athletes. They're professional and under a lot more scrutiny." Thus, on the one hand, as a minority playing group, the retired players said that they felt deeply exploited during their playing careers; on the other, they shared a strong sense of support for and satisfaction from today's playing cohort, who earn much higher salaries compared with those of the amateur and semi-professional era of Australian Rugby League competitions.

Empowering Voices of the Past

Drawing on Hau'ofa's notion of "Pacific empowerment,"[80] we observe that the fascination with Pasifika athletic prowess has increased curiosity about the significant influence and heterogeneous nature of Pasifika culture in Australian sport. Previous studies of Pasifika footballers have not dealt with historical pathways in Australian Rugby League histories and competitions. The empowering voices captured here through talanoa and from a "cultural insider" view add much-needed scholastic value through Pasifika sport lenses, interpretations, and perspectives. They also help us to better understand the complex cultural milieu of retired Pasifika athletes and their communities and clubs.

The lived experiences of Pasifika pioneers reveal the heavy influence of familial motivation and the subsequent role of mana by placing collective needs above their own needs, especially in negotiating the pressures and successes of upward mobility and labour migration. This is included in the politics of salary or contract negotiations for Pasifika athletes and their families. Our study also found that maintaining connections with their respective ethnic identities and the concept of mateship were of great importance to retired Pasifika footballers, even though misinformed stereotypes and labels of retired players' ethnic identities were common. Considering their minority status in Australian Rugby League competitions and the regularity of racial abuse experienced by Pasifika players, their tremendous humility, strength, and resilience were shown in overcoming adversity. The evidence presented here affirms that a sense of mana is critical to any discussion of Pasifika sport performance. Furthermore, family, faith, and culture are hallmark values of retired Pasifika footballers, as has been established for contemporary players.[81]

Although mateship was highly valued, the politics of unequal salaries also sometimes led to feelings of exploitation or being used by football administrators. More broadly, further research is needed to examine the practices of diversity management between Pasifika employees and non-Pasifika employers and improving Pasifika cultural competencies in the sport workplace. In sum, this study will help one to better understand the lived experiences of retired Pasifika players in past Australian Rugby League competitions by giving primacy to their voices. The findings suggest a rethink of approaches to and sensibilities in understanding Pasifika players by all dimensions of the sporting code brought about by the "Pasifika turn," or substantial participation of Pasifika athletes, past and present.

NOTES

1 Epeli Hau'ofa, "Our Sea of Islands," in *A New Oceania: Rediscovering Our Sea of Islands*, ed. Eric Waddell, Vijay Naidu, and Epeli Hau'ofa (Suva, Fiji: School of Social and Economic Development, University of the South Pacific, 1993), 2–16.

2 Ibid, 11.

3 Samantha Rose, Max Quanchi, and Clive Moore, *A National Strategy for the Study of the Pacific* (Brisbane: Australian Association for the Advancement of Pacific Studies, 2009); Konai H. Thaman, "Decolonizing Pacific Studies: Indigenous Perspectives, Knowledge, and Wisdom in Higher Education," *Contemporary Pacific* 15, no. 1 (2003): 1–17; Katerina Teaiwa, "Reframing Oceania: Lessons from Pacific Studies," in *Framing the Global: Entry Points for Research*, ed. Hilary E. Kahn (Bloomington: Indiana University Press, 2014), 67–96.

4 Edward W. Docker, *The Blackbirders: A Brutal Story of the Kanaka Slave-Trade* (Sydney: Angus and Robertson, 1981).

5 Helen Lee and Steve Francis, *Migration and Transnationalism, Pacific Perspectives* (Canberra: Australian National University E Press, 2009).

6 Paul Hamer, "'Unsophisticated and Unsuited': Australian Barriers to Pacific Islander Immigration from New Zealand," *Political Science* 66, no. 2 (2014): 93–118.

7 Australian Bureau of Statistics, *Counting Persons, Place of Usual Residence* (Canberra: Australian Bureau of Statistics, 2016).

8 Paul Hamer, "One in Six? The Rapid Growth of the Maori Population in Australia," *New Zealand Population Review* 33, no. 1 (2008): 153–76.

9 Teaiwa, "Reframing Oceania," 68–70.

10 Jioji Ravulo, *Pacific Communities in Australia* (Sydney: University of Western Sydney, 2015).

11 Judith Kearney and Matthew Glen, "The Effects of Citizenship and Ethnicity on the Education Pathways of Pacific Youth in Australia," *Education, Citizenship and Social Justice*12, no. 3 (2017): 277-289; Ravulo, *Pacific Communities in Australia*, 11–25.

12 Australian Bureau of Statistics, *Counting Persons*.

13 Katerina Teaiwa, "Niu Mana, Sport, Media and the Australian Diaspora," in *New Mana: Transformations of a Classic Concept in Pacific Languages and Cultures*, ed. Matt Tomlinson and Ty P. Kawika Tengan (Canberra: ANU Press, 2016), 107–30.

14 P.J. Borell, "He iti hoki te mokoroa: Maori Contributions to the Sport of Rugby League" (MA thesis, University of Canterbury, 2012); Mark Falcous, "Rugby League in the National Imaginary of New Zealand Aotearoa," *Sport in History* 27, no. 3 (2007): 423–46.

15 John Coffey and Bernie Wood, eds., *100 Years: Maori Rugby League 1908–2008* (Wellington, NZ: Huia Publishers, 2008).

16 John Haynes, *All Blacks to All Golds* (West Yorkshire: League Publications, 2007).

17 Gary Lester, *The Story of Australian Rugby League* (Sydney: Lester Townsend Publishing, 1988).

18 Sean Fagan, *The Rugby Rebellion: Pioneers of Rugby League* (Sydney: RL1908, 2007).

19 Coffey and Wood, *100 Years*.

20 Andrew Stevenson, "Polys Put the Mettle On," *Sydney Morning Herald*, 28 February 2009, https://www.smh.com.au/sport/nrl/polys-put-the-mettle-on-20090228-gdte5i.html (accessed 27 April 2013).

21 Paul Bergin, "Maori Sport and Cultural Identity in Australia," *Australian Journal of Anthropology* 13, no. 3 (2002): 257–69.

22 David Lakisa, Daryl Adair, and Tracy Taylor, "Pasifika Diaspora and the Changing Face of Australian Rugby League," *Contemporary Pacific* 26, no. 2 (2014): 347–67; Lameko Panapa and Murray Phillips, "Ethnic Persistence: Towards Understanding the Lived Experiences of Pacific Island Athletes in the National Rugby League," *International Journal of the History of Sport* 31, no. 11 (2014): 1374–88; Frank Puletua, "Chocolate Soldier: The Emergence of Pacific Players in the NRL," 15th Annual Tom Brock Lecture (Sydney: Tom Brock Bequest Committee and Australian Society for Sports History, 2014).

23 David Rowe, "Rugby League in Australia: The Super League Saga," *Journal of Sport and Social Issues* 21, no. 2 (1997): 221–26; Greg Ryan, *The Changing Face of Rugby: The Union Game and Professionalism since 1995* (Newcastle, UK: Cambridge Scholars Publishing, 2008).

24 Robert F. Dewey, "Embracing Rugby and Negotiating Inequalities in the Pacific Islands," paper presented at the Traditional Knowledge Conference 2008: Te Tatau Pounamu—The Greenstone Door, Knowledge Exchange Programme, Auckland, 2010.

25 Dwight Zakus and Peter Horton, "Pasifikas in Australian Rugby: Emanant Cultural, Social and Economic Issues," *Sporting Traditions* 26, no. 2 (2009): 67–86.

26 Brendan Hokowhitu, "Tackling Maori Masculinity: A Colonial Genealogy of Savagery and Sport," *Contemporary Pacific* 16, no. 2 (2004): 259–84; Matani Schaaf, "Elite Pacific Male Rugby Players' Perceptions and Experiences of Professional Rugby," *Junctures: The Journal of Thematic Dialogue* 7 (2006): 41–54.

27 Robert F. Dewey, "Pacific Islands Rugby Alliance (PIRA): Rugby in 'Our Sea of Islands,'" *International Journal of the History of Sport* 31, no. 11 (2014): 1406–20; Gyozo Molnar and Yoko Kanemasu, "Playing on the Global Periphery: Social Scientific Explorations of Rugby in the Pacific Islands," *Asia Pacific Journal of Sport and Social Science* 3, no. 3 (2014): 175–85.

28 Niko Besnier, "The Athlete's Body and the Global Condition: Tongan Rugby Players in Japan," *American Ethnologist* 39, no. 3 (2012): 491–510.

29 National Rugby League Game Development, *Pasifika Participation Data* (Sydney: National Rugby League, LeagueNet, 2017).

30 Panapa and Phillips, "Ethnic Persistence," 1376.

31 Roannie Ng Shiu, "Sports Diplomacy in the Pacific: Developing Pacific Rugby League Elite Athletes for Diplomacy and Development," *State, Society and Governance in Melanesia*, 30 November 2016, http://bellschool.anu.edu.au/sites/default/files/publications/attachments/2016-04/ib-2016-11-ngshiu.pdf (accessed 16 January 2017); National Rugby League Game Development, *Pasifika Participation Data.*

32 Niko Besnier, "Sports Mobilities across Borders: Postcolonial Perspectives," *International Journal of the History of Sport* 32, no. 7 (2015): 849–61.

33 Fa'anofo L. Uperesa and Tom Mountjoy, "Global Sport in the Pacific: A Brief Overview," *Contemporary Pacific* 26, no. 2 (2014): 263–79.

34 Peter Horton, "Pacific Islanders in Global Rugby: The Changing Currents of Sports Migration," *International Journal of the History of Sport* 29, no. 17 (2012): 2388–404; Lakisa et al., "Pasifika Diaspora," 361; Brent McDonald and Lena Rodriguez, "'It's Our Meal Ticket': Pacific Bodies, Labour and Mobility in Australia," *Asia Pacific Journal of Sport and Social Science* 3, no. 3 (2014): 236–49; Puletua, "Chocolate Soldier," 5; Chris Valiotis, "Suburban Footballers of Pacific Islander Ancestry: The Changing Face of Rugby League in Greater Western Sydney," in *Centenary Reflections: 100 Years of Rugby League in Australia*, ed. Andrew Moore and Andy Carr (Melbourne: Australian Society for Sports History, 2008), 141–56; Patrick Skene, "The Forgotten Story of Olsen Filipaina, the Polynesian Who Tamed Wally Lewis," *Guardian News*, 30 April 2015, http://www.theguardian.com/sport/blog/2015/apr/30/the-forgotten-story-of-olsen-filipaina (accessed 30 April 2015).

35 Lakisa et al., "Pasifika Diaspora," 361; Puletua, "Chocolate Soldier," 5.

36 Ibid.; Gregory Mumm and Donna O'Connor, "The Motivational Profile of Professional Male Fijian Rugby Players and Their Perceptions of Coaches' and Managers' Cultural Awareness," *Asia Pacific Journal of Sport and Social Science* 3, no. 3 (2014): 202–21.

37 Robert H. Codrington, *The Melanesians: Studies in Their Anthropology and Folk-Lore* (1891; reprinted, New Haven, CT: Human Relations Area Files Press, 1957); Mason H. Durie, *Te Mana, Te Kāwanatanga: The Politics of Māori Self-Determination* (Auckland: Oxford University Press, 1988); Farah Palmer and T.M. Masters, "Māori Feminism and Sport Leadership: Exploring Māori Women's Experiences," *Sport Management Review* 13, no. 4 (2010): 331–44; Teaiwa, "Niu Mana," 108; Matt Tomlinson and Ty P. Kawika Tengan, eds., *New Mana: Transformations of a Classic Concept in Pacific Languages and Cultures* (Canberra: ANU Press, 2016).

38 Niko Besnier and Margaret Jolly, "Afterword: Shape-Shifting Mana: Travels in Space and Time," in *New Mana: Transformations of a Classic Concept in Pacific Languages and Cultures*, ed. Matt Tomlinson and Ty P. Kawika Tengan (Canberra: ANU Press, 2016), 349–68; Vicente Diaz, "Tackling Pacific Hegemonic Formations on the American Gridiron," *Amerasia Journal* 37, no. 3 (2011): 90–113; Ty P. Kawika Tengan and Jesse M. Markham, "Performing Polynesian

Masculinities in American Football: From 'Rainbows to Warriors,'" *International Journal of the History of Sport* 26, no. 16 (2009): 2412–31.

39 Teaiwa, "Niu Mana," 113.

40 Ibid.

41 Ibid.; Lakisa et al., "Pasifika Diaspora"; Peter Horton, "Pacific Islanders in Professional Rugby Football: Bodies, Minds and Cultural Continuities," *Asia Pacific Journal of Sport and Social Science* 3, no. 3 (2014): 222–35; C.P.E. Marsters, "Young Pacific Male Athletes and Positive Mental Wellbeing" (Master of Public Health thesis, University of Auckland, 2017).

42 Saili Lilomaiava-Doktor, "Beyond Migration: Samoan Population Movement (Malaga) and the Geography of Social Space (Va)," *Contemporary Pacific* 21, no. 1 (2009): 1–32.

43 Setsuo Otsuka, "Talanoa Research: Culturally Appropriate Research Design in Fiji," paper presented at the International Education Research Conference, Melbourne, 2005; Rochelle Stewart-Withers, Koli Sewabu, and Sam Richardson, "Talanoa: A Contemporary Qualitative Methodology for Sport Management," *Sport Management Review* 20, no. 1 (2017): 55–68.

44 Trisia Farrelly and Unaisi Nabobo Baba, "Talanoa as Empathic Apprenticeship," *Asia Pacific Viewpoint* 55, no. 3 (2014): 319–30.

45 Barbara Burns McGrath and Tevita O. Ka'ili, "Creating Project Talanoa: A Culturally Based Community Health Program for U.S. Pacific Islander Adolescents," *Public Health Nursing* 27, no. 1 (2010): 17–24; Tamasailau Suaalii-Sauni and Saunimaa M. Fulu Aiolupotea, "Decolonising Pacific Research, Building Pacific Research Communities and Developing Pacific Research Tools: The Case of the Talanoa and the Faafaletui in Samoa," *Asia Pacific Viewpoint* 55, no. 3 (2014): 331–44.

46 Mo'ale Otunuku, "How Can Talanoa Be Used Effectively as an Indigenous Research Methodology with Tongan People?," *Pacific-Asian Education* 23, no. 2 (2011): 43–52; Timote M. Vaioleti, "Talanoa Research Methodology: A Developing Position on Pacific Research," *Waikato Journal of Education* 12, no. 1 (2006): 21–34.

47 Vaioleti, "Talanoa Research Methodology," 21.

48 Tevita O. Ka'ili, "Tauhi va: Nurturing Tongan Sociospatial Ties in Maui and Beyond," *Contemporary Pacific* 17, no. 1 (2005): 83–114.

49 Brij V. Lal and Kate Fortune, eds., *The Pacific Islands: An Encyclopedia, Vol. 1* (Honolulu: University of Hawaii Press, 2000); Kathleen S. Samu and Tamasailau Suaalii-Sauni, "Exploring the 'Cultural' in Cultural Competencies in Pacific Mental Health," *Pacific Health Dialog* 15, no. 1 (2009): 120–30.

50 Farrelly and Nabobo-Baba, "Talanoa as Empathic Apprenticeship."

51 Gina Hawkes, David Pollock, Barry Judd, Peter Phipps, and Elinor Assoulin, "Ngapartji Ngapartji: Finding Ethical Approaches to Research Involving Indigenous Peoples, Australian Perspectives," *Ab-Original: Journal of Indigenous Studies and First Nations and First Peoples' Cultures* 1, no. 1 (2017): 17–41; Lakisa et al., "Pasifika Diaspora," 361.

52 Megan Stronach and Daryl Adair, "Dadirri: Using a Philosophical Approach to Research to Build Trust between a Non-Indigenous Researcher and Indigenous Participants," *Cosmopolitan Civil Societies: An Interdisciplinary Journal* 6, no. 2 (2014): 117–34.

53 Farrelly and Nabobo-Baba, "Talanoa as Empathic Apprenticeship."

54 Tagaloatele Peggy Fairbairn-Dunlop, "Reconnecting to Our Sea of Islands: Pacific Studies in the Next Decade," *AlterNative: An International Journal of Indigenous Peoples* 4, no. 1 (2008): 45–56; Rose et al., *A National Strategy*; Thaman, "Decolonizing Pacific Studies."

55 Melani Anae, Eve Coxon, Diane Mara, Tanya Wendt-Samu, and Christine Finau, *Pasifika Education Research Guidelines* (Auckland: Auckland Uniservices, University of Auckland, 2001); Teresa Teaiwa, "On Analogies: Rethinking the Pacific in a Global Context," *Contemporary Pacific* 18, no. 1 (2006): 71–87.

56 Greg Fry, "Framing the Islands: Knowledge and Power in Changing Australian Images of the South Pacific," *Contemporary Pacific* 9, no. 2 (1997): 305–44.

57 Hau'ofa, "Our Sea of Islands."

58 Teaiwa, "Reframing Oceania," 68.

59 Ibid.

60 Fuimaono K. Pulotu-Endemann et al., *Seitapu Pacific Mental Health and Addiction Clinical and Cultural Competencies Framework* (Auckland: Te Pou, 2007).

61 Unaisi Nabobo-Baba, "Decolonising Framings in Pacific Research: Indigenous Fijian Vanua Research Framework as an Organic Response," *AlterNative: An International Journal of Indigenous Peoples* 4, no. 2 (2008): 140–54.

62 Linda T. Smith, *Decolonizing Methodologies: Research and Indigenous Peoples*, 2nd ed. (London: Zed Books, 2012).

63 Lakisa et al., "Pasifika Diaspora," 351; Brent McDonald, "Developing 'Home-Grown' Talent: Pacific Island Rugby Labour and the Victorian Rugby Union," *International Journal of the History of Sport* 31, no. 11 (2014): 1332–44; Puletua, "Chocolate Soldier," 6.

64 Anae et al., *Pasifika Education Research Guidelines*, 14; Cluny Macpherson, Paul Spoonley, and Melani Anae, *Tangata o te Moana Nui: The Evolving Identities of Pacific Peoples in Aotearoa/New Zealand* (Palmerston North, New Zealand: Dunmore Press, 2001).

65 Joseph Maguire and Mark Falcous, eds., *Sport and Migration: Borders, Boundaries and Crossings* (Oxon, UK: Routledge, 2011).

66 Paul Darby, "The New Scramble for Africa: The African Football Labour Migration to Europe," *European Sports History Review* 3 (2001): 217–44; Jonathan Magee and John Sugden, "The World at Their Feet: Professional Football and International Labor Migration," *Journal of Sport and Social Issues* 26, no. 4 (2002): 421–37.

67 Bevan Erueti and Farah R. Palmer, "Te Whariki Tuakiri (the Identity Mat): Māori Elite Athletes and the Expression of Ethno-Cultural Identity in Global Sport," *Sport in Society* 17, no. 8 (2013): 1061–75.

68 Gary Osmond, "The Nimble Savage: Press Constructions of Pacific Islander Swimmers in Early Twentieth-Century Australia," *Media International Australia* 157 (2015): 133–43.

69 Kristen McGavin, "Being 'Nesian': Pacific Islander Identity in Australia," *Contemporary Pacific* 26, no. 1 (2014): 126–54.

70 Copped is a slang term meaning "to catch" or "to receive."

71 Stan Grant, "How Rugby League Player Dean Widders Stared Racism in the Face and Won," *Guardian*, 22 January 2016, https://www.theguardian.com/australia-news/2016/jan/22/how-rugby-league-player-dean-widders-stared-racism-in-the-face-and-won (accessed 6 May 2016); Daniel Lewis, "Civoniceva Urges NRL to Educate Racist Minority," *Brisbane Times*, 8 March

2011, https://www.brisbanetimes.com.au/sport/nrl/civoniceva-urges-nrl-to-educate-racistminority-20110308-1bmn4.html (accessed 27 March 2011).

72 Dean Ritchie, "Warriors' Culture Slammed as Club Sinks to 'Soul-Destroying' Nine-Game Losing Streak," *Daily Telegraph*, 6 March 2016, https://www.dailytelegraph.com.au/sport/nrl/warriors-culture-slammed-as-club-sinks-to-souldestroying-ninegame-losingstreak/news-story/daf5a011898cdcbfb67b285c9c292014 (accessed 7 March 2016).

73 Neil Ratley and Shane de Barra, "Former Queensland State of Origin Star Billy Moore under Fire over 'Coconut' Remark," *Sydney Morning Herald*, 30 July 2015, https://www.smh.com.au/sport/nrl/former-queensland-state-of-origin-star-billy-moore-under-fireover-coconut-remark-20150730-gioa9l.html (accessed 1 August 2015).

74 Steve Mascord, "Discord: Pronouncing Polynesian Players' Names Correctly Not Just a Matter of Sticks and Stones," *Sydney Morning Herald*, 31 August 2017, http://www.smh.com.au/rugby-league/discord-its-not-just-sticks-and-stones-20170830-gy7lyi.html (accessed 3 September 2017).

75 Joseph Pearson and Clay Wilson, "Nigel Vagana Says Ignorance Is No Excuse after Matty Johns Show Is Accused of Casual Racism," Stuff, 31 August 2017, https://www.stuff.co.nz/sport/league/96183528/nigel-vagana-says-ignorance-is-no-excuse-after-matty-johns-show-isaccused-of-casual-racism (accessed 31 August 2017).

76 Nick Dyrenfurth, *Mateship: A Very Australian History* (Melbourne: Scribe Publications, 2015).

77 Panapa and Phillips, "Ethnic Persistence," 1377, 1381.

78 Ibid., 1383.

79 Ravulo, *Pacific Communities in Australia*.

80 Hau'ofa, "Our Sea of Islands."

81 Lakisa et al., "Pasifika Diaspora."

CHAPTER 3

My Mom, the "Military Mohawk Princess": kahntinetha[1] Horn through the Lens of Indigenous Female Celebrity

Kahente Horn-Miller

The media tried to set me up as a media plaything, inviting me to publicity occasions. As an onkwe-hon-weh I was uncomfortable standing out from the crowd and being looked at as an object.[2]

Where Did My Mother Go?

The public life of kahntinetha[3] Horn has been largely shaped by the camera lens and reporters' pens. In the early 1960s, she modelled fashion for print and then the runway in Montreal, Toronto, and New York City, garnering attention as a rare Indigenous face in an industry populated by whiteness. She turned this early attention into activism that had been fuelled years earlier by the destruction of her grandparents' home on the Caughnawaga[4] Indian Reserve after the expropriation of their land for the St. Lawrence

Seaway. kahntinetha became the Indian Princess of the Indigenous and Canadian imaginations. She just might be one of the first modern-day Indigenous celebrities.[5] She was an outspoken advocate for Indigenous rights throughout the 1960s. She stepped back from public life in the early 1970s and had four daughters. kahntinetha worked for the Department of Indian and Northern Affairs until the late 1980s, retiring after winning her court case against the department for firing her during the 1990 Oka Crisis. She continues to remain active in advocating for Indigenous rights as she enters her eighties.

This chapter is an account of the years that my mother spent in the eye of the storm as an Indigenous celebrity. What kind of Indian spoke out? Said anything? Was heard? no less. Especially an Indigenous woman. This look at the celebrity of our mother comes out of the thoughts and conclusions that my three sisters—Ojistoh, Waneek, and Kaniehtiio—and I have made about our mother. This story is based on our lived experiences and her stories, which illustrate her life that can be best described as lived with spirit and resilience. This is how many continue to describe her. We can attest to the impact that her notoriety has had on us and the legacy that she has passed on to us. We have had to live with her legacy, and sometimes it has been hard. My sisters and I have worked hard to make our own lives unique in our own ways.

Since I was a child, I have encountered the "Military Mohawk Princess" in different ways.[6] The first way was through beautiful fringed leather jackets and furred hats carefully put away in hall closets. These were items that my sisters and I were not allowed to use for dress-up play. There was ornate silver jewellery stored in cookie tins. I remember looking at these things as a child and thinking how beautiful they were and wondering what it all meant. Was my mother someone special? Was she someone famous? My sisters and I asked her about these things. She would always give us a vague answer: "Oh, you know, they are just things I wore a long time ago." She would give a small smile and nothing else. So, in time, I forgot about them until I encountered her in history textbooks that we used in grade school. When does this ever happen? Finding your mother on the page before you is unique to say the least. To this day, people constantly have asked "aren't you kahntinetha Horn's daughter?" Or they have said "I was in love with your mother!" Even worse, sometimes they have said "my father was so in love with your mother!" Imagine how that feels as a young girl, or an adult, for that matter. Often when I encounter

"Military Mohawk Princess; Kahn-Tineta Horn; last night angrily tells Robert K. Andras; minister without portfolio; that only Indians on the government payroll are being heard at the meetings on Indian policy Andras is holding across Canada. Miss Horn ambushed Andras in Lord Simcoe Hotel." This photo and caption, which appeared in the *Toronto Star* on 27 September 1968, inspired the title for this chapter. This depiction illustrates how kahntinetha was viewed at that time and was meant to minimize her efforts. Photo by Mario Geo/*Toronto Star*, via Getty Images, 502337435.

people of her generation who remember her from the 1960s, they do a half bow to me, as though in reverence of their memories and of her. At some point, my sisters and I learned to nod graciously, smile, and move on in the conversation. What can we say? We are our own women. In these contexts, it becomes an act of reclaiming as we give a non-answer, in a sense distancing that person from our mother and pushing his or her attention back to the focus of the meeting.

The woman whom so many knew in the 1960s disappeared for a time. Away from the spotlight, she spent over twenty years working for the Canadian government and raising us, her daughters. She didn't carry on with her modelling, only going back to it briefly in her fifties. This was the mother whom I knew—a high-energy, charismatic, and hard-working mom who drove us to swimming lessons at five in the morning six days a week or taught aerobic weight classes at the local YMYWCA. When I was preparing to write this chapter, I had a long conversation with my oldest sister, Ojistoh, about which memories to include. She and I talked of many things, and most importantly she told me an incredible story about the experiences of three Indigenous women whom she had encountered. She described the traumas that they had suffered because they are Indigenous and because they are women. She did this in part because that is what we do as sisters and because Indigenous peoples tell stories to impart messages. Her message to me was to focus on the resilience of our mother.

It was when she was behind the lines during the Oka Crisis in 1990 that I really began to question who she was and is. Here was a woman whom I had never really known. A glimpse of our mother here and there didn't prepare me for her. After 1990, she was a woman who had something to say. She had been fired from her job at Indian and Northern Affairs, and the press called attention to this fact, which placed her in the public eye once again. She was committed to the men and women at the blockade and not only defended herself at the Saint-Jérôme, Quebec, courthouse but also attended all of their trial proceedings. At this time, she began to write letters, notes, and eventually a book titled *Mohawk Warriors Three*. She talked of the Great Law of Peace (Kaienerekowa). kahn-tinetha began to speak Kanien'keha (Mohawk) again. She seemed to be more vibrant, almost manically so. Years later, when we asked her about her previous activism, she said that she had put it aside to raise her daughters quietly. It was at that point that I headed off to university to begin my undergraduate degree. I was questioning my own identity as a Mohawk and began to ask my mother questions about who we are and the community we come from. I read all of the resources that I could find on the Mohawk and Iroquois in the University of British Columbia library. When that wasn't enough, she would fax me papers written by Louis Karonhiaktajeh Hall or other things written about our people. I think that this was her way of teaching me about the perspective that she came from and what informed her actions before, during, and after the summer of 1990. She still didn't speak of her activism of the 1960s. It was as though life began again for kahntinetha after the Oka Crisis, and writing this chapter has helped me to understand why that was so. I think that she never stopped being a fighter and was ready to enter the Indigenous rights movement once again. As I read those faxed papers and asked her questions in our long phone conversations, or even now as I examine our interview for this chapter, a story has emerged: rich with complexity, humour, and an abiding sense of responsibility to the Mohawk people.

The Seaway or Bust

My mother was born at Queens County Hospital in Brooklyn, New York, on 14 April 1940. She is the second oldest of nine children. Her father, Joe Horn, was an ironworker, and her mother, Margaret Diabo, was a homemaker. Her father died when she was thirteen in a work-related accident, slipping and falling off a bridge in Vermont. kahntinetha also has a half-brother around the same age who entered her life as an adult. Her formative years were spent living with her mother's parents on their farm near the St. Lawrence River. She grew up with some of her siblings hearing and speaking the old Mohawk language and being exposed to the longhouse traditions.[7] It was in the Indigenous tradition of visiting and sharing food that our mother would have been exposed to many conversations among Elders about our history, culture, and traditions in the Mohawk language around a wood stove late into the evening. This tradition would later inform her activism. We know that with the old language comes a deep understanding of the philosophy of the Kaienerekowa.[8] My sisters and I know that hearing and speaking this language from an early age enabled our mother to gain a perspective on the world unique and different from learning about the world through the English language. She did not speak English until she went to school. Her father told her to go to school but not to learn anything.

She didn't speak English until she was about nine years old.[9] My older sister and I were provided with a similar foundation and spoke and were spoken to in the Mohawk language until we began school in French and English.

Over our lifetimes, my sisters and I have heard bits and pieces of what our mother's early life was like—the piss pot story is a beloved memory,[10] as is the story of her relatives teaching each other how to drive as preteens on the reservation. The stories that our mother tells describe the love that our great-grandmother had for her grandchildren; life with family members in Brooklyn's Little Caughnawaga;[11] her beloved aunts Francis, Lylie, and Josie; life lived on a small farm; and being part of a Mohawk community that was somewhat isolated from the rest of the world. That isolation ended when the St. Lawrence Seaway project was initiated in 1954. Our mother has recounted many times the story of her grandfathers Horn and Diabo, who tried to stop its construction. Stephanie Phillips documents the impact of the project on the community in her thesis "The Kahnawake Mohawk and the St. Lawrence Seaway" (2000). She writes of the factionalism that emerged as a result of the project, for some families took money in settlement for their expropriated lands, and on principle others did not.[12]

This project, my sisters and I believe, informed our mother's activism. Her celebrity comes from her efforts to fight the Canadian government on various issues using any weapon that kahntinetha had, including beauty, celebrity, and fashion. The international seaway project was the first community political struggle that she witnessed, and it was a hard lesson to learn. Her grandfathers Horn and Diabo worked hard to lobby the Canadian and American governments to stop the project, but they were unsuccessful. It was completed in 1957. Our mother recounts the impact that their fight and subsequent defeat had on her and describes it as a railroading of the project through the community. She was a teenager at that time and can recall with sadness how her grandfather Diabo had to be carried from his house just before it was dynamited. Most vivid in her mind are the seaway excavations that left his house on a peninsula, her grandmother climbing down a steep embankment to get fresh water, and the deep sense of loss and defeat that her grandfathers carried with them until her grandfather Diabo died not long after and her grandfather Horn a few years after the project was completed.[13] She says that she swore and shook her fist at the queen's yacht as it travelled through the man-made channel in celebration of the completion. Watching their effort and defeat, we think, sparked her desire to fight and resist.

The Power of the Pen

Our mother has used and continues to use a mixture of letter writing, public speaking, marching on front lines, supporting blockades, and showing physicality to engage in activism. She came of age in a time when one's Indigenous identity arose from being an active participant in the movement rather than from proficiency with the Mohawk language or involvement in ceremonial life. You were Indian if you had braids, wore fringe, fought hard, spoke out, rallied, and tuned in.[14] While at a funeral in Akwesasne of a cousin and activist who had worked alongside my mother, I had the opportunity to witness how people of her generation viewed her and how they engaged with her at that event. The three women and the one man who stood talking with her had participated in the Cornwall Bridge Blockade in 1969[15] and reminisced with her about old times, laughing and chortling over their actions of over fifty years ago. One woman said twice that our mother had taught them that they had to stand up and fight back: "She taught us to stand on our own two feet." Our mother had taken the air out of car tires with a small camera tool as an act of resistance. Doing so made it difficult to move the cars out of the way and let the police through. This woman saw that act as inspiring. At that blockade, our mother was arrested and charged with carrying a concealed weapon. You can see this happening in the film *You Are on Indian Land* (1969).[16] In that brief moment at the funeral, the three Elders who conversed with my mother relived that day as if time had never passed. They spoke appreciatively of her and pointed out how her actions inspired them to act. In fact, one remarked that my mother said "this is how you protest" as she let the air out of a car tire.

Later that day I saw the same appreciation as she stood among some men of our extended family in a related event. They spoke admiringly of her beauty and strength, saying that she is still the leader, the first Indian supermodel. In turn, she pointed out that she was a model only for a short time because she couldn't stand the industry. My mother waved it away and said, "I got out of it. You know the Harvey Weinstein stuff? Well, I got lots of that. I hated it, and I got out of the business."[17] I think that sometimes she doesn't want to focus on this part of her life, for good reason. Instead, she chooses to focus on the more vocal and violent activism in which she has taken part. Some of her actions have been just that, violent altercations, as at Oka and her arrest at the Canada-U.S. border in 2008, which caused her to go into cardiac arrest.[18] As I reflect on this, I ask where does one learn to respond with a fist?

People comment that in meeting kahntinetha they quickly realized the resilience and energy with which she approaches life. I think that what they remember most about her is her fighting spirit. Where does that come from? Our mother has told us this story about her father and the boxing gloves. She says that she learned how to fist-fight at an early age. One day her father came home from an ironworking job and brought with him two pairs of boxing gloves. If there were any disputes among the older children, then the gloves would be taken out, and the children would be encouraged to duke it out on the front lawn as a way to resolve the issue. Her father and his brothers "would then place bets on us," she says.[19] Our mother recounts this story with great fondness. For her, it seems that the memory is of learning how to defend herself with her fists, which is important to her. Never back down, she has said, and never let anyone see you, so you can't be charged. Good advice if you are going to be punching people out.

Our mother tells her stories with great embellishment and humour, laughing uproariously throughout. It's that Horn laugh, mouth wide, head thrown back—a whole body experience. You can't help but join in, especially when she tells the one about the *Toronto Telegram* reporter and the fist fight. During Expo '67, she was continually harassed by the reporter for a date.[20] She refused again and again. He went on to write three scathing articles about her. She went to Toronto to the head office to confront him and demand a retraction. He refused, calling her "an Indian whore" and told her to get out of his office.[21] She refused in turn, saying that she wouldn't leave until he did the retraction. They got into a physical altercation in which she punched him in the face and left. He called security, and she was escorted roughly down the escalator to the main lobby. He followed her, and on the escalator they began to fight again, and she managed to get in another good punch, she says. She was arrested and charged with assault. In the court proceedings, she is described as "wearing a fringed suede jacket and mid-thigh mini skirt" when she pleaded not guilty to assault causing bodily harm. In court, the reporter testified that "his face and neck were cut and that a strip of flesh was gouged away under his left eye from the attack."[22] This story is a good example of the kinds of direct action that our mother took. She approaches life without fear. She tells the story to us as a way to illustrate what we should do as women, as Indigenous women, never back down.

A famous story of her particular brand of activism is about when our mother let rats loose in Indian Affairs. It is documented in *The Canadian Encyclopedia*, and I remember reading it many years ago.[23] We asked her about it, and she told us the story. It has stayed with me, and I have shared it with my own daughters to illustrate their grandmother's character. They were not surprised but entertained. The way that she tells it is that the City of Montreal was dumping its garbage on the Caughnawaga Reserve, and the community couldn't stop it. As a result, many homes were infested with rats. It was when she encountered rats in her home that she decided to take action.

At a speech given at the old Indian Affairs building in downtown Ottawa, she lifted a dead rat by the tail above her head as she made her point. There were also live rats in the box in front of her, and they became excited. As they moved around, the box fell from the podium, and the rats escaped. This was the 1970s, and bell bottoms were in style, so you can just imagine the reaction of the audience. Many men and women jumped up on their chairs in fright. They did not want the rats climbing up their wide-legged pants or skirts. Her aunties and cousins who had accompanied her sat stoically in the audience and did not move. It was not until they left the building and went around the corner that they began to laugh and laugh. Her aunt Francis liked to tell this story. Our mother says that they had to fumigate the entire building afterward. She had made her point. The dumping eventually ceased. It was this kind of activism that made her popular among other Indians. No one else was doing this kind of thing. Infusing humour into her serious statements on the affairs of our people seemed to make for effective change.

Our mother in her retirement, if you can call it that, reads widely and writes daily. She has her own internet site called *Mohawk Nation News* that she uses as a platform for her ideas on local, provincial, federal, and international politics. It is her way of sending a figurative punch over the web. But this kind of activism is not new for her. She has used writing as a method of engagement with the issues for many years. One of her earliest acts, she recounts, was to help Margaret Deer and her family. In her teens, kahntinetha attended school and worked in Montreal.[24] Margaret had been trying to obtain disability benefits on behalf of her husband, Reginald, who had been injured and could no longer work. The young kahntinetha decided that Margaret should send a letter to the minister of Indian and Northern Affairs demanding compensation. She typed the letter and sent it by registered mail on behalf of the family. It worked, and Margaret and Reginald eventually received the much-needed money. My sisters and I think that the effectiveness of this kind of action at the age of seventeen had a lasting impact on our mother, and it was probably something that she witnessed her grandfathers doing in relation to their actions against the St. Lawrence Seaway project, though without success. Letter writing and writing in general she has seen as powerful tools for change and continues to use them.

Library and Archives Canada contains three files of letters in an online archive titled Complaints and Petitions Received on Behalf of the Indian People of Canada from Kahn Tineta Horn that she wrote to the government between 1963 and 1969. Although it is not known exactly how many letters she has written, there are many private collections in official archives throughout Canada that contain correspondence from her to various government officials.[25] Many of these archives are not available to the public and according to her contain letters about major concerns such as pollution, access to clean water and adequate housing on reserves, particular policies in the Indian Act, forced sterilization, and child welfare. kahntinetha was an early critic of Indian policy before there were any Native women's organizations. Most such organizations were formed in the 1970s. It appears that she was one among a few women who did this kind of activism, and her letter writing was prolific.

The writing aspect of her activism is important for the fact that the internet didn't exist until the mid-1990s. It puts into context her activism of the day. In the 1960s, if people wanted to share ideas, they did so face to face or held protest marches, sit-ins, public rallies, and letter-writing campaigns. This was witnessed during the Red Power movement that paralleled the Black Power movement of that time. It was not until the 1980s that the fax machine became a more widely used technology. So there is something to be said about the impact of her letter writing on Indigenous activism. There was no such thing as online social media. In her speeches and writing, kahntinetha expressed views on colonization, theft of Indigenous lands and resources, poverty, forced sterilization, and the taking of babies from their mothers now known as the Sixties Scoop. These topics now have a wide international audience thanks to the internet. Social activism spreads quickly and powerfully online, as with the #NODAPL protests of 2016–17. But the 1960s and 1970s were a different time.

Never shy or quiet about her views, in her early activism kahntinetha was an outspoken critic of the Canadian government and its bureaucrats who served as the vanguard for the new relationship forming between Indians and Canada that coalesced into organizations such as the National Indian Brotherhood and, later, the Assembly of First Nations. She was highly critical of urban Indians who held public positions and spoke for those on reserves. She thought that they did not speak for her and called attention to their collusion with the Canadian government and their soft tactics.[26] Her criticisms did not sit well with many of the Indian leaders of that time, particularly the National Indian Council which was created as an umbrella group to advocate for Status Indians, Métis, and Non-Status Indians. Her feud with Executive Director William Wuttunee is well known. My sisters and I think that these men were not used to someone like our mother. With her grounding in the Mohawk language and culture, intellect, and willingness to speak out, they did not know how to uphold her on her path as a strong Indian woman. Indian men did not know how to support a woman like her.

In 1964, kahntinetha was made the Canadian Indian Princess, a title created by the National Indian Council. She says that she showed up at a meeting one day and was bestowed with the title. She believes that she was a distraction, brought in for her looks. There was no pageantry or context for the appointment, she says. She was the first one.[27] The allure that our mother held because of her youthful and exotic beauty in the eyes of both Native and non-Native men and women is something that my sisters and I believe had an impact on her activism. This is one of the first things commented on when we are approached by people who knew of her in the 1960s. "Your mother was so beautiful," they say. "She still is," we reply. This continual recognition, and our ongoing interventions in the narrative, are part of her celebrity.

In *Indigenous Women, Work, and History 1940–1980*, Mary Jane McCallum explores the recognition that kahntinetha garnered for how she looked and its influence on her activism. McCallum examines the Indian politics of beauty and style. She writes of the involvement of Indigenous women in hairdressing and discusses it as a context for the ability of women to exhibit choice in look and dress in contrast to the enforced bodily conformity experienced in residential schools. McCallum, quoting Agnes Grant, writes that, "for Indigenous people, consciously making a choice about one's appearance was also a political act."[28] Our mother never cared what people thought of her. Her beauty was a weapon, and she learned early on how to wield it with panache. That is agency. Beauty is either a weapon or allows others to objectify the person. Our mother has always had a style and flair for colour. My younger sisters agree that she was conscious of her looks and their impact on her activism. As Kaniehtiio writes, "I think she knew how to navigate in that time through all those snakes. . . . She knew the game and how to play it even though it was a hard game."[29] Of course, there is a fine line between being strategic and being objectified when one plays the gender/race game. When asked about it, our mother clarified that she was in fact strategic about using her looks. Her looks got her through the door, and then she would have the opportunity to speak. In fact, Mohawk Elders Peter Deome[30] and Louis Karonhiaktajeh Hall told her that, if anyone criticized her for using her looks to get attention to our issues, she was to ask them, "well, what are you doing?" as a challenge. They encouraged her to use what she could to bring Indian issues forward, but she says that they made sure she understood the history of our people and colonization and was well grounded in the Kaienerekowa first.

McCallum also links African American beauty culture to the role of First Nations women in the hairdressing trade and asks questions about how beauty and style influence politicized racial and national identities. There are questions about the link between First Nations women who moved to cities to work and their uptake of the latest Western styles in the postwar period that are not answered here. Yet, in the many photographs of her from the 1960s, kahntinetha appears with long straight black hair and eye makeup, and she is dressed in the latest styles of the time. It is almost as though she is making a visual counterpoint to the stereotypical image of the "drunken squaw." Her beauty and dress are the first to be commented on in newspaper articles, and second is her message, or it is not commented on at all. When asked about this, our mother says that she was told it was okay to use her beauty to get the message out. However, years later, in retrospect, she says that she sometimes felt objectified. I take up the challenge here of reconciling these two points of view and examine how and why beauty is a part of her celebrity.

The importance of the role of kahntinetha's beauty in her celebrity lies in the fact that her beauty is the first thing to be referenced followed by her words by those who remember her activism of the 1960s, much like the reporters of the time. kahntinetha is fondly remembered as the outspoken and militant Indian Princess. I propose that this identity goes beyond mere objectification and is tied directly to what she sees as her responsibilities as a Mohawk. It is important as we examine kahntinetha in the context of Indigenous celebrity, different from non-Indigenous celebrity. This difference was outlined briefly by Waneek and Kaniehtiio as we discussed our mother. Both of my sisters have extensive experience with this issue and can speak to it with knowledge. Indigenous celebrities, they agreed, are held accountable to their communities of people, whereas non-Indigenous celebrities seem to be able to leave the places in which they grew up, severing all ties.[31] As we spoke further, they said that when our mother spoke or acted, she always did so with the idea in mind that she was accountable to her community, Kahnawake, and the Mohawk Nation at large. Our women are beautiful, and our people are strong. This was the image that she wanted to project to her audiences. As a result, she was criticized and vilified by women of the community for putting her looks front and centre. In her view, she had no choice. It made people mad, she said, and a little jealous.

Shedding light on these views of strategic beauty and celebrity in the era of the birth of white Western feminism is fraught with its own controversies, for obvious reasons. How could kahntinetha use her image to get her message across? Wasn't she perpetuating the objectification of women by her actions? She speaks fondly of Louis Karonhiaktajeh Hall and Peter Deome, who have had a lasting influence on her political activism. Hall's drawings and written works advocated for the reimagining of the Indigenous self in all of her or his corporeal glory.[32] The images that Hall drew and painted were of muscular men and beautiful women. Sculpted muscles and defined facial features are often seen as stereotypical, but he had a point to make. He viewed our mother as a muse along with a few other beautiful Kanien'kehá:ka women, such as Lorraine Montour.

If you take a look at some of Hall's artwork, then you can see kahntinetha's and Lorraine's features in the drawings and paintings. What Hall advocated by using imagery of strong men and beautiful women was the empowerment of our people. He thought that it was important to reinvigorate a sense of pride in our physical selves and to begin to take care of ourselves politically, socially, and spiritually so that we could be independent, strong, and self-determined.

Hall's work spoke of a different kind of sovereignty, one that came from the individual and radiated outward, and part of that was taking pride in one's appearance.[33] One only has to look at the photos of our mother taken in the 1960s to understand this point. In them, her hair is in the latest style. Her makeup is impeccable, her clothing stylish. She makes a statement by her appearance. kahntinetha was the urban Indian Princess of the day, and she had something to say. But what does that really mean? I asked my mother one time if she was a feminist. She replied, "we have our roles, and they are different," meaning that the roles of men and women are different and that no one role is more powerful than another. Over time, patriarchy has infused our communities and cultures with misguided beliefs, but kahntinetha has tried to remain true to our traditions. Her roles and responsibilities in speaking out come, she says, from the Kaienerekowa, the Great Law of Peace, about balance. In fact, everything that she does she frames within the context of the law, including having children. In it, all of us are instructed to stand up and do what is right. If it is about deep accountability, and maintaining balance and peace, then it is the right thing to do.

The Shitty Pocahontas Princess

They could not believe that I did not want to become famous except under my own terms. Not possible. I was supposed to talk about how we want to escape being onkwe-hon-weh and be their shitty or Pocahontas type character. The world would be better off without us.[34]

I found their attitude to be vulgar. They wanted to use me to make money on my image, which made me hate modeling.[35]

Carmen Robertson states that Indian Princess contests evoked a sense that Indian women's beauty was derived from two contexts: being trapped in a romanticized and conciliatory past and being integrated into a modern and non-Indigenous present.[36] My mother experienced both in her modelling and activism. Pocahontas, to her credit, is probably one of the most recognizable Indigenous women, and it is through her story that we can find links to the celebrity status of kahntinetha. The life of Pocahontas is the tale of colonization itself—her invasion, her subordination, her socialization, and her total subjugation. She is the Indian Princess of the North American imagination.[37] Pocahontas serves as the ideal stereotype of the Indigenous woman as the "promiscuous female body, as fecund and wild and seductive as the land,"[38] whereas kahntinetha, by her activism and outright refusal to be what was expected, pushed back against the system, in essence saying that this is who I am, this is who you are, and these are my rights.[39] Whereas Pocahontas could not speak back, kahntinetha used television, print, and radio to fight colonization and its impacts.

She came of age during the emergence of the Red Power movement and the Sexual Revolution, and this influenced her view of the world and fuelled her activism. kahntinetha unabashedly addressed Canadian leaders and intellectuals with a speech, a shout, or a letter to the editor. One only has to look at the many photographs of her talking to Canadian politicians to see how she addressed them and the issues head on. In them, she stands close, almost face to face, projecting her words into their faces so that they could not ignore them. Canadians didn't know what to make of her because she did not match the stereotypes that most had been socialized to—she was Indigenous, beautiful, smart, vocal, and could throw a good punch. kahntinetha was shaped externally by the multiple narratives of Indigenous feminine identity. In turn, she countered them with stories of her own making informed by Kanien'kehá:ka traditions.

McCallum, quoting Phillip Deloria, invites us to rethink dichotomies built upon crude notions of difference and assimilation such as white and Indian, primitive and advanced, in order to discover what she describes as "complex lineaments of personal and cultural identity."[40] These linkages among particular personal, physical, cultural, and communal identities shape kahntinetha's activism and ultimately her celebrity. kahntinetha is both complex and simple. Her story is about beauty, visibility, and resistance. Kanien'kehá:ka artist Shelley Niro describes it best when she says that "people have a stereotypical idea of what Native women are all about. . . . We are portrayed in the movies as cardboard cut-outs and when you try to present a different image, people are disappointed."[41] Niro works in her own artistic practice to counter these images. My mother fit the fantasy of the Indian Princess much like the Indian Princess Barbie. She was cosmopolitan yet also a real Onkwe-hon-we. Yet, take off the imagined feathers, war paint, and fringed clothing, and you could put her in a suit and high heels.

Robertson also describes the objectification of our women as princesses or squaws depending on how they satisfied political aims. Highlighting the passivity of women who needed the protection of mainstream Canadian justice, the women were pawns in the ongoing rhetoric that championed the government's progressive treatment of First Nations at that time. The imaginary princess would ultimately embrace and endorse assimilationist policy. The squaw was also a binary found in some of the same reports. Squaws were seen as Indigenous women who were threats to Indigenous traditional cultures and future efforts to secure autonomous strength with regard to the Canadian government.[42] As Betty Louise Bell points out, the Native woman's experience is "repressed and distorted, colonized by the settlers' imagination and reduced to a silent and fixed image."[43] At first, my mother was the Indian Princess, and then when she gained a voice she became the squaw and was vilified for her point of view and strength of character.

kahntinetha was named Miss Indian Princess Canada in August 1963 by the National Indian Council, which then removed the title a year later. According to the *Winnipeg Free Press*, some members of the council took issue with her public political stances on various issues. They thought that she was projecting her own point of view as council policy.[44] McCallum also discusses the Indian Princess title in her work: "The figure of the Indian princess was thus more than a simple, one- or two-dimensional depiction of Indian women."[45] She finds that, in the speeches given by the women who held the title they focused on volatile topics such as racism, Native–non-Native relations, the war in Vietnam, welfare, and Indian policy. Feminist scholar Patrizia Gentile, as cited by McCallum, considers postwar beauty contests as defining moments for portraying new definitions of gender, sexuality, and labour practices that, as she writes, "reflected changing cultural, political, and social needs." Gentile asserts that a new and more modern middle-class image of the Indian woman challenged racist notions of Indian women as beasts of burden.[46] My mother was perhaps one of a few well-known First Nations activists, both male and female, who spoke their traditional languages and practised their cultural traditions. She was an Indian from the reserve but polished in her appearance. Many activists of her generation were urban Indians who had lost touch with their home communities or grassroots activists who did not get noticed. She therefore had the cultural and communal grounding when she talked to the urban male First Nations intellectuals and government officials about issues relevant to Indians across Canada. It was this culturally grounded perspective and foundation that many found intimidating. This seems to be an important element of her celebrity.

As Cherokee scholar Rayna Green describes in relation to Pocahontas, both her nobility as a princess and her savagery as a squaw are defined in terms of her relationships with male figures.[47] Green describes this within the virgin-whore paradox. As a princess, the Indigenous woman must save or give aid to white men. As a model, kahntinetha served in this role. Double burdened, she was also desired sexually by white men because of her beauty. Yet, as Green describes, she also had to remain the virtuous mother goddess-queen. It was when kahntinetha opened her mouth or swung a fist that the image of her shifted in the mainstream. At one point, kahntinetha expressed the desire to have seven children with different men, with no intention of getting married. This was her strategy to diversify the gene pool, and she was criticized in the media for it.[48] To her, this was about enacting Mohawk matrilineality, in which our lineage is determined solely through the mother. She has always said that what matters most is your mother, not your father. This is a central tenet of Rotinonhsiónni culture that was not understood at that time. She did succeed in having seven children, and four of us survived. Yet, despite this view, in Indian Country she remains the epitome of Indigenous strength. Through the stories of Pocahontas and kahntinetha, we see that Indigenous women's actions are cast in sexual terms. It is this fine line between elevation and degradation that also defines Indigenous female celebrity.

Indigenous women, then, are victims of the "Pocahontasis" suffered by the dominant society. That is a term coined by Kanien'kehá:ka scholar Thohahoken and describes the process whereby women of one society are simultaneously elevated and degraded by the dominant society. For example, Indigenous women are viewed as virgin princesses and fallen squaws concurrently when they are considered to have accepted domination by Euro–North American white men.[49] Indigenous women who gain position and power in the dominant society benefit from the effects of this Pocahontasis, at least within the terms of that society. But it comes at a cost. The dominant society's perennial view of Indigenous women colours its ability to see each Indigenous woman as unique in her own right. My mother is no exception. She achieved success when she played the role of Indian Princess, yet when she spoke she shattered the image that was placed on her. Her refusal to accept the domination of the white man enabled her to escape the impacts of Pocahontasis.

The Last Word on Indigenous Celebrity

When they turned against me for not conforming and shut the cameras and sound off, I felt relief. I got my real life back.[50]

In 1969, kahntinetha tried to present concerns to Queen Elizabeth II in London about the Trudeau White Paper of that year. A few things happened after that attempt to visit the queen. kahntinetha lost the focus of the media; she was no longer the pretty Indian Princess, and the public turned against her, deciding to focus on the next celebrity. So where did she go once the cameras were turned off and the reporters went home? She stepped out of that life and became just mom for us. She says that she was happy. She came up once in a while in the media, especially when she had her first child, which was news because she did not declare the father. It was not until twenty years later that our mother was once again in the public eye during the Oka Crisis in 1990. She went back into the spotlight because she had a cause, a platform on which to stand. She became socially and politically active again. It was her reawakening as she entered the struggle once again.

In the context of the 1960s, we can view kahntinetha's celebrity from the perspective of settler colonial desire, though Indigenous men were caught up in such desire too. Is this idea of desire about sexualizing Indigenous bodies, as Robertson, Green, and Bell propose? How can we take that back? The way that kahntinetha functioned with complete knowledge of the desire that people have had for her decentralizes the notion of Pocahontas as victim and actually puts her in a place of power. Were Pocahontas able to meet her, I think that they would have a lot to talk about.

From a young age, my mother understood the context in which she was living. She had full mastery of the tools at her disposal. She could think. She could write. She could punch. What more do you need? She also knew that she was coming from a strong grounding in the language, culture, and history of her people. She was never a naive and manipulated figure, and at times she was rash, obnoxious, and violent. That is why she is such a controversial figure. She was never an Indian Princess.

My mother has always been somewhat confusing to me. This writing has put her into better perspective. I can see now that some of her approach to life she has passed on to us, her daughters. My memories of her and of the impacts of her celebrity on my life are like the haze on a photograph or a filter. You see it, but you don't. Time can make something more beautiful or inscrutable. I have always thought that my mother is contradictory. She says one thing, then does another. Is that what celebrity is all about? It does not work on fact. It works on half a conversation. It is a one-sided conversation. We know only part of the story, that which she decides to share. Of course, I am not telling everything about my mother, how can I? She's still here doing what she does. Her story is not over yet. Celebrity is not about the whole person anyway. Her celebrity is about that moment when she was puncturing tires or defiantly marching down the street to 10 Downing Street to deliver a message to the queen via the prime minister after she couldn't get near Buckingham Palace. My mother knew exactly what she was doing. She managed her image, always. Will you ever really get to see the entire picture? Probably not. I will not either, because she is her own person.

In my view, celebrity is about the tension between a real life lived and that which is constructed for us through the media. No matter how authentic that life is, celebrity culture requires and engenders a sort of mystery and fetishization. That was a function of colonization, to disempower our women and "other" them, to lock them in an ossified image. I believe that this is what has gone on here with my mother's beauty and activism. This is the consequence of celebrity. kahntinetha has become larger than life, but when you learn about her the message is really simple and brings you back to reality. Live life to the fullest. Fight for what is right. And do not let anyone or anything hold you back. Perhaps that is her greatest legacy, what she taught us, her daughters. You do not need to be exotic to be real. Our mother is and always has been accountable to her community, and she has not forgotten that.

My mother sums it up best. I asked her about how she saw her beauty in relation to celebrity and activism. She wrote that

> your question reminds me of what Vine Deloria said when he came here [Kahnawake]. He said that he had never

> seen so many beautiful native women before. I explained "ionkwatenikorakwenies" (youn-gwa-deh-ni-gora-gwenyes) which is self-pride. Not just in appearance but how we carry ourselves. We are very proud about every aspect of ourselves, our relationships, families, people and children. If someone said something negative, we do not let anyone unfairly criticize. Criticism has to be constructive. We try to continue to do this. Like not committing suicide or leading a degrading lifestyle because we love our children and are here for them. We stay alive to take responsibility for their future and to do what is right for them. If we don't do that then we are cowards. We will always defend our family, children, and land. We adapt to social, economic circumstances but never abandon the way we are. Yes, many have. The invaders want us to be nothing more than basket makers and make earrings to sell by the side of the road or at pow wows. We don't have an inferiority complex. . . . I told Vine that is the beauty he sees when he looks at our women.[51]

NOTES

1 kahntinetha is spelled with a lowercase k throughout this chapter. In her review of it, she specifically asked that her name be lowercase because capitals denote a corporate designation, she says.

2 kahntinetha Horn, email message to the author, 1 October 2017. Onkwe-hon-weh means "original people" in Kanien'keha and is used as a term to describe Indigenous peoples.

3 kahntinetha means "she walks through tall grasses." Her father gave her his mother's name. It was not allowed on her birth certificate. Her father tried to register her in school with her Kanien'keha name, but that was not allowed either. He told her to use it when she was older. So she did, she says. kahntinetha Horn, email message to the author, 5 November 2017. Her name has been spelled in different ways as Kahn-Tinetha, Kahn-Tineta, Kahntinetha, and Kahentinetha.

4 Caughnawaga was the name of the original village in the Mohawk Valley. The people are the descendants of those who established a village site near Montreal in 1667.

5 Throughout, the terms "Indian" and "Indigenous" are used interchangeably. The terms "Kanien'kehá:ka" and "Mohawk" are used interchangeably to reflect the time in which they were used. The term "Kanien'kehá:ka" came to be more widely used after the 1990 Oka Crisis as a sign of self-determination.

6 The title "Military Mohawk Indian Princess" or a derivative of it is used to label various photos and in newspaper articles about kahntinetha Horn.

7 The Kaienerekowa or Great Law of Peace encompasses social, ceremonial, and political aspects of Rotinonhsiónni tradition (also known as Haudenosaunee or Iroquois). When one uses the term "longhouse," it means practising these traditions.

8 Kaienerekowa is the Kaienkeha (Mohawk) word for the Great Law of Peace.

9 kahntinetha Horn, email message to the author, 2 December 2017.

10 This story is about her grandmother walking through the house to dump the urine pot out the kitchen window in front of everyone and meant to highlight the frank acknowledgement of poverty of her upbringing in a time before there was running water and electricity on the Caughnawaga farm.

11 The area in Brooklyn where many Mohawk iron workers and their families lived. See Reaghan Tarbell, dir., *Little Caughnawaga: To Brooklyn and Back* (National Film Board of Canada, 2008).

12 Stephanie Phillips, "The Kahnawake Mohawk and the St. Lawrence Seaway" (MA thesis, Concordia University, 2000).

13 kahntinetha Horn, "Experiences with the Seaway Construction," class lecture, Indigenous Politics and Resurgence, Carleton University, 5 October 2017.

14 For an examination of symbolism, rhetoric, and language of the Red Power movement, see Randall A. Lake, "Enacting Red Power: The Consummatory Function in Native American Protest Rhetoric," *Quarterly Journal of Speech* 69 (1983): 127–42; and John Sanchez and Mary E. Stuckey, "The Rhetoric of American Indian Activism in the 1960s and 1970s," *Communication Quarterly* 48, no. 2 (2000): 120–36.

15 See Michael Kanentakeron Mitchell, dir., *You Are on Indian Land* (National Film Board of Canada, 1969).

16 Ibid.

17 This was a public discussion witnessed at a funeral gathering in Akwesasne in November 2017.

18 See Kaniehtiio Horn, "Ma Takes on *The Toronto Telegram*," *Coffee with My Ma* (podcast audio), 16 April 2018, https://www.stitcher.com/podcast/coffee-with-my-ma/e/55615698 (Accessed 30 November 2019).

19 kahntinetha Horn, email message to the author, 2 December 2017.

20 The reporter is not named because, as kahntinetha said, "I don't want to give that bastard any notoriety." Ibid.

21 See Horn-Miller, "Ma Takes on *The Toronto Telegram*."

22 "The *Ottawa Journal* from Ottawa, Ontario, Canada · Page 8," 8 May 1968, Newspapers.com, https://www.newspapers.com/newspage/44459699/ (accessed 27 November 2017).

23 See Bennett McCardle, "Kahn-Tineta Horn," 4 February 2008, updated by Michelle Filice, 25 January 2016, in *The Canadian Encyclopedia*, http://www.thecanadianencyclopedia.ca/en/article/kahn-tineta-horn/ (accessed 18 November 2017).

24 She began working right after high school in Montreal, untrained. She lied about her age.

25 See James Gladstone Family fonds, Glenbow Museum; Fonds, Mennonite Archives of Ontario; Fonds, University of Regina; Harry Hawthorn fonds, University of British Columbia; Pierre Burton fonds, McMaster University; and Canadian Speakers' and Writers' Service fonds, York University Library.

26 LAC (Library and Archives Canada), "(Miss) Kahn-Tineta Horn, Miscellaneous Correspondence re: Indian Affairs," n.d. RG 22, 6-10-3, vol.1, 271–75. Described by Andrew Gemmell as one of the most important letters in Canadian history (Gemmell, "Chapter 7. Defending Indigenous Rights against the Just Society" in *1968 in Canada: A Year and Its Legacies*, edited by Michael Hawes, Andrew C. Holman, and Christopher Kirkey, 149–76. Ottawa: Canadian Museum of History and Ottawa University Press, 2021), this is kahntinetha's letter to former Director of Indian and Northern Affairs Peter Laing calling attention to corruption on the Caughnawaga reserve where

she characterized the elected council members as well-bought Indians and encouraged Laing to look at what the Canadian government funds under the Indian Act.

27 kahntinetha Horn, email message to the author, 13 November 2017.

28 Mary Jane McCallum, *Indigenous Women, Work, and History, 1940–1980* (Winnipeg: University of Manitoba Press, 2013), 109.

29 Kaniehtiio Horn, email message to the author, 18 November 2017.

30 Deome was a condoled chief in the longhouse.

31 Interview with Waneek Miller, Kaniehtiio Horn, Kahnawake, 15 October 2017.

32 See Kahente Horn-Miller, "From Paintings to Power: The Meaning of the Mohawk Warrior Flag Twenty Years after Oka," *Socialist Studies: Journal of the Society for Socialist Studies* 6, no. 1 (2010): 96–124; and Kahente Horn-Miller, "A Symbol of Indigenous Unification and Impetus to Assertion of Identity and Rights Commencing in the Kanienkehaka Community of Kahnawake" (MA thesis, Concordia University, 2003).

33 Ibid.

34 kahntinetha Horn, email message to the author, 1 October 2017.

35 Ibid.

36 Carmen Robertson, "'Indian Princess/Indian Squaw': Representations of Indigenous Women in Canada's Printed Press," in *Culture and Power: Identity and Identification*, eds. Martin-Albo, Angel Mateos-Aparicio, and Eduardo de Gregorio-Godeo (Newcastle upon Tyne, UK: Cambridge Scholars, 2013), 112.

37 See Clara Sue Kidwell, "What Would Pocahontas Think Now? Women and Cultural Persistence," *Native American Literatures* 17, no. 1 (1994): 149–59.

38 Betty Louise Bell, "Pocahontas: 'Little Mischief' and the 'Dirty Men,'" *Studies in American Indian Literatures* 6, no. 1 (1994): 68.

39 See Audra Simpson, *Mohawk Interruptus: Political Life across the Borders of Settler States* (Durham, NC: Duke University Press, 2014); and Audra Simpson, "On Ethnographic Refusal: Indigeneity, 'Voice' and Colonial Citizenship," *Junctures* 9 (2007): 67–80.

40 McCallum, *Indigenous Women, Work, and History*, 119.

41 *Mohawks in Beehives + Other Work*, Mercer Union: A Centre for Contemporary Art, http://www.mercerunion.org/exhibitions/mohawks-in-beehives-other-work/ (accessed 18 November 2017).

42 Robertson, "'Indian Princess/Indian Squaw,'" 137.

43 Bell, "Pocahontas," 67.

44 McCallum, *Indigenous Women, Work, and History*, 114.

45 Ibid.

46 Ibid.

47 Rayna D. Green, "The Pocahontas Perplex: The Image of Indian Women in American Culture," *Massachusetts Review* 16, no. 4 (1975): 698–714.

48 Chris Allan, "Baby by the Falling Waters Joins the Fight," *Gazette* [Montreal], 23 February 1971, collection of kahntinetha Horn.

49 Thohahoken, conversation with the author, 2007.

50 kahntinetha Horn, email message to the author, 1 October 2017.

51 kahntinetha Horn, email message to the author, 27 November 2017.

CHAPTER 4

Indigenous Activism and Celebrity: Negotiating Access, Inclusion, and the Politics of Humility

Jonathan G. Hill and Virginia McLaurin

Indigenous celebrities intersect with activist roles for myriad reasons. With the relatively increased access to spaces of influence, some Indigenous celebrities are motivated, or even pressured, to take the opportunity to speak on behalf of causes and concerns stemming from their own experiences as Indigenous people, their home communities, and other First Nations. During these moments, Indigenous celebrities operate in complex spaces. In doing so, they manage multiple identities, roles, and obligations, and they are often held accountable for maintaining them all according to varied expectations, depending on the context.

This complex negotiation was evident in the recent struggles over the oil pipelines in which Indigenous celebrities working in activist roles and spaces experienced their status as sites of extreme complications. Complex bundles of expectations emerging from multiple contexts intersected with their heightened visibility, requiring a dynamic negotiation of status relative to the fight for Indigenous rights and sovereignty.

In this chapter, we draw from interviews and published accounts of Indigenous activists involved in recent pipeline struggles and illuminate the relational complexities that they manage as celebrity status intersects with activist work. We address the impacts and implications of celebrity in the navigation of constellations of expectations, roles, and obligations among audiences and communities that they engage, with an emphasis on the negotiations between the politics of celebrity status legitimized in popular culture and Indigenous notions of status legitimized by humility.

To define and illustrate the negotiation between these expressions of Indigenous celebrity status, we will discuss prevailing theoretical definitions of celebrity and how they relate to Indigenous celebrity. We will then illustrate how celebrity was negotiated by looking at established Indigenous celebrities who engaged in the events around the Standing Rock reservation located on the North Dakota/South Dakota border in the United States, including major Indigenous film and movie stars, as well as non-Indigenous celebrities who became involved. Then we will look at a different form of "celebrity" that includes those known primarily in Indigenous circles, some known only in the context of their activist work, local leaders who nevertheless engaged with media to gain support for their people, and individuals who gained personal status through their connection with the events at Standing Rock. These expressions of celebrity status call attention to the identity politics at play in activist work and are mobilized through Indigenous notions of humility and the critique/rejection of mainstream notions of celebrity bolstered by capitalist stratification.

Defining Celebrity

Western studies of celebrity are said to start generally with Max Weber's analysis of charismatic leadership, which Weber identified as the sole form of leadership in extremely small communities but which are still extant in large-scale, complex societies in the form of celebrities.[1] This broad framing of celebrity is inclusive of both pop culture notions of celebrity and types of celebrity that disavow the capitalist features found in the pop mainstream. This broad framing is necessary for our considerations since the charismatic individual with heightened visibility and influence in local Indigenous communities—for instance, an Elder who gives moving interviews—can emerge from a context wholly different from the Indigenous celebrity embedded in the pop culture mainstream—such as an Indigenous movie star who enters a local community to lend his or her support.

The status of local activists is bolstered through community-based efforts directly opposed to the state and the inequality inherent in the mainstream marketplace. Their visibility is often articulated through resistance to material gain, authority, and iconic status. Conversely, pop culture celebrity status is inextricably tied to capitalism. Celebrity status and capitalism are viewed as mutually founding and fostering one another. Richard Dyer emphasizes this relation as he situates stardom in a capitalist society as a status that furthers the goals of capitalism and, to that end, emphasizes individuality.[2] This reading of celebrity status is also central to other Marxist interpretations of celebrity, proffered by Theodor Adorno and Max Horkheimer as well as Guy Debord.[3] Celebrity is theorized in these interpretations as being embedded in a systemic set of relations in which it operates as a point of fixation and distraction and fosters capitalism using spectacle and the naturalization of individual ascension to elite status and influence.

These critical approaches highlight the hegemonic and oppressive nature of the media industry and the "bread and circus" models of spectacle in which all entertainment is a mere distraction from systemic issues of inequality. However, their emphasis on the celebrity's bolstering of capitalism does not account for the Indigenous people at Standing Rock who did not arise from the mainstream industry, did not support its commerciality or the capitalist mainstream media, yet accrued visibility and status that sometimes surpassed those of Indigenous mainstream pop celebrities during the resistance. The tensions arising from the politics of inclusion were rooted in many factors, the most visible of which emanated from the dissonant intersection between mainstream features of celebrity such as self-promotion, exploitation, and elitism—the kinds of celebrity that the above literature addresses well—and Indigenous community-based notions of leadership anchored in humility.

What followed was a dynamic negotiation on the incorporation of differing notions and definitions of celebrity that generally included mainstream celebrity status, often brought by Hollywood stars who lent their support, and local status that existed before and during the media attention to activism and was not allied with or did not emanate from pop culture industries. In the following section, we trace the negotiation in the intersection between these kinds of celebrity and the responses to their inclusion by Indigenous people during the course of the Standing Rock resistance.

Events at Standing Rock

In February 2015, the Army Corps of Engineers proposed the Dakota Access Pipeline project, intending to connect the Bakken Oil Fields in North Dakota to southern Illinois. The proposed route runs under the Mississippi and Missouri Rivers, with the Missouri River crossing initially routed near Bismarck, North Dakota. In response to concerns about the threat to Bismarck's municipal water supply, the pipeline was rerouted to cross the Missouri River and Lake Oahe near the Standing Rock Sioux Indian Tribe Reservation.

After the proposed rerouting of the pipeline, the Standing Rock Sioux Tribe opposed the pipeline construction through the waterways, citing the imminent potential for devastating impacts on those who relied on the water in the immediate area and downstream. By April 2016, tensions among Energy Transfer Partners, the Army Corps of Engineers, other government agencies, the Standing Rock Sioux Tribe, other tribal nations, and their supporters escalated. The first resistance camp, Inyan Wakanagapi Oti (Camp of the Sacred Stones), was established on the land of Standing Rock Sioux Elder LaDonna Brave Bull Allard, located at the confluence of the Cannonball and Missouri Rivers, on 1 April 2016. By that summer, the Oceti Sakowin (Seven Council Fires) was established to house the overflow, intertribal, and international populations. This camp was placed on land that had been taken by the Army Corps of Engineers from the Standing Rock Sioux Tribe on the north bank of the Cannonball River running directly along Highway 1806. A third camp also emerged in late August, located along the river between Oceti Sakowin and Inyan Wakanagapi Oti, called Sicangu Oyate (named for the federally recognized Sicangu Oyate people of the Rosebud Reservation, also known as the Sicangu Lakota).

These camps housed "water protectors" from over 300 tribal communities and their allies, and over the course of the resistance their population grew into the thousands, gaining both national and international attention, support, and participation in their efforts to protect water and tribal sovereignty. It is difficult to detail the full significance, reality, and meaning of the resistance. It meant many things to many people, and volumes could be written on it. It can be stated factually that the pipeline construction was another iteration of the American settler colonial legacy, in which private interests secured gains using the instruments and tactics of the state, including violence, intimidation, theft, and disregard for both treaty and human rights.

Water protectors and their allies resisted using tradition, culture, laws, bodily sacrifice, and other non-violent means. In the end, the pipeline was completed, and little was done to address the actions of the state. For a short time, there were moments of recognition of tribal sovereignty and spreading of awareness of the historical and cultural underpinnings of sovereignty and the threats to it. The traditional Sioux Treaty Council was reunited, and ceremonies brought many nations together. There were also intergenerational collaborations in which effort and investment resulted in shared intention, leadership, and action. Moreover, these moments and more were shared as participants took advantage of their ability to communicate and connect on a global scale across multiple media platforms.

"Standing Rock Stars"

With daily live feeds, updates, and social media posts, several activists from different camps and entities within the camps gained visibility and status over the course of the resistance. The individuals with the most visibility accrued large followings through social media and were sought out to speak on activities within the camps, to educate the public and allies, and to help coordinate resources. Dallas Goldtooth, Linda Black Elk, and Chase Iron Eyes were among those with a highly visible media presence. Their involvement was not the same even though they experienced many of the same conditions associated with their heightened visibility, including having their names used to legitimize people, actions, and activities, many times without their permission. They were also targets of criticism for purportedly using resources and elevated status for personal gain. Status in relation to activism in general was found at different levels within the camps and in the surrounding support generated outside the camps.

Physical presence at the camps was often used to legitimize authority among activist groups and communities supporting the pipeline resistance. Films were proposed and produced based on an individual's or community's involvement with the resistance. Non-Indigenous allies who visited Standing Rock gave talks on Natives and their experiences in the camps, and they were featured in their local media. Some Indigenous and non-Indigenous activists who never attended Standing Rock, or had minimal presence there, became local spokespeople and gained status as authorities on the pipeline resistance by giving talks, screening films, leading events, and being the faces of the resistance in their local media. This illustrated what Alice Marwick and Danah Boyd observed in that "people are rewarded with jobs, dates, and attention for displaying themselves in an easily-consumed public way using tropes of consumer culture."[4]

As a result, the term "Standing Rock stars" began to be heard when a person referred to those who used the resistance as a means of elevating their status. Simultaneously, and contradictorily, the term was also used to refer to and compliment humble activists who were not using the movement as a source of social capital or for personal gain. In each instance, the meaning was articulated around perceptions of a person's motives with regard to humility, self-promotion, exploitation, or personal gain.

Dallas Goldtooth (Mdewakanton Dakota and Diné) was one of the activists who garnered a large following on social media. Over time, his updates on the struggle and his live feeds on Facebook logged millions of views. Goldtooth's identity as an Indigenous community member and activist was always emphasized first. Outside his role in the Indigenous Environmental Network and as a member of the sketch comedy group the 1491s, Goldtooth had not achieved mainstream celebrity status according to theoretical metrics that measure status as a positive correlation with the bolstering of capitalism in the mainstream media. He gained notoriety among a primarily Indigenous audience through the 1491s, with their self-produced videos and sketch comedy performances. Goldtooth had made appearances on MSNBC, Vice's Motherboard, National Geographic, and other news outlets spanning the United States and the globe.[5] In these mainstream spaces, his engagement was largely self-directed. His narrative was anti-colonial and anti-capitalist in his assessments of the impacts of the fossil fuel industry and the systemic havoc wielded by neocolonial resource extraction.

At the end of April 2016, when the camps were still being built and people and resources were being mobilized, Goldtooth began providing regular public updates, and his audiences grew. During his time in the camps, he was not merely one of the faces of the movement, for he occupied many roles. Goldtooth worked as an organizer for the Indigenous Environmental Network, and he served as a representative and member of his nation, fulfilling obligations and acting in roles defined by kinship, operating as a liaison, and working with the leaders in the camps. These roles were mentioned in some threads, but his ties to the community were never detailed or promoted in ways that could be used to increase his social capital as part of his public "spectacle." Still, despite his continued criticism of capitalism, neocolonialism, and imperialism, his being embedded in the community, and the dominant acceptance of the narratives that he provided over the course of the resistance, his elevation to the status of a "face" of the movement was met with some criticism.

The wary attitude toward elevated status and visibility was expressed on occasion in social media threads and videos produced by other people in the movement. They alluded to power, authority, and financial gain for several faces in the movement. These accusations were intended to link community members to features of celebrity that are not parts of community values or ideals of leadership. Goldtooth, for example, often had to dispel accusations and made definitive statements for the Facebook record. Posts on the individual Facebook pages of several Indigenous people accused him of being linked to controversial figure Dave Archambault, and one post featured a doctored image of Goldtooth holding cartoon bags of money, indicating an accusation of financial gain. His direct responses to such posts allayed fears of corruption and drew out acknowledgement of no capital gain for him, legitimizing his status as an activist. The comments that he posted in response on his own page often showed support for his work and acknowledged the divisive and unfounded nature of the accusations. Supporters of Goldtooth, and especially activists, mostly agreed that these accusations operated to factionalize communities and create distrust. One comment in defence of Goldtooth pointed out that airing unproven and hateful grievances via Facebook had "DAPL [Dakota Access Pipeline] laughing at us," thus anthropomorphizing the pipeline as a sentient representation of capitalist and colonialist interests. Still, others persisted in critiques of Goldtooth and argued that, despite his lack of financial profit, he was nonetheless garnering something just as valuable as money: increased celebrity status. The absence of financial gain but the elevation in status, as reflected in the chapters of this book, exemplifies Weber's observation that "charismatic and economic power do not necessarily overlap."[6]

In this instance, Goldtooth's Indigenous celebrity did not meet with the celebrity frameworks of Dyer and Marshall, but we can see that expectations rooted in the relationship between celebrity status and capital gain did drive suspicions, rumours, and accusations. Attention and influence, regular visibility, and work alongside mainstream celebrities were employed as rationales for these accusations. Goldtooth was able to use his long history of well-documented activist work to counter these claims.

Here again anti-state and anti-capitalist discourses were used to diffuse these claims and to realign, bolster, and legitimize Goldtooth's status as an activist with some degree of celebrity but without economic gain. The roles and receptions of Indigenous celebrities who had mainstream celebrity status in movies and films were different from those of Goldtooth, Black Elk, and Iron Eyes. In contrast to the experiences of other Indigenous celebrities discussed within this book, when pop culture celebrities engaged the media about the resistance, they were often delegitimized and criticized because of their affiliations with pop culture, already visible before and primary to their identities.

Mainstream Celebrities at Standing Rock

A variety of both Indigenous and non-Indigenous allies from beyond the local Standing Rock community visited the site throughout the events there or engaged in acts of support across the country. These celebrities were met with mixed responses from within the camps and from a pan-Indigenous audience who expressed critiques, concerns, or commentaries online. Having a connection to the capitalist marketplace and engaging in these activist efforts without engendering suspicion of self-serving motives made for a difficult undertaking.

Jaime Luis Gomez, better known under the name Taboo, is a striking example of how Indigenous celebrities face identity critiques based on how they engage with activist efforts. Taboo was under ethnic scrutiny prior to the pipeline struggles. Addressing the confusion about his appearance and ethnicity, Taboo joked in 2016 "I'm not the Asian guy from the Black Eyed Peas, I'm the Native guy from the Black Eyed Peas!"[7] Although Taboo offered clarity about his mixed Mexican and Shoshone ancestry before the pipeline struggles, his seemingly recent stylistic change from hip hop–influenced clothing to Indigenous styles attracted claims that he was suddenly highlighting his heritage to become a "face" of Indigenous struggles—a status that detractors claimed might be used to further his own image or give him access to major media networks focused on Standing Rock. In fact, for the past several years, Taboo has been consciously shifting his public image to reflect his heritage better, wearing Indigenous-created clothing and speaking openly on Native representation in music, film, art, and athletics. However, some of his projects, such as his collaboration with Nike fostered by Indigenous artist Bunky Echo Hawk, might have furthered the sense that Taboo's recent public embrace of his Native American ancestry was in fact a market-based strategy.

In March 2017, Taboo was featured in an MSNBC interview conducted by Ali Velshi in which Taboo highlighted his group's work and his own role at the frontlines of Standing Rock just after Thanksgiving 2016.[8] During the interview, he emphasized peaceful protest, collaboration with non-Indigenous allies, and the role of youth in creating a movement at Standing Rock. This interview was one of several that Velshi conducted with Taboo over the several months of his involvement with Indigenous environmental movements.

Following this, in July 2017, Taboo took part in an online Marvel series entitled "Becoming Marvel," which allows cosplayers to demonstrate their skills. In this case, Taboo acted as the model while cosplay designer Lauren Matestic created the costume for the 1970 Marvel superhero Red Wolf.[9] Although the public supported Taboo's embodiment of the minority superhero character, as evidenced by the generally positive comments on the original YouTube video that Marvel released on its official Marvel Entertainment Channel, comments by Indigenous people on the same video posted to Facebook were far more mixed.[10] Some comments called attention to how his portrayal of Red Wolf further stereotyped Indigenous people, to the "B-rated" mix of tribal aesthetics used in the costume, and to accusations that Taboo "never once" claimed to be Indigenous until doing so benefitted him.[11] In addition to the costume, equal attention was paid to his non-costume clothing—visibly Indigenous in design—at the beginning of the video. Although he never appeared to wear recognizably Indigenous clothing in his performances with the Black Eyed Peas, Taboo has adopted for the past several years increasingly visible Indigenous clothing, incorporating graphic designs, beadwork, eagle feathers, southwestern metalwork and turquoise, and even the "Billy Jack"[12] felt hats extremely popular among Indigenous people on the Plains in the late 1800s and again among Indigenous Americans in the 1970s. This shift in clothing style was critiqued as a rediscovery of Indigenous heritage in service to career, not culture, and it was frequently attacked as an attempt at "rebranding," underscoring the relationship between celebrity and capitalism that Adorno and Horkheimer[13] and Debord[14] emphasize.

Taboo's affiliation with mainstream pop culture continued in his anthem to Standing Rock, "Stand Up."[15] Although the song was given positive publicity on *Indian Country Today*, the comments section often featured questions about why a non-Indigenous person was highlighted reading a poem written from an Indigenous perspective and voice. Shailene Woodley's role in the video is by far the most visible female role, which might further contribute to the kind of marginalization that Indigenous women have faced in Native American rights movements and their public representations. Kyle Mays highlighted this trend further by pointing to the Indigenous cultural heroes whom Taboo lists in the song—all Indigenous men, taken from a pan-Indigenous rather than a local context.[16] The song won an MTV music award,[17] and Taboo was generally acknowledged as the singular "winner" of the award despite his insistence that it "has nothing to do with my group or with me as an artist."[18] The rapper has gone on to host pro-environmental events in New York City, performing the Standing Rock anthem far away from the treaty lands that inspired it but nevertheless raising awareness and money. It is worth noting that Taboo has performed in multiple fundraising concerts for Standing Rock.[19]

In the case of Taboo's involvement in the No Dakota Access Pipeline struggles, there are several issues at play. His seemingly recent embrace of highly visible cultural symbols can be viewed as akin to the behaviour of a newcomer that is generally anathema to subcultural and minority groups. There is a concern as well that the public might embrace as authentic anyone who appears to represent "Native Americans" as a group. "The signs are so intertwined that it is nearly impossible to separate the 'real' from the constructed image."[20] Given his celebrity, it is likely that insiders within the movement and, even more likely, outsiders who recognized his name through his Black Eyed Peas fame pressured Taboo to become a speaker in order to draw attention to the issue. Events such as the New York City charity performance undoubtedly boosted ticket sales because of his presence. However, at the heart of Indigenous concerns about such visible spokespersons' embrace of

Native ancestry is likely the tension between Taboo's close connections to mainstream popular culture and its ties to capitalism, a point supported by the common understanding of the Black Eyed Peas as "bubblegum pop."

Several feature film actors who have enjoyed longer public recognition as Indigenous actors also made appearances at Standing Rock. One such figure was Adam Beach, known for his work in major feature films, including *Windtalkers*, *Flags of Our Fathers*, *Smoke Signals*, and *Suicide Squad*.[21] Beach was featured prominently as a camper at Standing Rock in the CNN program *United Shades of America*.[22] He used his time with host Kamau Bell to discuss the different mindsets of Indigenous actors, citing a story about him asking permission from the Navajo or Dine to play a Navajo code talker in the 2002 film *Windtalkers*.[23] Although Beach did not directly address the pipeline, his presence at the camp and his incorporation of group values and permissions regarding his film roles proffered a community-oriented narrative in distinction to his generally privileged status and visibility. Perhaps most importantly, Beach self-consciously joked about being a "Hollywood Indian" while expressing gratitude for the position. Although humility is vaunted for all Hollywood stars, it seems to be an especially important aspect for Indigenous actors if they want to remain in good standing with Indigenous communities. As with Kahente Horn-Miller's discussion in Chapter 3 on the legacies of the activism of her mother, kahntinetha Horn, and kahntinetha's assessment of her stereotyping as the "Indian Princess," this self-effacing behaviour speaks to the widely shared Indigenous value of humility, a difficult value for highly charismatic personalities in high positions to express.

Riffing off his joke, host Bell commented directly on the juxtaposition between Beach's Hollywood status and his "real" status as an Indigenous person.[24] If it appears to be ironic that authenticity is being touted on yet another media product, a popular TV show no less, it is a well-established trend in the world of celebrity studies: "It is, in part, the blurring of the boundaries between private and public or the idea of an authentic individual behind the public persona that makes celebrity images particularly potent ideological symbols."[25]

Although Beach is certainly known to the Native American community as one of the primary Indigenous actors in Hollywood, CNN's YouTube channel posts his interview with the title "Actor on Native American Roles," listing him by name only in the comments section.[26] This reminder that

Beach is largely known within Indigenous spheres, as well as his self-effacing comments, grateful acknowledgement of privilege, and apparent reluctance to discuss directly the pipeline struggles and become "the face" of the resistance, perhaps worked to soften potential critiques from Indigenous viewers. Certainly, the online comments about Beach, on the whole, were less harsh than those about Taboo.[27]

Actor Wes Studi also had some involvement in the Standing Rock movement. In October 2016, he tweeted that he was "on my way to Standing Rock today. I'll be there as long as I can to help with the movement!" He included a picture of himself driving.[28] For the five days that he was there with his son, he was active on his Facebook and Twitter accounts and obliged fans with pictures. However, mainstream media coverage of his presence was slim, consisting mainly of two articles, one in *Tribal Tribune* and the other in *White Wolf Pack*. In his interview with Cary Rosenbaum, also known as the Travelling NDN (NDN being a shorthand for "Indian," a term Indigenous people in the United States still occasionally use self-referentially), Studi emphasized his "commitment to being part of the American Indian community" and to the young people at Standing Rock whom he saw as taking up the torch of activism from earlier Indigenous generations.[29]

Later, in December 2016, Studi became involved with the Standing Rock camp again, this time from afar. He performed with the band Drums for Peace in a "Stand and Rock for Standing Rock" event at the Skylight in Santa Fe.[30] His celebrity from his acting career and previous local music performances likely gathered a substantial crowd for the charity event. This was not the first time that Studi was involved in large-scale Indigenous activism. As the interview in *Tribal Tribune* pointed out, he was present at the Wounded Knee protests in 1973.[31] His discussion of Standing Rock through personal media outlets such as Facebook and Twitter stood in stark contrast to the widely viewed CNN interviews that other Indigenous Hollywood celebrities and Indigenous activists were conducting, effectively keeping the mainstream spotlight off him despite his long career as a Hollywood star. This appears to have been the result of strategic low-level media engagement given that Studi is one of the most recognizable Indigenous actors in Hollywood.

Other Indigenous celebrities used their status in ways similar to that of Studi, albeit without an in-person visit to the camp. In September 2016, First Nations actor Graham Greene tweeted about "the evil being done by the money grubbing bastards at Standing Rock," followed by a strong condemnation of the police action there.[32] Gary Farmer used Twitter to provide timely updates on the events at the camp, and he used his frequently touring musical group, Gary Farmer and the Troublemakers, to put on a fundraising event for Standing Rock in Taos, New Mexico.[33] Jason Momoa, with his *Justice League* co-stars, held up a pro–Standing Rock sign passed around news sites and social media.[34] Tommy Lee Jones, not often recognized as Indigenous but outspoken and knowledgeable about his Cherokee descent, put his name on an anti–Dakota Access Pipeline ad that ran in the *Dallas Morning News* despite his earlier endorsements of the equally controversial practice of fracking.[35] Although such actions were generally helpful in increasing media exposure and financial support for the camps, these stars did not garner much celebrity status within the resistance itself. Their participation was peripheral; although some had their Indigenous identities more entrenched in their work, their status as Indigenous celebrities in film did not translate into their ties to the mainstream or become incorporated into or tapped by the movement. This foundational aspect marked their identities as outside the activist celebrity sphere of Indigenous identity, making some of their participation less visible and excluding them from being "faces" of the movement.

The inclusion of non-Indigenous celebrities in the Dakota Access Pipeline protests adds complexity to the discussion of the limitations of pop culture's integration with this moment in Indigenous activism. Actors such as Shailene Woodley, Mark Ruffalo, and Leonardo DiCaprio offered their support and criticism, and some even took part in actions with Indigenous people during their resistance to the neocolonial tactics enacted by Energy Transfer Partners. Non-Indigenous celebrity participation illustrates how celebrity agency can be used to reject and resist capitalism. In such moments, among this class of celebrities, we observe what Kim Allen and Heather Mendick acknowledge with regard to celebrity agency: "Negotiations of celebrity . . . combine compliance and resistance to dominant discourses. People can and do mobilize counter-discourses in their relationships to celebrity."[36] Although the narratives and acts of resistance by some celebrities fully immersed in the pop culture mainstream reveal opposition to the dominant ideals of neocolonial capitalism in a resource extraction industry, they did not divorce themselves from their status as movie stars. In fact, they and their Indigenous allies often used that status strategically to garner public attention. They were identified as "outsiders" from the start and self-consciously employed their status to help bring more visibility and support to those who lacked the same traction in the mainstream. The participation of mainstream Indigenous celebrities immersed in mainstream entertainment industries was more constrained than that of non-Indigenous mainstream celebrities. Although they mobilized counterdiscourses that decried capitalism and injustice, their status as Indigenous people was often criticized and scrutinized, and their words and actions lacked the same legitimacy conferred on community-based activists because of their identities as defined through their pop culture industry status.

Non-Indigenous celebrities helped the resistance to garner access to mainstream circuits and audiences, allowing Indigenous people in the resistance to leverage anti-colonialist, anti-imperialist, and anti-capitalist sentiments in full view of the mainstream. In these instances, spectacle was used to subvert the capitalist state, in part, through selectively employed celebrity agency. Some critiques of their participation and the infiltration of their mainstream status into the pipeline struggle—especially as non-Natives, whites, and elites among Indigenous people—were still present, but they were far less barbed than the critiques of Indigenous celebrities. Perhaps this was because the boundaries between Indigenous and non-Indigenous participants were addressed from the beginning as an open part of the organizational discussions regarding access, legitimacy, and protocol.

Indigenous Activism and Celebrity

Criticisms levelled at popular celebrities embedded in the mainstream often addressed the commercialization of the cause and the perception that they were using the Dakota Access Pipeline resistance for personal gain. Some online comments, particularly via individual activists' Facebook pages, also delegitimized the status of some celebrities as speakers for the movement, insisting that their identities were not sufficiently Indigenous, or locally connected, to allow them to act as representatives of the activists at Standing Rock. Examples of such online comments could be seen clearly in the case of Taboo,[37] criticized as someone who sought attention and claimed Indigenous identity suddenly for his own benefit, in spite of several discussions of his heritage prior to the events at Standing Rock. Contrary to the celebrities in the mainstream, activists who did not have ties to the pop culture industry and were more rooted in Indigenous communities did not suffer the same degree of delegitimization or accusations of using their Indigenous identities as a source of profiteering. Although some concerns were voiced about these activists, as evidenced by Dallas Goldtooth's need to maintain a Facebook record of his conduct, often they were able to point to community relations to demonstrate the legitimacy of their actions. They had long histories of anti-capitalist and anti-imperialist narratives reflected in the material circumstances of their work.

This differentiation in status between non-mainstream Indigenous activists who critique capitalism and those embedded in relations that appear to bolster it has been found historically and across different contexts. These two approaches to activism—resisting the system versus participating in it in order to bend it toward the fight for equality—seem to have persisted in the relationship between Indigenous people and colonial culture, thus making these juxtaposed celebrity statuses nothing new and the ensuing identity politics nothing different.

The politics of visibility have always produced limited access to and representation in mainstream media for Indigenous people. Popular culture has always been profit driven in the United States, and Indigenous representation within pop culture media has been shaped largely by colonial projections rooted in the exploitation of Indigenous images, cultures, and spaces. Occasionally, moments of the colonial critique rendered by Indigenous artists have gained attention in mainstream pop culture.

The development of film and recorded sound in the United States included Indigenous participation and emphasis, but the roles that Indigenous people played in their development have been overlooked and underplayed, and few Indigenous celebrities arose from the more than 100 involved in the development of these technologies. In the American mainstream, celebrity status has its emphasis in Eurocolonial populations, their tastes, and the individuals who represent and produce them.[38]

Indigenous performers in American pop culture past and present—such as Red Wing, Will Rogers, Jay Silverheels, Chief Dan George, Will Sampson, Tantoo Cardinal, Irene Bedard, Wes Studi, Graham Greene, Buffy Sainte-Marie, Russell Means, and John Trudell—have had direct but differentiated engagements with Indigenous advocacy and activism while either gaining celebrity status or keeping close to celebrities and pop culture industries.

Similarly, in these instances, when activism is paired with celebrity, the structural dominance of capitalist pop culture co-occurs with anti-capitalist sentiment and action. We can see this relationship operating in the benefit concerts at which Indigenous activists such as John Trudell have collaborated with pop music stars such as Bonnie Raitt and Jackson Browne to address the threats posed by corporations and the state's use of nuclear energy, weapons, and waste and their consequences for land and water. These issues particularly affect Indigenous people living in spaces where ecological degradation from industry is often experienced first.[39]

The bolstering of capitalism is delineated in these moments, marked by narratives that overtly critique the oppression and misrepresentation of Indigenous people and their plight by the mainstream. This kind of demystification and activism is exemplified in other historical moments as well, such as when Indigenous people were first taken and exhibited in European courts, world fairs, human zoos, and Wild West shows, key instances of their exploitation by the state in its desire for Indigenous people as entertainment. Despite the limited agency of Indigenous people in these sites of constrained political engagement, well-known icons among Indigenous North Americans, including Geronimo and Sitting Bull, often attempted to use these spaces to advocate for their people. They held meetings with people of power and influence in the United States in the hope of altering policies and the conditions in which their people lived, and they asked for the removal of corrupt agents of the state stealing resources secured by treaty rights. The use of these spaces for these purposes is not well known in the mainstream culture. However, the later rise of social movements that produced Indigenous leaders who represented a more visible Indigenous community, with an explicit anti-state identity, came during the Red Power era.

With the rise of Red Power, a new wave of visibility emerged, with an emphasis on activism that included more community involvement with opportunities for activists to become engaged eventually in mainstream film, music, and art. Leaders of the Red Power movement were aware of the role of the media and strategically engaged the media to assert the agendas. They could represent, reorient, and rearticulate Indigeneity across the nation, gaining the necessary attention through television and print media.[40]

Their accrued status through the Red Power struggle often put them close to mainstream musicians, movie stars, and other celebrities who aided in bringing visibility to Indigenous struggles and, at times, collaborated artistically with Indigenous activists as they endeavoured to perform in mainstream circuits. Although the visibility and status of these activists changed in the mainstream, community issues, interests, and complications continued to intersect and shape their identities. Community expectations garnered more visibility in the mainstream, and the critique of the Red Power movement revealed dialogues within communities that had not been given a public ear in previous movements. Furthermore, the legacy of the Red Power movement and the American Indian Movement, and how organizations chose representatives for mainstream representation, have continued to be topics in many Indigenous communities.

Critiques of representation, of Indigenous actors in the mainstream, of movements that gave rise to celebrity, and of celebrities themselves are often born from the same conflicts between Indigenous people and colonization. These critiques arise out of Indigenous confrontations with capitalism and its symptoms, leaving little room for pop culture celebrity status within Indigenous activist communities in which the face of an activist movement is not the same as that on the silver screen or in sold-out arenas. Sterlin Harjo's commentary in response to multiple requests for pointers and advice on producing films about Standing Rock reflects this conflict with celebrity culture since, as he states, "humility is built into our cultures."[41]

Although it is important to steer clear of typologizing, it is safe to say that there is consensus among many Indigenous people that those who seek attention or act as authorities on culture, politics, and other affairs pertaining to Indigenous people are not the ones who should be trusted to speak on these subjects. As Harjo affirms in his advice regarding filmmaking,

> my biggest advice is to never interview the people that are trying to get in front of the camera. I've seen bits and pieces of Standing Rock documentaries made by non-Natives that suffer from this—people sticking their mug in the camera, playing up their "Native mysticism," and placing themselves in leadership roles. Those are the people that make us look bad. . . . So the people you really want to talk to are the ones not trying to be on TV. Those are the ones that will have the most knowledge and be most comfortable

> with their Native identity. . . . The way indigenous people live and carry themselves is very different from non-indigenous worlds.[42]

Many express gratitude for the increased visibility gained through film and media; however, along with the increased access to and control over representation facilitated by new technology and media platforms, the politics of humility is still a metric that finds its way into critiques of Indigenous community members.

This ethic is found among activists across the generations. Tom Porter, Kanien'kehá:ka Bear Clan Elder and educator in the activist group the White Roots of Peace, which arose in response to termination policy in the United States, affirmed that, in advocacy groups and community life prior to the rise of Red Power, self-promoting behaviour was a clear indicator that a person was questionable and would often be avoided. Generally speaking, being the face, commentator, spokesperson, educator, performer, or principal orator creates a conflict and—as we saw during several critiques of Indigenous activists by online commenters—exposes individuals in these roles to both criticism and skepticism.

The Dakota Access Pipeline struggle brought heightened awareness to Indigenous issues, aided by the use of new technology that provided individuals and communities with even more visibility and outreach. Over the course of the pipeline struggle, Indigenous activists and communities, as well as activist groups among the mainstream American public, participated directly in efforts that included raising funds and resources for the various camps, organizing solidarity efforts, and engaging in discourses on the pipeline. The politics of Indigenous people operating in spaces with heightened public visibility provided the conditions for both mainstream Indigenous celebrities and local Indigenous activists who gained media attention to occupy the same space at the same time. As we have seen, this provided an opportunity to assess the dynamics of similarity and difference in how these celebrity types represented themselves, utilized national media outlets, and were received by the wider pan-Indigenous audience.

Social media users were able to observe and critique or praise Indigenous people in front of the camera, which included Indigenous activist celebrities and Indigenous pop culture celebrities. The examples in this chapter detail how status was differentiated based on celebrities' relations to mainstream pop culture and how critiques of their involvement were founded on a larger denunciation of their relations to capitalism and the use of activism as a means of making personal gains, thereby exploiting Indigenous people.

Conclusion

The frequency of messages ranging from adoration to attack demonstrates the precarious position of the charismatic Indigenous celebrity. Indeed, the position of Indigenous stars is made more precarious by their ambiguous status in the public sphere. They are stars, but usually only among a small minority, and only rarely are Native American artists known by name to the overall American populace. They are leaders, and might have ceremonial roles, but they do not represent their nations as legal representatives in the eyes of the colonial government. And, perhaps more fundamentally, their status as celebrity activists fighting against the abuses of capitalism places them in a somewhat paradoxical position: they are individuals who must stand for group cohesion, they must appear to be authentically traditional while engaging new media, and their images are distributed by those new media, which rely on the very capitalistic system that they are resisting. However, in spite of theories declaring that "celebrity is inextricably bound up with capitalist consumer culture and attempts to individualize cultural production," it is possible to use mainstream media to enhance activist efforts rather than individual careers.[43]

The potential contradictions are not lost on Indigenous celebrities, on whom both the spotlight and significant responsibility have been placed because of their recognizable heritage and status in the wider pan-Indigenous community. In attempting to negotiate the criticisms and levelling mechanisms directed at them, they frequently deny desires for individual attention or monetary gain, and they redirect audiences toward environmental causes and Indigenous heritage more broadly.

With the arrival of new technologies and Indigenous-produced media, there are opportunities for a more broadly defined continuum of celebrity that includes resistance to the mainstream, rejection of capitalism and personal gain, and acknowledgement of the need for speakers to address the masses while living according to community values that contradict pop culture celebrity. Yet how this space is engaged is rife with complications, especially with regard to integrating the mainstream. Although there were many advantages of incorporating agents of the pop culture industry as participants in the pipeline resistance, their proximity to the identity of the movement and Indigenous culture was constrained by their pop culture celebrity status.

In the integration of non-Indigenous celebrities, the rejection of neocolonial resource extraction and its consequences did not require the rejection of the whole entertainment industry by these participants. Media that could be controlled by Indigenous activists were embraced as providing a desperately needed alternative to the mainstream media and state-based narratives in circulation. This differed from the complications of participation by Indigenous celebrities with mainstream status. Celebrity status did not translate from the mainstream to the movement. The access to mainstream circuits brought by Indigenous celebrities and their actions within the movement were suspect among Indigenous community members concerned about self-promotion and other features of pop culture in contrast to Indigenous community leadership values.

Although some celebrity activists occupied roles that met Indigenous cultural standards of leadership, they faced similar suspicions, which they had to refute with the reassertion and community-based affirmation of their rejection of self-interest. Although these artists fit within broader general framings of celebrity as "charismatic leadership," they are not limited by compliance with capitalism, and their status is maintained through contradiction to and critique of the mainstream. The contradictions arising from being the "face in front of the camera" have become more complex, and negotiations have become more public with greater access to platforms and technologies that provide more visibility. These negotiations display the complexity of contradictions not easily smoothed over by the dominance of the pop culture spectacle and systemic reaffirmation of the status and legitimacy of celebrity stardom. As a result, we were also able to witness the complex negotiation of celebrity status as it was shaped by different values related to Indigenous identity, its relationship to capitalism, and its relationship to community leadership protocols. In this negotiation, it is important to note that Indigenous celebrity, as it related to the pipeline resistance, was not valued in the ability to commercialize one's involvement or the resistance itself. Instead, values associated with Indigenous leadership that conflicted with commercial interests were the legitimizing criteria used to negotiate the politics of inclusion.

In the past, conversations on these politics of inclusion and legitimacy were not visible, and the dominance of the mainstream cast a large shadow over these values and the struggle over their viability in communities. With the increase in Indigenous-controlled media, we see a broader range of celebrity exemplified, including post-Marxist critiques of celebrity with their emphasis on agency and their potential to reject the mainstream. Still, the cultural contrast to the mainstream in the charismatic leadership displayed by activists is a new articulation of Indigenous celebrity, especially in its mainstream reach, as these individuals arise out of Indigenous contexts, are legitimized by Indigenous people, and are anchored in anti-imperialist, anti-colonialist, and anti-capitalist orientations toward the mainstream. As these individuals selectively engage in the mainstream while being rooted in community-based notions of identity and leadership, they outperform the visibility and viability of their Indigenous pop culture celebrity counterparts. These instances display the possibility of a dominant mainstream Indigenous celebrity that does not have its origins in the pop culture industry and is not infiltrated to a large degree by its commerciality. Although gains have been made and doors have been opened by mainstream Indigenous celebrities, the more dominant circulation of Indigenous people arising from communities, as the faces of community issues and conducting themselves according to the cultural metrics of humility, marks a new mediation of Indigenous celebrity articulated to the masses.

NOTES

1 Sean Redmond and Su Holmes, "Introduction," in *Stardom and Celebrity: A Reader,* Sean Redmond and Su Holmes, eds. (Los Angeles: SAGE, 2007), 14.

2 Richard Dyer, *Heavenly Bodies: Film Stars and Society* (London: Routledge, 2004).

3 Theodor Adorno and Max Horkheimer, "The Culture Industry: Enlightenment as Mass Deception in *Dialectic of Enlightenment*, trans. John Cumming (New York: Herder and Herder, 1972), 121–67; Guy Debord, *Society of the Spectacle* (New York: Zone Books, 1967).

4 Alice E. Marwick and Danah Boyd, "I Tweet Honestly, I Tweet Passionately: Twitter Users, Context Collapse, and the Imagined Audience," *New Media and Society* 13, no. 1 (2010): 890–907.

5 "Deadline Arrives for Dakota Access Protesters to Leave," MSNBC, 22 February 2017, https://www.msnbc.com/msnbc-news/watch/deadline-arrives-for-dakota-access-protesters-to-leave-882700867856 (accessed 7 March 2019); Paul Spencer, "Native Americans Are Resisting the Dakota Pipeline with Tech and Media Savvy," Motherboard, 29 October 2016,

https://motherboard.vice.com/en_us/article/78kmw4/tech-behind-the-dakota-access-pipeline-protests (accessed 7 March 2019); Michael McBride, "Resource Extraction and American Indians: The Invisible History of America," National Geographic blog, 14 December 2017, https://blog.nationalgeographic.org/2017/04/28/resource-extraction-and-american-indians-the-invisible-history-of-america/ (accessed 7 March 2019).

6 Kerry O. Ferris, "The Sociology of Celebrity," *Sociology Compass* 1, no. 1 (2007): 371–84.

7 Chelsey Luger, "From the Black Eyed Peas to N7: Nike and Taboo Form Unique Collaboration," Indian Country Media Network, 28 September 2016, https://indiancountrymedianetwork.com/culture/health-wellness/from-the-black-eyed-peas-to-n7-nike-and-taboo-form-unique-collaboration (accessed 6 March 2019).

8 "Taboo from Black Eyed Peas Speaks Out for Indigenous Rights," MSNBC, 10 March 2017, https://www.msnbc.com/msnbc-news/watch/taboo-from-black-eyed-peas-speaks-out-for-indigenous-rights-894974531542 (accessed 7 March 2019).

9 Dan Wickline, "Taboo of the Black Eyed Peas Becomes Marvel's Red Wolf," Bleeding Cool News and Rumors, 24 July 2017, https://www.bleedingcool.com/2017/07/24/taboo-black-eyed-peas-marvels-red-wolf/ (accessed 6 March 2019).

10 Marvel Entertainment, "Taboo of Black Eyed Peas Becomes Red Wolf—Marvel Becoming," YouTube, 24 July 2017, https://www.youtube.com/watch?v=LLHVtsIqdeA (accessed 6 March 2019); "Marvel Becoming," Facebook, 31 August 2017, https://www.facebook.com/MarvelBecoming/videos/10155561865232488/?eid=ARAaVWgf3AB3JseoITAbsy-4wLQIMiCpVO-uEDGRo1IW3dU5Pm6VuouosCB9gOi17w-C21A51GNtFA9GK (accessed 7 March 2019).

11 "Marvel Becoming."

12 *Billy Jack*, dir. and perf. Tom Laughlin (National Student Film Corporation/Warner Brothers, 1971).

13 Adorno and Horkheimer, "The Culture Industry."

14 Debord, *The Society of the Spectacle*.

15 Taboo, "Stand Up/Stand N Rock #NoDAPL (Official Video)," YouTube, 4 December 2016, https://www.youtube.com/watch?v=Onyk7guvHK8 (accessed 7 March 2019).

16 Kyle Mays, "Indigenous Dreamin': How Indigenous Hip Hop Rejects the Colonial Politics of Authenticity and Recognition," presentation at Decolonization in Comparative Context, Amherst College, Amherst, MA, 27 October 2017.

17 Brandi Morin, "Standing Rock Music Video Hip-Hop Artists Take Home MTV VMA," CBC News, 28 August 2017, https://www.cbc.ca/news/indigenous/standing-rock-music-video-hip-hop-artists-take-home-mtv-vma-1.4265830 (accessed 7 March 2019).

18 Luger, "From the Black Eyed Peas to N7."

19 Toyacoya Brown, "The Sights and Sounds from the Mni Wiconi Benefit Concert," PowWows.com—Native American Pow Wows, 24 January 2017, http://www.powwows.com/sights-sounds-mni-wiconi-benefit-concert/ (accessed 6 March 2019).

20 Erin Meyers, "'Can You Handle My Truth?' Authenticity and the Celebrity Star Image," *Journal of Popular Culture* 42, no. 5 (2009): 890–907.

21 *Windtalkers*, dir. John Woo, perf. Adam Beach, Nicolas Cage, and Peter Stormare (Lion Rock Productions and Metro Goldwyn Mayer/MGM Distribution Company, 2002); *Flags of Our Fathers*, dir. William Broyles, Clint Eastwood, and Paul Haggis, prod. Robert Lorenz and Steven

Spielberg (Paramount Pictures, 2006); *Smoke Signals*, dir. Sherman Alexie, prod. Sherman Alexie, Chris Eyre, Scott Rosenfelt, and Larry Estes (Miramax, 1998); *Suicide Squad*, dir. David Ayer, perf. Will Smith, Jared Leto, and Margo Robie (Warner Brothers Home Entertainment, 2016).

22 CNN, "Actor on Native American Roles: 'They Like Us in the . . . ,'" YouTube, 9 May 2017, https://www.youtube.com/watch?v=rBrFBxaFz-o (accessed 7 March 2019).

23 *Windtalkers*.

24 CNN, "Actor on Native American Roles."

25 Meyers, "'Can You Handle My Truth?,'" 891.

26 CNN, "Actor on Native American Roles."

27 Ibid.

28 Wes Studi, "I'm on my way to Standing Rock today. I'll be there as long as I can to help with the movement!," Twitter, 3 October 2016, https://twitter.com/wesleystudi/status/782951231031390208?lang=en (accessed 6 March 2019).

29 Cary Rosenbaum, "Wes Studi Shares #NoDAPL Experience with the Traveling NDN," *Tribal Tribune*, 21 October 2016, http://www.tribaltribune.com/opinion/article_bc3f91f4-955a-11e6-86f2-fb306f47a8dc.html (accessed 6 March 2019); White Wolf, "From Standing Rock to Washington: Actor Wes Studi Is Everywhere as a Water Protector," *White Wolf Pack*, March 2017, http://www.whitewolfpack.com/2017/03/from-standing-rock-to-washington-actor.html (accessed 7 March 2019).

30 Jennifer Levin, "A Benefit for Protectors: Stand and Rock," *Santa Fe New Mexican*, 29 December 2016, https://www.santafenewmexican.com/pasatiempo/music/in_concert/a-benefit-for-protectors-stand-and-rock/article_eae4dba0-1880-5323-af5a-2023917dd710.html (accessed 7 March 2019).

31 Rosenbaum, "Wes Studi Shares #NoDAPL Experience."

32 Graham Greene, "Has Anyone Noticed the Evil Being Done by the Money Grubbing Bastards at Standing Rock. . . . It's Just Deplorable. So Much for Police Protection," Twitter, 16 September 2016, https://twitter.com/rafeolla/status/776924873809592320?lang=en (accessed 6 March 2019).

33 M. Elwell Romancito, "Two Taos Concerts Set to Benefit Standing Rock," *Taos News*, 28 November 2016, https://taosnews.com/stories/two-taos-concerts-set-to-benefit-standing-rock,20177 (accessed 7 March 2019).

34 *Justice League*, dir. Zack Snyder, perf. Gal Gadot, Ben Affleck, and Jason Momoa (DC Films/Warner Brothers Pictures, 2017); Melissa Leon, "Jason Momoa on Speaking Out for NoDAPL: 'I Don't Mind Standing Up for What I Believe In," *Daily Beast*, 4 February 2017, https://www.thedailybeast.com/jason-momoa-on-speaking-out-for-nodapl-i-dont-mind-standing-up-for-what-i-believe-in (accessed 7 March 2019).

35 Jeffrey Weiss, "Celebs Line Up to Oppose a Pipeline across Rural West Texas Landscape," *Dallas News*, 10 June 2016, https://www.dallasnews.com/business/energy/2016/06/10/celebs-line-oppose-pipeline-across-rural-west-texasnbsplandscape (accessed 7 March 2019).

36 Kim Allen and Heather Mendick, "Young People's Uses of Celebrity: Class, Gender and 'Improper' Celebrity," *Discourse: Studies in the Cultural Politics of Education* 34, no. 1 (2013): 77–93.

37 "Marvel Becoming."

38 Andrew J. Weaver, "The Role of Actors' Race in White Audiences' Selective Exposure to Movies," *Journal of Communication* 61, no. 2 (2011): 369–85.

39 Rob Pegoraro, "The 'No Nukes' Concert, with Bonnie Raitt," *Washington Post*, 27 September 1997, https://www.washingtonpost.com/archive/lifestyle/1997/09/27/the-no-nukes-concert-with-bonnie-raitt/0d0f8d8a-e4e5-4a39-a44f-a40397150 52f/?noredirect=on&utm_term=.5e51531ed8ab (accessed 7 March 2019).

40 Jason Heppler, "Framing Red Power: The American Indian Movement, the Trail of Broken Treaties, and the Politics of Media" (MA thesis, University of Nebraska Lincoln, 2009).

41 Lauren Wissot, "Sterlin Harjo on the Dos and Don'ts of Filming in Indian Country," International Documentary Association, 18 October 2017, https://www.documentary.org/online-feature/sterlin-harjo-dos-and-donts-filming-indian-country (accessed 6 March 2019).

42 Ibid.

43 Philip Drake and Andy Miah, "The Cultural Politics of Celebrity," *Cultural Politics: An International Journal* 6, no. 1 (2010): 54.

CHAPTER 5

Rags-to-Riches and Other Fairytales: Indigenous Celebrity in Australia 1950–80

Karen Fox

When nineteen-year-old tennis player Evonne Goolagong won the ladies' singles championship at Wimbledon in 1971, she was elevated to Australian sports stardom. Known as the "Sunshine Supergirl," she was one of a number of Indigenous Australians to emerge as celebrities in the middle decades of the twentieth century. Among others making their marks in these years were artist Albert Namatjira, opera singer Harold Blair, boxers Dave Sands and Lionel Rose, poet Kath Walker (later known as Oodgeroo Noonuccal), actor David Gulpilil, singers Georgia Lee and Jimmy Little, and footballer and activist Doug Nicholls. Yet as late as the 1960s Indigenous Australians in many parts of the country remained subject to a wide range of restrictions on their lives, including in their employment, movements, finances, and relationships, and in some cases they were denied the vote, legal responsibility for their children, or the right to possess alcohol. Indigenous activism, intensifying from the 1960s on, sought an end to such restrictions as well as the granting of civil and land rights and self-determination, and gradually both federal and state governments began to respond to these demands. By the 1980s, though many concerns remained unaddressed, much had changed for Indigenous Australians: the right to vote had been granted in all states and federally, so-called protection regimes had been dismantled, the first land rights legislation and a Racial Discrimination Act had been passed, and self-determination had been accepted as federal government policy.

In this chapter, I examine the historical context of Indigenous celebrity in Australia during these years of social, cultural, and political transformation. Beginning with a brief overview of the history of Indigenous affairs policies and of Indigenous activism in Australia, I then explore a range of media framings of several Indigenous Australian men and women who were nationally or internationally prominent between 1950 and 1980 and some of the ways in which they engaged with and challenged those media representations. Portrayals of Indigenous Australian celebrities often elided differences in their lives, experiences, and cultural backgrounds, deploying similar representational tropes and drawing on visions of Aboriginality that tended to be differentiated only through binaries such as assimilated/traditional or authentic/inauthentic. In a climate of widespread concern about Indigenous affairs, Indigenous Australian celebrities were often placed under considerable pressures to represent both their people and—in the context of increased international criticism of racially restrictive societies—a positive view of Australian race relations.

A relatively new field, celebrity studies is a lively and growing one, in Australia as elsewhere.[1] The subject has developed to such a degree that it is difficult—if not impossible—to provide a brief survey, with scholars exploring both the broader cultural phenomenon and specific types of fame, from sports celebrity to celebrity feminism and many others.[2] Within this rapidly expanding field, however, relatively little attention has yet been given to Indigenous Australian experiences of celebrity.[3] Much of what has appeared has focused on contemporary figures.[4] Indeed, though the historical antecedents of modern celebrity are increasingly attracting scholarly interest, comparatively little work has been done to explore historical manifestations of celebrity in Australia in general.[5] Considerable scholarship exists, however, on a related topic: the representation of Indigenous Australians, and Indigenous affairs, in the media. While this literature does not necessarily concern celebrities, given the nature of celebrity as a media-driven phenomenon, it has much to say that is of use and interest to scholars concerned with the subject of Indigenous celebrity.[6] My own earlier research has drawn on this body of work to explore print media depictions of prominent Indigenous women in both Australia and New Zealand in the second half of the twentieth century.[7] In this chapter, I consider the historical context of Indigenous celebrity in Australia during a period of considerable change in Indigenous affairs, and I reflect on some common themes in the media representation of Indigenous Australian celebrities during those decades.

Absorption, Assimilation, and Protection

By the middle of the twentieth century, only a small number of Indigenous Australian men and women had become household names among white Australians. Investigating texts celebrating famous or significant Australians, from biographical dictionaries to children's books, one finds relatively few Aboriginal or Torres Strait Islander people who lived and died before 1950 included. Among those often represented, one of the most famous—and certainly the most well-known woman—is Trukanini (spelled variously as Truganini, Trucanini, and Trugernanner). Known erroneously as the last Tasmanian Aboriginal person, whose death marked the extinction of a people, Trukanini has been described as "the most famous Aborigine in white Australian history."[8] Colonial Australia was not a fertile ground for Indigenous celebrity, at least outside archetypes such as the tragic "last" member of a tribe or the heroic guide to European explorers.[9] Yet some did gain prominence, and even ongoing fame, outside such moulds. The first Indigenous celebrity to emerge after federation, according to John Ramsland and Christopher Mooney, was David Unaipon, an inventor, scholar, and preacher whose portrait today graces the country's fifty-dollar note.[10] From the 1940s on, however, a small cohort of Indigenous celebrities began to emerge in a range of fields, changing the face of fame in Australia in lasting ways.[11]

European settlement of Australia began with the arrival of the First Fleet—six ships laden with convicts, two Royal Navy escort ships, and three supply ships—in Botany Bay in January 1788. Only a few days were needed to reveal that Botany Bay was not an ideal location for a permanent settlement, and before the end of the month the fleet moved to Sydney Cove, in Port Jackson, where the city of Sydney would begin to take shape. Considerable violence attended European settlement as it expanded, continuing into the early twentieth century in the central, northern, and western parts of the continent.[12] The legal doctrine of *terra nullius*, applied in the Australian context from the late nineteenth century, deemed the land empty and thus able to be settled without regard for its occupation by Indigenous peoples.[13] Although humanitarian concern was expressed in some quarters about the welfare of Indigenous Australians, a key outcome of that solicitude was regimes of Aboriginal protection, which in practice meant oppressive regulation of Indigenous lives and for many people a restricted existence on reserves and missions. A widespread belief that Aboriginal Australians were a "doomed race" perhaps helped to alleviate any guilt felt by European settlers about the dispossession and suffering that accompanied them and to render unnecessary questions about the place of Indigenous peoples in a white settler nation.[14] Expressions of "sadness" and "nostalgia" began to replace representations of Aboriginal people as "violent" or "savage," as it came to be believed that their eventual disappearance was inevitable.[15]

Although the belief that Aboriginal Australians were a "dying race" persisted into the early twentieth century, by then it was becoming clear that Indigenous populations were no longer declining but in fact growing. Disquiet developed within the settler society over the growth of a mixed-descent population, and in Western Australia and the Northern Territory during the 1930s policies of biological absorption attempted to "breed out the colour" through practices such as requiring state sanction for marriages.[16] At a national conference of administrators of Indigenous affairs in 1937, it was resolved that "the destiny of the natives of aboriginal origin, but not of the full blood, lies in their ultimate absorption by the people of the Commonwealth," a declaration that has sometimes been understood as endorsing biological absorption.[17] Other voices, however, advocated cultural rather than biological absorption or that Aboriginal Australians ought to be able to retain their culture while also gaining equal rights and living standards.[18]

Significant change took place in relation to Indigenous affairs policies in the aftermath of the Second World War. With the extremes of Nazi racial ideology revealed to the world, ideas of racial science came into disrepute, and efforts to end discrimination based on race began to be made at the international level. The possibility of international scrutiny—and especially the potential for comparison with the apartheid regime of South Africa—now came to be a factor in policy-making decisions.[19] At the same time, sections of the Aboriginal population were becoming urbanized, and this too drove alterations in government policy. Assimilatory approaches were adopted around the country, seeking to incorporate Indigenous Australians into white modes of living. Such approaches potentially offered equality in standards of living, as well as in opportunities and civil rights, but at the cost of largely obliterating Indigenous cultures.[20] One of the key engineers of Australia's assimilationist policy, Minister for Territories Paul Hasluck, expected only folkloric elements to remain.[21] Those of mixed descent were the major focus of such policy since it was thought that they were most capable of adapting to white ways of living.

Despite the possibility of equality held out by assimilationist rhetoric, the reality of life for many Indigenous Australians was of daily oppression and fear. Children continued to be removed from their families, girls and boys were indentured as domestic servants or labourers, private lives were subjected to intrusive surveillance, and benefits and civil rights were tied to requirements to live in European ways. Exemption from protection legislation was necessary in order to access many of the rights of citizenship, a humiliating and resented system. In 1962, when Shirley Andrews, a campaign organizer for the Federal Council for Aboriginal Advancement, prepared a report summarizing the positions of Indigenous Australians in the various states and federally, she found differing practices across the country but a uniform pattern of restriction and bureaucratic control of Indigenous lives. In some states and territories, Aboriginal people were unable to travel freely or determine their own places of residence, to control their own properties or finances, to marry without permission or hold legal guardianship of their children, to socialize freely with non-Indigenous Australians, to vote in state government elections, or to purchase or possess alcohol. Restrictions were particularly severe in some parts of the country, such as Queensland, where the director of Native affairs had sweeping powers over the lives of Indigenous people.[22]

Nor was assimilation ever a straightforward concept; indeed, its meanings and practices continue to be debated. Although it could refer simply to the achievement of equality between Indigenous and non-Indigenous Australians, it could also mean the disappearance of Indigenous cultures as Indigenous people were subsumed into white Australian culture.[23] Leading proponents disagreed about exactly what the policy might involve, and how much might remain of Indigenous cultures.[24] As well, though many scholars have taken the term "assimilation" to describe a particular policy that existed between the 1930s and the 1970s, the concept can also be understood as referring to a destructive approach that has continued since 1788.[25] In the view of Anna

Haebich, assimilation can be considered "a powerful act of national imagining."[26] Such a vision was tied to the concept of white Australia, an ideal that was enshrined in the nation's immigration policy from the time of federation in 1901 and that would gradually be abandoned from the late 1950s on. Indigenous Australians might not have vanished physically, but they were expected to do so in a cultural sense—or at least to retain only those folkloric elements of culture referenced by Hasluck. They would thus become part of a culturally homogeneous nation, and no longer would their presence raise the spectre of dispute over "who owns, and whose identity is fused with, the land."[27] Such a vision of the nation, celebrating cultural if not racial homogeneity, had significant implications for the place that highly successful or well-known Indigenous figures might hold in that nation and in its narratives about itself.

Protest, Foment, and Change

Protest by Indigenous Australians against the injuries of colonization has been continual since the first arrival of Europeans in Australia. One aspect of early resistance to colonization was armed opposition to white settlement; another was the writing of letters and the signing of petitions. Organizations calling for improvements in the welfare of Indigenous people, and for the extension of civil or land rights to Indigenous Australians, began forming in the early twentieth century. Described by John Maynard as "the first united politically organised Aboriginal activist group" in the country, the Australian Aboriginal Progressive Association was founded in New South Wales in 1924.[28] The following decade saw the establishment of both the Aboriginal Progressive Association in Sydney and the Australian Aborigines' League in Melbourne as well as the holding of a Day of Mourning as white Australians celebrated 150 years of European settlement in 1938.

New organizations were formed in the middle of the century, often focused on advances in welfare and the cessation of discrimination as well as the granting of civil rights to Indigenous Australians. In many of these bodies, Indigenous and non-Indigenous people worked alongside each other, as they did—at least to begin with—in the first national organization formed to push for Indigenous rights, the Federal Council for Aboriginal Advancement (later the Federal Council for the Advancement of Aborigines and Torres

Strait Islanders or FCAATSI), founded in 1958.[29] Among other objectives, FCAATSI campaigned for a referendum on changing the constitution to remove two sections considered discriminatory: Section 51, which limited the federal government's ability to make laws relating to Indigenous people, and Section 127, which dealt with the use of census data. More than 90 percent of voters supported these changes when the referendum was held in May 1967, a result that produced a surge of optimism among Indigenous Australians, who hoped that positive changes would follow.

Activism for Indigenous rights had increased and intensified during the 1950s and 1960s, and as the 1960s drew to a close a new generation of Indigenous activists emerged, often adopting more militant stances than had their predecessors. Indigenous organizations began to focus more closely on specifically Indigenous rights, especially land rights, as well as the extension of civil rights to Indigenous people and the cessation of discrimination. A number of young, urban Aboriginal leaders began to employ more militant tactics and to speak of "Black Power," drawing on the movement of that name in the United States.[30] Many of these younger leaders were disappointed at the apparent lack of change following the referendum in 1967, and many were no longer willing to work through white-dominated organizations.[31] More strongly than had previous generations of activists, they articulated "an Aboriginal or black consciousness," and they advocated self-determination rather than assimilation or integration.[32] Connected to such ideas of consciousness in the 1970s was a growth in Indigenous "pride and identity" as manifested in the formation of a range of community projects that sought to advance Indigenous welfare, in the creation of Aboriginal studies courses, and in the rise of cultural and artistic groups and productions.[33]

Although inequality and disadvantage remained realities, and the struggle of Indigenous activists would continue, significant changes took place in Indigenous affairs from the 1960s on, driven by the increasing protests of Indigenous Australians as well as changing public opinion and international pressure. Oppressive policies such as those that restricted the movements and choices of Indigenous Australians were gradually dismantled. By the end of 1965, all states had granted Indigenous people the right to vote, and by 1969 each had repealed its legislation permitting Indigenous children to be removed from their families for assimilatory purposes.[34] The socially progressive federal government of Labor Prime Minister Gough Whitlam, in power from December 1972 on, adopted a policy of self-determination in place of assimilation. A Racial Discrimination Act was passed in 1975, making it unlawful to discriminate on the ground of race in contexts such as employment, housing, and provision of services and goods. The first moves were also made to extend land rights to Indigenous Australians when, in 1973, the government appointed Justice Edward Woodward to hold a royal commission to determine how best to introduce such rights. At a ceremony in 1975, in a visual moment that has become iconic, Whitlam symbolized the handing back of a parcel of land to the Gurindji people by pouring soil into the hand of Vincent Lingiari, the Gurindji spokesman who had led the fight for the return of his people's land.

Assimilation and Indigenous Celebrity

In the years during and after the Second World War, at the height of the assimilationist era, a number of Indigenous Australians began to gain prominence in their fields and become well known to white Australians. One of the earliest to do so was Arrernte artist Albert (Elea) Namatjira, whose story has since become emblematic of the injustices of assimilation. Born in 1902 at Hermannsburg in the Northern Territory, Namatjira was educated at the Hermannsburg mission school, living in the boys' dormitory and regularly visiting his parents at their camp on the edge of the mission. At the age of eighteen, he married Ilkalita (Rubina), and the couple departed from the mission, returning with their children in 1923. Working in various jobs, including as a stockman, cameleer, blacksmith, and carpenter, Namatjira also began to create wooden plaques decorated with pokerwork, which he sold to visitors. Among those visitors were the artists Rex Battarbee and John Gardner, who in 1934 exhibited their images of Arrernte country at the mission. Eager to learn to paint, Namatjira began practising with watercolours himself, and in 1936 he travelled with Battarbee about the Macdonnell Ranges, working as a cameleer while being taught the techniques of watercolour painting. Ten of his images were shown at the Lutheran synod conference in 1937 by the mission's superintendent, Friedrich Albrecht, and three were included in an exhibition of Battarbee's work in Adelaide the same year. Namatjira's first solo show was held in Melbourne the following year.[35] He would soon become famous as "the first prominent Aboriginal artist to work in a modern idiom."[36] Included in *Who's Who in Australia* in 1944, he received the Queen Elizabeth II coronation medal in 1953 and was presented to Her Majesty during her tour of Australia in 1954.[37]

One representation of Namatjira was as "the public face of assimilation," as he had been portrayed in a government documentary put out by the Commonwealth Film Unit in 1947.[38] As Haebich has shown, Indigenous individuals who could be depicted as successful in white terms were held up at times in official discourse as exemplars of assimilation.[39] Similar portrayals are evident in other texts produced about the lives and achievements of Indigenous celebrities in this era. In a booklet entitled *Sketches of Outstanding Aborigines*, likely produced around 1956, the secretary of the Aborigines' Friends' Association in Adelaide, Reverend Gordon Rowe, explained that he told their stories "for the purpose of showing that the Australian aborigines are capable of qualifying to fill a variety of useful positions in the community."[40] Rowe included Namatjira in his cast of successful individuals, together with a number of other men and women, some well known and others relatively unknown. Analyzing Rowe's portrayal of the life of singer Harold Blair in an earlier radio version of the sketches, Ramsland and Mooney observed that Rowe presented government officials and institutions positively and emphasized "the supposed largesse of the . . . assimilation policy," though no such support had in fact existed during Blair's early life.[41] Such representations of Indigenous celebrities as exemplars of assimilation potentially served to alleviate white Australians' feelings of guilt at the situations of Indigenous Australians and to present a positive view of race relations that glossed over embedded prejudice and disadvantage.

Yet depictions of Indigenous celebrities as models of assimilation were often not simply uncomplicated, feel-good tales of success. A common theme, evident perhaps especially in portrayals of Namatjira, was that of living "between two worlds," embodying assimilation, and its promise of equality, and simultaneously struggling to achieve it, held back by continuing ties to community and culture. Echoing "a long history of fascination in the West with the experiences of Indigenous individuals negotiating" this dilemma, Australians' mid-twentieth-century "anxieties about crumbling race barriers and Aboriginal assimilation found expression in . . . popular narratives of individuals seeking to lead marginal lives 'between two worlds.'"[42] Reflecting on time spent with Namatjira and his sons in Central Australia, for example, author and journalist Frank Clune remarked that he had returned "to civilisation, pondering over the problem of these sensitive Stone Age artists" who were "too advanced to live in the bush, and not enough advanced to stand the strain of living in cities."[43] Artist Noel Counihan described Namatjira as "occupying the unenviable position of the artist of transition, a bridge between two cultures," while an article by critic and gallery director Laurie Thomas was introduced with the idea that he had "been set the impossible task of obeying two contradictory ways of life."[44] Journalist and author Douglas Lockwood, meanwhile, painted a sad picture of a broken-down man, asserting that "the tragedy of Namatjira is that he was brought up too quickly into the dazzling lights of publicity" and thrust into a life for which he was unprepared. He had been "projected," wrote Lockwood, "into space and left there—a lost, unhappy wanderer between two worlds."[45] As Haebich concludes, rather than "the official government message of fairytale endings in comfortable suburban homes," such portrayals judged "that it was impossible for Aboriginal people to become assimilated, that it was impossible for them to remain unassimilated, and that it was impossible for them to live between the two cultures."[46]

In Namatjira's case in particular, such narratives were imbued with a powerful air of tragedy, for his success in the white world was seen to have created inconsistencies and pressures that had proved not only impossible to navigate but ultimately fatal. Granted "a form of citizenship rights" in 1957, he had been released from the constraints consequent on being deemed a ward of the state.[47] Now able to purchase alcohol, he found himself charged with supplying it to a fellow artist not similarly emancipated. For this, he was sentenced to six months in prison, a term eventually lowered to three months. In the end, he served only two, in "open" detention at the Aboriginal settlement at Papunya. Less than three months after being released, however, in August 1959, he died.[48] For many media commentators, both at the time and since, his death was a tragedy caused by the flawed policy of assimilation, the pressures of which had broken him. Shortly after his death, for example, artist Herbert McClintock challenged the statement that he had "died of a heart failing of long standing," asking "would it not be more true to say he died of a broken heart?"[49] Some years later a feature on his life appeared in the *Daily Mirror* under the headline "Fame Was Death to Aboriginal Artist." Although Namatjira had "achieved enormous success as a painter," the writer suggested, he had "never [been] able to bridge the gap between the codes of the white man and the Aboriginal," and, when he had continued to act according to Indigenous customs of sharing, "the white man's law gave him little sympathy or understanding."[50]

More recently, Ramsland and Mooney have reinterpreted this aspect of Namatjira's life, arguing that his refusal of white expectations that he ought to "conserve wealth rather than use and expend it," and his continuing "faithful[ness] to the Aboriginal doctrine of sharing," represented a repudiation of the concept of assimilation "in favour of maintaining his cultural identity, responsibilities, links and heritage."[51] Namatjira's art has also been re-evaluated. During his lifetime, he was sometimes applauded for having "learnt to paint like a white man," and at other times his work was disparaged by artists and critics who were enthusiastic about modernism, or the idea of primitivism, as having lost "a pure 'tribal' expression" or "authenticity."[52] Later assessments have instead recognized that his work "blended Aboriginal and European modes of depiction" and showed places of ancestral significance.[53]

Such arguments about Namatjira's art reveal a related binary sometimes evident in representations of Indigenous celebrities, particularly those whose fame stemmed from their creative works. Whereas prominent Indigenous figures were liable to be depicted in terms of the twin poles of assimilated/modern and tribal/traditional, those celebrated for their artistic and literary works could also find themselves subject to portrayal as either authentic or inauthentic. One who experienced this representational tension was poet and activist Kath Walker (later known as Oodgeroo Noonuccal). Born in Queensland in 1920, Walker grew up with her family on Minjerribah, or North Stradbroke Island, where she attended Dunwich State School. After leaving school, she worked as a domestic before joining the Australian Women's Army Service during the Second World War.[54] She began writing poetry and prose, publishing her first volume of poetry, *We Are Going*, in 1964. Often claimed to be the first collection of poems published by an Indigenous Australian, the book sold well, and Walker quickly became famous.[55] As well as continuing to publish, she became deeply involved in activism on behalf of Indigenous Australians, for which work she also became nationally prominent. Involved in the Queensland Council for the Advancement of Aborigines and Torres Strait Islanders and in FCAATSI, she played an important part in the campaign for the 1967 referendum.

Representations of Walker and her poetry demonstrate the connection between notions of assimilation and notions of authenticity. One response to her work in the 1960s was indeed to greet it as the expression of an authentic Indigenous voice. Reviewing her second volume of poetry, *The Dawn Is at Hand*, in 1966, for example, author and critic T. Inglis Moore described her as "the authentic voice of the Aborigine."[56] On other occasions, however, her work was disparaged as less than authentic because she could be regarded as assimilated. In the words of Bob Hodge, "earnest white critics who claimed to understand Aboriginality better than she did said that they would have liked the work better if it had been more obviously Aboriginal."[57] Penny van Toorn too has noted that "essentialist beliefs about Aboriginality" meant that Walker was considered by some "too modern to be authentically Aboriginal" and by others too "old-fashioned and rhetorical to be a proper poet."[58] Along with "other non-Anglo-Celtic Australian writers," van Toorn observes, Indigenous Australian authors tended to be "required to prove their authenticity and put their cultural identity on display."[59] This pressure, and the constant identification and evaluation of individuals and their work in terms of race, could irritate. "When I'm written up in the papers or the media or whatever," Walker noted in 1982, "they always call me an 'Aboriginal poet.'" She rejected the label, preferring to consider herself "a poet who is proud to be of Aboriginal descent."[60] It was an important distinction, asserting her right to enter the literary field and be judged as more than a mere curiosity.

Rags-to-Riches and the Myth of Discovery

Another common framing in media depictions of Indigenous Australian celebrities in the mid-twentieth century was what might be called a "rags-to-riches" narrative. In such framings, individuals were depicted as having escaped from a life of poverty and deprivation—perhaps implied to be the usual lot of Indigenous Australians—through their talent and success in a particular field. As with the representational tropes discussed above, ideas of assimilation were central to this narrative frame, which presented success on white terms as a road away from disadvantage and toward equality. Tenor Harold Blair, for example, was sometimes portrayed in such a way. Growing up on the Purga mission in Queensland, Blair lived apart from his mother, who worked as a domestic and was not permitted to have him with her, and he received only a minimal education before taking up employment on a dairy farm and later working as a cane cutter on Queensland's sugar plantations.[61] The contrast between his early life and his later years, studying at the Melbourne (Melba) Conservatorium of Music and in the United States, and performing in concert halls around Australia and in New York, was irresistible to journalists. "Harold Blair: Cane-Cutter to Top Tenor" was the headline in the Melbourne *Age* at his death in 1976.[62] The *Daily Mirror*, meanwhile, had not only transported him from poverty to fame but also transmuted him in the process from "Aboriginal" to "Australian": after outlining his early life and work as a labourer, the author remarked that "from such a beginning that young uneducated Aboriginal youth rose to achieve fame as the talented Australian tenor Harold Blair."[63] Rags-to-riches representations can also be found in media coverage of boxer Lionel Rose, who catapulted to national fame when he won the world bantamweight championship in Tokyo in 1968. He was, claimed one headline, "A Rose from the Dust" who had lived with his family as a child "in a humpy with a dirt floor [with] neither electricity nor water and . . . only an open fire in the yard for cooking," but who had "rise[n] from rags to riches, from an under-privileged boy out of a bush shack to a civic welcome through the streets of Melbourne."[64]

Although such narratives might be a common framing for media stories about celebrities in general, those related to Indigenous individuals potentially carried additional meanings. In 1968, the New South Wales Aborigines Welfare Board publication *Dawn* explained the "extraordinary appeal" of tennis star Evonne Goolagong as a result of her being viewed "not only as a rising champion, but also as an Aborigine who has made good."[65] As this statement hints, a subtext of salvation could thus be implanted in these rags-to-riches tales, potentially assuaging white Australians' feelings of guilt about past injustices toward Indigenous Australians. Moreover, just as depictions of Indigenous celebrities as models of assimilation could present government departments and officials positively, and thereby Australian race relations, so too rags-to-riches stories could highlight the roles of white mentors and supporters. In some media portrayals of Goolagong, for example, her coach, Vic Edwards, was depicted as having discovered her talent and worked to develop it—just as, perhaps, white Australians were imagined to have discovered and developed the land. Goolagong herself resisted this narrative, once being quoted as stating that she thought "some people think that Mr. Edwards plucked me out of Barellan [her hometown] and, presto, I became a Wimbledon champion." Such an idea, she said, gave her "no credit as a person."[66] She was well aware of the negative implications of the rags-to-riches version of her life. "I have been painted many times in the media as an Eliza Doolittle, an Aboriginal urchin who was saved from the savages and taught civilised ways by the Edwards family," Goolagong observed in an autobiography co-authored with journalist Phil Jarratt in 1993, commenting that "it wasn't like that."[67] She recalled being upset on one occasion in 1971 by the behaviour of a film crew from the Australian Broadcasting Commission who, she thought, had probably been seeking "to illustrate beyond any shadow of doubt the rags-to-riches element of my story" by portraying Barellan as disadvantaged and her family as ostracized "fringe dwellers."[68]

In telling her own story in an autobiography, and in choosing to narrate such episodes, Goolagong actively engaged with and contested media representations of her life, as did other Indigenous celebrities. Moreover, if many of the representational tropes often applied to Indigenous celebrities placed them as representatives of all Indigenous Australians, and particularly of their potential for successful assimilation, celebrity also provided opportunities to speak and be heard and a platform from which to make representations on behalf of their people.[69] Blair, for example, is reported to have commonly responded to comments about his being the first Indigenous person to achieve in particular ways by observing "isn't it awful . . . that I'm the only one."[70] Or, as the *Daily Mirror* reported, to have pointed out that "people don't know . . . how many Aboriginals could do the same thing," for "we have the same talents as white people and lack only equal opportunities."[71] Blair took the opportunities provided by his celebrity to advocate for a better deal for Indigenous Australians, once telling a reporter that, "now that I am doing well, my main objective is to show Australia and the world that Australian aborigines must be given a chance."[72] In a radio interview in 1956, for example, he talked of the difficulties faced by Indigenous people, and his sorrow that so many still experienced poverty and disadvantage, as well as his hopes for the future.[73] Of course, for some Indigenous celebrities, it was their work as activists that had led to their fame in the first place. Pastor Doug Nicholls, for instance, was well known for his activism on behalf of Indigenous Australians, and in the 1950s his name was "synonymous" with "the Aboriginal cause."[74] A capable media operator, he "both exploited and was exploited by the media."[75] Celebrity, and the media visibility that it brought, could thus be a double-edged sword, at times a source of pain and frustration but also a means by which to make one's voice heard.

Conclusion

As these examples demonstrate, historical context is crucial to understanding celebrity as it has been manifested in particular places, times, and situations. Reflecting on the ways in which historians might analyze the heroes of the past, Max Jones has advocated "locating heroic reputations in historical context" and examining individuals "as sites within which we can find evidence of the cultural beliefs, social practices, political structures and economic systems of the past."[76] Likewise, close attention to the historical contexts in which celebrities have come to prominence, and in which their media profiles and public images have been constructed, can reveal much not only about the nature of celebrity but also about the social, cultural, and political worlds within which they gained fame. Indigenous Australians who became celebrities during the mid-twentieth century did so in a context of anxiety among white Australians about Indigenous affairs. Media representations of well-known Indigenous Australians in this era, as well as official government portrayals, were shaped by the policy dilemmas and concerns of the assimilationist era, making ideas of race ever present in framings of their lives and achievements and creating or perpetuating tropes such as the exemplar of assimilation or the rags-to-riches success story. Yet Indigenous celebrities were never only the subjects of media representations. Whether by actively contesting and challenging those representations, or by using their fame to advocate for change, or simply by offering the examples of their lives, they disrupted embedded narratives of race in ways that continue to resonate today.

NOTES

1 One indication of the growth of celebrity studies as a field is the founding of a dedicated journal of *Celebrity Studies* in 2010. Australian contributions to the literature include both work on celebrity in general and research on the specific contours of the phenomenon in Australia. For examples, see Graeme Turner, Frances Bonner, and P. David Marshall, *Fame Games: The Production of Celebrity in Australia* (Cambridge, UK: Cambridge University Press, 2000); and Robert van Krieken, *Celebrity Society* (London: Routledge, 2012). For an overview of the development of Australian celebrity studies, see Frances Bonner, "Kylie Will Be OK: On the (Im-)Possibility of Australian Celebrity Studies," *Cultural Studies* 29, no. 4 (2015): 527–45.

2 As examples, see David L. Andrews and Steven J. Jackson, eds., *Sport Stars: The Cultural Politics of Sporting Celebrity* (London: Routledge, 2001); Sandra Lilburn, Susan Magarey, and Susan Sheridan, "Celebrity Feminism as Synthesis: Germaine Greer, *The Female Eunuch* and the Australian Print Media," *Continuum: Journal of Media and Cultural Studies* 14, no. 3 (2000): 335–48; and Anthea Taylor, *Celebrity and the Feminist Blockbuster* (London: Palgrave Macmillan, 2016).

3 Exceptions include Toni Bruce and Christopher Hallinan, "Cathy Freeman: The Quest for Australian Identity," in *Sport Stars: The Cultural Politics of Sporting Celebrity*, ed. David L. Andrews and Steven J. Jackson (London: Routledge, 2001), 257–70; Felicity Collins, "The Ethical Violence of Celebrity Chat: Russell Crowe and David Gulpilil," *Social Semiotics* 18, no. 2 (2008): 191–204; Felicity Collins, "Resisting the Ethical Violence of Coercive Aboriginality: David Gulpilil," in *Celebrity Colonialism: Fame, Power and Representation in Colonial and Postcolonial Cultures*, ed. Robert Clarke (Newcastle upon Tyne, UK: Cambridge Scholars Publishing, 2009), 189–207; Glenn D'Cruz, "Breaking Bad: The Booing of Adam Goodes and the Politics of the Black Sports Celebrity in Australia," *Celebrity Studies* 9, no. 1 (2018): 131–38; and Celia Lam and Louise St. Guillaume, "'Grant'ing a Voice: The Representation, Activity and Agency of Stan Grant," *Celebrity Studies* 9, no. 1 (2018): 139–46. Some few Indigenous Australian celebrities also receive brief mention in Turner et al., *Fame Games*.

4 Examples considering earlier Indigenous celebrities include Catherine Bishop and Richard White, "Explorer Memory and Aboriginal Celebrity," in *Indigenous Intermediaries: New Perspectives on Exploration Archives*, ed. Shino Konishi, Maria Nugent, and Tiffany Shellam (Canberra: ANU Press, 2015), 31–66; Christopher Mooney and John Ramsland, "Growing Up and Breaking Away from the Mission: The Formative Years of Aboriginal Celebrities of the 1950s," *ISAA Review* 6, no. 1 (2007): 6–15; John Ramsland, "Images of Albert Namatjira in Australian Popular Culture of the 1950s," *Inter-Cultural Studies* 2, no. 2 (2002): 11–26; John Ramsland and Christopher Mooney, "Out of the Dark: The First Successful All-Black Musical: Aboriginal Celebrity and Protest," *Victorian Historical Journal* 78, no. 1 (2007): 63–79; and John Ramsland and Christopher Mooney, *Remembering Aboriginal Heroes: Struggle, Identity and the Media* (Melbourne: Brolga Publishing, 2006).

5 A recent example of the former is Antoine Lilti, *The Invention of Celebrity* (Cambridge, UK: Polity, 2017). Examples of work on historical instances of celebrity in Australia include Anna Johnston, "George Augustus Robinson, the 'Great Conciliator': Colonial Celebrity and Its Postcolonial Aftermath," *Postcolonial Studies* 12, no. 2 (2009): 153–72; Lilburn et al., "Celebrity Feminism as Synthesis"; Leigh Straw, "Celebrating Kate: The Criminal-Celebrity of Sydney Underworld Figure, Kate Leigh," *Journal of Australian Studies* 40, no. 1 (2016): 59–73; Julie Ustinoff and Kay Saunders, "Celebrity, Nation and the New Australian Woman: Tania Verstak, Miss Australia 1961," *Journal of Australian Studies* 28, no. 83 (2004): 61–73.

6 Among others, see Kim Bullimore, "Media Dreaming: Representation of Aboriginality in Modern Australian Media," *Asia Pacific Media Educator* 6 (1999): 72–80; John Hartley and Alan McKee, *The Indigenous Public Sphere: The Reporting and Reception of Aboriginal Issues in the Australian Media* (Oxford: Oxford University Press, 2000); Ruth McCausland, "Special Treatment: The Representation of Aboriginal and Torres Strait Islander People in the Media," *Journal of Indigenous Policy* 4 (2004): 84–98; and Michael Meadows, *Voices in the Wilderness: Images of Aboriginal People in the Australian Media* (Westport, CT: Greenwood, 2001).

7 See especially Karen Fox, *Māori and Aboriginal Women in the Public Eye: Representing Difference, 1950–2000* (Canberra: ANU E Press, 2011).

8 Lyndall Ryan, "Truganini (Trukanini)," in *The Oxford Companion to Australian History*, ed. Graeme Davison, John Hirst, and Stuart Macintyre (Melbourne: Oxford University Press, 1998), 651.

9 On the latter, see Bishop and White, "Explorer Memory."

10 Ramsland and Mooney, *Remembering Aboriginal Heroes*, x–xi.

11 See ibid., ix, 319–39, especially 327.

12 Ann McGrath, "A National Story," in *Contested Ground: Australian Aborigines under the British Crown*, ed. Ann McGrath (St Leonards, NSW: Allen and Unwin, 1995), 18–19.

13 Bruce Buchan, "Traffick of Empire: Trade, Treaty and *Terra Nullius* in Australia and North America, 1750–1800," *History Compass* 5, no. 2 (2007): 387.

14 Russell McGregor, *Imagined Destinies: Aboriginal Australians and the Doomed Race Theory, 1880–1939* (Carlton South, Vic.: Melbourne University Press, 1997), ix; Anthony Moran, "White Australia, Settler Nationalism and Aboriginal Assimilation," *Australian Journal of Politics and History* 51, no. 2 (2005): 172.

15 Richard Waterhouse, "Australian Legends: Representations of the Bush, 1813–1913," *Australian Historical Studies* 31, no. 115 (2000): 209.

16 Anna Haebich, *Broken Circles: Fragmenting Indigenous Families 1800–2000* (Fremantle, WA: Fremantle Arts Centre Press, 2000), 205; Russell McGregor, "'Breed Out the Colour': Or the Importance of Being White," *Australian Historical Studies* 33, no. 120 (2002): 287–90.

17 *Aboriginal Welfare: Initial Conference of Commonwealth and State Aboriginal Authorities Held at Canberra, 21st to 23rd April, 1937* (Canberra: Commonwealth Government Printer, 1937), [3]; Haebich, *Broken Circles*, 205; Stuart Macintyre, *A Concise History of Australia*, 2nd ed. (Port Melbourne, Vic.: Cambridge University Press, 2004), 188.

18 See the discussion in Cora Thomas, "From 'Australian Aborigines' to 'White Australians,'" *Australian Aboriginal Studies* 1 (2001): 22–23.

19 On the significance of the fear of international scrutiny in changing Australian race policies, see John Chesterman, *Civil Rights: How Indigenous Australians Won Formal Equality* (St Lucia, Qld: University of Queensland Press, 2005); and Jennifer Clark, *Aborigines and Activism: Race, Aborigines and the Coming of the Sixties to Australia* (Crawley, WA: University of Western Australia Press, 2008).

20 Anna Haebich, "Imagining Assimilation," *Australian Historical Studies* 33, no. 118 (2002): 62.

21 Russell McGregor, "Assimilationists Contest Assimilation: T.G.H. Strehlow and A.P. Elkin on Aboriginal Policy," *Journal of Australian Studies* 75 (2002): 46.

22 Shirley Andrews, "The Australian Aborigines: A Summary of Their Situation in All States in 1962," State Library of Victoria, Council for Aboriginal Rights (Vic.), Papers, MS 12913, Box 3/4,

http://indigenousrights.net.au/resources/documents/the_australian_aborigines_a_summary_of_their_situation_in_all_states_in_1962 (accessed 14 December 2017).

23 Rani Kerin, "Charles Duguid and Aboriginal Assimilation in Adelaide, 1950–1960: The Nebulous 'Assimilation' Goal," *History Australia* 2, no. 3 (2005): 85.1–85.2.

24 See, for example, McGregor, "Assimilationists Contest Assimilation."

25 Tim Rowse, "Contesting Assimilation," in *Contesting Assimilation*, ed. Tim Rowse (Perth: API Network, 2005), 1–2.

26 Haebich, "Imagining Assimilation," 62.

27 Moran, "White Australia," 169–70.

28 John Maynard, "Vision, Voice and Influence: The Rise of the Australian Aboriginal Progressive Association," *Australian Historical Studies* 34, no. 121 (2003): 91.

29 For the history of FCAATSI, see Sue Taffe, *Black and White Together FCAATSI: The Federal Council for the Advancement of Aborigines and Torres Strait Islanders, 1958–1973* (St Lucia, Qld: University of Queensland Press, 2005).

30 Bain Attwood, *Rights for Aborigines* (Crows Nest, NSW: Allen and Unwin, 2003), 321–24; Richard Broome, *Aboriginal Australians: Black Responses to White Dominance 1788–2001*, 3rd ed. (Crows Nest, NSW: Allen and Unwin, 2002), 188; Clark, *Aborigines and Activism*, 203–21.

31 Gary Foley, "Black Power in Redfern 1968–1972," updated 5 October 2001, The Koori History Website, http://www.kooriweb.org/foley/essays/essay_1.html (accessed 19 May 2008); Attwood, *Rights for Aborigines*, 322–26; Clark, *Aborigines and Activism*, 214–17; Macintyre, *Concise History*, 235.

32 Attwood, *Rights for Aborigines*, 322–23; Macintyre, *Concise History*, 235.

33 Broome, *Aboriginal Australians*, 201–3.

34 Australian Human Rights Commission, "Track the History Timeline: The Stolen Generations," https://www.humanrights.gov.au/track-history-timeline-stolen-generations (accessed 11 January 2018).

35 Sylvia Kleinert, "Namatjira, Albert (Elea) (1902–1959)," *Australian Dictionary of Biography*, National Centre of Biography, Australian National University, http://adb.anu.edu.au/biography/namatjira-albert-elea-11217/text19999, published first in hardcopy 2000 (accessed online 4 January 2018); Ramsland and Mooney, *Remembering Aboriginal Heroes*, 33–39.

36 Kleinert, "Namatjira, Albert."

37 Ibid.; Ramsland and Mooney, *Remembering Aboriginal Heroes*, 41, 51.

38 Anna Haebich, *Spinning the Dream: Assimilation in Australia 1950–1970* (North Fremantle, WA: Fremantle Press, 2008), 355; Ramsland and Mooney, *Remembering Aboriginal Heroes*, 51.

39 Haebich, *Spinning the Dream*, 152, 355. Other scholars too have observed that successful Aboriginal people were sometimes praised for exemplifying assimilation. See, for example, Mooney and Ramsland, "Growing Up and Breaking Away," 6; Ramsland, "Images of Albert Namatjira," 16–17; and Adam Shoemaker, *Black Words White Page: Aboriginal Literature 1929–1988* (Canberra: ANU E Press, 2004), 73.

40 Gordon Rowe, *Sketches of Outstanding Aborigines* ([Adelaide?]: [Aborigines' Friends' Association?], [1956?]), cover.

41 Ramsland and Mooney, *Remembering Aboriginal Heroes*, 90–91.

42 Haebich, *Spinning the Dream*, 348–49. This has been an enduring trope in media representations of Indigenous Australian celebrities. Collins, for example, has identified it in media depictions of actor David Gulpilil across his decades-long career. Collins, "Ethical Violence of Celebrity Chat," 197–98.

43 Frank Clune, "Albert Namatjira: Aboriginal Artist," *Trans-Air* 7, no. 11 (1956), cutting held in National Library of Australia, Canberra, Biographical Cuttings on Albert Namatjira, Artist, Containing One or More Cuttings from Newspapers or Journals.

44 Noel Counihan, "The Tragedy of Albert Namatjira," *Tribune* [Sydney], 1 April 1959, 6; Laurie Thomas, "Namatjira: Tragic Symbol of a Lost People," *Woman's Day with Woman*, 27 October 1958, cutting held in National Library of Australia, Canberra, Biographical Cuttings on Albert Namatjira, Artist, Containing One or More Cuttings from Newspapers or Journals. The description by Counihan is also quoted by Ramsland and Mooney, *Remembering Aboriginal Heroes*, 44. The depiction from the *Woman's Day* article by Thomas is also quoted by Ramsland and Mooney, *Remembering Aboriginal Heroes*, 45; and Haebich, *Spinning the Dream*, 356.

45 Douglas Lockwood, "Rise and Fall of a Great Aborigine," *Advertiser* [Adelaide?] 2 August 1958, cutting held in National Library of Australia, Canberra, Biographical Cuttings on Albert Namatjira, Artist, Containing One or More Cuttings from Newspapers or Journals; Douglas Lockwood, "The Tragedy of Albert Namatjira," *Herald* [Melbourne?] 2 August 1958, cutting held in National Library of Australia, Canberra, Biographical Cuttings on Albert Namatjira, Artist, Containing One or More Cuttings from Newspapers or Journals.

46 Haebich, *Spinning the Dream*, 350.

47 Ibid., 354; Ramsland and Mooney, *Remembering Aboriginal Heroes*, 41.

48 Haebich, *Spinning the Dream*, 355; Kleinert, "Namatjira, Albert"; Ramsland and Mooney, *Remembering Aboriginal Heroes*, 42, 48.

49 Herbert McClintock, "Homage to Namatjira," *Tribune* [Sydney], 19 August 1959, 6.

50 "Fame Was Death to Aboriginal Artist," *Daily Mirror* [Sydney?] 24 July 1967, 28, cutting held in National Library of Australia, Canberra, Biographical Cuttings on Albert Namatjira, Artist, Containing One or More Cuttings from Newspapers or Journals.

51 Ramsland and Mooney, *Remembering Aboriginal Heroes*, 59.

52 Sylvia Kleinert, "The Critical Reaction to the Hermannsburg School," in *The Heritage of Namatjira: The Watercolourists of Central Australia*, ed. Jane Hardy, J.V.S. Megaw, and M. Ruth Megaw (Port Melbourne: William Heinemann Australia, 1992), 222, 227–30; Daniel Thomas, "Albert Namatjira and the Worlds of Art: A Re-Evaluation," in *Albert Namatjira: The Life and Work of an Australian Painter*, ed. Nadine Amadio, Anne Blackwell, Jonah Jones, and Daniel Thomas (South Melbourne: Macmillan, 1986), 24.

53 See, for example, Haebich, *Spinning the Dream*, 357; Kleinert, "Critical Reaction," 240, 243; Kleinert, "Namatjira, Albert"; and Thomas, "Albert Namatjira," 26.

54 Sue Abbey, "Noonuccal, Oodgeroo (1920–1993)," *Australian Dictionary of Biography*, National Centre of Biography, Australian National University, http://adb.anu.edu.au/biography/noonuccal-oodgeroo-18057/text29634, published online 2017 (accessed online 8 January 2018).

55 For example, "Her Poems to Be Published," *Courier-Mail* [Brisbane], 6 July 1963, 6.

56 T. Inglis Moore, "Aboriginal Poet: Technique Has Matured," *Canberra Times*, 17 December 1966, 13.

57 Bob Hodge, "Poetry and Politics in Oodgeroo: Transcending the Difference," *Australian Literary Studies* 16, no. 4 (1994): 67.

58 Penny Van Toorn, "Indigenous Texts and Narratives," in *The Cambridge Companion to Australian Literature*, ed. Elizabeth Webby (Cambridge, UK: Cambridge University Press, 2000), 30.

59 Ibid., 41.

60 Personal interview with Oodgeroo Noonuccal, conducted by Cliff Watego, Stradbroke Island, August 1982, quoted in Shoemaker, *Black Words White Page*, 188.

61 Alan T. Duncan, "Blair, Harold (1924–1976)," *Australian Dictionary of Biography*, National Centre of Biography, Australian National University, http://adb.anu.edu.au/biography/blair-harold-9520/text16761, published first in hardcopy 1993 (accessed online 12 January 2018); Ramsland and Mooney, *Remembering Aboriginal Heroes*, 62–65.

62 "Harold Blair: Cane-Cutter to Top Tenor," *Age* [Melbourne], 22 May 1976, 2, cutting held in National Library of Australia, Canberra, Biographical Cuttings on Harold Blair, Opera Singer, Containing One or More Cuttings from Newspapers or Journals.

63 "Aboriginal Mission Boy Won Fame as World Class Tenor," *Daily Mirror* [Sydney?], 11 August 1976, 70, cutting held in National Library of Australia, Canberra, Biographical Cuttings on Harold Blair, Opera Singer, Containing One or More Cuttings from Newspapers or Journals.

64 "A Rose from the Dust," *Daily Mirror* [Sydney?], 10 December 1984, 32, cutting held in National Library of Australia, Canberra, Biographical Cuttings on Lionel Rose, Boxing Champion, Containing One or More Cuttings from Newspapers or Journals.

65 "Two Years till Wimbledon?," *Dawn* 17, no. 3 (1968), 1. Similarly, Peter Kell has suggested that the media liked Goolagong and Rose for their "heartwarming" rags-to-riches stories. Peter Kell, *Good Sports: Australian Sport and the Myth of the Fair Go* (Annandale, NSW: Pluto Press, 2000), 44.

66 Peter Bodo, *The Courts of Babylon: Tales of Greed and Glory in a Harsh New World of Professional Tennis* (New York: Scribner, 1995), 110.

67 Evonne Goolagong Cawley and Phil Jarratt, *Home! The Evonne Goolagong Story* (East Roseville, NSW: Simon and Schuster, 1993), 115.

68 Ibid., 208–10.

69 On the possibility for a famous Indigenous individual to be "a celebrity spokesperson," and thereby a "powerful political device," see Turner et al., *Fame Games*, 167–68.

70 "Harold Blair—A Big Smile Helps Him in a White Man's World," *People*, 4 July 1951, 18–20, quoted in Ramsland and Mooney, *Remembering Aboriginal Heroes*, 92.

71 "Aboriginal Mission Boy."

72 Ramsland and Mooney, *Remembering Aboriginal Heroes*, 75; "Harold Blair to Study in United States," c. 1949, unidentified newspaper clipping, Harold Blair Papers, quoted in ibid., 78.

73 Harold Blair, "Does the White Man Expect Too Much of the Australian Aborigines," in *The Aboriginal Friends Association Annual Report*, 1956, 26–30, cited in ibid., 93–94.

74 Ibid., 225.

75 Ibid., 243.

76 Max Jones, "What Should Historians Do with Heroes? Reflections on Nineteenth- and Twentieth-Century Britain," *History Compass* 5, no. 2 (2007): 439–40.

CHAPTER 6

"Pretty Boy" Trudeau Versus the "Algonquin Agitator": Hitting the Ropes of Canadian Colonialist Masculinities

Kim Anderson and Brendan Hokowhitu

Celebrity, or "the state of being celebrated," typically involves success that is performed and measured through colonial hegemonic values; it involves role-playing within well-worn narratives of what it means to be successful in a largely capitalist, heteropatriarchal world. Given these criteria, what might celebrity look like for Indigenous men? And to what end do Indigenous men serve in the celebrity narratives of others? In this chapter, and as scholars of Indigenous masculinities in our respective contexts (Anderson in Canada and Hokowhitu in Aotearoa), we will address these questions through our reading of an event that occurred in March 2012: a celebrity boxing match between Justin Trudeau, then a Member of (the Canadian) Parliament, and Patrick Brazeau, a Canadian senator. The two would play out a narrative that seemed to be an incredulously crass version of the well-worn frontier/colonial narrative of gentleman versus savage but that nonetheless received largely positive feedback from the press, the Canadian political establishment, and the Canadian public.

On the face of it, our task in this chapter is simple: that is, to analyze a celebrity event staged by two Canadian men for political status, employing fairly rudimentary gentleman/savage tropes that go a long way toward explaining the dominant discourses surrounding the fight. There are multiple reasons why this fight became a celebrity event, but none is more important than the narrative of defence of unsettler[1] patriarchy embodied by Trudeau, who represented not only his celebrity father (former prime minister Pierre Elliott Trudeau) but also the white heteropatriarchal line passed on to him. Indeed, our prima facie concern in this chapter is to reveal the "viewing relations" of Indigenous celebrity.[2] In so doing, we hope to disrupt the unconsciousness of white heteropatriarchy that remains to structure celebrity events inductive of Indigenous peoples. Celebrity, in relation to Indigenous masculinity in particular, allows for a horizontal analysis related to the narrowness or broadness of representation—from the narrow simplistic tropes of sports mascots, for instance, to a broader analysis of mimicry.[3] Of particular interest is how the celebrated performance of masculinities in this fight informs a theoretical analysis of power.[4] We will begin by describing "the main event" and follow with a discussion.

The Main Event

Staging the Players

The fight begins with Justin Trudeau, son of one of Canada's most notable prime ministers, Pierre Elliott Trudeau. Trudeau-the-father held office from 1968 to 1979 and again from 1980 to 1984, a figure both loved and hated by the Canadian population. As much as Canadian prime ministers become "celebrities," he was noted for his bold "just watch me" attitude along with his intellect.[5] Among Indigenous peoples, Trudeau-the-father is also remembered as the prime minister who commissioned the 1969 White Paper, a policy proposal aimed at bringing about total and final assimilation of Indigenous peoples into whitestream Canada, under the guise of equality but at the cost of eliminating Indigenous rights. It was one more attempt to reckon with Canada's "Indian problem": that is, Indigenous peoples who held fast to their cultures and rights.

Trudeau-the-younger thus grew up in the spotlight as the son of one of Canada's most "famous" prime ministers, and, after a brief career as a teacher, he followed his father's footsteps into Canadian politics. In 2012, when this story takes place, Trudeau was serving as the Member of Parliament for the riding of Papineau in Montreal, but he was on the rise to become leader of the Liberal Party of Canada and later the second youngest prime minister in

Canadian history. After becoming prime minister in 2015, he received international adulation because of his youth and charismatic good looks as well as his gentlemanly comportment and self-declared feminist positioning. But the path to leadership for Justin Trudeau wasn't without challenges, and the one of interest to us concerns his masculinity.

During his campaign to become leader of the Liberal Party, the Conservative Party of Canada issued attack ads calling his masculinity into question. In one, Trudeau is surrounded by fairy dust, swirling stars, and text that reads "bungee jumping coach; [d]rama teacher for two years," and "when it comes to Canada's economy, Justin Trudeau just isn't ready." That slogan—he "just isn't ready"—became a primary tool that the Conservatives would employ. Because of the campaign to discredit him according to these gendered tropes of leadership, Trudeau needed an image makeover that would position him as a strong leader, ready to take charge. Someone on his team must have decided that using a farcical, blatant device such as a fight would help with this image. So they staged a celebrity boxing match, a "Fight for the Cure" (for cancer), that would take place in March 2012.

The team needed an adversary for the fight, and they found one in Patrick Brazeau, an Indigenous senator affiliated with the Conservative Party. In an interview with *Rolling Stone* magazine, Trudeau was quoted as saying that "I wanted someone who would be a good foil, and we stumbled upon the scrappy tough-guy senator from an Indigenous community. He fit the bill, and it was a very nice counterpoint." Trudeau later expressed regret about making this comment, stating that it was not in keeping with Liberal Party discourse of Indigenous-settler reconciliation.[6] Brazeau, however, did not hesitate to fulfill his role as the perfect villain for Trudeau. An Algonquin man from the community of Kitigan Zibi, Brazeau grew up not far from the nation's capital but under obviously different circumstances in terms of race and class privilege. As a lesser-known public figure, Brazeau had served in Indigenous politics as the president of the Congress of Aboriginal Peoples. Toward the end of his tenure, his leadership came under fire with allegations of creating a culture of sexual harassment and heavy drinking, but he moved from this position into the Senate, where, at the age of thirty-four, he was appointed to a lifetime seat by Conservative Prime Minister Stephen Harper.[7] Trudeau was well on his way to becoming the leader of the country, but Brazeau would soon find himself mired in further controversy after insulting Indigenous and settler women with misogynistic tweets and later facing charges of cocaine possession and sexual assault and a suspension for investigation of fraud in the "Senate scandal."[8] He was later acquitted of charges related to the Senate and pleaded guilty to charges of cocaine possession and simple assault.

The Thrill on the Hill

The promotional material and pre-fight discourse played up the differences between the two, mimicking the theatrics typical of entertainment fighting. Class differences were notable. Trudeau, we learned, had been keeping in shape over the years by training in boxing, something purportedly introduced to him by his father. Brazeau had a military background, was a kick boxer, and had a black belt in karate. As they posed side by side for photos at the weigh-in, Brazeau hunched over, aping a muscle pose, with only black bikini briefs, a watch, and a skullcap covering his bulky body. In contrast, Trudeau stood with his arms raised up in a bicep flexor, boxer/boarders covering from waist to knees of his more lanky frame.

Posters for the event promoted "The Thrill on the Hill" between "Justin 'Pretty Boy' Trudeau" and "Patrick 'Ponytail' Brazeau." The question of masculinity was central since there were references to Trudeau as the "shiny pony" by Conservative commentator Ezra Levant and online comments calling his masculinity into question: "Brazeau should knock him out if it is a real fight and send 'Justine' back to the comforting arms of his wife who can twirl her fingers through his metrosexual locks."[9] Brazeau, nicknamed the "Senator Soldier," indulged in pre-fight banter that included "dick jokes": "I've got a lot of length over here," he said to Trudeau at the weigh-in while pulling out the waistband of his bikini briefs and looking down.[10]

The media played with the "savagery" of Brazeau, at best making him out to be a Harlequin book cover brave—"his hair is unponytailed, long and flowing, full of power and eroticism"—but more often playing into one of the prime tropes of Indigenous men: the bloodthirsty warrior.[11] Trudeau joined in creating the savagery of Brazeau. In response to pre-fight social media banter between the two, Trudeau tweeted "are you ok, Pat? That's even more unintelligible than usual. Stick to your usual grunting and snarling."[12] As for the fight itself—it was anticlimactic, lasting only a few minutes. Trudeau won. The press delighted in photos of Trudeau taking a victory kiss from his wife, clad in a tight black dress fitting for a ringside groupie.

After All

The consequence of losing was to don a hockey jersey in the colour of the winner's political party and wear it in the halls of the Parliament buildings. Brazeau thus appeared in the press the next day wearing a red jersey with "Trudeau" and the number "1" on his back. The loser also had to suffer the humiliation of the winner cutting his hair in public, again in the Parliament buildings. Trudeau reportedly said that he chose the stakes because First Nations warriors historically cut their hair as a sign of shame.[13] Hair cutting is a marker of grief among many North American Indigenous cultures, but this was never raised. More importantly, what was invisible in the public discourse should be familiar to all Canadians in the wake of the Truth and Reconciliation Commission of Canada: the involuntary cutting of Indigenous hair is a marker of colonial violence since it was the first in a series of violations committed against Indigenous children as they entered residential schools. Hair cutting was thus part of a systemic strategy of assimilation and subjugation of Indigenous peoples; in the now infamous words of Duncan Campbell Scott, it was part of "taking the Indian out of the man," a victory over savagery.

In the days that followed the fight, there was a lot of banter about how "classy" Trudeau was, countered by calling attention to the brutish behaviour of Brazeau. In honour of the victorious Trudeau, one of the Liberal Members of Parliament recited a poem in the House of Commons in the style of Robert Service—a late-nineteenth-century and early-twentieth-century Canadian poet—much celebrated for his ballads on the frontier hero. Whether deliberate or not, the boxing match thus helped to bolster Trudeau's masculinity, a necessary ingredient in his being perceived as "prime ministerial."

Discussion

The folk monster of the earlier period was replaced by a new category, the Savage Man. This figure was usually pictured as naked, very hairy though without facial or feet fur, apelike but not ape, carrying a large club or tree trunk. . . . The generic image of the savage represented violence, sexual license, a lack of civility and civilization, in a word, morality—that confronts each human being.[14]

One of the first points to be made in relation to masculinity and celebrity is that Trudeau entered a long list of unsettler men who have tried to overcome Indigeneity through demonstrations of physical dominance. Ironically, though, it was his alternative form of masculinity (i.e., his femininity) that was attacked directly in relation to his capacity to lead the nation, and he tried to prove himself by participating in this celebrity fight. In turn, this points to the constructedness of masculinity, a useful analytic here. First, as this particular case highlights, battles for political kudos can often boil down to gender politics, which can be as base as the dick-size banter prevalent in the lead-up to the fight and as complex as linking morality and immorality to gender and sexuality, as also seen in this celebrity fight.[15] Second, the uncomplicated nature of the celebrity boxing match at face value serves to highlight that gender, though seldom discussed, is always a part of celebrity construction, particularly in relation to masculinity because the everyday activities that men choose often serve to reassert the masculine dividend: "Gender domination often sustains itself in very mundane and practical ways. . . . In competitive male team sport, for example, the ritualized outpourings of aggression shown through the clenching of fists, the self-magnifying chant, and the invitation into others' personal space in the celebration that often accompanies victorious moments are typical acts of practical and symbolic masculine domination."[16] Hence, this celebrity boxing event between two high-profile Canadian men cannot be read outside the context of colonization, which in turn demands a genealogical analysis of masculinity and sport.

There is not the space here to elaborate fully Michel Foucault's expansive genealogical method,[17] yet there are several points salient to this discussion. Typically, in the colonial context, power is seen as something performed *on* the Indigenous subject. Yet, as Brazeau's presence implies, Indigenous peoples are not without agency even when that agency is repulsive to other Indigenous peoples. In relation to a key underpinning of Foucault's work, then, we ask how do Indigenous cultural truths enact a variety of operations on Indigenous bodies, thoughts, and actions to enable self-understanding as Indigenous subjects, including Indigenous celebrities often chosen by unsettler peoples to represent Indigenous peoples (i.e., Brazeau was hand-picked to be a senator by former Conservative Prime Minister Stephen Harper)?[18] Which Indigenous subjectivities came to fill the postcolonial field? In particular, how did Indigenous masculinities manifest themselves to be nameable and desirable?

In the first volume of *The History of Sexuality*, Foucault argues that the biopolitical regulation of a population operates beyond the conscious production and control of knowledge.[19] That is, crucial to biopolitical control is internalization: the self-imposition of regulatory mechanisms so that the material, the corporeal, and the ethos function in unison, albeit a unison achieved via heterogeneous statements. In the context of this chapter, then, it could be argued that the conditioning of Indigenous masculinities throughout colonization has not only a symbolic genealogy but also a material existence. Here the etiological importance of the word *genealogy* should not be underestimated, for it does not merely mean a textual genealogy. Foucault's nomenclature literally refers to the material and biological descent of corporeality, in which the body is "totally imprinted by history."[20] A genealogical analysis would suggest, then, that what is witnessed today in celebrity boxing matches between men, for example, is overlaid with historical meaning that unconsciously reifies white heteropatriarchy. Moreover, central to a celebrity boxing match in particular are the body and its constitution by dominant historical discourses. Through a Foucauldian lens, then, masculinity is not an ethereal concept; rather, in this case, Indigenous and non-Indigenous bodies are the materialization of discourse. The genealogist thus asks, why do masculinities exist in their present forms?

Again, there is simply not enough space to provide a full analysis of the genealogical production of Indigenous masculinities.[21] Yet this particular celebrity event occurred in the realm of sport, which (as has been demonstrated) has been a significant, if underanalyzed, cog in various colonial machines, particularly in relation to masculinities.[22] Sport has often been understood within dominant discourses as closely linked to masculine morality partly because various sports in the British colonial context at least (in particular rugby, cricket, and boxing) were seen as training grounds for male leaders who would be loyal team players: "Physical training was patriotic and chauvinistic: it prepared men's bodies for war. . . . The male body required physical discipline not solely for the sake of a state threatened with military and economic collapse: it also required discipline in the pursuit of social harmony."[23] Also, most sports were originally conceived of as "manly" ventures and, consequently, beyond the influence of feminine qualities commonly aligned with weakness and emotional immorality. As John Beynon discusses, "in the latter half of the [nineteenth] century sport became the main nurturing ground for what were regarded as 'typical' British values of never-say-die competition and fair play.... Masculinity was both attained and displayed through athleticism, strength, speed, fitness and muscularity. Men dominated nineteenth century sport and women participants were ridiculed, being regarded as too weak to play games, whereas for men it was 'natural.'"[24] Moreover, physical training and exercise have a long association with politics and nationalism: "The Fabian Society, founded in 1884, joined in the call for an able-bodied citizenry as the best antidote to the moral and physical virus held to be devouring Britain's martial and economic sinews. The health of the nation was equated with the state of the male body, in particular an athletic soldier-citizenry. More than ever the bodies and minds of both workers and soldiers were, it was felt, in urgent need of control and rationalization if the cycle of threatened instability at home and regular humiliation abroad was to be averted."[25] Hegemonic British culture, in particular, was in a constant apprehensive state regarding the contamination of the masculine by the feminine, leading to the production of private boys' schools and the explicit inculcation of stoicism through sports such as cricket and rugby.

In relation to the celebrity boxing match, Trudeau literally fought to demonstrate that, though he might be a feminist, he also had the classically masculine traits of fortitude, stamina, and guile typically associated with pugilism. The end game for Trudeau was not to beat Brazeau but to demonstrate his white heteromasculinity to be as virulent as his father's and to show corporeal control: "A large part of the success of physical culture was its assertion of the male body as heroic rather than erotic, in the body's depiction as 'under control' rather than 'out of control.'"[26] Pugilism, though possibly largely misunderstood, if anything is about controlling desire, so for Trudeau to produce such a stoic, self-restrained, and measured fight plan spoke to his will to align himself with a constructed heroic morality that lies at the core of white heteropatriarchy: the rational achievement of mind over body. In contrast, Brazeau was lambasted for his poor discipline while heavily underscoring his own narrative via exotic and highly sexualized motifs.

Fighting has its own specific genealogy—at least partly linked to land ownership—that, in the context of unsettler colonialism, speaks volumes to the import of this celebrity event. "Gentry masculinity," as analyzed by Raewyn Connell, was a class of hereditary landowners "who dominated the North Atlantic world of the eighteenth century" based on land ownership and an emerging capitalism: "The gentry provided army and navy officers, and often recruited the rank and file themselves. At the intersection between this direct involvement in violence and the ethic of family honour was the institution of the duel. Willingness to face an opponent in a potential lethal one-to-one combat was a key test of gentry masculinity, and it was affronts to honour that provoked such confrontations."[27] Reading this celebrity bout in light of Connell's historical analysis of gentry masculinity elucidates what was at stake for Trudeau at least: gentlemanly reputation and the defence of his father's White Paper. The mere presence of Brazeau was the affront.

The celebrity boxing match, pitting the Indigenous man against the unsettler man, far from being an event signifying Indigenous resistance, was an event of complicity. As Beynon points out, since "fighting has long been a culturally sanctioned and distinctively male way of conflict resolution, in this respect, violent men can be viewed as over-conformists,"[28] yet Brazeau's conformity also served to disrupt colonial discourse. This brief genealogical contextualization of this celebrity pugilist bout reveals the stakes of the fight: the upholding of a particular form of morality underpinned by manly virtues, repressive of feminine qualities, tied to the ongoing suppression through violence of Indigenous land rights, and generally the apprehension that unsettler cultures have regarding Indigenous masculinity.

The second point to be made about masculinity in relation to celebrity events is that, when celebrity masculinity is put through its paces, the unconscious framework is inevitably related to morality, indeed more than anything else revealing its fragility as per the so-called masculinity in crisis, first noted in the groundbreaking work of Connell. Masculinity in crisis has been central to discourses over the past forty years that have bolstered, for instance, the anti-feminist "men's movement" prominent in both the United States and Canada. Connell found that men's groups in the 1980s sought to "overcome their resistances to encountering 'the hairy man,' the deep masculine. Once the deep masculine was found, they helped initiate each other into it. The main direction taken by masculinity therapy in the 1980s was this attempt to restore a masculinity thought to have been lost or damaged in recent social change" (where "damaged in recent social change" can be read as the establishment of feminism and women's rights).[29] Anthony Clare also refers to this phenomenon, suggesting the growing perception of a crisis of masculinity because of the breaking down of men's traditional roles: that is, the postmodern fracturing of traditional performances of men in work, education, family, sexuality, and health.[30] In reality, this phenomenon should be renamed as "patriarchy in crisis" and further refined as "white heteropatriarchy in crisis."

It is our contention that the tag masculinity in crisis was best represented in this celebrity bout by Brazeau. That is, typically (and unsurprisingly), analyses of this crisis have focused on the debilitation of North American and British white, middle- to upper-class, and straight masculinities even though the fracturing of traditional masculine roles has probably been most keenly felt by those men most disenfranchised in the working class and by colonization.[31] Moreover, since colonization, Indigenous masculinity can be said to have been in a constant state of crisis and fragility. Here fragility refers not only to the precarious nature of being Indigenous but also to the notion that hypermasculine behaviours, far from signalling power, actually gesture toward a deep self-loathing manifested in behaviours that underscore brute physical prowess. The dominant discourse, at least, certainly reinforces the fragility of Indigenous masculinity as produced via the prevalence of violence, drug and alcohol abuse, heightened sexuality and physical and sexual abuse, and spousal abuse. Connell explains that this "protest masculinity" arises from an experience of powerlessness and leads to an exaggerated claim to the gendered position of masculine power.[32] In many ways, Brazeau was the poster child for such an analysis, his well-documented misogyny serving simultaneously to reinforce the "savage" trope and, in this particular celebrity event, to give allegorical credence to Trudeau's claims to gentry masculinity. The predictable outcome of the fight, then, reinforced what dominant colonial discourses are founded on—the immorality of the Native man and the morality of the Western man.

Indeed, Brazeau was merely an allegorical figure in this celebrity event; the headline act was Trudeau's masculinity in crisis and its linkage to morality. At the time and after, the Conservative Party's clearly articulated anti-feminine message was central to the campaign to smear Trudeau by associating him with typically "artsy" and/or feminine qualities such as "drama teacher." The campaign resonated with the Victorian-era public school system set up to inculcate boys into masculinity via numerous rights of passage, including "intimidation and violence [and] mental and physical toughness."[33] The questioning of Trudeau's readiness to lead the nation because of a lack of specific masculine traits resembled the qualities that the Victorian system attempted to promote in boys: that is, "self-reliance, independence, emotional control and the deep suspicion of intimacy."[34] The use of "fairy dust" in the imagery was also suggestive of an anti-gay undertone that, through the lens of the Conservative Party spin doctors at least, reflected a masculinity not trusted to lead a modern economy.

The highlighting of Trudeau's femininity and "gay tendencies" recalls the work of David Buchbinder, who employed psychoanalytic theory to proffer the idea that successful performances of masculinity have been as much about disavowing one's feminine and/or gay attributes as about manly displays.[35] That is, dominant white heteropatriarchal masculinity attempts to hold on to its framing of morality by attacking other forms of masculinity as inauthentic and untrustworthy. Ironically, the Conservative Party's campaign mirrored colonial discourses underpinned by morality judgments on Indigenous gender roles. Gail Bederman outlines how, in the late nineteenth century, clear gender roles were an essential component of civilization; advanced civilizations were identifiable by the degree of sexual differentiation.[36] Civilized white women were womanly—delicate, spiritual, dedicated to home. And civilized white men were the most manly ever evolved—firm of character, self-controlled, protectors of women and children. In contrast, gender differences among "savages" seemed to be blurred. Indigenous women were aggressive, carried heavy burdens, and did all sorts of masculine hard labour. Indigenous men were emotional and lacked a white man's ability to restrain their passions. Indigenous men were creatures of whim who, like women, even wore dresses and jewellery.[37]

The signification of savagery with androgyny in historical colonial discourses read in relation to both Brazeau's and Trudeau's celebrity makes visible the violence of colonization and the morphing of morality in relation to gender—Trudeau the androgynous SNAG (sensitive new age guy), Brazeau the hypermasculine Native buffoon. Commentary on the fight and particularly the rhetoric produced by Trudeau's political opposition make clear the Conservative Party's investment in white heteropatriarchy via anti-feminine rhetoric. As Connell points out, "hegemonic masculinity establishes its hegemony partly by its claim to embody the power of reason, and thus represent the interests of the whole society."[38] This is the critical point: the hidden agenda of the Conservative Party's attack on Trudeau's masculinity was grounded in the white masculine possessive of reason and morality and thus the right to rule. At face value, the Conservative tagline in relation to Trudeau, he "just isn't ready," was imbecilic because it affirmed that at some stage he would be ready. Of course, the slogan was really saying that the nation was not ready for that type of masculinity to lead it, and, as the election result in 2015 would show, the slogan got it horribly wrong.

This question could rightfully be asked: "What if Brazeau had won, wouldn't that have reaffirmed Indigenous rights?" Our answer would be "no." All celebrity events involving Indigenous peoples must always be read via a colonial genealogical method (i.e., the production of Indigenous bodies through discourse), so in this case winning or losing the fight was unimportant. Many representations of Indigenous peoples are inherently violent because they are produced by a system underpinned by an apparatus designed to subjugate Indianness regardless of the outcome. Brazeau's loss, in simple terms, represented another victory for colonial white masculinity over the less evolved and self-restrained "savage." If Brazeau had won, however, then the sight of a frenzied Indian pummelling a skinny white guy would have played into the trope of the "ignoble savage," reaffirming the colonial state's right to control the violence of the "savage." This celebrity boxing match reminds us that the creation of the discourse of the "Indian problem" was never about resolving the issue; it was always about Indian presence being "the problem." At least Brazeau's presence in the ring, though highly problematic, disrupted the logic of elimination.

Conclusion

The Trudeau-Brazeau fight demonstrates how the study of Indigenous masculinities can aid in the theoretical analysis of power. As has been said elsewhere, "Indigenous masculinities and their associated cultural performances in particular can and should be treated as a largely untapped rubric for examining the propagation of power in the colonial context. Accordingly, Indigenous masculinity, in serving two essentialised binary masters (i.e., colonised/coloniser and men/women), creates a model for looking at power within the colonial context where the two essentialised notions associated with the dominance of [the] colonised man over the Indigenous man, and man over woman, create the ambivalent figure of the Indigenous heterosexual patriarch. Both oppressor and oppressed."[39] The analysis of colonized masculinities thus allows for a widening of the space beyond simplistic analyses of tropes. It allows for the dialectic between heteropatriarchal masculinity and feminism, for instance, to be complicated since Indigenous men are suppressed by white privilege yet enjoy the privilege of being men or what Connell would refer to as the "masculine dividend." That notion is limited when we consider a triangulation among hegemonic masculinities, femininities, and colonized masculinities, however, because reliance on the binary of men's power over women accounts for the privilege that Indigenous men accept simply for being men but does not account for the loss and violence (epistemological, material, and corporeal) that Indigenous men experience when they are either complicit with or resistant to dominant discourses.

The latter point here is important because tropes of Indigenous men tend toward worship (e.g., "noble savage") or demonization (e.g., "savage"), enabling what Homi Bhabha refers to as "ambivalence" within colonial discourses.[40] This ambivalence stems from the production of hybrid Indigenous identities that fuse Indigenous and unsettler cultures. As Bhabha outlines further, authoritative tropes of colonial discourse only come to be following the "traumatic scenario of colonial difference, cultural or racial, return[ing] the eye of power to some prior archaic image or identity. Paradoxically, however, such an image can neither be 'original'—by virtue of the act of repetition that constructs it—nor identical—by virtue of the difference that defines it."[41] Although possibly an extreme example because Brazeau was hardly the ambivalent figure whom Bhabha would describe, in that he was both loathsome and pitiful, his mimicry of unsettler masculinity in this public ring nonetheless served to disrupt colonial discourse. That is, his presence as a Canadian senator served to disrupt the narrow colonial discourse within which Indigenous men are usually celebrated while highlighting the ongoing neocolonial violence that Indigenous peoples continue to suffer. This intensifies both the glare on the wrongs of white patriarchy and the harm caused to Indigenous men and women by patriarchy and colonization: "In 'normalizing' the colonial state or subject, the dream of post-Enlightenment civility alienates its own language of liberty and produces another knowledge of its norms."[42] Brazeau, then, in many ways, was an ideal Indigenous celebrity because the fact that he was a Canadian senator was symbolic of the liberty supposedly inherent to the Canadian state, yet his lack of civility heightened the awareness of the normative violence of colonialism.

Similarly, Trudeau was Brazeau's ideal sparring partner because Brazeau's mere presence spoke to the legacy of Trudeau's father's infamous (for Indigenous communities at least) White Paper. In terms of biopower, Brazeau became the celebrity embodiment of the "Indian problem," which has been Canada's subject of erasure since colonization began and for which Trudeau Senior provided the theoretical blueprint forty-three years earlier. Brazeau's mere presence highlighted the violence of the White Paper's assimilatory and normative intent. To paraphrase Bhabha, articulated in this celebrity boxing match was the postcolonial state of Indigenous men and the idealism and ultimate violence of the White Paper as embodied by Trudeau Junior.[43] The imagery within this celebrity fight was palpable, the white empty canvas prior to the fight symbolic of the freedom and meritocracy espoused by Canada in general, and in particular by Pierre Trudeau via the White Paper, which attempted to blank out the rights of Indigenous peoples. Undoubtedly, this white canvas and that White Paper symbolized elimination.

Finally, reflecting on this farcical spectacle in 2021 offers one more lens through which to view the ubiquitous narratives that underpin the hetero-patriarchal, capitalist nature of the colonial state. Now that it's 2021, we find ourselves in recovery from the ultimate farce, the Trump presidency. The path to that presidency involved a celebrity fight too, Trump's 2007 "Battle of the Billionaires," in which a Black fighter (Trump's surrogate) took on a Samoan fighter (World Wrestling Federation Chairman Vince McMahon's surrogate). The narrative involved a beaten Indigenous contestant (Umaga), a head shaving for the loser, a white working-class hero (referee Steve Austin), and a victorious billionaire (Trump). Theatre and performance studies scholar Sharon Mazer cites masculinities scholar Michael Kimmel to show how such a spectacle, the fight, and now Trump's presidency have allowed "angry white men to focus their rage downwards—towards persons of colour, women, sexual minorities, and immigrants—rather than upwards at the more privileged white men who both exploit and condescend to them."[44] Although the Canadian context is different, the similarities demonstrate how we must pay attention to such theatrics, to what celebrity has to offer to Indigenous men, and to what this study of masculinities teaches us about power in our contemporary world.

NOTES

1 We employ "unsettler" as opposed to the more common parlance "settler" because we write from an Indigenous perspective. That is, from an Indigenous perspective, there was nothing "settling" about colonization. Colonization was an invasion into Indigenous lands and lives and thus was wholly an unsettling experience. We use the nomenclature not as a metre quip, but to highlight that "settler colonialism" was a violent disruptive experience for Indigenous peoples.

2 Laura Mulvey, "Visual Pleasure and Narrative Cinema," *Screen* 16, no. 3 (1975): 6.

3 Homi Bhabha, "Of Mimicry and Man: The Ambivalence of Colonial Discourse," *October* 28 (1984): 125–33.

4 We wrote this chapter prior to the media attention on Justin Trudeau's blackface and brownface incidents in the 1990s and early 2000s. Although relevant here, there is not enough space to address adequately the racialized politics involved. To read about these incidents, see Anna Purna Kambhampaty, Madeleine Carlisle, and Melissa Chan, "Justin Trudeau Wore Brownface at 2001 'Arabian Nights' Party While He Taught at a Private School," *Time*, 18 September 2019, https://time.com/5680759/justin-trudeau-brownface-photo/ (accessed 13 September 2020).

5 "Just watch me" was the response that Pierre Trudeau gave to a reporter when questioned about how far he would go to suspend civil liberties during the October Crisis in Quebec in the 1970s. It defined an iconic style of bold leadership for which Trudeau was known.

6 Katie Simpson, "Trudeau 'Regrets' Comments in *Rolling Stone* about Senator Patrick Brazeau," CBC News, 1 August 2017, https://www.cbc.ca/news/politics/trudeau-regrets-rolling-stone-comments-brazeau-1.4230498 (accessed 13 September 2020).

7 Mark Bourrie, "From the Archives: The Rise and Fall of Patrick Brazeau," *Ottawa Magazine*, 29 October 2015, https://ottawamagazine.com/people-and-places/from-the-archives-the-rise-fall-of-patrick-brazeau (accessed 13 September 2020).

8 Huffington Post Canada, "Patrick Brazeau Suggests Theresa Spence Gained Weight during Protest," *Huffington Post Canada*, 31 January 2013, https://www.huffingtonpost.ca/2013/01/31/patrick-brazeau-theresa-spence_n_2589799.html (accessed 13 September 2020); National Post, "Tory Senator Apologizes for Calling Reporter a Bitch after Report on Poor Attendance Record," *National Post*, 27 June 2013, https://nationalpost.com/news/canada/patrick-brazeau-jennifer-ditchburn (accessed 13 September 2020); Ottawa Citizen, "Patrick Brazeau's Two-Year Downward Spiral," *Ottawa Citizen*, 20 May 2014, https://ottawacitizen.com/news/local-news/brazeaus-two-year-downward-spiral (accessed 13 September 2020).

9 Tristan Hopper, "Rivals Justin Trudeau and Senator Patrick Brazeau Facing Off in Charity Boxing Bout," *National Post*, 18 January 2012, https://nationalpost.com/news/canada/rivals-justin-trudeau-and-senator-patrick-brazeau-facing-off-in-charity-boxing-bout (accessed 13 September 2020).

10 Michel Bolen, "Justin Trudeau Boxing Match Tonight After Liberal MP Hit with Loss of Grandmother Kathleen Sinclair," *The Huffington Post*, 31 March 2012, https://www.huffingtonpost.ca/2012/03/31/justin-trudeau-boxing-grandmother-dies-kathleen-sinclcair_n_1393680.html (accessed 13 September 2020).

11 Steve Murray, "No One Said There Would Be Blood: Steve Murray at the Justin Trudeau Boxing Match," *National Post*, 2 April 2012, https://nationalpost.com/news/canada/no-one-said-there-would-be-blood-steve-murray-at-the-justin-trudeau-boxing-match (accessed 13 September 2020).

12 Steve Rennie, "Justin Trudeau Beats Tory Sen. Patrick Brazeau in Charity Boxing Match," *The Canadian Press, Associated Press, Yahoo News*, 1 April 2012, https://www.yahoo.com/news/justin-trudeau-beats-tory-sen-patrick-brazeau-charity-032151014.html (accessed 13 September 2020).

13 Michael Bolen, "Justin Trudeau Defeats Patrick Brazeau in Charity Boxing Fight," *Huffington Post*, 31 March 2012, https://www.huffingtonpost.ca/2012/03/31/trudeau-brazeau-boxing-justin-patrick_n_1394122.html (accessed 13 September 2020).

14 David Theo Goldberg, *Racist Culture: Philosophy and the Politics of Meaning* (Oxford: Blackwell, 1993), 23–24.

15 David Buchbinder, *Performance Anxieties: Re-Producing Masculinity* (St Leonards, Australia: Allen and Unwin, 1998).

16 David Brown, "Pierre Bourdieu's 'Masculine Domination' Thesis and the Gendered Body in Sport and Physical Culture," *Sociology of Sport Journal* 23, no. 2 (2006): 166.

17 Michel Foucault, *Power/Knowledge: Selected Interviews and Other Writings, 1972–1977*, ed. Colin Gordon (Brighton, UK: Harvester Press, 1980).

18 CBC News, "Patrick Brazeau: Harper's Strategic Aboriginal Appointment," CBC News, 13 February, 2013, https://www.cbc.ca/news/canada/patrick-brazeau-harper-s-strategic-aboriginal-appointment-1.1411015 (accessed 13 September 2020).

19 Michel Foucault, *The History of Sexuality: Volume 1, An Introduction*, trans. Robert Hurley (New York: Pantheon, 1978).

20 Michel Foucault, "Nietzsche, Genealogy, History" in *The Foucault Reader*, ed. Paul Rabinow (New York: Pantheon Books, 1984), 83.

21 For further reading, see Robert Alexander Innes and Kim Anderson, eds., *Indigenous Men and Masculinities: Legacies, Identities, Regeneration* (Winnipeg: University of Manitoba Press, 2015).

22 For further reading, see Brendan Hokowhitu, "Tackling Maori Masculinity: A Colonial Genealogy of Savagery and Sport," *Contemporary Pacific* 16, no. 2 (2004): 259–84; and Brendan Hokowhitu, "Foucault, Genealogy, Sport and Indigeneity," in *Examining Sport Histories: Power, Paradigms, and Reflexivity*, ed. Richard Pringle and Murray Phillips (Morgantown, WV: FiT Publishing, 2013), 225–48.

23 Joanna Bourke, *Dismembering the Male: Men's Bodies, Britain and the Great War* (London: Reaktion, 1996), 176, 179.

24 John Beynon, *Masculinities and Culture* (London: Open University Press, 2002), 42.

25 Ibid., 40.

26 Michael Budd, *The Sculpture Machine: Physical Culture and Body Politics in the Age of Empire* (London: Palgrave Macmillan, 1997), 77.

27 Raewyn Connell, *Masculinities*, 2nd ed. (Berkeley: University of California Press, 2005), 190.

28 Beynon, *Masculinities and Culture*, 82.

29 Connell, *Masculinities*, 207.

30 Anthony Clare, *On Men: Masculinity in Crisis* (London: Chatto and Windus, 2000).

31 Tim Edwards, *Cultures of Masculinity* (New York: Routledge, 2006).

32 Connell, *Masculinities*, 113.

33 Beynon, *Masculinities and Culture*, 41.

34 Clare, *On Men*, 88.

35 Buchbinder, *Performance Anxieties*.

36 Gail Bederman, *Manliness and Civilization: A Cultural History of Gender and Race in the United States, 1880–1917* (Chicago: University of Chicago Press, 1995).

37 Ibid., 25.

38 Connell, *Masculinities*, 164.

39 Brendan Hokowhitu, "Taxonomies of Indigeneity: Indigenous Heterosexual Patriarchal Masculinity," in *Indigenous Men and Masculinities: Identities, Legacies, Regeneration*, ed. Robert Alexander Innes and Kim Anderson (Winnipeg: University of Manitoba Press, 2015), 83.

40 Homi Bhabha, *The Location of Culture* (London: Routledge, 1994).

41 Ibid., 107.

42 Bhabha, "Of Mimicry and Man," 126.

43 Ibid., 127.

44 Sharon Mazer, "Donald Trump Shoots the Match," *TDR: The Drama Review* 62, no. 2 (2018): 185.

CHAPTER 7

Famous "Last" Speakers: Celebrity and Erasure in Media Coverage of Indigenous Language Endangerment

Jenny L. Davis

Famous "Last" Indians

In this chapter, I focus on Indigenous celebrity, or famous Indians, as a form of celebrity that entails the recognition or celebration of Indigenous individuals by settler colonial audiences. Such celebrity gains its popularity and circulation within these audiences because it perpetuates long-standing myths of the inevitable disappearance of Indigenous peoples. Specifically, I explore the role of Indigenous languages in the celebrity of "last" Indians and the increasing circulation of "last" speakers as a subgenre of that category. "Last" Indian celebrity is a robust genre of famous Indians, one that has existed, as historian and Native studies scholar Jean O'Brien has demonstrated,[1] almost as long as European presence in North America. "Last" speakers also fit a long-existing trend in which Indigenous celebrity has been tied to linguistic knowledge and ability. Tisquantum (Patuxet) and Sacagawea (Shoshone), for example, are two of the most celebrated Native Americans in United States popular culture for their role as translators for the pilgrims and the Lewis and Clark Expedition respectively. In fact, in her book on the rhetorical practices of "firsting" and "lasting," O'Brien notes that Tisquantum (also known as Squanto) was perhaps the first famous "last" Indian (but not actually the last). Her excavation of seventeenth-century colonial texts and histories yields numerous examples of Indians made famous in New England in the 1800s for being the "last," but famous "last" Indians were not limited to New England or the seventeenth century. Although the earliest examples discussed circulated via newspapers, books, and even monuments, the latter examples are found most frequently in digital media and social media platforms such as Twitter, Reddit, and Facebook. I focus here on media discussions of "last Indians/speakers" because, as Nancy Rivenburgh notes in her own examination of how English-language media frame the causes and implications of language endangerment, "for better or worse, people rely heavily on media to understand how these global phenomena touch their lives."[2]

I will examine here the increasing circulation of "last" speakers of Indigenous and endangered languages as celebrities in media in which the reporting represents a centuries-old practice of creating famous Indians as a means of counting down to the inevitable end of Indigenous peoples, assuming an unavoidable loss of culture, space, and eventually existence. I will show how these "last" speakers join Martha Simon (Narragansett) of seventeenth-century New England and the man known as Ishi (Yahi) of twentieth-century California as "last" Indian celebrities. Although the individuals named and circulated as "last speakers" represent a particular type of speaker within much larger communities, they are represented as "the last of [their] kind." Such rhetoric directly mirrors not only seventeenth-century descriptions of the "last" of the tribes in New England but also popular accounts such as *The Last of the Mohicans* and *The Last of the Dogmen*, in which specific individuals (historical or fictional) were held up as the "last" of their communities, thereby marking the extinction, or vanishing, of specific groups of Indians and all Native Americans more generally.[3] This superlative enumeration makes spectacularly famous (and famous spectacles of) those individuals, like the man named Ishi, deemed to be the "last." This process is replicated in discussions about "last speakers" and the overemphasis on declining speaker populations[4] rather than new speakers and positive impacts of language reclamation. By examining these widely circulating rhetorics, within studies of broader colonial framings of Indigenous peoples within Native American and Indigenous studies, I will demonstrate how such circulation of "last" speaker celebrities both draws on existing trends within settler societies and continues to influence them.

"Last Indians"

O'Brien demonstrated that seventeenth-century New England claims to modernity were upheld through a contrast to the "myth of Indian extinction," whereby Indians were "deemed inauthentic if they did not comply with the expectation that they be persistently ancient, [and] the collective project of local narrations cast Indian peoples as teetering on the brink of extinction if they did not relegate them explicitly to the past by declaring them extinct."[5] The role of expectation in this process is significant, particularly to the role of Indigenous celebrity in this process. Philip Deloria argues that the depiction of Native Americans as already always something of the past occurs via the co-constructive nature of expectation and anomaly: "To assert that a person or event is anomalous cannot help but serve to create and to reinforce other expectations."[6] In the case of "last" Indians, celebrities are thus held up as anomalies through the discursive process of *lasting*, in which Indigenous populations are framed as "vanishing" first by defining Indians based on a singular characteristic—full-blood quantum in the case of seventeenth-century New England. Lasting, then, is a process of what Judith Irvine and Susan Gal call iconization (rhematization) and erasure.[7] Specific individuals or characteristics are made iconically representative of larger wholes—groups, languages, or cultures. Erasure happens in two concomitant processes: other characteristics or people that could be representative of the larger whole are erased, and then the larger whole is erased through the countdown, or "lasting," of those iconic few. In other words, though they circulate as individuals, "last" Indians are seen to be stand-ins for their whole tribal community, nation, and Indigenous people more generally. They are anomalous for still existing in the present instead of only in the past, and by embodying this anomalous present existence they maintain the expectation that all Indians are in the past.

Indigenous celebrity in this context was predicated on its bolstering of settler nostalgia for an imagined Indianness assumed to be already or almost already extinct. Although these discourses depended predominantly on the concept of blood as a location of race, or Indigeneity, and therefore identified "last Indians" based on assumptions of racial mixing, blood was not the only factor. Critically, blood was assumed to be a correlate to culture. O'Brien summarizes the characteristics assumed to diminish in proportion to lessening Indian blood:

> possession of unbroken homelands,
> defense of those homelands through diplomacy and warfare,
> *speaking their language*,
> living in wigwams,
> engaging in hunting and fishing (and sometimes agriculture),
> displaying mastery of Native pharmacology and
> producing Native material culture through craft work such as
> basket weaving.[8]

Here blood is at the forefront, but it entails cultural knowledge of traditional dwellings (wigwams), practices (pharmacology and material culture), and, critically, language(s). O'Brien notes that in mid-seventeenth-century New England Martha Simon (Narragansett) was famous as the "last full-blooded Indian," so much so that she was visited by Henry David Thoreau in 1856. He wrote in his journals after his visit with Martha that, "to judge from her physiognomy, she might have been King Philip's own daughter. *Yet she could not speak Indian*, and knew nothing of her race."[9] In this description, we see that Thoreau's expectation of Martha as a "last" Indian was met by her appearance but not by his evaluation that she could not "speak Indian." Thus, speaking an Indigenous language, being full blooded, and looking Indian were all assumed to be co-occurring qualities of "last" Indians even as early as the 1800s.

The circulation of famous "last" Indians in seventeenth-century New England continued and later could be found throughout the United States. The twentieth century provided one particularly famous "last Indian" celebrity, commonly referred to as Ishi.[10] In 1911, a Yahi man in his fifties was discovered in northern California and arrested for being Indigenous in the twentieth century. Anthropologists Alfred Kroeber and Thomas Waterman from the nearby University of California, Berkeley, were called in to evaluate him and determined that he was, in fact, a living member of a tribe that they had assumed to be gone. They took custody of him, gave him the name Ishi (meaning "man" in the Yana language), and brought him to the university museum and campus area, where he lived until his death in 1916.[11] During that five-year period, the man known as Ishi was the subject of numerous newspaper articles and exhibits, and he has since been the subject of several books and documentaries.

His "celebrity" has much in common with the "last Indians" described by O'Brien's work on seventeenth-century New England and the contemporary celebrity culture of the "last speakers" of Indigenous languages. News coverage at the time frequently used the same discursive frames to describe him. In 1911, he was described in newspapers as the "last of the cavemen," the "last 'uncontaminated' aboriginal American Indian in the US," and a "primordial man, the only really wild Indian in existence, and the last of his tribe," in the *San Francisco Sunday*, and the "last of the Deer Creeks," in the *Oroville Register*.[12] These framings continued into the twenty-first century as the man known as Ishi was described as "the last wild Indian in North America,"[13] "the last Yahi,"[14] "the last of his tribe,"[15] and "the last of his people"[16] in texts, documentaries, and music recordings targeting both academic and general public audiences. These framings explicitly invoke ideologies that relegate Indians to the past as the determiner of "real" Indianness ("last of the cavemen," "primordial man") and view Indigeneity as based in blood in danger of being corrupted ("last 'uncontaminated' aboriginal"). It was exactly this presumed link to the past with no possibility of a future that made the man known as Ishi such a celebrity. He was famous because he was the "last." Although Kroeber, Waterman, and other anthropologists emphasized the importance of their work with this individual for academic research, the man known as Ishi nonetheless circulated as a form of entertainment, and he was put on display for visitors to the museum. In 1911, the *San Francisco Examiner* reported that "theatrical offers poured in upon Waterman. A Sacramento man offered Thomas Waterman $2,000 spot cash to show Ishi for two weeks in Sacramento."[17] But his appeal to researchers and audiences alike was not simply in his presumed genetic background but also in the ways that this background was linked to his position as the last speaker of the Yana language, as these two excerpts from news coverage at the time demonstrate:

> "Indian Enigma Is Study for Scientists"
> Mary Ashe Miller, *San Francisco Call*, 6 September 1911
> Deciphering a human document, with the key to most of the hieroglyphics lost, is the baffling but absorbing delightful task which Dr. A.L. Kroeber and T.T. Waterman of the University of California have set for themselves. The document is the Deer Creek Indian captured recently near Oroville, who should by

> every rule and reckoning be the loneliest man on earth. *He is the last of this tribe; when he dies his language becomes dead also* [emphasis added]; he has feared people, both whites and Indians to such an extent that he has wandered, alone, like a hunted animal, since the death of his tribal brothers and sisters.

> "Untainted Life Revealed by Aborigine"
> Philip H. Kinsley, *San Francisco Examiner*, 6 September 1911
>
> "The capture of this man is of the utmost importance," said Professor Kroeber. "*He represents a new and supposedly extinct dialect* [emphasis added]. He says he is of the Yahi tribe. He is more of an aborigine than any of the Indians we have been working with for ten years."

These examples make it clear that being a speaker of his heritage language was part of what made him "more aborigine than any of the Indians we have been working with for ten years" and that language "death" via the death of the last speaker is an important element in framing "last Indians" and the eventual demise of all Indigenous peoples. And, though never described as such, this earlier body of media on "last Indian" celebrities exists as the rhetorical foundation on which contemporary media on "last speakers" are understood.

"Last Speakers"

More than a century after the original celebrity of the man known as Ishi, famous "last" Indians still abound, particularly as the "last" speakers of Indigenous and endangered languages. From BBC News and the *Guardian*, the *New York Times*, and the *Huffington Post* to Vodafone promotional materials, endangered languages comprise an increasingly pervasive topic in the media. The rhetorical strategies deployed in these media discussions are intended to raise public awareness of language endangerment. Here I examine rhetorics of Indigenous celebrity that surround language endangerment and their implications for Indigenous languages in North America and for many endangered language communities more broadly. These rhetorics create a status quo that Barbra Meek argues "constantly presents barriers, challenges, or constraints that need to be destroyed, unpacked, and deconstructed, or just changed."[18] In doing so, I join a growing number of scholars who examine closely the rhetorics surrounding Indigenous languages and their impacts on public and community conceptualization, language reclamation efforts, and even language policy in order to begin to unpack these discourses.[19]

Marie Wilcox (Wukchumni), Manuel Segovia (Ayapa), and Isidro Velázquez (Ayapa) are part of an increasingly public discourse on "last speakers" of Indigenous and endangered languages. The reporting on these speakers thus continues the longer-standing genre of counting down the inescapable end of Indigenous peoples, this time foregrounding the (always assumed) loss of culture. Take the first words of Judith Thurman's 2015 *New Yorker* article, "A Loss for Words: Can a Dying Language Be Saved?": "It is a singular fate to be *the last of one's kind*. That is the fate of the men and women, nearly all of them elderly, who are—like Marie Wilcox, of California; Gyani Maiya Sen, of Nepal; Verdena Parker, of Oregon; and Charlie Mungulda, of Australia—*the last known speakers of a language*."[20] Here being "the last of one's kind" is made explicitly parallel with being "the last known speakers of a language." The circulation of "last speaker" celebrity is so prevalent that *National Geographic* hosts a webpage that invites readers to "See and Hear Last Speakers of Dying Languages," Wikipedia lists fifty-nine individuals from around the globe in an article titled "List of Last Known Speakers of Languages," and BBC Online, the *Huffington Post*, and other news outlets circulated a story throughout 2011 and subsequent years titled "Last Two Speakers of Dying Language Refuse to Talk to Each Other," among many others.[21]

Critically, the individuals circulating as celebrities within these discussions are usually selected by researchers and media outlets rather than volunteering themselves, and the broadly circulating discussions of them within the celebrity framework do not reflect their positions in their own communities. In fact, being selected as one of these celebrities can become disruptive as the push to frame them within the expectations of "last (Indian) speakers" creates narratives that can position "last" speakers as the agents of language attrition in the media. In such instances, particular individuals are often scapegoated as the cause of the decline of language transmission. Perhaps the most widely discussed example of this is the (partially fictionalized) story of two speakers of the Indigenous language Ayapaneco in Mexico. In a 2011 *Huffington Post* article about the now infamous feud between two men, Manuel Segovia and Isidro Velázquez, the author summarizes the situation: "Though the language has been spoken in what is now Mexico for centuries, there are only two people left who can speak Ayapaneco fluently. Like so many other indigenous languages, *it's at risk of extinction—even more so because*, as the *Guardian* reports, *the last two speakers are refusing to talk to each other*."[22] Within this widely circulated and reworked story that was shared directly from the *Huffington Post* page alone over 3,500 times and became the focal point of a British telecommunications company (Vodafone) campaign and ad series, the two fluent speakers of Ayapaneco are repeatedly identified as the reason that the language will not be spoken by future generations through rhetoric that parallels the placing of all agency in language endangerment on Indigenous communities.[23] Phrasing such as "it's [Ayapaneco] at risk of extinction . . . because the last two speakers are refusing to talk to each other" directly links language dormancy—here problematically called "extinction" (discussed further below)—to the late-in-life actions of two individuals whose personal feelings toward each other are of no consequence for a world desperate to extract valuable knowledge hidden within the treasure chest of Indigenous languages. From this external evaluative perspective, Indigenous peoples are not only to provide aspects of their cultures, lives, and knowledge of the world to outsiders on demand but also to be friends with anyone else involved in accommodating those demands. Such articles never lament the decline or demise of Indigenous sovereignty or autonomy; the loss of political, economic, or geographic stability and power; or even the strong correspondence between language attrition and actual necropolitical[24] dynamics in marginalized communities. In fact, as I will discuss in a subsequent section, Indigenous (language) death is noteworthy only when it is the "last."

Three elements of the creation of "last speaker" celebrities are of particular importance. The first element is that, like those identified as "last Indians," those identified as "last speakers" of languages are only specifically and narrowly defined iterations of "speaker." Usually, the collocation "last speakers" assumes classification within most if not all of these arenas of language: native speakers (those who learned the language in childhood); monolingual (those who speak only the language of interest); fully fluent (those able to participate in all domains of communication in the language); mentally sound; heritage language speakers (those who have ethnic and/or cultural origins within the communities associated with the language); and so on. However, these are not the same criteria applied to speakers of non-endangered languages, and such a narrow restriction in terms of who gets counted as a speaker, or holding linguistic expertise and knowledge, erases those who fit one or more, but not all, of those speaker qualities. As Wesley Leonard and Erin Haynes point out, researchers' determinations of who is and is not a speaker "without having come to understand what being a speaker means within the cultural context extends the historical colonialist practice of imposing Western ways of knowing without acknowledging that other ways of knowing exist."[25] Furthermore, narrow, linguistically derived definitions of speakerhood effectively erase bilingual speakers and learners and exclude potential members of multilingual communities.[26]

The second element of concern is the direct connection between lasting and the already critiqued discourses of some endangered and Indigenous languages as dead. As enumerations go, "last" is a superlative, and it evokes the same level of irreversible finality as "dead."[27] In nearly all classification systems for language vitality and endangerment, the end point is extinction—borrowing from ecological and biological discourses. The UNESCO Language Vitality and Endangerment Report of 2003, for example, divides language endangerment into a six-degree scale, with "Safe (5)" being the most robust, with no threat of endangerment, and "Extinction (0)" being the least robust, defined as follows: "There is no one who can speak or remember the language."[28] This discourse of extinction has been challenged by groups whose languages were previously classified as extinct, such as Myaamia and Wampanoag, but have since regained speakers. As Miami linguist and language activist Wesley Leonard points out, the problem with the category of "extinct" is that "extinct means forever."[29] Once classified as extinct, as the Miami language was, it is extremely difficult for existing language practices to be recognized as legitimate—or even as existing. In contrast, language activists call for the term "dormant" or "sleeping" to be used for languages that do not currently have living speakers—a semantic frame assuming that such a status might be only temporary. Bernard Perley suggests that shifting the metaphor from "dead" to "dormant" or "sleeping" is powerful enough to "provide new hope for sleeping languages, as community members conceive emergent vitalities for their heritage languages as they awaken them."[30] I believe that the same consideration of the metaphorical framing of "last" can be equally powerful and the inverse equally detrimental. The origin of the category of "last" speakers in the longer circulating "last" Indians is also apparent here, since the framing of extinction was also central to discourses of lasting in seventeeth-century New England, where "the relentlessness of this message of extinction figured crucially in the large project of lasting in which local histories participated."[31]

The third element of these rhetorical strategies to consider is that they contribute to "depictions of indigenous languages as shifting toward nonexistence in direct correspondence to shifts across generations of speakers," where "younger generations are depicted as failing to acquire a language, in this case their ancestral or heritage tongue."[32] As such, these rhetorics contribute to what Meek identifies within media depictions of Indigenous language dynamics as the "doom-and-gloom" narrative of Indigenous languages, their communities having "failed" to maintain them.[33] Such tropes leave endangered language communities in seemingly impossible positions. Bilingual and multilingual speakers and contexts are usually uncounted, and, when new speakers emerge against great odds in communities already slated as dead, their last speaker gone, those communities must argue against the archive of coverage to declare their language "undead." Indigenous language communities with reawakened languages are then tasked with convincing settler colonial audiences of the reality of their accomplishments. Revitalized and reawakened languages—with their (often bilingual) new speakers and regular use—cannot completely escape from the pervasive expectation of the vanishing Indian (language) trope and are perceived as unnatural at best.

Conclusion

The circulation of famous "last" speakers works against language reclamation efforts in Indigenous communities, in which language activists work to counter the ideologies that Indigenous language dormancy is inevitable, that Indigenous languages are not relevant in the present and future, and that new speakers are not possible. Indigenous and endangered language community efforts and narratives also offer counterstrategies to the dominant trend of lasting, which assumes an inevitable "countdown" and end to endangered and Indigenous language speakers[34] and limited definitions of both "speaker" and the contexts of language use and reclamation. From Wendat[35] to Miami[36] to Wampanoag,[37] researchers and Indigenous communities are demonstrating that languages can "awaken" after periods of dormancy. These examples also demonstrate that individuals, groups, and communities can "save" languages, not just lose them as popular media representation suggests. They also provide examples in which declarations of language "extinction" or "dormancy" prove to be overly enthusiastic, such as those that declared Plains Indian Sign Language long dormant, when in fact it was—and still is—known and used within a variety of communities throughout the United States and Canada.[38] We are increasingly offered evidence that endangered language communities can, and do, pull together to maintain their knowledge with language documentation resources and comparative linguistic analyses of related languages to create new generations of speakers and new contexts of language use. This includes genres—old and new—within Indigenous and endangered language communities often erased by dominant rhetorics of language endangerment focused exclusively on quantifications of "speakers" and "languages." The contributors to the book edited by Paul Kroskrity,[39] for example, highlight the role of narrative and lesser-discussed genres such as poetry in the language maintenance and reclamation efforts of Indigenous communities.

Overwhelmingly, discourses of endangered and Indigenous language failure[40] are attributable to which questions are asked, how, and by whom. The differences between the proposed questions above and the questions being answered in dominant rhetorics about endangered languages represent what Meek calls "sociolinguistic disjunctures," or "points of discontinuity or contradiction, moments where practices and ideas about language diverge."[41] In these cases, the disjunctures exist among Indigenous communities, their languages, and broader institutionalized ideologies and representations of those communities and languages. Such representations or dominant discourses have a far greater circulation within broader publics and might therefore disproportionately shape both public opinion and policy. However, as "sociolinguistic disjunctures," the differences highlighted in this chapter can also "create opportunities for resetting patterns, for reschematizing some system of semiotic value, for transforming everyday communicative practices and expectations."[42] This resetting of patterns can be supported by asking new questions and reframing old stories in ways that demonstrate the full depth of the challenges facing Indigenous communities through recent years, decades, and centuries while also highlighting the incredible extent of Indigenous language and cultural maintenance against all odds as a decolonial act of breathtaking resistance, resilience, and survivance.

Rather than a new phenomenon emerging out of some twenty-first-century increased awareness of language endangerment, the widely circulating narratives about famous "last speakers" of Indigenous languages are simply a variation on much older narratives about "last Indians." It is a continuation of the practice of "writing Indians out of existence,"[43] both the circulation of "last Indians" and the relationship between the lasting of Indians and the Indigenous languages assumed to disappear with them. By ignoring the plentiful examples of language reclamation efforts that create new speakers and demonstrate that language is multifaceted and multifunctional, and instead continuing the practice of "lasting" through Indigenous celebrity, it becomes clear that the concern with such representations is not for maintaining Indigenous communities and culture(s) but for continuing the long-standing tradition of counting, and counting down, Indians.

NOTES

1 Jean O'Brien, *Firsting and Lasting: Writing Indians Out of Existence in New England* (Minneapolis: University of Minnesota Press, 2010).

2 Nancy K. Rivenburgh, "Media Framing of Complex Issues: The Case of Endangered Languages," *Public Understanding of Science* 22, no. 6 (2013): 704.

3 O'Brien, *Firsting and Lasting*; James Fenimore Cooper, *The Last of the Mohicans* (London: Ward, Lock and Company, 1888); *The Last of the Dogmen*, dir. Tab Murphy (HBO Home Video, 1995).

4 Shaylih Muehlmann, "Von Humboldt's Parrot and the Countdown of Last Speakers in the Colorado Delta," *Language and Communication* 32, no. 2 (2012): 160–68.

5 O'Brien, *Firsting and Lasting*, 4.

6 Philip J. Deloria, *Playing Indian* (New Haven, CT: Yale University Press, 2004).

7 Judith T. Irvine and Susan Gal, "Language Ideology and Linguistic Differentiation," in *Regimes of Language: Ideologies, Polities, and Identities*, ed. Paul V. Kroskrity (Santa Fe: School of American Research Press, 2000), 35–83.

8 O'Brien, *Firsting and Lasting*, 118; emphasis added.

9 Quoted in ibid., 113; emphasis added.

10 This individual refused to share his given name(s) with Alfred Kroeber and others while at Berkeley. Kroeber called him Ishi, but that was not his given name, and the fact that the individual who circulated globally as Ishi refused to give those in settler society his name was an important act of refusal that should not be ignored.

11 Upon his death, doctors at the University of California Berkeley medical school went against the traditions of the Yahi people, which keep bodies intact after death, and conducted an autopsy on the man known as Ishi to remove the brain before cremating the body. The brain was then sent to the Smithsonian Institution, where it remained until 2000, when it was finally repatriated to Indigenous communities in northern California. See Orin Starn, *Ishi's Brain: In Search of America's Last "Wild" Indian* (New York: Norton, 2004).

12 Robert F. Heizer and Theodora Kroeber, eds., *Ishi, the Last Yahi: A Documentary History* (Berkeley: University of California Press, 1979).

13 Theodora Kroeber, *Ishi in Two Worlds: A Biography of the Last Wild Indian in North America* (Berkeley: University of California Press, 1976).

14 Heizer and Kroeber, *Ishi, the Last Yahi;* Ishi and Bernie Krause, *Ishi: The Last Yahi* (San Francisco, CA: Wild Sanctuary, 1992); Jed Riffe, Pamela Roberts, and Anne Makepeace. *Ishi: The Last Yahi: A Film*, Rattlesnake Productions (Berkeley Media, 1992).

15 Theodora Kroeber, *Ishi, Last of His Tribe* (Berkeley, CA: Parnassus Press, 1964).

16 David Petersen, *Ishi: The Last of His People*, Picture-Story Biographies (Chicago: Children's Press, 1991).

17 Heizer and Kroeber, *Ishi, the Last Yahi.*

18 Barbra A. Meek, "Failing American Indian Languages," *American Indian Culture and Research Journal* 35, no. 2 (2011): 55.

19 Jane H. Hill, "'Expert Rhetorics' in Advocacy for Endangered Languages: Who Is Listening and What Do They Hear?," *Journal of Linguistic Anthropology* 12, no. 2 (2002): 119–33; Wesley Y. Leonard, "When Is an 'Extinct Language' Not Extinct? Miami, a Formerly Sleeping Language," in *Sustaining Linguistic Diversity: Endangered and Minority Languages and Language Varieties*, ed. Kendall A. King, Natalie Schilling-Estes, Lyn Fogle, Jia Jackie Lou, and Barbara Soukup (Washington, DC: Georgetown University Press, 2008), 23–33; Wesley Y. Leonard, "Producing Language Reclamation by Decolonizing 'Language,'" *Language Documentation and Description* 14 (2016): 15–36; Barbra A. Meek, *We Are Our Language: An Ethnography of Language Revitalization in a Northern Athabaskan Community* (Tucson: University of Arizona Press, 2010); Meek, "Failing American Indian Languages"; Bernard C. Perley, "Zombie Linguistics: Experts, Endangered Languages and the Curse of Undead Voices," *Anthropological Forum* 22, no. 2 (2012): 133–49.

20 Judith Thurman, "A Loss for Words: Can a Dying Language Be Saved?," *New Yorker*, 30 March 2015, http://www.newyorker.com/magazine/2015/03/30/a-loss-for-words (accessed 16 February 2016); emphasis added.

21 Ker Than and Chris Rainier, "See and Hear Last Speakers of Dying Languages," *National Geographic*, 18 February 2012, http://news.nationalgeographic.com/news/2012/02/pictures/120217-talking-dictionaries-vanishing-languages-science-hear-audio/ (accessed 27 January 2016); "List of *Last Known Speakers* of Languages," Wikipedia, https://en.wikipedia.org/wiki/Talk%3A_List_of_last_known_speakers_of_languages; Rachel Nuwer, "Languages: Why We Must Save Dying Tongues," BBC Future, 5 June 2014, https://www.bbc.com/future/article/20140606-why-we-must-save-dying-languages (accessed 12 August 2015); "Last 2 Speakers of Dying Language Won't Speak to Each Other," *Huffington Post*, 14 April 2010, https://www.huffpost.com/entry/ayapaneco-dying-languages_n_849319 (accessed 14 July 2014).

22 "Last 2 Speakers of Dying Language"; emphasis added.

23 See Daniel F. Suslak, "Ayapan Echoes: Linguistic Persistence and Loss in Tabasco, Mexico," *American Anthropologist* 113, no. 4 (2011): 569–81.

24 Achille Mbembe, "Necropolitics," *Public Culture* 15, no. 1 (2003): 14. Mbembe defines necropolitics as "the relationship between sovereignty and power over life and death." In other words, necropolitical dynamics are those in which a sovereign—often colonial—power is capable not only of deciding when and how a subject dies but also of claiming the right to enslave others, to impose social or civil death, and other forms of cultural and political violence.

25 Wesley Y. Leonard and Erin Haynes, "Making 'Collaboration' Collaborative: An Examination of Perspectives that Frame Linguistic Field Research," *Language Documentation and Conservation* 4 (2010): 279.

26 Haley De Korne, "The Multilingual Realities of Language Reclamation: Working with Language Contact, Diversity, and Change in Endangered Language Education," *Language Documentation and Description* 14 (2016):111–35.

27 See Kendall A. King and Mary Hermes, "Why Is This So Hard? Ideologies of Endangerment, Passive Language Learning Approaches, and Ojibwe in the United States," *Journal of Language, Identity and Education* 13, no. 4 (2014): 268–82; Leonard, "When Is an 'Extinct Language' Not Extinct?"; Meek, "Failing American Indian Languages"; and Perley, "Zombie Linguistics."

28 UNESCO Ad Hoc Expert Group on Endangered Languages, "Language Vitality and Endangerment," 2003, 8.

29 Wesley Y. Leonard, "Challenging 'Extinction' through Modern Miami Language Practices," *American Indian Culture and Research Journal* 35, no. 2 (2011): 137.

30 Perley, "Zombie Linguistics," 145.

31 O'Brien, *Firsting and Lasting*, 139.

32 Meek, "Failing American Indian Languages," 51.

33 Ibid., 53.

34 Muehlmann, "Von Humboldt's Parrot."

35 Megan Lukaniec, "From Archives to Adult and Child Language Learning: Reconstructing and Revitalizing Wendat (Iroquoian)," poster presented at the 89th Annual Meeting of the Linguistic Society of America, Portland, Oregon, 10 January 2015.

36 Daryl Baldwin, Karen Baldwin, Jessie Baldwin, and Jarrid Baldwin, "Myaamiaataweenkioowaaha: 'Miami Spoken Here,'" in *Bringing Our Languages Home: Language Revitalization for Families*, ed. Leanne Hinton (Berkeley, CA: Heyday Books, 2013), 3–18; Leonard, "When Is an 'Extinct Language' Not Extinct?"

37 jessie little doe baird, "Wampanoag: How Did This Happen to My Language?," in *Bringing Our Languages Home: Language Revitalization for Families*, ed. Leanne Hinton (Berkeley, CA: Heyday Books, 2013), 19–32.

38 Brenda Farnell, *Do You See What I Mean? Plains Indian Sign Talk and the Embodiment of Action* (Austin: University of Texas Press, 1995).

39 Paul V. Kroskrity, ed., *Telling Stories in the Face of Danger: Language Renewal in Native American Communities* (Norman: University of Oklahoma Press, 2012).

40 Meek, "Failing American Indian Languages."

41 Meek, *We Are Our Language*, 50.

42 Ibid., 51.

43 O'Brien, *Firsting and Lasting*.

CHAPTER 8

Celebrity in Absentia: Situating the Indigenous People of the Andaman and Nicobar Islands in the Indian Social Imaginary

Aadita Chaudhury

Introduction

A number of scholars of celebrity have studied the phenomena of personas, fame, and the process by which an ordinary individual can become famous, for either desirable or undesirable reasons, but little attention has been paid to cases in which the subject of celebrity is reluctant to be in the proverbial spotlight to begin with or has categorically refused engagement with structures and social systems that lead to such types of public recognition. How does this relate to the ways in which we understand celebrity, especially in contemporary times, in which social media, the internet, and other forms of mass communication have enabled the creation of celebrity, even momentarily, for a larger number of people, leading to what some have called the "democratization" of celebrity? As such, the concept of "celebrity in absentia" sounds paradoxical at best. But fame, or infamy, without intending the effects thereof, is at least as old as settler colonialism. It could be argued that the first subjects of what I am calling celebrity in absentia were Indigenous peoples of the Americas, starting from their first contact with Europeans.

Because of the proliferation of the printing press, transatlantic travel, and increasing rates of literacy that originally facilitated European settler colonialism, information about and colonial representations of Indigenous peoples of the Americas reached Europe in unprecedented ways. They created the first instances of celebrity in absentia, whereby the people subjected to fame, speculation, and curiosity had little, if any, input in the narratives surrounding them. In this chapter, I explore how Indigenous and non-Indigenous groups interact in the context of postcolonial state making, specifically with regard to social imaginaries around literature, media, and tourism when it comes to the Andaman and Nicobar Islands, an archipelago considered to be a union territory of India. I also discuss how the phenomenon of celebrity in absentia underlies these dynamics.

Celebrity in absentia has created long-lasting myths and prejudices about Indigenous peoples that have extended from and proliferated beyond the early days of European settler colonization to this day. It has greatly harmed the aims of their sovereignty while providing tangible benefits to the colonial project, which seeks to justify its methods by portraying the Indigenous as inherently inferior and ungovernable within the context of settler laws. Celebrity in absentia is therefore something constructed for and by the colonial project that purports to be about Indigenous peoples but ultimately is an interpretation of them in a light that facilitates further colonial and capitalist expansion. What I am calling celebrity in absentia is forced on Indigenous peoples even with their continued refusal,[1] as I will describe later with the example of the Sentinelese people of the Andaman and Nicobar Islands.

Early colonial ethnographers and historians, such as Bartolomé de Las Casas,[2] Adriaen Cornelissen van der Donck,[3] Fray Juan de Torquemada,[4] and many others became instrumental as the first scholars who represented the Indigenous peoples of the Americas to lay Europeans. Although many of these accounts by Europeans about the Indigenous peoples of the Americas are read as sympathetic to their plight under colonization, others are not, and regardless of the tone and content, European ethnographers and historians often entirely left out the voices of their ethnographic subjects in order to give accounts that spoke more about their preconceived notions of race, gender, class, and culture than anything else. This orientalist, exoticized fetishization laid the groundwork for Euro-American, and sometimes global, perceptions of the Indigenous peoples of the Americas while their own voices remained elusive. Indigenous peoples became subjects of fascination for centuries to come, and their fame and mystique only led to further interest in the extraction of cultural artifacts and resources for the colonial project.

Nonetheless, while the colonial project was creating this kind of celebrity in absentia, Indigenous peoples resisted it in their own ways. In the past few decades, concerns about Indigenous rights and sovereignty, and traditional knowledge, languages, and cultures, have been represented to the world by Indigenous peoples themselves. Increasingly, the perceptions rooted in colonial accounts are being challenged squarely by Indigenous agents, and in many ways Indigenous peoples around the world are fighting back against the perils of celebrity in absentia through the use of their own media, research and writing, and the arts. The damage done by the original colonial project of celebrity in absentia, however, continues to persist.

Still, some Indigenous communities remain celebrities in absentia in ways that others simply do not. Many of these tribes resist contact with outsiders, which only fuels further exploitative curiosity about them. Some of these tensions are played out in contemporary postcolonial landscapes, where the history of imperial occupation and exploitation is palpable, yet the same gaze that these landscapes were subjected to by their former colonial overlords now extends to certain isolated Indigenous communities as a function of the postcolonial state. In many instances, the postcolonial state creates its own narratives of celebrity in absentia in order to fulfill its functions in nation building and creating social imaginaries that sustain its presence and legitimacy, sometimes in contested areas.

India is one such postcolonial state. It is home to countless ethnic groups, a trait often highlighted by the Indian state to promote national unity, a model of multiculturalism, and tourism among its citizens and the world at large. However, since the Hindu nationalist Bharatiya Janata Party (BJP) came to power in 2014, Indian national unity has begun to crack, especially as majoritarian values aligning with northern Indian, Hindu, upper-caste, and conservative publics are imposed on lower-caste, Muslim, Dalit, and Indigenous people.[5] Although the Hindu nationalist project of the BJP is based on myth rather than history,[6] and goes squarely against the secular foundations of the Indian constitution,[7] it is one of many permutations of the Indian state, what many scholars and activists have termed "Brahminical patriarchy,"[8] which has used a number of essentialist tactics to promote national unity, sometimes at the expense of minority and Indigenous sovereignty.

The Indian Subcontinent has been peopled by numerous waves of migration, starting at least 1.5 million years ago. At present, there are over 780 languages spoken in India, with many of them nearing extinction.[9] Among the many ethnic groups in India, many are considered Adivasis (which literally translates into "ancient inhabitants" or "original inhabitants") or Indigenous peoples.[10] Many of these groups are recognized by the national governments of India, Bangladesh, and Pakistan, but their status and sovereignty vary widely. Interestingly, though South Asian scholars have long contributed to the tradition of postcolonial thought, much of it has been within the context of recent waves of European colonization, and in discussions many of the dynamics between Indigenous and non-Indigenous populations of India have been flattened. However, scholars in South Asia and the diaspora, in particular Adivasi and Dalit scholars, continue to reflect on the various ways in which the postcolonial states of India, Bangladesh, and Pakistan deal with their Indigenous subjects.[11]

Although the notion of "strategic essentialism," as per Gayatri Chakraborty Spivak's definition, has been mobilized to support both state-sponsored narratives and independent cultural programming to represent all regions of India, its Indigenous peoples, specifically those inhabiting the union territories of Andaman and Nicobar Islands, occupy a special niche in the Indian state's image. Located in the Bay of Bengal, the Andaman Islands, which make up the Andaman and Nicobar Islands union territory, are home to several Indigenous groups that are among the least contacted communities in the world.[12] Despite government-sponsored settlement schemes to bring thousands of mainland Indians to the islands in the 1950s and on,[13] the relative isolation of the Indigenous Andamanese has become fodder for national legend and widespread curiosity. Although Indigenous-inhabited areas are technically off limits to mainlanders and non-Indigenous settlers of the Andaman and Nicobar Islands, as dictated by Indian law,[14] increasing settler presence in the area has meant a continued fascination with things Indigenous and even the fetishization of Indigenous cultures and bodies. In this way, Indigenous Andamanese cultures and bodies are sometimes propelled to celebrity status, often without the agency of the Andamanese themselves being considered. Ironically, the celebrity of the Indigenous Andamanese is created with little, if any, of their sovereign input and agency. Although India's mainland Indigenous tribes are often visibly present in the media, politics, education, and beyond (albeit still underserved and systemically disenfranchised by majoritarian, especially Hindu, nationalist politics), the fame of the last of India's unadulterated Indigeneity of the Andaman Islands is mobilized as part of tourism campaigns, popular books and movies set on the islands, and even human safaris.

In this chapter, I seek to investigate the paradox of Indigenous celebrity without sovereign Indigenous representation within a liberal, secular democracy—one that has dealt for decades with the perils of Hindu nationalism. I will use the framework of celebrity established by Olivier Driessens, and the respective processes of celebrification and celebritization as per his theorization, to guide my understanding of how the Indigenous peoples of Andaman and Nicobar Islands are framed within the Indian social imaginary. I will intertwine this framework with critical reflection on my personal experiences and exposures to the social imaginaries crafted by mainstream Indian culture as a non-Indigenous Indian, and I hope that doing so will help me to consider how Adivasis are positioned within Indian society today and how I have become part of the very cultural narratives that sustain the caricatures of Adivasis while aiding the state-sponsored narratives. I will investigate renewed international interest in the Indigenous Andamanese, especially in the aftermath of the Indian Ocean tsunami of 2004, which left them unharmed thanks to traditional knowledge, and more recently the death of an American missionary who reached North Sentinel Island illegally with the hope of proselytizing the Sentinelese. With this in mind, I will consider what it means for an Indigenous group to gain fame in absentia, without having much active sovereignty in the process, in the context of the postcolonial Indian state. I will also focus on the role of the settler gaze on Indigenous bodies and how it perpetuates the problematic celebrity of the Indigenous Andamanese. Finally, I will reflect on the function of this peculiar kind of celebrity in the nationalistic imagination of India at large.

The Andaman and Nicobar Islands and Cascading Colonialisms

The Andaman and Nicobar Islands are an archipelago located in the Indian Ocean. According to archaeological studies, they were first settled by humans between 70,000 and 50,000 years ago by a wave of migrants moving along the Indian coastline toward southeast Asia and Oceania.[15] There might have been subsequent arrivals of newer groups of people, and these communities form what we now know as the Indigenous inhabitants of the archipelago. In the nineteenth and twentieth centuries, under British colonial rule, a number of prisons were set up in the Port Blair region, the headquarters of the Andaman Islands.[16] These prisons were meant to isolate many political prisoners under British rule from resistance and freedom movements happening on the Indian mainland. Moreover, unfamiliarity with the local territory meant that prisoners could do little to escape or build resistance movements on site. Yet the prisoners themselves were an unwilling extension of the British settler colonial project. As prisoner and non-prisoner populations from the mainland of the Indian subcontinent were brought to the islands, the British used them to establish and legitimize their territorial claims to the islands. This in turn affected the islands' Indigenous populations, for many of them were reluctant to make contact or engage in any way with the new settlers.

Amidst the various Indigenous groups, those from North Sentinel Island, known as the Sentinelese, captured the most interest because of their immense reluctance to make contact with other populations.[17] In the history of the Andaman Islands, the Sentinelese would remain the most elusive while adding much fodder to the public and social imaginations about the islands and being a significant aspect of the celebrity and allure of the islands for tourism and ethnographic and artistic interests. After the end of British occupation, the islands were briefly used as a Japanese prisoner of war colony.[18] Then, when they changed hands to India, refugees (as well as other groups from the subcontinent) from Bangladesh were given large plots of land to settle the islands.[19] At present, the islands are inhabited by many settlers from the mainland Indian subcontinent, and Indigenous populations who have resisted contact inhabit lands recognized by the government with reserves that span much of the archipelago. According to Indian law, unauthorized visits to and photographs of these tribes are strictly prohibited.[20] However, over the years, there have been many instances of both Indian and foreign nationals making unauthorized contact with the tribes, sometimes even in the context of exploitative human safaris run by contentious tour operators.

In the next section, I will discuss the official definition of being Indigenous in India and relate it to the larger context of identity formation for different groups within the Indian Subcontinent and the significance thereof within broader socio-political history.

Indigeneity in India

India has a number of recognized Indigenous tribes and populations. How Indigeneity is defined in the Indian context is difficult to pinpoint, but it often refers to various populations that are not part of the large Indo-European- and Dravidian-speaking populations that settled India much later than the original settlers known as Adivasis.[21] Indigenous tribes have had an interesting history in the Indian subcontinent, wherein their nationhood and sovereignty have been recognized to varying degrees. However, despite the political landscapes, Adivasis have been subjected to discrimination by wider society influenced by ideas from the Hindu caste system and attempts to establish a system of Hindu supremacy.[22] Although many Indigenous tribes, officially recognized as Scheduled Tribes (STs), are often in regular contact with other populations in the subcontinent, the isolation of the Andamanese, Nicobarese, and Sentinelese tribes makes them objects of fascination precisely because of how "unfamiliar" and "exotic" they are. The STs are distinguished from the SCs (Scheduled Castes) in that SCs belong to the predominant Indo-European and Dravidian ethnic groups but come from historically marginalized castes. As such, STs have retained a distinct identity because of language, custom, religion, and livelihood, which distinguish them from other similarly marginalized populations in the subcontinent.

With this information about the context in which the Indigenous peoples of the Andaman and Nicobar Islands are recognized, and their unique positionality within the various ethnic groups in the Indian Subcontinent, we can begin to delve deeper into the social, political, and material ingredients that create their celebrity. In the next section, I will discuss the theoretical frameworks that help to uncover the phenomenon of celebrity in absentia further.

What Is Celebrity?

To understand how the Indigenous peoples of the Andaman and Nicobar Islands are propelled into the Indian national imaginary, we must understand the nature of celebrity itself as well as the processes and labour relations that go into its production. Celebrity can be an elusive concept. What makes the Andamanese a cultural celebrity is not the same thing as what makes an individual entertainer, politician, performer, or artist one. Part of celebrity is facilitated by mystery, unfamiliarity, fantasy, and fixation that go beyond the ordinary,[23] and the elusiveness, isolation, and distance of the cultures of the Indigenous peoples of the Andaman and Nicobar Islands create the ideal ingredients for celebrity. Yet the lack of ordinariness itself can act as a kind of objectification and a flattening of identities that create constrictions for the celebrated subject. Driessens explains the processes and co-production of the social construction of celebrity: namely, the acts of "celebrification" and "celebritization":

> Celebrification . . . entails commodification: stars and, by extension, celebrities "are both labour and the thing that labour produces." They are manufactured by the celebrity industry and produce and help to sell other commodities. In this sense, the celebrity presents and personifies "[t]he two faces of capitalism—that of defaced value and prized commodity value." Celebritization, on the other hand, occurs not at the individual, but at the social fields level. Scholars have discussed celebritization particularly in relation to (electoral) politics but also (environmental) activism, fashion, literature, academia and medicine have been studied or mentioned as examples. Importantly, celebritization does not equal increased celebrification, nor does the celebritization of a social field imply the celebrification of all the agents in this field. Similar to other power resources, celebrity is distributed unequally.[24]

Other scholars of celebrity, such as Chris Rojek, have conceptualized "attributed celebrity." Rojek, who defines celebrity as the accumulation of attention capital,[25] notes that in certain instances celebrity occurs because of the "concentrated representation of an individual [or, in the case of the Indigenous Andamanese, a group] as noteworthy or exceptional by cultural intermediaries."[26] However, I argue that celebrity in absentia is distinct from attributed celebrity in that, though some level of consent and/or contact with the machinations of the world that produce celebrity is required from the subject of attributed celebrity, celebrity in absentia happens even in the face of continued refusal of contact with and no desire for cultural recognition[27] from worlds that create celebrity.

With this framework, it is important to disentangle carefully the tensions between celebrification and celebritization in the case of the Indigenous peoples of the Andaman and Nicobar Islands and the ends to which the respective processes of celebrification and celebritization are mobilized. In the next section, I will explore the various ways that celebrification of the Indigenous peoples of the Andaman and Nicobar Islands are produced and the means by which their celebritization at the national scale further legitimizes the presence and territorial control of the Indian state over the islands.

Indian Cultural Fascination with the Andaman and Nicobar Islands

Since independence, the Indian state has included the Andaman and Nicobar Islands in its development programs under its various five-year plans. Part of this has resulted in the construction of the Andaman trunk road, which enables easier movement of resources and people from the interior areas of the archipelago to the ports.[28] This road goes through the traditional territories of the Indigenous peoples of the islands and over the years has been the site of many encounters that exploit the Indigenous peoples but nonetheless add to the global "intrigue" about them, compounding their exoticization.

As a child growing up in India, I heard about the "mysterious" tribes of the Andaman and Nicobar Islands. I was exposed to them through books such as one of the novels of esteemed Bengali author Sunil Gangopadhyay, in his series of detective/adventure novels with protagonist Kakababu (which translates into "uncle"), the nickname for Raja Roychowdhury, a fictional former director of the Archaeological Survey of India. Perhaps my first notable exposure to the Indian fascination with the mysteries of the Andaman and Nicobar Islands came from the novel *Sabuj Dwiper Raja* ("The King of the Green Island"),[29] adapted as a feature film in 1979. The novel follows the adventures of Kakababu and his nephew and assistant, Shontu, who embark on an investigative trip to the islands in search of a notorious smuggler who has been plotting to steal a mysterious material or metal from a meteorite that has fallen on an island where the sole inhabitants are Jarawas, one of the Indigenous tribes of the islands. Implied in the story are the apparent "backwardness" of the Jarawas and their inability to comprehend the value of the meteorite to civilization, hence their lack of interest in defending it from capture by the wrong parties and their inability to defend themselves in general. At the same time, the narrator and characters praise the Jarawas for their peaceful existence and their lack of interest in material wealth and capital. A subplot of the story involves the fate of a freedom fighter from the era of the British Raj who has befriended and "gone Native" with the Jarawas, becoming the tribe's leader by the time Kakababu begins his investigation in order to reach the meteorite before the smugglers do. The significance of the subplot is multifold: to show that a non-Indigenous Indian might be better equipped to govern the Jarawas than the Jarawas themselves, to indicate the history of colonialism in the Indian Subcontinent, and to show how Indigenous and non-Indigenous Indians are positioned within that context. Through this narrative, Gangopadhyay's novel shows us and corroborates the perception that non-Indigenous Indian involvement in the governance of the tribes is legitimate, especially as they are subjected to contact by relatively "more exploitative" forces, for instance the British. Kakababu is not simply any non-Indigenous Indian person but a man from a presumably upper-caste Hindu background (though caste and its implications are never explicitly stated in Gangopadhyay's series) who formerly worked for an Indian state agency, which had its roots in the British colonial government. The Archaeological Survey of India was established by British army engineer, explorer, and archaeologist Sir Alexander Cunningham,[30] through whose efforts the British Empire was effectively able to plunder much of South Asia's cultural artifacts through a formalized bureaucratic process for British museum collections.[31] It is perhaps no accident that in the world of *Swabuj Dwiper Raja* the protagonist is a representative of the former colonial state agency, from a Hindu high-caste mainland Indian background, who—like his British imperial predecessors—drives an account of "noble savages" unable to govern or defend themselves effectively.

Gangopadhyay's narrative in *Sabuj Dwiper Raja* employs many of the tropes associated with Indian adventure fiction as it relates to the Indigenous populations of India as well as the general public's perception of Indian Indigeneity. As mentioned, as with most depictions of Indigenous Indians, *Sabuj Dwiper Raja* portrays Jarawas as a technologically unsophisticated and anti-materialistic people increasingly threatened by and needing protection from nefarious external forces that seek to destroy their livelihoods. In a subtle way, it also nods to the piece of legislation titled The Protection of Aboriginal Tribes, Article 243, Clause 2, of the Andaman and Nicobar Islands (Protection of Aboriginal Tribes) Regulation, 1956,[32] created to ensure that the Indigenous peoples of the region would not have their lives and cultures interrupted by settler presence, but to what extent this legislation has been enforced is uncertain. The novel also underscores that, with the creation of the Andaman Trunk Road, "an increasing number of visitors as well as settlers had become interconnected by the road, effectively creating a 'work of the imagination' within Andamanese culture."[33] As Vishvajit Pandya explains further,

> the road facilitated the reconstruction and mediation of more visible Jarwas. As Jarwas could now be seen on the roadside, those visitors and settlers who had only imagined Jarwas could now use the road to visualize the actual Jarwa. . . . The public sphere, in which Jarwas were restricted to a reserved territory, rapidly expanded to contacts with those outside the reserve, along the roadside. The imagined Jarwa and the Jarwa images now had "its own life" for people and authority. . . . This set the stage for encounters in which the line of distinction between primitive and ex-primitive Jarwa became blurred. The notion of modernization, while protecting primitive Jarwas, was now counter-posed. People on the islands were demanding the modernization of the protected primitive, as the category of "once-were-primitives" or "ex-primitives" came to be called. Settlers, as well as some administrators and tourists, were keen to see the Jarwas brought into the main fold of society and made to fit into their collective imagination of ex-primitive, who had become non-foraging, disciplined, decipherable, and controllable.[34]

The fascination with the Andaman and Nicobar Islands is now manifest in various ways within the Indian imagination. There are books, movies and television shows, and tourism programs that exploit the trope of the pristine "noble savages" of the islands along with the promotion of ecotourism. Popular imaginings of the Andaman and Nicobar Islands as well as tourism-related publications invoke the "exotic" in the islands. Centred within the exotic is the Indigenous body, and its juxtaposition with the "civilized" body, where the former is unclothed or minimally clothed, and that in itself is key in the creation of Indigenous celebrity in the islands. This type of celebrity, however, is created with little, if any, input from the Indigenous peoples themselves and therefore subjected to settler standards of modesty, civilization, and sexuality. Indigenous peoples themselves do not drive tourism in the Andaman and Nicobar Islands; rather, tourism operators are either backed by the Indian state or businesses run by non-Indigenous Indian settlers in the islands. As a result, Indigenous bodies are exploited to create sensationalized narratives that ultimately benefit settlers and increase their presence in Indigenous traditional territories. Therefore, the celebrification of the Indigenous peoples of the islands is produced by the labour of non-Indigenous Indians, with the use of the labour of the Indigenous body, under the exploitative gaze of the settler imagination, to further settler aims. It is noteworthy that the celebrification, as Driessens would put it, is not enacted by the Indigenous peoples themselves, the object of celebrity, but enforced through various exploitative means. If we see this process of celebrification as "two sides of capitalism," as Driessens puts it, the "defaced value" and the "prized commodity value," then specific power relations between the Indigenous peoples of the Andaman and Nicobar Islands and others also become visible. We can begin to see that the "prized commodity value" refers to the cultural production of the mystique of the Indigenous peoples of the islands, whereas the "defaced value" refers to the livelihoods and bodies of the same people. Those who benefit from the "prized commodity value" in this context are directly in an exploitative relationship with the Indigenous peoples of the Andaman and Nicobar Islands, and their "defacement" makes them unwilling participants in this process of celebrification.

As mentioned, one salient way that this fascination has emerged is with the preoccupation with the Jarawas or, more broadly, the Indigenous body itself. In 2014, two French filmmakers were charged with illegal trespassing in the territories of the Jarawas in order to create a documentary, apparently to be titled *The Organic Jarawa*.[35] Even before then, many human safaris disguised as other types of tourism activities were observed in the Andaman and Nicobar Islands. Large numbers of tourists would be taken illegally into the Tribal Reserve Territory of the Jarawas simply to gaze at them. *Vice* magazine reported that

> the tours to see the Jarawa, who appear by the side of the Trunk Road, were disguised as trips to some caves and a mud volcano. . . . Sophie Grig of Survival International told me that, when she asked people why they wanted to see the Jarawa, the most common reply was, "Because they're not civilised." Sunil—a British visitor to the Andaman Islands, who a friend put me in touch with—told me over the phone that he thought going on the human safari was "not a big deal." He even told me he thought the Jarawa benefited from it.[36]

Guido Abbattista elaborates:

> In 2008 the Indian government had to adopt measures to safeguard the aborigines, prohibiting vehicle traffic and direct contacts in the settlement zones which are home to the few surviving Jarawas. In spite of these measures, mass arrivals of tourists continued, driven by the interests of the private companies, until in 2012 a news story hit the headlines. It featured a video taken by a tourist showing half-naked Jarawa women being persuaded by tourists in a Jeep to dance with the inducement of food and other offerings in what was actually styled not just a "human zoo" but a "human safari." . . . The local police were not only disposed to turn a blind eye but actually participated in the activities of the local organizers, and columns of vehicles were allowed to enter the settlement zones, with hundreds of tourists not only photographing and videoing the Jarawas but treating them like animals on display and curiosities, exactly as had occurred for decades in the "human zoos" in the European expositions in the nineteenth and twentieth centuries.[37]

As with the French video that surfaced in 2014, the fixation seems to be on naked Jarawa bodies and the performance of those bodies for the touristic gaze. The colonial project is not simply to conquer lands and resources within traditional territories of Indigenous peoples but also to use their bodies for othering entertainment. To situate this phenomenon, we need to understand the role of tourism in providing fodder for various social imaginaries. Noel Salazar's reflections on the relationship between anthropology and global tourism might offer us a place to start:

> Anthropologists have been consequential proponents of the great nostalgic narrative of loss and possible contact with a disappearing object that forms a major motivating background to many tourism activities. . . . It is very difficult to disentangle colonial thought, ethnographic stereotypes, and other cultural models of difference that continue to circulate within global tourism. It is not anthropology alone that is to blame, and contemporary anthropological scholarship recognizes that dominant imaginaries and discourses do not reflect the actual situation on the ground and often silence the voice of the powerless. The hard question that begs an answer is how anthropologists should deal with the discipline's deep implication in contemporary tourism and other cultural dynamics around the globe.[38]

Salazar gives us a glimpse of how certain social imaginaries become normalized and taken up by the state and its affiliates (e.g., through tourism). Indeed, rooted in colonial anthropology, tourism recycles many colonial stereotypes and proliferates them to larger masses. Thus, tourism, both that privately run and that encouraged by the state, functions to normalize and market the social imaginaries of the Andaman and Nicobar Islands in a way that propels the fame of the Indigenous islanders without their consent. In turn, this strategy becomes a way for the Indian state and mainland Indian settlers to establish further their presence and socio-political, -economic, and -cultural control over the islands.

However, the recent uptick in international attention to the Indigenous peoples of the Andaman and Nicobar Islands can perhaps be traced back to the aftermath of the 2004 Indian Ocean tsunami. Although much of South Asia and Southeast Asia directly impacted by the tsunami was devastated, with countless lives lost and properties and resources destroyed, the Indigenous peoples of the Andaman and Nicobar Islands were found unharmed.[39] NBC News in the United States reported that "Stone Age Cultures Survive

Tsunami Waves."[40] Just as the tsunami itself became international news, so too the survival of the Indigenous peoples *in spite of* their apparent lack of technological prowess was noteworthy and became one of the most sensational news items to carry their celebrity into the twenty-first century.

In 2013, an interview with a member of the Jarawa tribe was conducted by Denis Giles, a journalist for the *Andaman Chronicle* and the founder of SEARCH, a human rights organization that works on causes related to Indigenous peoples of the Andaman and Nicobar Islands. During this interview, the impacts of the enforced celebrification through the human safari of the tribe were elaborated by a young Indigenous man named Enmay:

> [Giles]: How do you feel when outsiders photograph you?
> [Enmay]: I don't feel good. I don't like it when they take photos from their vehicles. I snatch the camera and break it. The [non-Indigenous Indians] told us how to break the cameras.[41]

The tourist's camera and the photographs taken without consent can be seen as the microcosm of the celebrification and celebritization of the Indigenous peoples of the Andaman and Nicobar Islands as well as the phenomenon of celebrity in absentia. The concern presented here about being photographed by non-Indigenous Indians is salient and notable. Indeed, the celebrification of the Indigenous peoples of the islands begins with photographs, often blurry, taken by tourists passing through Indigenous territories on the Andaman Trunk Road on buses and in cars. I remember in 2012, during my first visit to the Andaman Islands, that I was on a bus taking me from one area to another through traditional Jarawa territories. Because of the aforementioned laws, visitors and non-Indigenous people of the islands are not allowed to make stops along the Andaman Trunk Road, which traverses Indigenous territories. Nonetheless, when the bus driver saw a Jarawa near the road perhaps thirty metres ahead, maybe a mother breastfeeding her child, he would signal to the passengers her presence, and they would then look out, equipped with their cameras, hoping to get a snapshot of the relatively unclothed Jarawa body. I was told that this was one of the most compelling aspects of the bus journey, to catch sight of an elusive Jarawa person alongside the road. Although more blatant attempts at human safaris might be rarer still, the mystique surrounding the Jarawas, the entitlement to view their bodies, and the othering behind human safaris are palpable every day along the Andaman Trunk Road. The celebrification of the Jarawas, facilitated by tourists and furtive efforts to capture on film what they are denied legally, feeds into the celebritization of them in larger culture as elusive forest beings who refuse clothing, modern technology, and contact with outsiders. The celebritization helps to create interest in tourism on the islands, which in turn brings more visitors to the Andaman Trunk Road, leading to the self-perpetuating cycle of celebrification and celebritization. In both cases, the processes are exploitative, for the Jarawas prefer not to be contacted or made party to the narratives of elusive Indigeneity of the outside world. All of this is possible thanks to the Andaman Trunk Road, a potent device of statecraft that only helps to produce increasing settler presence in the traditional territories of the Indigenous peoples of the Andaman and Nicobar Islands.

Most recently, the Sentinelese of the archipelago's North Sentinel Island, famous for being the most elusive of the Indigenous inhabitants of the archipelago, attracted international attention once again as an American tourist, John Allen Chau, travelled illegally to the island, which he described as "Satan's last stronghold," in order to covert the tribe to Christianity.[42] Chau was killed immediately by spears and arrows as he set foot on the island.[43] In the aftermath, it was discovered that—influenced by the myths and legends surrounding the Sentinelese in the settler imagination—Chau had prepared for years to undertake his illegal voyage to North Sentinel Island.[44] As of late 2018, the Indian government had no plan to go to the island to recover Chau's body,[45] for doing so would violate its own laws against contact with the Sentinelese. Various Christian groups, however, celebrate Chau as a missionary who died for the gospel.[46] Rise on Fire Ministries wrote the following to accompany a video on the incident: "Earlier this week a missionary was killed by the Sentinelese people on a remote island along India. The world's reaction was shocking, but the reaction from many Christians was even more shocking. John did not die for nothing :) The reason for why Father allowed things to go this way is clear! The entire world knows about John's death today, about the unreached Sentinelese people, and thousands are convicted to walk in boldness for the great commission as John did. John's testimony is a message to western Christianity to pick up their cross."[47] The imperial entitlement that Chau and his apologists represent goes back to the origins of settler colonial creations of celebrity in absentia that enabled the destruction of Indigenous legal orders, genocide, and forced conversions in the early days of colonialism in the Americas. In Chau's actions, we see the logical extreme of celebrity in absentia, as echoed by the call "to pick up their cross," in order for the eliminationist process of cultural genocide to begin. Of course, much has been written about depictions of "savagery" in colonial encounters and alliances between Christianity and colonialism, and Chau's actions and fate add yet another case study.

In the next section, I will discuss what postcolonial theorist Gayatri Chakraborty Spivak meant by "strategic essentialism" and how such ideas are used within the practices of celebrification and celebritization to magnify and intensify their effects toward the creation of celebrity in absentia.

Strategic Essentialism and Celebrity in Absentia

In many ways, the presentations of the Andaman and Nicobar Islands—through works of fiction such as *Sabuj Dwiper Raja*, tourism posters, sensationalist human safaris, and missionary interest in the Sentinelese—often make me think of the concept of strategic essentialism.[48] In her work on subalternity and strategic essentialism, Spivak talks about how ethnic groups often marginalized historically use their perceived essential characteristics strategically to campaign for their needs and demands. But when I think of the Andaman and Nicobar Islands, whose essentialist beliefs am I actually using? Certainly not those of the Jarawas. Of course, I am a mainland Indian using images and narratives put forth by other mainland Indian settlers on these islands, propelling a view of Indian state making. This is perhaps not strategic essentialism in the same way that Spivak originally intended but strategic essentialism outside her frame of subalternity. Within that frame, Spivak talks about the difference in power between the colonizer and the colonized but flattens other dynamics implicated when the colonized are complicit in their colonizing and go on, independently, to colonize further and essentialize the identities of others and represent them in such a way. The Andamanese Indigenous subalterns have chosen not to or cannot represent themselves in these larger conversations, and indeed they have not given informed consent to the publication of their stories and photographs across different media. Additionally, as various Dalit, Adivasi, and even non-Indigenous Indian scholars and activists have highlighted and documented numerous times, Indigenous and Dalit peoples of India were not only subjected to European colonization but also millennia of efforts of colonization by, subjugation under, and assimilation into the fold of Hindu supremacist politics.[49] Spivak's framework of strategic essentialism and subalternity is therefore insufficient in fully elucidating the nuances and tensions within Dalit-Adivasi struggles in the context of India as a postcolonial nation-state. Strategic essentialism has been used against the Indigenous peoples of the Andaman and Nicobar Islands by non-Indigenous Indians to cement their claims to Indigenous territories and justify their influence in them.

It might be argued that the Andamanese have repeatedly made use of a form of what Audra Simpson has called "ethnographic refusal,"[50] and settlers and invaders, whether non-Indigenous Indians or foreigners, have failed to heed this boundary. Perhaps this failure also takes form in how the Sentinelese are described in international media and even Indigenous rights organizations such as Survival International as an "uncontacted tribe," implying that nobody has attempted to make contact with them, while erasing the history of their explicit, unambiguous, and active refusal each time that they have had contact with outsiders, thus ascribing a certain passivity to them. The first instance of contact with the Sentinelese that appears in the colonial record occurred in 1867 when survivors of a shipwreck landed on the beach of North Sentinel Island and were attacked with arrows by the islanders.[51] Later, in 1880, British naval officer Maurice Vidal Portman led an armed party into the island to establish contact with the Sentinelese,[52] but he found their settlements empty as the Sentinelese hid in the forested areas from him and his party. Eventually, he was able to capture six individuals on the island—a man and a woman and four children. The adults died shortly after, and the children fell sick, after which they were promptly returned to the island with gifts in another effort to establish contact,[53] which remained unsuccessful. Portman continued in vain to establish further contact with the Sentinelese throughout his tenure as an administrator in the British-ruled Andaman and Nicobar Islands. He also indulged his interest in posing and photographing various Indigenous groups of the islands, with salient colonial sexualization of their bodies,[54] similar to the imagery and language used today to describe the Sentinelese and other Indigenous groups around the world. It is clear that the Sentinelese have had multiple instances of contact with other groups throughout their history and are therefore not "uncontacted"; they have made a deliberate decision not to reciprocate contact. In this light, further problematization of the notion of "uncontacted tribes" is warranted, not only in the case of the Sentinelese but also in general. The implied passivity among Indigenous groups described in such ways erases the history of their sustained and deliberate refusal to engage with outside influences.

Thus, though their celebrity is used to attract attention to the islands, the Indigenous Andamanese, especially the Sentinelese, have little input in the creation of this public attention. These subalterns cannot, or deliberately do not, speak, at least on the terms of colonizers and outsiders, and their essentialism has been hijacked by a series of settler colonial projects for strategic purposes. This one-sided desire to learn more about Indigenous groups in the face of their continued refusal of contact is a core characteristic of colonial versions of celebrity in absentia.

By using the likeness of the Andamanese in their essentialist understanding for the rest of the Indian publics, the Indian state, various actors within India, and the world at large can mobilize interest in and support for their settlements and developments in the Andaman and Nicobar Islands. So, in effect, the Indian state and its apparatuses strategize using commonly held essentialist beliefs about Indigenous peoples of the islands to advance the colonial state-building project, both necessitating and justifying the continued presence and traffic of settlers within the traditional territories of the Indigenous peoples of the islands. According to settler law itself, however, it is forbidden to go into these areas and disrupt the governance, life, and culture of the Indigenous Andamanese.

This peculiar application of what Spivak calls strategic essentialism is central to the processes of celebrification and celebritization discussed above, and it creates a dynamic whereby the more represented the Andaman and Nicobar Islands become in mass media, and the multitude of interpretations that emerge from those representations, the less political power the Indigenous peoples of the islands have over the narratives. This is no different from the cases of celebrity in absentia that I alluded to in the introduction to this chapter: colonizers, as part of their strategy, have always used some form of celebrity in absentia to control the perceptions of Indigenous peoples and the justifications required for their colonization.

Conclusion

In this chapter, I have investigated the tensions between the sensationalized exoticization of Indigenous people and their bodies and the means by which, without their input, their existence and bodies are used to attract attention to the Andaman and Nicobar Islands. The phenomenon by which Indigenous peoples become sensationalized and famous without their sovereign input I have named celebrity in absentia. I have argued that this process of creating celebrity for a community dates back to the early days of Spanish colonization of the Americas and continues today in a variety of forms. Within the Indian context, celebrity in absentia is used in tandem with other strategies to extend governance by the postcolonial state to Indigenous territories. I have also argued that the categorization of groups such as the Sentinelese as "uncontacted tribes" erases their agency and history of deliberate refusal to partake in dialectic exchanges with outsiders and colonizers. In this context, though legal means exist to leave the Tribal Reserve Territory of the Andamanese undisturbed from settler interference, the constant stream of cultural production focused on half-naked bodies and differences in lifestyle between settlers and Indigenous peoples of the islands runs counter to these aims. As a result, the postcolonial state continues to justify its presence in the area.

When considering the tensions between the processes of celebrification and celebritization, it becomes clear who benefits from the ever-increasing fascination with the Indigenous peoples of the Andaman and Nicobar Islands. As with the original cases of celebrity in absentia crafted by European colonial ethnographers and historians, the narratives of the Indigenous peoples of the islands, whether works of adventure fiction such as Sunil Gangopadhyay's *Sabuj Dwiper Raja* or tourism campaigns with images of "exotic" Jarawa bodies, celebrity in absentia is a cyclical phenomenon that feeds into itself and magnifies its effects over the years. Its ultimate impacts are especially troubling considering that the subjects of this unwanted celebrity, tribes such as the Jarawas and Sentinelese, prefer to have limited contact with the non-Indigenous settlers in their territories, and the impacts of celebrity in absentia are always counterproductive to the wishes of the Indigenous peoples of the Andaman and Nicobar Islands and their sovereignty.

From the standpoint of understanding the phenomenon of enforced celebrification and consequent celebritization and celebrity in absentia from the framework of strategic essentialism, as per Spivak, certain power relations within a postcolonial population become apparent. Indigenous subjects of celebrity in absentia are beholden to the postcolonial state (which itself battles with the continued presence of the politics of Hindu supremacy despite its secular constitution), which chooses to represent them in ways suited to its state-building project. As in many multicultural societies, this introduces a tension between the rights of minority groups, such as Indigenous peoples, and the overall aim of the state to exert and legitimize its governance within its borders. In this way, a postcolonial government continues to borrow strategies from its former colonial rulers, using images and narratives to present essentialized portraits of some of its subjects in order to expand control over them and their territories.

In light of the recent rise and century-long history of Hindu nationalism and supremacy, it would be interesting to examine how strategic essentialism and the concept of Indigeneity have also been employed by the Hindu right to position itself as "indigenous" and therefore the rightful guardian of India while marginalizing the actual Indigenous peoples of India and other minority groups. As described with the example of Kakababu in *Swabuj Dwiper Raja*, there is the danger that the colonizer will only change form in the postcolonial nation-state of India—from the British to the upper-caste Hindu, continuing the millennia-long legacy of Hindu subjugation and exploitation of Indigenous peoples.

The phenomenon of celebrity in absentia needs to be studied further, especially in the contexts of postcolonial landscapes and their own purportedly decolonial and anti-colonial initiatives. Even when Indigenous subjects are the sovereign craftspeople of their celebrity or their celebrity personas, their reception and perception are often guided by the same tropes and notions rooted in former or ongoing colonial projects. An increased awareness of these dynamics, and how they interact with the performance of celebrity, might lead to more radical responses in line with more transparent, anti-oppressive, and equitable decolonial and anti-colonial aims, for Indigenous and non-Indigenous subjects of colonialism alike.

NOTES

1 Audra Simpson, "On Ethnographic Refusal: Indigeneity, 'Voice' and Colonial Citizenship," *Junctures* 9 (2007): 67–80.

2 Bartolomé de Las Casas, *The Devastation of the Indies: A Brief Account* (Baltimore, MD: Johns Hopkins University Press, 1992).

3 Ada van Gastel, "Van Der Donck's Description of the Indians: Additions and Corrections," *William and Mary Quarterly* 47, no. 3 (1990): 411–21, https://doi.org/10.2307/2938095(accessed 8 August 2018).

4 D.A. Brading, *The First America: The Spanish Monarchy, Creole Patriots and the Liberal State 1492–1867*, reprint ed. (Cambridge, UK: Cambridge University Press, 1993).

5 Aarefa Johari, "Dalits, Adivasis, Muslims Targeted in at Least Five Incidents since BJP Won the Election," *Scroll.In*, 27 May 2019, https://scroll.in/article/924841/dalits-adivasis-muslims-targeted-in-at-least-five-incidents-since-bjp-won-the-election (accessed 5 March 2020); Sidharth Yadav, "Modi Must See Dalit-Adivasi Unity against CAA: Yogendra Yadav," *Hindu*, 28 January 2020, sec. "Other States," https://www.thehindu.com/news/national/other-states/modi-must-see-dalit-adivasi-unity-against-caa-yogendra-yadav/article30670311.ece (accessed 28 January 2020); Sonia Sarkar, "India's Marginalised Minorities Unite against Hindu Nationalism," *South China Morning Post*, Hong Kong, 23 February 2020, sec. "This Week in Asia," https://www.scmp.com/week-asia/politics/article/3051781/marginalised-under-modi-how-indias-minorities-are-starting-stand (accessed 5 March 2020); Akshay Deshmane, "10 Lakh Adivasis Face Eviction from Their Land: It All Hinges on One SC Order," *HuffPost India*, 3 July 2019, sec. "News," https://www.huffingtonpost.in/entry/modi-govt-tribal-rights-forests-supreme-coure_in_5d1c4b46e4b03d6116443090 (accessed 5 March 2020).

6 Romila Thapar, "They Peddle Myths and Call It History," *New York Times*, 17 May 2019, sec. "Opinion," https://www.nytimes.com/2019/05/17/opinion/india-elections-modi-history.html (accessed 5 March 2020).

7 Government of India, "Constitution of India | National Portal of India," https://www.india.gov.in/my-government/constitution-india (accessed 5 March 2020).

8 Thenmozhi Soundararajan, "Twitter's Caste Problem," *New York Times*, 3 December 2018, sec. "Opinion," https://www.nytimes.com/2018/12/03/opinion/twitter-india-caste-trolls.html (accessed 5 March 2020); Uma Chakravarti, "Conceptualising Brahmanical Patriarchy in Early India: Gender, Caste, Class and State," *Economic and Political Weekly*, 3 April 1993, 579–85; Sonja Thomas, "The Women's Wall in Kerala, India, and Brahmanical Patriarchy," *Feminist Studies* 45, no. 1 (2019): 253–61.

9 David Lalmalsawma, "India Speaks 780 Languages, 220 Lost in Last 50 Years: Survey," *Reuters Blogs*, 7 September 2013, http://blogs.reuters.com/india/2013/09/07/india-speaks-780-languages-220-lost-in-last-50-years-survey/ (accessed 5 March 2020).

10 India Parliament House of the People and India Parliament Lok Sabha, *Lok Sabha Debates*, Lok Sabha Secretariat, 1995.

11 Asoka Kumar Sen, *Indigeneity, Landscape and History: Adivasi Self-Fashioning in India* (New Delhi: Routledge India, 2017); V. Srinivasa Rao, *Adivasi Rights and Exclusion in India* (New York: Routledge, 2018); Nicolas Jaoul, "Beyond Citizenship: Adivasi and Dalit Political Pathways in India," *Focaal* 76 (2016): 3–14.

12 Lantz Fleming Miller, "Rights of Self-Delimiting Peoples: Protecting Those Who Want No Part of Us," *Human Rights Review* 14, no. 1 (2013): 31–51.

13 Philipp Zehmisch, "Between Mini-India and Sonar Bangla: The Memorialisation and Place-Making Practices of East Bengal Hindu Refugees in the Andaman Islands," in *Partition and the Practice of Memory*, ed. Churnjeet Mahn and Anne Murphy (Cham, Switzerland: Springer, 2018), 63–88.

14 Sunita Reddy, "Mega Tourism in Andaman and Nicobar Islands: Some Concerns," *Journal of Human Ecology* 21, no. 3 (2007): 231–39; Govindasamy Agoramoorthy and Chandrakasan Sivaperuman, "Tourism, Tribes and Tribulations in Andaman Islands," *Current Science* 106, no. 2 (2014): 141.

15 Malliya Gounder Palanichamy et al., "Comment on 'Reconstructing the Origin of Andaman Islanders,'" *Science* 311, no. 5760 (2006): 470, https://doi.org/10.1126/science.1120176 (accessed 5 March 2020).

16 Clare Anderson, "Colonization, Kidnap and Confinement in the Andamans Penal Colony, 1771–1864," *Journal of Historical Geography* 37, no. 1 (2011): 68–81, https://doi.org/10.1016/j.jhg.2010.07.001 (accessed 5 March 2020); Clare Anderson, "The Politics of Convict Space: Indian Penal Settlements and the Andaman Islands," in *Isolation: Places and Practices of Exclusion*, ed. Carolyn Strange and Alison Bashford (New York: Routledge, Taylor and Francis, 2003), 40–55.

17 Miller, "Rights of Self-Delimiting Peoples."

18 Jayant Dasgupta, *Japanese in Andaman and Nicobar Islands: Red Sun over Black Water* (New York: Berghahn Books, 2002).

19 Vishvajit Pandya, "Contacts, Images and Imagination: The Impact of a Road in the Jarwa Reserve Forest, Andaman Islands," *Bijdragen Tot de Taal-, Land-En Volkenkunde* 158, no. 4 (2002): 805.

20 Ibid.

21 Sanjukta Das Gupta and Raj Sekhar Basu, *Narratives from the Margins: Aspects of Adivasi History in India* (New Delhi: Primus Books, 2012).

22 C.R. Bijoy, "The Adivasis of India: A History of Discrimination, Conflict, and Resistance," *PUCL Bulletin* 1, no. 1 (2003): 54–61; Amita Baviskar, "Adivasi Encounters with Hindu Nationalism in MP," *Economic and Political Weekly*, 26 November–2 December 2005, 5105–13.

23 Olivier Driessens, "The Celebritization of Society and Culture: Understanding the Structural Dynamics of Celebrity Culture," *International Journal of Cultural Studies* 16, no. 6 (2013): 641–57.

24 Ibid., 645.

25 Chris Rojek, "Celebrity," in *The Wiley-Blackwell Encyclopedia of Consumption and Consumer Studies*, ed. Daniel Thomas Cook and J. Michael Ryan (New York: Wiley-Blackwell, 2015), 1–3.

26 Chris Rojek, *Celebrity* (London: Reaktion Books, 2001), 18.

27 Simpson, "On Ethnographic Refusal."

28 Pandya, "Contacts, Images and Imagination," 809.

29 Sunil Gangopadhyay, *Sabuj Dwiper Raja* (Kalakātā: Ananda Publishers, 2014).

30 Abu Imam, "Sir Alexander Cunningham (1814–1893): The First Phase of Indian Archaeology," *Journal of the Royal Asiatic Society of Great Britain and Ireland* 3–4 (1963): 194–207.

31 Nayanjot Lahiri, "Archaeology and Identity in Colonial India," *Antiquity* 74, no. 285 (2000): 687–92.

32 Press Information Bureau, Ministry of Tribal Affairs, Government of India, "Punishment for Exploitation of Tribals in Andaman and Nicobar Islands," 30 November 2012, https://pib.gov.in/newsite/PrintRelease.aspx?relid=89726 (accessed 5 March 2020).

33 Pandya, "Contacts, Images and Imagination," 809.

34 Ibid.

35 "French Filmmakers Shoot Jarawa Tribe, Booked," *Indian Express*, 25 October 2014, http://indianexpress.com/article/india/india-others/french-filmmakers-shoot-jarawa-tribe-booked/ (accessed 5 March 2020).

36 Oscar Rickett, "An Interview with a Member of a Human Safari Tribe," *Vice*, 18 February 2013, https://www.vice.com/en_au/article/bnykw5/everyone-needs-to-stop-exploiting-the-jarawa-tribe (accessed 5 March 2020).

37 Guido Abbattista, "Humans on Display: Reflecting on National Identity and the Enduring Practice of Living Human Exhibitions," in *Moving Bodies Displaying Nations. National Cultures, Race and Gender in World Expositions. Nineteenth to Twenty-First Century*, ed. Guido Abbattista, 241–71 (Trieste, EUT Edizioni Università di Trieste, 2014), 264.

38 Noel B. Salazar, "Imagineering Otherness: Anthropological Legacies in Contemporary Tourism," *Anthropological Quarterly* 86, no. 3 (2013): 690–92.

39 Subir Bhaumik, "Tsunami Folklore 'Saved Islanders,'" BBC News, 20 January 2005, http://news.bbc.co.uk/2/hi/south_asia/4181855.stm (accessed 5 March 2020).

40 Neelesh Misra, "Stone Age Cultures Survive Tsunami Waves," NBCnews.com, 4 January 2005, http://www.nbcnews.com/id/6786476/ns/world_news-tsunami_a_year_later/t/stone-age-cultures-survive-tsunami-waves/ (accessed 5 March 2020).

41 Rickett, "An Interview with a Member of a Human Safari Tribe."

42 Ajay Saini, "The Lesson from This Missionary's Death? Leave the Sentinelese Alone," *Guardian*, 27 November 2018, sec. "Opinion," https://www.theguardian.com/commentisfree/2018/nov/27/missionary-death-sentinelese-andaman-islands (accessed 5 March 2020).

43 Annie Gowen, "'He Lost His Mind': Slain Missionary John Allen Chau Planned for Years to Convert Remote Tribe," *Washington Post*, 27 November 2018, https://www.washingtonpost.com/national/he-lost-his-mind-slain-missionary-john-allen-chau-planned-for-years-to-convert-remote-tribe/2018/11/27/eb13d7ad-4685-4748-951b-790d671f655d_story.html (accessed 5 March 2020).

44 Ibid.

45 Michael Safi and Denis Giles, "India Has No Plans to Recover Body of US Missionary Killed by Tribe," *Guardian*, 28 November 2018, sec. "World News," https://www.theguardian.com/world/2018/nov/28/india-body-john-allen-chau-missionary-killed-by-sentinelese-tribe (accessed 5 March 2020).

46 Rise on Fire, *A Missionary Dies for the Gospel—John Allen Chau*, 2018, https://www.youtube.com/watch?v=DMhCPfA4RTk (accessed 5 March 2020).

47 Ibid.

48 Kristina Wolff, "Strategic Essentialism," in *The Blackwell Encyclopedia of Sociology* (Malden, MA: John Wiley and Sons, 2007), https://doi.org/10.1002/9781405165518.wbeoss268 (accessed 5 March 2020).

49 Kancha Ilaiah, *Post-Hindu India: A Discourse in Dalit-Bahujan, Socio-Spiritual and Scientific Revolution* (Thousand Oaks, CA: SAGE, 2009); Pradnya Waghule, "Reading Caste in Holi: The

Burning of Holika, a Bahujan Woman," *Feminism in India*, 12 March 2017, https://feminisminindia.com/2017/03/13/caste-holi-burning-holika-bahujan/ (accessed 5 March 2020); Equality Labs, "Why Do We Say No to Holi? A Guide to Challenge Casteism," *Medium.com* (blog), 2 March 2020, https://medium.com/@EqualityLabs/why-do-we-say-no-to-holi-a-guide-to-challenge-casteism-ad592d0735cb (accessed 5 March 2020).

50 Simpson, "On Ethnographic Refusal."

51 Adam Goodheart, "The Last Island of the Savages," *American Scholar* 69, no. 4 (2000): 13–44.

52 Satadru Sen, "Savage Bodies, Civilized Pleasures: MV Portman and the Andamanese," *American Ethnologist* 36, no. 2 (2009): 364–79.

53 Goodheart, "The Last Island of the Savages."

54 Sen, "Savage Bodies, Civilized Pleasures."

CHAPTER 9

Marvin Rainwater and "The Pale Faced Indian": How Cover Songs Appropriated a Story of Cultural Appropriation

Christina Giacona

Cherokee descendant and singer-songwriter John Loudermilk, though not a household name, is a legend in Nashville. His 1959 composition "The Pale Faced Indian," originally recorded by country and western musician Marvin Rainwater, is a story about the plight of the Cherokee and the effects of assimilation. It was not until 1968, when English pop singer Don Fardon recorded the cover and gave "The Pale Faced Indian" a new title—"(The Lament of the Cherokee Reservation Indian) Indian Reservation"—that the song gained in popularity and more artists started covering it. Interestingly, each rendition of the song not only changed the arrangement but also introduced changes to the lyrics and thus the meaning. Fardon's cover of the song, however, takes the focus on post-assimilation contemporary Native identity found in "The Pale Faced Indian" and changes it to a lament for an extinct and lost people, and this trend continued with each version. Through musical and lyrical analysis, I will explore the history of "The Pale Faced Indian" and how voice appropriation, idealized sympathy, the prevalence of misappropriation in the artistic mainstream of popular music, and the revolutionary actions of artistic and cultural reappropriation affected the narrative, narrators, and meaning of Loudermilk's composition.

This chapter revolves around the idea of subject appropriation and how it has applied to Indigenous peoples in the realm of popular music. James Young and Susan Haley indicate that "subject appropriation occurs when members of one culture (call them outsiders for the sake of brevity) represent members of other cultures (insiders for the sake of convenience) or aspects of insiders' culture. (Subject appropriation has sometimes been called voice appropriation, particularly when outsiders represent the lives of insiders in the first person)."[1] Young and Haley also recognize the difficulty in generalizing subject appropriation as morally good or bad without discussing individual cases. Using this case-by-case approach, many previously mentioned acts of subject or voice appropriation mentioned in this essay fall squarely into the morally suspect realm, especially those propagated by and resulting in celebrity. I call this specific kind of subject or voice appropriation cultural misappropriation, defined as "the intentional theft of tangible or nontangible cultural commodities by an outsider with the intent to be used for economic gain or to intentionally create a stereotype."[2] Blackface, Hollywood "Injuns," cowboys and Indians, and the plethora of "Indian giver" songs are all obvious examples of cultural misappropriation that claim authenticity through the propagation of negative racial stereotypes.

In *Playing Indian*, Philip Deloria highlights America's appetite for Native voice appropriation by drawing attention to the history of "playing Indian" that the counterculture movement drew on: "Whenever white Americans have confronted crises of identity, some of them have inevitably turned to Indians. . . . It should come as no surprise that the young men and women of the 1960s and 1970s . . . followed their cultural ancestors in playing Indian to find reassuring identities in a world seemingly out of control."[3]

It is important to understand from Deloria that playing Indian has remained an element of American culture from the beginning of colonization. The first displays of American Indians at the World's Fair in 1851 sparked an even greater entertainment-driven Western fascination with American Indian and Aboriginal culture that continued in radio stories, dime novels, classical and popular music, stage performances, fashion, and cinema. Our infatuation with recreating and staging Western contact and expansion in the "New World" has contributed to a worldwide epidemic of playing Indian. On playgrounds, children mock-kill each other as "Cowboys and Indians," at Halloween "Indian warrior" and "sexy Indian" costumes are ubiquitous, in arenas sports teams use "Indian" mascots, elementary schools reimagine and re-enact the "first Thanksgiving," and concertgoers wear feathers, headdresses, and "Indian" face paint. Others have tried to capture the "ways" of Indigenous peoples by creating games such as finding your "Indian" spirit guide, recognizing your "Indian" name, and finding your "Indian" tribe. In fact, playing Indian has been done so often that it can practically be considered an integral part of American culture, and we do not have to look far back to see where this pastime came from.

This fascination with Indigenous culture and playing Indian, despite its laudatory contemporary goal of raising awareness and empathy for Native peoples, has actually furthered inauthentic "Indianism." Rather than being taught about different Indigenous nations and understanding their different cultures, children are exposed to music and role-playing that promote the stereotyped notion of a singular Native identity. With centuries of misinformation and the perpetualization of Native stereotyping and homogenization, the world has become inundated with renderings of inauthentic Native tropes.

Most commonly seen representations of Indigenous peoples in American media are actually derived from stereotypes and "performed" by whites. Even a cursory glance at Native-themed musical performances in the past century reveals a history of Western performance rife with what I call "singing Redface." Singing Redface artists have promoted racial slurs, mock Indian languages, and inauthentic Native music. To "become Native," artists literally and figuratively dress up as "Indians" in live performances, music videos, album covers, and song lyrics.

Around the turn of the twentieth century, minstrelsy performances employed these practices of "acting" as a different race for entertainment, but they created a situation in which a different ethnicity affected the cultural traits of the culture that they were emulating in a sort of recursive cultural feedback loop. Blackface minstrelsy is often tied directly to music and dance, but Blackface itself is the act of "becoming Black" by "acting" and "looking" Black. Like Blackface, "Redface" is a general term associated with actions taken by a non-Native person in order to be perceived as Native. In this chapter, I will use the archetypes formed through Blackface minstrelsy performance studies as a model for better understanding singing Redface as a creation that propagates inauthentic cultural understanding.

Following the tradition of minstrelsy and vaudeville shows, Buffalo Bill's Wild West shows introduced some of the first "Indian" dances seen by the Western world. Whites were intrigued by Native American culture, but traditional Native American dancing did not necessarily make for a good show. To meet the demands of the audience, Native performers started to create a more energetic style of dancing while promoting it as a traditional Native American dance. These "Show Indians" re-enacted battles, raided stagecoaches, showcased their equestrian and archery skills, and performed stylized dances. In 1894, footage was taken of Native American dances, labelled Buffalo and Ghost Dances. According to the Edison film historian Charles Musser, these images were actually of Buffalo Bill's Wild West show Indians[4]—they were not actual depictions of Native American dances but staged versions that catered to white Americans. These were and frequently still are presented as and believed to be traditional Native American dances.

The shift from minstrel shows employing white artists who pretended to be Black before the Civil War to minstrel and Wild West shows employing African American and Native American artists who pretended to be "Black" and "Indian" stereotypes is part of a complex change in how agency and race were culturally tied to music in the United States. This complex history is explored by Karl Hagstrom Miller in *Segregating Sound: Inventing Folk and Pop Music in the Age of Jim Crow*, in which he describes the process by which "a variety of people—scholars and artists, industrialists and consumers—came to compartmentalize southern music according to race."[5] Hagstrom Miller posits that in the 1880s and 1890s the combination of segregation laws, academic folklorists in search of Southern music untainted by popular American culture and explained by racial and cultural traditions, and the record industry's view of the South as both an object of northern fantasy and a potential customer base coalesced into a new "correlation between racialized music and racialized bodies: black people performed black music and white people performed white music."[6] Before this philosophical change in how musical agency was viewed, and showcased by minstrel shows, "black and white performers regularly *employed* racialized sounds."[7] After this philosophical change, and showcased by the Wild West shows and African American–performed minstrel shows, "most listeners expected artists to *embody* [the racialized sounds]."[8] However, both the aesthetic employment and the aesthetic embodiment of racialized sounds have continued in popular

American music through the twentieth century and into the twenty-first century. According to Hagstrom Miller, these two ideals—the mutability of what he terms minstrel authenticity and the permanence of non-commercial, folkloric authenticity—formed the push/pull of racialized musical voice appropriation so important in understanding American popular music of the twentieth century.

Yet, though examples of voice appropriation that misrepresent Indigenous peoples in a negative manner are easy to lambaste, the problems present in the counterculture movement's voice appropriation of Indigenous identities were hidden beneath an overly sympathetic tone. Compared with earlier instances of singing Redface, these suddenly sympathetic songs come across as a quantum leap forward in race relations. However, as Young and Haley state, "it is conceivable that even sympathetic portrayals of a minority culture could be harmful.... Such works can convey and perpetuate stereotypes of the noble savage that are, in the long run, of no benefit to Indigenous peoples."[9] It is in songs that feature "idealized sympathy," or sympathy for an imaginary Indigenous caricature, that the issues of voice appropriation and misrepresentation become clearly visible.

Voice appropriation of this type occurs when a non-Native American artist or author seemingly speaks for or as a Native American. This kind of idealized, sympathetic voice appropriation in search of some kind of Native spirituality is defined by Lenore Keeshig-Tobias in her famous 1990 *Globe and Mail* article "Stop Stealing Native Stories" as "mostly escapist, and people... would rather look to an ideal native living in never-never land than confront the reality of what being native means in Canadian society."[10]

Here I will analyze popular songs that are examples of voice appropriation: one that is transformed from an empathetic but strangely caricatured example of singing Redface to an example of idealized sympathy and finally to a reappropriated, pan-Indian anthem and another that attempts both to empathize with and to humanize a specific character study. The first song is best known as "Indian Reservation (The Lament of the Cherokee Reservation Indian)" and was made famous by Paul Revere and The Raiders. Loudermilk's "Indian Reservation" is often viewed as an anthemic song expressing Cherokee pride, but the first rendition by Marvin Rainwater under the title "The Pale Faced Indian" showcases a different message. The second song that I analyze is the empathetic single "The Ballad of Ira Hayes," written by folk singer Peter La Farge and recorded and promoted by Native-rights activist Johnny Cash.

The Transformation of "The Pale Faced Indian" to "Indian Reservation (The Lament of the Cherokee Reservation Indian)"

Loudermilk has had a very successful career in the music industry, and throughout the years his songs have been recorded by musicians such as Eddie Cochran, the Everly Brothers, Chet Atkins, Linda Ronstadt, Marianne Faithful, Jewel, and Johnny Cash.[11] His 1959 composition "The Pale Faced Indian," originally recorded by Marvin Rainwater, was unique for mainstream media at the time because the song told the story of the Cherokee and the effects of assimilation not only for the Cherokee but also for Indigenous peoples in the United States and Canada. Unlike other songs at the time, the storyline depicted its Native subjects not as "braves" or "warriors" but as a nation that had lost its identity through forced assimilation. Although the lyrics project a strong message, the Native-inspired accompaniment most likely sounds comical to contemporary listeners. Rainwater's audiences were often confused by his persona, stage presence, and songwriting because Rainwater was an Indian who, much like African American minstrel troupes in the aftermath of the Civil War, seemed to be appropriating the white man's racist stereotype of his people and using it to gain celebrity.

As a performer, Rainwater used his Cherokee heritage to set himself apart from other recording artists while trying to break into the country scene during the 1950s. His full-regalia stage costume and performance of songs such as "Half-Breed" reminded audiences of the Native whom they had seen in Hollywood films—a disconnect from the white country-rockabilly singer whom they were expecting on stage.[12] His unique appearance allowed Rainwater to become one of the first successful crossover artists, piquing the interest of rock 'n' roll audiences who sympathized with the plight of Indigenous peoples in addition to fans of his country-rockabilly songwriting style. "The Pale Faced Indian" did not garner the same success as Rainwater's other songs until it was covered in 1968 by the English pop singer Don Fardon, who gave it a new title: "(The Lament of the Cherokee Reservation Indian) Indian Reservation." His recording sold more than a million copies. Eager to ride the momentum of "Indian Reservation," Fardon quickly recorded other Native-themed songs, including "Running Bear (Loves Little White Dove)," "Cheyene," and "Follow Your Drum." Not only did his cover popularize the song, but also the changes that he made in his version of "Indian Reservation" altered the meaning of the song and influenced all future renditions of it.

In 1971, the American rock band Paul Revere and The Raiders, inspired by Fardon's cover, used similar orchestration to create their own interpretation of Loudermilk's song. Although The Raiders replaced the horn section with an electric keyboard, their version keeps the same anthemic rock feel of Fardon's rendition. Their single, "Indian Reservation (The Lament of the Cherokee Reservation Indian)," reached top spot on the American charts and eventually became a certified platinum record. The American civil rights movement and unrest over the Vietnam War laid the foundation for the single to appeal to a suddenly empathetic public.

Interestingly, each rendition of the song changed not only the arrangement but also the lyrics. Rainwater's original version[13] told the story of the Cherokee and their dealings with broken treaties, the Trail of Tears, and assimilation. Rainwater appropriated Redface in order to gain agency and begin to control the message being relayed by Native characters on stage. He avoided popular and clichéd one-dimensional characters such as the "chief" or "noble brave." Although Rainwater recorded "The Pale Faced Indian" using traditional Redface musical stylings, the lyrics were about actual Cherokee cultural elements. His version was about the struggles of a people forced to "become white." Although the Cherokee Nation abided by the rules of assimilation, in the song Rainwater defiantly states that he will remain "a red man till I die." Rather than relying on generic Redface stereotypes, Rainwater's version includes references to specific Cherokee cultural practices. In the line "they put our papoose in a crib / and took the buckskin from our rib," Rainwater references how Cherokee children, prior to assimilation, slept and were carried in cradleboards. The line "and they took away our native tongue / and taught their English to our young," highlights the banning of Native cultural practices when Native children were forced to attend boarding schools where they were taught only English and "American" ways of life. Regardless of the seemingly stereotypical and heavy-handed nature of Rainwater's music, dress, and mannerisms, "The Pale Faced Indian" is a song about Cherokee pride and identity in contemporary America.

Fardon's cover of the song, however, takes the focus on post-assimilation contemporary Native identity in "The Pale Faced Indian" and changes it to a lament for an extinct and lost people. In Rainwater's original rendition, the Cherokee Nation has been moved, its language and cultural heritage have been stolen, and its people are now dressed in the apparel of the white man, yet Rainwater still proudly states that his heart and soul remain Cherokee. His statement that he will remain a "red man" until he dies emphasizes the idea that, though the Cherokee Nation as an entity might have been changed forever, the Cherokee people continue to live within white society. The added chorus in Fardon's cover,[14] however, implies the opposite: "Cherokee people / Cherokee tribe / So proud you lived / So proud you died." The later line "Cherokee Injun will return" further implies that both the Cherokee Nation and the Cherokee people are dead. The use of past tense and inclusion of the term "Cherokee people" actually serve to shift the song's focus completely from contemporary Native identity and turn it into a fantasy-drama focused on the mythical reimagining of the Cherokee Nation as a dead race of "noble savages" who will return only when "the world has learned" and become worthy.

In his performance, Fardon, a white artist, also confusingly becomes both the "Indian" whom he sings about and the sympathetic "white" who mourns the Indian's demise. Even though Fardon keeps the first-person narrative of the lyrics the same in the verses, he creates a distinction between "us whites" and "you Indians" in the chorus "Cherokee people / Cherokee tribe / So proud you lived / So proud you died." Obviously influenced by the tropes of other singing Redface songs, Fardon changes his speech pattern near the end of the song to become more "Indian." He sings the line "big built houses by the score / won't need tipis anymore" only once, obviously drawing on "Tonto speak" or "Hollywood Injun English." Instead of saying "*we built big* houses by the score / *so we* won't need *our* tipis anymore," the song turns to caricature that is almost impossible to imagine as anything but a white person impersonating an Indian. In addition to the other changes, Fardon even changes the last line of the song to "Cherokee *Injun*" rather than "Cherokee *Indian*" or Cherokee *Nation*" in keeping with the stylized speech patterns of what Barbra Meek termed "Hollywood Injun English" in "And the Injun Goes 'How!' Representations of American Indian English in White Public Space."[15]

Rainwater's and Fardon's versions of the same song provide an incredible example of the difference between a Native performer and a white performer singing Redface. Every element that specifically references Cherokee culture is removed in Fardon's rendition and replaced with stereotypes. The line "they put our papoose in a crib / and took the buckskin from our rib," is completely removed. The line "and the old tipi we loved so / they're using now just for a show," which references both Rainwater's longing for the tipi and the fact that Indians are used for display in white culture, is replaced with the "Tonto speak" of "big built houses by the score / won't need tipis anymore." The lyric "they took away our way of life, our tomahawk, and the hunting knife" is replaced with "they took away our way of life—tomahawk and the bow and knife," adding the reference to a bow (necessary for any recognizable Indian stereotype) and removing the "our" before "tomahawk." This is a subtle change, but in Fardon's version the Indian way of life *is* the tomahawk, bow, and knife, whereas in Rainwater's original version the Indian way of life is separate and stolen in addition to the tomahawk and knife. The changes in the lyrics simplify Native culture to one of savagery and primitivism.

The interesting thing is that these changes were obviously not part of a calculated attempt to create a racist caricature but likely a series of small and probably thoughtless edits; they showcase exactly how Indigenous culture is trimmed and repackaged into the racist stereotypes that we so often see and hear in music. Those responsible for the edits were probably trying to make the song more marketable and to remove any lyrics that seemed to be confusing or off message. Seemingly small changes, such as inclusion of the phrase "Cherokee Injun will return" and removal of the image of the Indian wearing a white man's tie, drastically change the story being told. The best example of this is removal of the words *and* and *away* from the first stanza. Rainwater's original version, "they took away the whole Cherokee Nation / and put us on this reservation," implies that the entire Cherokee Nation was destroyed and that the remnants of its people were later placed on a reservation. In Fardon's rendition, "they took the whole Cherokee Nation / put us on this reservation," emphasis on the destruction of a society has disappeared and been replaced merely with relocation. These changes do not seem to be dramatic in isolation, but together they showcase how ingrained Native stereotypes have been in white performances of singing Redface.

The version by Paul Revere and The Raiders[16] is based on Fardon's cover, but it does not fall prey to the same stereotyped "Indian" image featured in Fardon's changes. Paul Revere and The Raiders still sing the lyrics in the first person and keep the added "Cherokee people" chorus but change the lyrics slightly. Instead of saying "Cherokee people / Cherokee tribe / So proud *you lived* / So proud *you died*," the chorus states "Cherokee people / Cherokee tribe / So proud *to live* / So proud *to die*" (emphasis added). This simple twist changes the spirit of the song to match Rainwater's version better. Influenced by Fardon's cover and retitling of the song, "Indian Reservation" by Paul Revere and The Raiders is a sympathetic lament rather than an empathetic story. This is highlighted near the end of the song when the band eliminates nearly all accompanimental musical lines and draws attention to the sympathetically sung "but maybe someday when they've learned." The rock band sound is replaced with sad-sounding strings; the song then picks up in feel, culminating with the line "the Cherokee Nation will return."

Although changes to the lyrics and music suggest that Paul Revere and The Raiders intended to use their cover of the song to show empathy for Indigenous peoples, their album cover depicts much the same message as Fardon's. The cover features a grassy landscape at sunset with a cross, covered in hanging feathers; the cross is meant as a metaphor for a tombstone. Although there are no obvious features that identify the scene as a cemetery, the cross suggests this meaning, thus referencing the Cherokee Nation as extinct.

Interestingly, what the band did acts as a great metaphor for the insidious nature of internalized racist stereotypes. Even though the majority of their changes to the lyrics of "Indian Reservation" make them less racist (taking out "Tonto speak" and the second-person narrative, replacing "Injun" with "Nation," etc.), the elements that made the song specific to the Cherokee Nation and drew attention to the severity of the Indigenous genocide remain missing in the transition from Rainwater's version, highlighting the difference between *empathy* and *idealized sympathy*. In the case of Paul Revere and The Raiders, creating a sympathetic lament to the Cherokee Nation through the use of Fardon's stereotyped revision of an earlier empathetic song by Loudermilk still retains elements of racist structure. Despite their best intentions, the version of the song by Paul Revere and The Raiders still assumes that the Cherokee Nation is only to be found on the reservation, emphasizes Native savagery, states that Cherokees are only "part" Indian deep inside, and still misses out on the specific elements of Cherokee culture taken out by Fardon.

Don Fardon and Paul Revere and The Raiders were not the only groups to cover Marvin Rainwater under the title of "Indian Reservation (The Lament of the Cherokee Reservation Indian)" or "Indian Reservation." The English punk band 999 and the Canadian First Nations group Billy ThunderKloud and the Chieftones each recorded a version. The success of Paul Revere and The Raiders spread the influence of this song past English-speaking borders, showcased by Slovenian industrial, dark wave band Laibach's version in 1994 titled "National Reservation," which appeared on their album *NATO*. By changing "Cherokee Nation" to "Eastern Nation," Laibach was able to use an understood Western metaphor about the plight of Indigenous peoples and compare it with their own hardships in Slovenia. The chorus of "Indian Reservation" even makes an appearance in Tim McGraw's 1994 song "Indian Outlaw" right before the outro.

In 1979, after representing Germany in the Eurovision Song Contest, the German space disco group Orlando Riva Sound released "Indian Reservation," which became their biggest hit. To help promote the single, they made a video similar to a music video that included their dancer-singer Sophia Reaney dressed in a shimmery bikini, mukluk-styled boots, and a headdress. Throughout the majority of the video, she dances what is essentially a strip tease until midway through the song, when she loosely emulates a Hollywood-style Native dance and then mimics using a bow and arrow to late 1970s synthesized laser sounds while the rest of the band members form a drum circle. As in the version by Paul Revere and The Raiders, the song ends with a sorrowful lament that builds in intensity while footage of a cemetery is shown in the background. Orlando Riva Sound also essentially mourns the Cherokee Nation by propagating the dangerous myth that it is extinct.[17]

These covers, and the cultural voices that they provided, allowed Oglala Lakota actor, musician, and activist Buddy Red Bow to release his own cover titled "Indian Reservation" on his first self-titled album. This 1980s country-inspired version took the power of Fardon's chorus and used its theme as an anthem for all Indigenous peoples. Instead of a song of remembrance of the Cherokee Nation, Red Bow's cover draws attention to the similarities of the struggles faced by all Native nations. In the song, the Trail of

Tears, the removal of the Cherokee, Choctaw, Chickasaw, Seminole, and Muscogee-Creek Nations to Indian Territory, becomes a metaphor for and a remembrance of how westward expansion affected all Native nations. Red Bow takes Fardon's removal of all specifics of Cherokee culture and turns it into a positive, for the stereotypical nature of his song allows it to be an anthem for any Native person who has experienced Western oppression.

Red Bow bases his lyrics on the version by Paul Revere and The Raiders; his main alteration is in the chorus, where he refers to a different nation with each rendition. The first time he sings "Cherokee people, Cherokee tribe," but the second time he changes the lyrics to "Lakota people, Lakota tribe."[18] To increase the energy of the message and music, the chorus is repeated five times, with each repetition invoking a new nation's name. To unite the message, the last chorus is sung with the lyrics "Indian people, Indian tribe." The stereotypical nature of the song, because of its reference only to pan-Indian attributes and its avoidance of lyrics specific to the experiences of the Cherokee Nation, becomes its strength as an anthem for pan-Indian unity.

It is an interesting historical arc for this song—from empathetic to sympathetic to anthemic. Although most versions of the song still do not deal with Indigenous peoples in a contemporary tone, all of them—from Marvin Rainwater and Buddy Red Bow to Don Fardon and Paul Revere and The Raiders and even to Orlando Riva Sound—were important in bringing Indigenous issues to the forefront. Rainwater's is by far the most Redface version of the song (with its stylized Native vocables and chants), but it also has by far the most culturally specific information and Native agency of any of the versions. Fardon's, though perhaps the most reprehensible, introduced the chorus that allowed the song to become a hit and brought it to a wider audience. Paul Revere and The Raiders, though hopelessly sentimental about a misunderstood fantasy of the Cherokee Nation, essentially made Fardon's somewhat racist rendition into a truly sympathetic work. And Orlando Riva Sound, despite its almost satirical on-point depiction of Native "enthusiasts," helped to bring Cherokee issues to the forefront on an international stage. Finally, Red Bow's cover, though leaving the stereotypical and generic nature of the "Indian Nation" present in the lyrics alone, used the stereotypical nature of the song as its strength to create an anthem for all oppressed Native peoples.

Johnny Cash and the Impact of Bitter Tears

After the success of his song "I Walk the Line," Johnny Cash believed that his 1964 protest album *Bitter Tears: Ballads of the American Indian* would have similar success.[19] The single "The Ballad of Ira Hayes," written by Native folk singer Peter La Farge, began its life with poor promotion, a lack of radio play, and little press. Cash, angry at the reception of *Bitter Tears*, blamed both radio DJs who declined to play the work and Columbia for not promoting the record strongly enough. However, as Antonino D'Ambrosio wrote, "controversy arose because La Farge's songs didn't whitewash history. Cash wanted to tell the 'Indians' side of the story' and present the 'Indians' viewpoint.'"[20] Cash believed that Columbia's lacklustre promotion of his 1963 single "Busted" allowed Ray Charles's cover of the song to become a top-ten hit just a few months later. Worried about the place of his newest album, Cash was determined not to let Columbia overlook "The Ballad of Ira Hayes."[21]

With the help of his manager, Saul Israel Holiff, Johnny Cash pressed Columbia for information on the lack of radio promotion and spin for "Ira Hayes." The promotional staff at Columbia told Cash that the song was too long for programming, claiming that most DJs preferred songs between two and three minutes long, whereas "Ira Hayes" is a little over four minutes long. However, it was the content of the song, based on the life of Ira Hayes, that was the root of the problem. A character piece about a Pima Indian who suffered from post-traumatic stress disorder while being paraded around as an American hero for raising the American flag on Iwo Jima, the song ends with its young hero becoming an alcoholic and dying at the young age of thirty-two. Country music DJ Hugh Cherry, who wrote the liner notes for *Bitter Tears*, said that the Columbia promotional staff were "gutless" and "missing in action."[22] As he noted, "they found a lot of resentment from country DJs over the subject matter; they feared their conservative listeners would tune out, so they buried the record, and Columbia just rolled over. They could have pressured them in all sorts of ways, but ultimately they decided against it because they didn't want to alienate the program directors."[23]

Determined to have "Ira Hayes" heard, Cash himself contacted the radio promotion company Great Western Associates to resend the single with personally signed promotional packets that included a picture of the raising of the American flag on Iwo Jima. In the 22 August 1964 issue of *Billboard* magazine, Cash took out a full-page ad criticizing DJs for shying away from the record's message in the light of current events related to Indigenous rights by stating that "'The Ballad of Ira Hayes' is strong medicine, so is Rochester—Harlem, Birmingham, Vietnam."[24] "Ira Hayes" eventually rose to number three in the *Billboard* charts, but *Bitter Tears* as a whole was given only a one-sentence mention, and Cash's own label ran an ad in the same *Billboard* issue without even mentioning the album. Columbia decided to focus on Cash's cover of Bob Dylan's "It Ain't Me, Babe."[25] By the end of the year, after alienating DJs and bruising egos in Nashville, *Bitter Tears* had only mediocre success before the album withered away to obscurity.

Bitter Tears was not just another protest folk album or another white record focused on playing Indian. It has an authenticity and a humanizing approach to Native protest that tie it closely to authentic Native culture's struggle to find a hold in the American consciousness. The eight-song concept album contained only "Indian protest songs," using five songs written by La Farge. Cash "insisted that he was a descendant of the Cherokee (and sometimes in a drug haze even claimed to be 'full-blood')."[26] However, he knew that having Native blood could not be enough to understand the hardships that Indigenous peoples had endured for centuries.[27] Cash empathized with the plight of Indigenous peoples, and he knew that his frustration at their mistreatment, paired with La Farge's music, would make a powerful album.

La Farge, listed in *The Encyclopedia of Native Music: More than a Century of Recordings from Wax Cylinder to the Internet* as Narragansett, grew up with an understanding of Native culture and politics partly because of his father, Oliver La Farge. An anthropologist and Pulitzer Prize–winning author, Oliver spent most of his adult life as an advocate for Indigenous rights, writing both fictional and non-fictional stories invoking Indigenous cultures. After returning home from fighting in Korea in the U.S. Navy, Peter became immersed in the Greenwich Village folk scene, often joining the stage with Bob Dylan, Pete Seeger, and Dave Van Ronk. Peter made a lasting impression on Cash; La Farge's music had a powerful message, and Cash was in the right place in his career to act as an influential mouthpiece for and proponent of change.[28]

Cash did exactly what he had set out to do: he recorded a folk Native-themed protest album that empathized with the past while allowing for the idea of a better future. Although *Bitter Tears* expressed Cash's grief at and unhappiness with the mistreatment of Native Americans, the songs themselves are narrative and sentimental ballads. *Bitter Tears* was one of a kind: Cash successfully recorded a popular, westernized album about Native Americans that did not stereotype them, employed songs by a Native artist, and attempted to empathize with them through the narration of historical and personal events. In "Re-Appropriating Cultural Appropriation," Kwame Dawes defines the difference between empathy and misappropriation exposed by the two examples in his essay. He states that, "when cultural appropriation is counteracted by the qualities of respect, sensitivity and equal opportunity, the result is work that is wonderfully developed and filled with the richness of cultural interaction and dialogue. It is the difference between stealing and getting permission to take, borrow, or share."[29]

The first song on the album, written by Cash and La Farge, "As Long as the Grass Shall Grow," speaks of broken treaties and the mistreatment of the Seneca Nation and how the same message holds true for all Native nations. Shattered promises, forced removals, and massacres were not isolated instances but expected parts of the all-too-familiar pattern of how Western nations chose to interact with Indigenous nations. "Apache Tears," the song inspired by the gift of an obsidian jewel given to Cash by Nancy Hayes, Ira Hayes's mother, is one of two songs on the album written solely by Cash.[30] Although the majority of the songs are based on historical events, "Apache Tears" is based on the myth that obsidian jewels were formed from the tears of Apaches who mourned for their murdered families. Yet the song also draws attention to the reality of the slaughtered Mescalero Apaches, another story little known to a white audience. *Bitter Tears* also includes La Farge's "Drums," a salute to Indigenous culture; "Custer," about how American history books claim that George Armstrong Custer is a hero despite his role in murdering both Sioux and Cheyenne at the Battle of the Little Bighorn; and "White Girl," about how prejudice against Native Americans and Anglos prevented a relationship from developing.[31]

The civil rights movement was a time of great change, but Indigenous protests were not readily featured on TV and in newspapers. Cash's approach to his album was not to sympathize with a "dying race" but to empathize with and draw attention to contemporary Indigenous issues. Yet it took decades of audience demand for the album, ignored or forgotten by many, to be rereleased by Sony Music in 2010. Although its songs are not readily known by white America, *Bitter Tears* has resonated strongly with many Indigenous peoples. Native activist Dennis Banks said that, "to me, Cash's album is one of the earliest and most significant statements on behalf of Native people and our issues."[32] In 2009, Native folk artists Joanne Shenandoah and Michael Bucher recorded the album *Bitter Tears—Sacred Ground*. In a promotional video recorded by Hondo Mesa Records, they state that they grew up listening to the songs on *Bitter Tears* along with millions of fellow Native Americans.[33] Their thirteen-song album honours the work of Johnny Cash, Peter La Farge, and Floyd Red Crow Westerman, who has also honoured Cash's work in his album *A Tribute to Johnny Cash*. The powerful songs on *Bitter Tears* have created their own legacy throughout Indian Country. *Bitter Tears—Sacred Ground* was recorded to honour music and musicians but also to continue that legacy and bring those songs to the next generation.

Fifty years after the release of Cash's *Bitter Tears*, Sony Music Masterworks released *Look Again to the Wind: Johnny Cash's* Bitter Tears *Revisited*. Famous country, Americana, and folk stars such as Kris Kristofferson, Steve Earle, Milk Carton Kids, Gillian Welch, David Rawlings, Nancy Blake, Norman Blake, Rhiannon Giddens, Emmylou Harris, and Bill Miller gathered to revisit these important songs. There is no doubt that this album tribute was meant to be an altruistic attempt to draw attention to Cash's original vision, but the fact that Miller is the only Native artist featured on the album reveals a troubling continuation of white sympathy at the expense of Native agency. Sony revealed that, in an act similar to the reinterpretation of "Indian Reservation" by Paul Revere and The Raiders, white sympathy continues the idea of mute and disempowered Native peoples who must be protected rather than becoming vibrant members of a contemporary society with the ability to speak for themselves and be heard. Although it is important for white artists with cultural clout to continue to advocate for Native interests, it is even more important that Native artists be given platforms on which they can speak for themselves.

Artists today are taking the hard-won cultural agency given to them by the work of Native artists such as Shenandoah and Bucher, Red Bow, La Farge, and Loudermilk and beginning to shape a new Native voice in the twenty-first century. Native musicians are also using their music to replace singing Redface tropes and to reinvent their image. The path forged by Native artists such as Buffy Sainte-Marie, XIT, Tom Bee, Keith Secola, Russell Means, Rita Coolidge, Robbie Robertson, Ulali, Pura Fé, John Trudell, Floyd Westerman, Joanne Shenandoah, Litefoot, and Blackfire has created a space for contemporary Indigenous musicians. Idle No More, an Indigenous sovereignty and environmental movement that began in Canada and "calls on all people to join in a peaceful revolution to honour Indigenous sovereignty and to protect the land & water & sky,"[34] has released *Idle No More: Songs for Life Vol. 1 and Vol. 2*, an ongoing series of free downloadable compilations of songs by artists who support the vision of Idle No More. The MTV documentary series Rebel Music explores real stories told through the medium of Indigenous popular music, and the message that holds true is "get your music out there." Soundcloud, YouTube, CBC Radio 3, and self-release platforms have allowed these artists to be heard. Now coming to the forefront are groups such as A Tribe Called Red, Tanya Tagaq, Supaman, Frank Waln, Inez Jasper, Sihasin, Tall Paul, Jesse "Red Eagle" Robbins, Naát'áaníí Means, and Mike Cliff a.k.a. "Witko."

Documentaries such as *Rumble: The Indians Who Rocked the World* along with articles that give agency and power to discussions of Native influence on popular culture are needed to understand the difference between cultural appropriation and artistic influence. As Dawes states, "interaction is inevitable; influences must occur. What need not be inevitable are exploitation and the movement toward a denial of one's own identity. As well, the kind of hierarchical structures that establish 'superior' cultures as the ultimate goal of 'inferior' cultures through the processes of so-called influence and change must be completely rejected as manifestations of genocidal tendencies."[35] Native art is not a passive commodity to be mined by a postcolonial Western art world but an active participant in influencing culture.

Because of contemporary Indigenous agency, the popularity of Indigenous artists, and the ease and immediacy with which the internet allows societies to react to social injustice and acts of misrepresentation, the chance is finally here to expose the centuries-old structure of Indigenous cultural misappropriation. As Dawes concludes, "it is in the context of such dialogue that we can then turn our minds to resolving the troubling question of cultural appropriation, for it is when the society begins to deal with this issue that we will start to see changes in the infrastructures that support the artists in this country."[36] It is my hope that the analyses and examples in this chapter will serve as tools for the agents of social change and that the cultural instances of singing Redface that seemed to be so integral to my childhood as an American will eventually be seen as an embarrassing racist past that future generations will struggle to understand.

NOTES

1 James O. Young and Susan Haley, "'Nothing Comes from Nowhere': Reflections on Cultural Appropriation as the Representation of Other Cultures," in *The Ethics of Cultural Appropriation*, ed. James O. Young and Conrad G. Brunk (Chichester, UK: Wiley-Blackwell, 2009), 268.

2 Christina Giacona, *The Indigenous of Turtle Island: Native American Music in North America* (Dubuque, IA: Kendall Hunt Publishing, 2018), 85.

3 Philip J. Deloria, *Playing Indian* (New Haven, CT: Yale University Press, 1998), 157–58.

4 Edison Manufacturing Company, *Sioux Ghost Dance*, 1894, www.loc.gov/item/00694139/.

5 Karl Hagstrom Miller, *Segregating Sound: Inventing Folk and Pop Music in the Age of Jim Crow*, Refiguring American Music (Durham, NC: Duke University Press, 2010), 2.

6 Ibid., 4.

7 Ibid.

8 Ibid.

9 Young and Haley, "'Nothing Comes from Nowhere,'" 274.

10 Lenore Keeshig [Tobias], "Stop Stealing Native Stories," *Globe and Mail*, 26 January 1990, A7.

11 Deborah L. Duvall, *Tahlequah and the Cherokee Nation* (Charleston, SC: Arcadia Publishing, 2000), 24.

12 Kurt Wolff and Orla Duane, *Country Music: The Rough Guide* (London: Rough Guides, 2000), 141–42.

13 Marvin Rainwater, *The Pale Faced Indian* [vinyl] (MGM Records, 1959).

14 Don Fardon, *(The Lament of the Cherokee Reservation Indian) Indian Reservation* [vinyl] (Pye Records, 1968).

15 Barbra A. Meek, "And the Injun Goes 'How!' Representations of American Indian English in White Public Space," *Language in Society* 35, no. 1 (2006): 93–128.

16 Paul Revere and The Raiders, *Indian Reservation (The Lament of the Cherokee Reservation Indian)* [vinyl] (Columbia, 1971).

17 Orlando Riva Sound, *Indian Reservation*, YouTube, https://www.youtube.com/watch?v=uZ5sAa-4IaJk (accessed 12 September 2016).

18 Buddy Red Bow, *Indian Reservation* [vinyl] (Native Spirit, 1981).

19 Johnny Cash, *Bitter Tears: Ballads of the American Indian* [vinyl] (Columbia, 1964)

20 Antonino Ambrosio, *A Heartbeat and a Guitar: Johnny Cash and the Making of* Bitter Tears (New York: Nation Books, 2009), 172.

21 Robert Hilburn, *Johnny Cash: The Life* (New York: Little, Brown, 2013), 265.

22 Ibid.

23 Ibid., 265–66.

24 Ibid., 266.

25 Ibid., 268.

26 Ambrosio, *A Heartbeat and a Guitar*, 165.

27 Ibid.

28 Brian Wright-McLeod, *The Encyclopedia of Native Music: More than a Century of Recordings from Wax Cylinder to the Internet* (Tucson: University of Arizona Press, 2005)

29 Kwame Dawes, "Re-Appropriating Cultural Appropriation," in *Borrowed Power: Essays on Cultural Appropriation*, ed. Bruce H. Ziff and Pratima V. Rao (New Brunswick, NJ: Rutgers University Press, 1997), 116.

30 Hilburn, *Johnny Cash*, 264.

31 Ibid.

32 Ambrosio, *A Heartbeat and a Guitar*, 171.

33 *Shenandoah and Bucher, Making* Bitter Tears—Sacred Ground, YouTube, https://www.youtube.com/watch?v=Tmij0O-T7JU (accessed 15 October 2016).

34 See the Idle No More website, http://www.idlenomore.ca (accessed 12 September 2016).

35 Dawes, "Re-Appropriating Cultural Appropriation," 118.

36 Ibid., 116.

CHAPTER 10

Collectivity as Indigenous Anti-Celebrity: Global Indigeneity and the Indigenous Rights Movement

Sheryl Lightfoot

In my book *Global Indigenous Politics: A Subtle Revolution,* I examine the nature and behaviour of the global Indigenous rights movement at the United Nations and in other international forums and argue that the Indigenous rights movement is a unique force in global politics.[1] I follow political scientist Franke Wilmer's definition of the Indigenous rights movement as a "case of political activism mobilized on a global scale to address problems grounded in the norms underlying the present system world order" with common impacts on Indigenous peoples everywhere.[2] In my book, I argue that the global Indigenous rights movement has created a set of potentially transformative structural changes in the international system through the advancement of Indigenous peoples' collective, land, and self-determination rights as articulated in the United Nations Declaration on the Rights of Indigenous Peoples. Yet I have also observed that the global Indigenous rights movement is actively reshaping how politics can be done, in practice, in ways that also serve as a counter to a wider cultural pull toward celebrity in political spaces.

In recent decades, social science scholars have increasingly taken up the study of celebrity as a media, cultural, and political phenomenon.

Overwhelmingly, these scholars describe celebrity as the intersection of two key elements: media and the elevation of individuals. Chris Rojek defines celebrity as the "attribution" of qualities to a particular individual,[3] and Graeme Turner similarly describes a celebrity as an individual with "star quality" who is considered to have a natural, immanent quality that an audience consumes because of "belief, desire or aspiration."[4] Furthermore, the widespread "mediatization" of contemporary society[5] produces the "accumulation of attention capital" by an individual akin to religious experiences.[6] Mark Wheeler analyzes how celebrity has cross-fertilized democratic politics in both national and transnational spaces. From politicians who package themselves as commodities for sale to voters to celebrities who position themselves as spokespersons for international humanitarian campaigns, political celebrity is produced through the mediatization of individuals and the reduction of complex issues to simple and emotional formulas.[7] Wheeler observes that this is a clear tendency in contemporary politics with troubling implications for democratic societies. In contrast to this wider societal and political tendency, the global Indigenous rights movement behaves very differently and offers an important alternative to the trend toward celebrity politics.

Grounded in transnational Indigenous ways of being, with grassroots activist origins that can be traced back to the founding in 1974 of the International Indian Treaty Council (IITC), the global Indigenous rights movement has followed the original tone, practice, and nature set by the IITC and other similar organizations in the 1970s. Over the decades, even while numerous and diverse Indigenous groups and organizations have joined from around the world, the nature and practice of the global Indigenous rights movement have remained remarkably consistent with its original roots in the IITC, which has served as a leader in the movement over the decades while maintaining a deliberate stance of collectivity and non-domination. The global Indigenous rights movement remains deeply anti-colonial in both nature and practice, and in multiple ways it challenges international structures of domination and subordination in order to gain and enhance the recognition of Indigenous rights to land, culture, and self-determination. Indigenous political actors are intelligent, strategic, creative, and articulate diplomats on the global stage and seek a global space of dignity and equality for Indigenous peoples. For four decades, the global Indigenous rights movement has been practising global politics in ways that differ fundamentally from predominant state-centric practices or Western leadership styles. By drawing on Indigenous ontologies, values, and commitments, the global Indigenous rights movement offers a new method of practice grounded in ancient and ongoing forms of Indigenous leadership that lack hierarchy and formal leadership but are horizontal, with equality of voice and the long-established practice of leading without dominating. The movement is counterhegemonic both in intent and in practice, working against hierarchies, both social and political. It is grounded in collectivism and behavioural norms that eschew individual praise or even attention in favour of the best interests of the community, whether broadly or narrowly defined. The behaviour of the global Indigenous rights movement can thus be conceptualized as a form of *deliberate anti-celebrity*.

Global Indigeneity is a supranational layer of Indigenous identity added to the already complex web of kinship, tribal, and national identities that Indigenous peoples maintain.[8] It is important to note that this Indigenous identity, though global in scope, is not intended as a *universalizing* force; rather, it seeks *unified* action. The distinction between unified and universalizing is key to understanding the movement and the anti-celebrity ethos that it embodies.

The global Indigenous rights movement deliberately aims to secure collectively the distinctiveness and singularity of individual Indigenous nations, cultures, and communities. One unifying force is what Māori lawyer and longtime Indigenous rights activist Moana Jackson describes as "an Indigenous worldview in which there are similarities of perceptions about the Earth as the mother and the importance of *whakapapa*, or relationships among human and non-human entities and spirits."[9] The other unifying force is a common experience of colonial oppression coupled with "a discourse of global indigeneity founded on the centrality of self-determination."[10] In sum, the global Indigenous rights movement is grounded in a unifying vision of Indigenous ontologies and composed of thoughtful and creatively strategic Indigenous political actors who represent the diversity of Indigenous peoples and enact common Indigenous values in their transnational political activities. These unifying forces have created a certain ethos of non-hierarchy and non-domination, what we might call anti-celebrity, grounded in a set of collectively held ideals and enacted through conscious and deliberate non-individualized political and strategic actions.

For this chapter, I draw on nearly ten years of qualitative research on and participant observation with the global Indigenous rights movement. Although I am a citizen of the Lake Superior Band of Ojibwe, I grew up in Minneapolis–St. Paul during the 1970s and 1980s, a heightened time of Indigenous activism. I worked in the American Indian community there as well during the 1990s and 2000s, so I have been surrounded by American Indian activism and advocacy, of many varieties, for most of my life. Inevitably, I draw partially on some of my own lived experiences, a kind of auto-ethnography that, as described by Paul Whitinui, connects my own lived experiences and personal observations to my formal qualitative research.[11] In my academic role, I have been interviewing activists and been a part of Indigenous UN meetings, including Indigenous Caucus meetings, since 2007. During that time, I have attended and participated in hundreds of meetings and interviewed dozens of participants. I also draw on the archival record of global Indigenous rights activity, though that record is extremely thin on the non-individualistic, non-hierarchical, anti-celebrity dynamics elaborated here.

In this chapter, I discuss in greater depth what I mean by "transnational Indigenous ways of being" followed by a closer exploration of an anti-celebrity ethos in the global Indigenous rights movement through three specific cases. First, I examine the International Indian Treaty Council's practice of "leading but not dominating," which illustrates the anti-celebrity ethos in place from the movement's beginning in a prominent Indigenous organization whose practices set the original tone for the Indigenous rights movement in the succeeding decades, a movement committed to maintaining and emphasizing Indigenous collectivity. Second, I look at the consensus decision-making model of the Indigenous rights movement. And third, I discuss the centrality of Elders, women, and youth within the movement. All of these factors contribute to the movement's anti-hierarchical, anti-celebrity ethos.

Transnational Indigenous Ways of Being

Obviously, no monolithic "Indigenous" culture exists in the world. Rather, the more than 5,000 distinct Indigenous nations around the world—more than 300 million Indigenous individuals—represent tremendous diversity. Yet a political identity of "Indigenous peoples" has emerged through transnational processes over the past several decades and taken on increasing levels of salience at local, national, and international levels. It is important to note that Indigenous identity, though often global in scope, is deliberately intended to secure collectively the distinctiveness and singularity of individual Indigenous nations, cultures, and communities.

Although Indigenous cultures vary widely, there does seem to be a broad tendency toward a shared vision of life and the universe as interconnected, and therefore respectful relationships must be cultivated and maintained—this type of vision also characterizes the Indigenous rights movement. Even with the long history of state oppression of Indigenous peoples, the norm of respectful relations prevails. For example, at the Seventh Session of the United Nations Permanent Forum on Indigenous Issues (UNPFII) in 2008, a representative from a large Latin American Indigenous organization rose and, with intense anger, expressed his frustration with the state-centric nature of the United Nations, speaking harshly of states and accusing them of using Indigenous peoples as mere puppets in their relations with each other. Many in the room interpreted his words as extremely disrespectful toward states and the United Nations. UNPFII Chair Victoria Tauli-Corpuz encouraged restraint and respect: "This is an organization of states, [international organizations], and Indigenous peoples. It will not be acceptable to cast aspersion on members of the Secretariat or even on states. We must show respect to all others who are engaging with us in this dialogue."[12] As this interaction demonstrates, the Indigenous rights movement prefers measured, respectful, diplomatic interactions among all stakeholders, even when long-term wrongs are obvious and there are perfectly valid grounds for angry responses by Indigenous groups. Although the movement encourages the airing of complaints and disagreements, it always conditions members to do so with dignity and respectful engagement, utilizing the methods and mores of respected, and respectful, diplomats. In short, they are to treat their harshest opponents as they themselves wish to be treated.

Although invoking the practices of international diplomats, the Indigenous rights movement remains simultaneously grounded in Indigenous ways of being. Both the current practice and the revitalization of Indigenous cultures are priorities for the movement. Long-time activist and IITC board member and co-founder Bill Means describes it as "part of our cultures, and certainly the idea is that our culture is still practised, and we haven't put it aside into a university or a history book, and so we're basically—we're not doing anything new for our people, we're carrying out our culture and our history."[13] What Means speaks of is the lived and living cultural grounding in Indigenous ways of being in the movement. This is also one of its primary political positions, which then aims reciprocally to support Indigenous cultural grounding.

Although guided politically in its orientation, the Indigenous rights movement also remains intensely grounded spiritually. One activist stated unequivocally that "a spiritual foundation laid the groundwork" for global Indigenous solidarity. He said that "at a lot of these meetings I've participated in a lot of ceremonies around the world where Indigenous peoples have come together in that way, and I think that's strengthened us and made the movement a little bit different than other movements."[14] Another activist stated that the tradition of spiritual grounding began at the first global Indigenous conference in Geneva in 1977, and this "phenomenon introduced by Indigenous people is a recognition of culture at least in terms of reminding ourselves where we come from."[15]

Another unique characteristic of the Indigenous rights movement is the tendency toward long-term thinking: decisions should be made with the impacts on multiple generations in mind. The idea is that actions taken in the past have direct impacts on peoples today and that decisions made in the present will likewise have direct future impacts. Māori activist and law professor Claire Charters spoke of the long-term vision of Indigenous rights implementation: "It's not necessarily about what happens in the short term, as is the case within the structure of democratic states, but the Indigenous perspective is much more long term and is seeking to protect our rights for generations to come—not just in the next one, two, five, or ten years."[16] As a result, Indigenous peoples have a responsibility to make decisions that are sustainable and will not cause harm well into the future. The late Tonya Gonnella Frichner—Onondaga lawyer, activist, president and founder of the American Indian Law Alliance, and expert member of the UNPFII—emphasized this approach as central to the transnational struggle for Indigenous rights: "As we say from the community that I'm from, the Haudenosaunee, when our leaders sit in deliberation, when they are in council, their decisions are going to be made with the seventh generation in mind. . . . [That's so] we don't stick with a quick fix or something that will only last for fifteen years. No, it must be until that seventh generation has arrived. The world needs to be intact for them when they arrive and are here to take on the challenges of this world."[17] All of these elements—connection of Indigenous peoples to the Earth, spiritual and cultural grounding, and seventh generation thinking—inform Indigenous practice and advocacy in the global Indigenous rights movement. In the following sections, I will examine three examples of how the movement enacts these elements of global Indigeneity in routine practices that centre collectivity, non-hierarchical relations, and community-based thinking over actions that could promote, benefit, or even credit the actions of single individuals, or even individual organizations, ahead of the collective.

Leading but Not Dominating: The International Indian Treaty Council

One of the keys to the success of the global Indigenous rights movement has been its ability to pull and hold together a strong Indigenous caucus, which has held fast to its consensus positions on land and self-determination. This tone was originally set by the International Indian Treaty Council, the first Indigenous organization with a focus on global organizing. The IITC was founded at the grassroots level, in 1974, at an American Indian Movement (AIM)–organized gathering at Standing Rock Reservation in Lakota territory, in what is also called South Dakota. A group of more than 5,000 Elders and traditional leaders representing ninety-eight Indigenous nations from nine countries gathered in the first council.

The IITC, also sometimes known as AIM's international diplomatic arm, developed a unique leadership model at that first meeting that was distinctive from that of AIM. Its practice of leading but not dominating has not only contributed to its consistency as a leading Indigenous organization and its longevity of leadership but also set the tone for the nature and practice of the global Indigenous rights movement as a whole.

My research has identified four factors that have contributed to the success of the IITC—success in helping to hold the Indigenous rights movement's consensus together through more than thirty years at the United Nations, success in leading but not dominating the movement, and success in finally celebrating the passage of the Declaration on the Rights of Indigenous Peoples. All four of these factors emanate from the roots of the IITC in AIM and its continued presence in the council. As one IITC board member stated at the board of directors meeting in 2007, "AIM is here. AIM has always been here."[18] As an extension of AIM, the IITC has been well equipped to lead because of the organization and resources provided by this legacy. At the same time, the IITC is not the equivalent of AIM and operates very differently from how AIM operated in the 1960s and 1970s and how it evolved over time, which did elevate a few key individuals as celebrities. In contrast, the IITC has developed its own identity and operation and shies away from the notion of North American domination of international Indigenous politics. It has chosen deliberately to avoid domination or any appearance of domination by invoking certain Indigenous ways of conducting international relations in both Indigenous and non-Indigenous spaces.

First and foremost, the IITC has had the longest and most consistent presence and participation at the United Nations of any Indigenous organization. At its founding meeting at Standing Rock Reservation in 1974, the Elders and leaders decided to take their treaty issues to the international level, especially the United Nations, so they officially founded the International Indian Treaty Council as their organizational vehicle. Their collective outcome document, *Declaration of Continuing Independence*, established the collective identity of the treaty peoples gathered there: "We, the sovereign Native Peoples recognize that all lands belonging to the various Native Nations now situated within the boundaries of the U.S. are clearly defined by the sacred treaties solemnly entered into between the Native Nations and the government of the United States of America."[19] Then the first IITC committed itself to a collective and unified struggle for the treaty rights of Indigenous peoples who have such relationships with the United States: "The Council further realizes that securing United States recognition of treaties signed with Native Nations requires a committed and unified struggle, using every available legal and political resource. Treaties between sovereign nations explicitly entail agreements that represent 'the supreme law of the land' binding each party to an inviolate international relationship."[20] Yet the rights of other Indigenous peoples beyond the borders of the United States were also mentioned, in a show of transnational unity, when the declaration stated that the IITC "recognizes the sovereignty of all Native Nations and will stand in unity to support our Native and international brothers and sisters in their respective and collective struggles concerning international treaties and agreements violated by the United States and other governments."[21]

The guiding principles of the IITC, articulated shortly after its genesis in 1974, demonstrate its larger commitments to collective and unified

Indigenous struggles within and beyond North America. The eight principles reflect the Indigenous rights movement's long-standing commitment to a horizontal structure and the lack of a formal leadership model. The eight principles are as follows:

> The IITC will reflect and support the values inherent in Traditional Indigenous cultures, including respect for the sacredness of all life and our Mother Earth, the wisdom of our elders, and the power of our traditional teachings and spiritual practices.
>
> The IITC recognizes that while sharing much in common, each Indigenous culture is also unique and each struggle reflects diverse historical conditions. Therefore in keeping with the principles of self-determination, the IITC respects the right of each member Nation, community and organization to define and pursue the objectives and strategies best suited to its specific situation, history and culture.
>
> The IITC respects and seeks the participation of both men and women in all aspects and levels of the organizations.
>
> The IITC will continue to seek the advice of our traditional elders and spiritual leaders, and will make efforts to increase the participation and develop the leadership of Indigenous youth.
>
> The IITC believes that Indigenous Peoples should speak for and represent themselves before the world community.
>
> The IITC believes in the consensus process as the means to building unity, based on mutual understanding and shared commitment, and will employ this process in its proceedings whenever possible.
>
> The IITC expects that its representatives, staff and leadership will demonstrate the highest level of respect and regard in their interactions with one another, and will resolve any difficulties or disagreements that may arise according to agreed upon internal procedures.

> The IITC expects that its staff, Board members and representatives will conduct themselves in accordance with the above principles as well as the highest level of accountability, diplomacy and ethical standards, and will keep the best interests of the IITC and the Peoples it represents foremost while representing the IITC in any capacity.[22]

The IITC was the first Indigenous organization to receive consultative status at the United Nations Economic and Security Council in 1977. It was also in 1977 that the IITC, along with the Indian Law Resource Center and the World Peace Council, organized the first international conference of Indigenous peoples at the UN headquarters in Geneva. A collectively drafted document, titled the Declaration of Principles, emerged from this first conference and formulated the core principles of what would eventually become the UN Declaration on the Rights of Indigenous Peoples. The Declaration of Principles centred the international Indigenous struggle on treaties, land rights, and self-determination. The UN record also shows that the IITC was present at every UN meeting and conference associated with Indigenous rights since 1977. As the IITC's Bill Means told me in an interview, "we were always there in Geneva, from 1977 until today. We probably have the most consistent representation in all fora that deal with Indigenous peoples—we have always had somebody there. And that was the key. And we not only had a continual presence in Geneva but also in New York City—at the UN in New York. So we were there on a daily basis. We have an office in New York, which no one else had—right across the street from the UN."[23]

My attendance at and observations of various international Indigenous meetings allow me to testify to the centrality of the IITC in international Indigenous politics at the United Nations. IITC representatives always have an important presence, offering numerous public statements, submitting draft documents for consideration, providing international legal counsel, and taking a lead role in shuffling diplomatically between and among Indigenous representatives. The UN record shows that the IITC played an important role as well during the development of the declaration, and during the negotiations on the declaration, and now takes a lead role in implementing the declaration on a state-by-state basis. The IITC holds human rights training sessions for tribal nations several times each year throughout the hemisphere, training elected tribal officials on how to leverage the declaration politically with their host states and how to take particular grievances through the available UN human rights apparatus.

Second, the IITC has important alliances with non-governmental organizations, churches, and funders that stem from its AIM legacy, and these alliances have been another key to the IITC's consistent participation at the United Nations. Even though foundation funding sources in the United States wax and wane over time, the IITC has built up a substantial network of regular and long-term funders, many of which are those that supported AIM in the 1970s. The ability of the late Vernon Bellecourt and Bill Means, both with long histories with AIM, to raise a steady stream of money for the IITC was and remains critical to its continual international presence and participation. As Means mentioned to me, "back in the 1980s, many times we went to Europe on one-way tickets, and then we'd go around and raise money while we were in Europe to get home. So that's a case of us being able to participate more than others because we had allies in Europe who believed in our cause, and not only in the foundation community but also in the religious community, the church community."[24] The IITC's good relationships with the "friendly" governments of Mexico, Guatemala, and Denmark also helped finally to propel the UN declaration to the floor of the General Assembly in 2006 and 2007.

These leadership factors—continual participation, critical alliances, and funding stream—stem largely from the history of the IITC and its AIM legacy. The next two factors of the IITC's success in international Indigenous politics relate to the stance of non-domination that the IITC has taken in building and holding consensus among the Indigenous Caucus at the United Nations. The IITC has deliberately chosen to engage in international relations in a new way, an Indigenous way. This also reflects the activist approach favoured by the reservation Elders—an approach grounded in sovereignty, treaty rights, and intellectual savvy that also incorporated Indigenous ways of doing things.

Third, then, the IITC has always represented a cross-section of Indigenous peoples by maintaining a network of grassroots support. The council's membership represents Indigenous nations from six continents. Although the organization began in North America, it quickly drew in members from Central and South America. By the 1980s, the IITC had added New Zealand and Australia, and by the 1990s its membership and affiliates had expanded to include Indigenous nations and organizations from Africa, Asia, and even the Saami in Northern Europe. So, even though some criticized the IITC for being North American based, the criticism later dissipated, according to an IITC member, as the council expanded to include broader participation.[25]

One IITC affiliate from the Caribbean also told me in an interview that one strength of the council is how it breaks down the legalese of the United Nations so that grassroots people all over the hemisphere can understand it. I witnessed this first hand at the IITC human rights training that I attended within a month of the passage of the declaration at the United Nations. At this meeting, two IITC board members, Chair Francisco Calí (Mayan from Guatemala) and Ron Lameman (Cree from Treaty 6 in Alberta), and Executive Director Andrea Carmen, spent an entire day with representatives from about a dozen tribal nations and organizations. Throughout the day, they patiently and clearly explained in detail what the declaration was and was not and how it could and could not be used. They also explained which avenues for grievance are available to Indigenous peoples through the international human rights system at the United Nations.

Fourth, the IITC has created unity in its diversity by conducting international relations in a new way, an Indigenous way. From the beginning of international Indigenous activity in 1977, the IITC has advocated for several characteristics of this new Indigenous way of undertaking international relations, often characterized by Indigenous cultural and spiritual practices. At the first international meeting in 1977, IITC representatives insisted on opening and closing the meeting with an Indigenous prayer. This tradition has carried through to the present day. In direct violation of standing rules and procedures prohibiting religious expressions at the United Nations, all Indigenous meetings there have opened and closed with an Indigenous prayer or cultural expression. The IITC often led, and certainly always participated in, the protests and pressures that made this possible. During one standoff in the UN Working Group on Indigenous Populations in the late 1980s, the UN-appointed chair actually walked out of the meeting when the Indigenous representatives asked to hold a prayer before starting the meeting. She returned to the meeting hall just in time to hear the end of the Indigenous prayer.

Finally, in the interest of Indigenous unity and solidarity, the IITC makes a serious attempt not to take individual credit for its successes but to give credit back to the group. For example, the UN record shows that the first draft of the UN Declaration on the Rights of Indigenous Peoples, which appeared in 1984, was likely drafted by the IITC since it bears a 95 percent resemblance to an earlier IITC document. However, no one from the IITC with whom I have spoken who was present during that process will attribute the document to the council. When questioned, each interviewee insisted that the first draft UN declaration was the product of a group effort by several Indigenous organizations and that there were many writers.

Consensus Decision-Making Model

The search for unifying Indigenous positions through consensus decision making appeared at the first global Indigenous conferences in the mid-1970s. Only three years after its grassroots founding at Standing Rock, the IITC co-sponsored the first global Indigenous conference at the United Nations in Geneva in 1977. Certain dynamics that emerged and became normalized at that first conference have continued for decades. One of these normalized dynamics is the consensus decision-making model, an already established organizational practice that the IITC took to Geneva.

The Geneva conference report notes that "nightly meetings were held during which consensus was reached concerning the content and structure of the next day's work."[26] As activist-scholar Roxanne Dunbar-Ortiz writes about the meeting,

> in all-night sessions, the Indigenous participants hammered out a document that they submitted collectively. This document, entitled "Draft Declarations of Principles for the Defence of the Indigenous Nations and Peoples of the Western Hemisphere," represented the dominant theme of the conference and set the basis for subsequent UN negotiations regarding the question of Indigenous peoples. . . . This declaration could be characterized as the fundamental political document of the international Indigenous movement, and would provide the basis for the elaboration of the Draft Declaration on the Principles for the Rights of Indigenous Peoples in the Working Group on Indigenous Populations that became the subject of more than

a decade of negotiations in the Commission of Human Rights, finally approved by the UN General Assembly in 2007.[27]

An Indigenous delegate at the 1977 Geneva conference explained how the traditional model of consensus works in his North American Native community and how that informs the practice of the larger global Indigenous rights movement:

> The whole idea of consensus is that all viewpoints are heard, and if there's a disagreement then we have to deal with the particular aspects/points of that disagreement and not just make some kind of blanket decision. As Indian people, we do that, have consensus, or try to go by consensus. I've been to meetings as a young person where the Elders appoint (and the English word they use is *critic*), after people have their say, then this person we call critic has the right to limit the debate and then to ask people or a council of chiefs, depending on the situation, a number of people, a smaller number of people, I should say, agree on how to go forward. Usually, it's not even a vote, it's just a smaller group of Elders—in our ways.[28]

In the Indigenous Caucus meetings that I have observed over a decade, consensus has been the primary objective and process. Since the Indigenous Caucus is constrained by time and resources as much as any other political decision-making body in any context, a vote is sometimes required in order to reach a final decision, though in the Indigenous Caucus this is viewed as a highly undesirable last resort. One activist described the difficulties of using consensus within the UN structure, noting that "the UN itself uses that word *consensus*, and it's fairly close to Indigenous peoples' view," though the United Nations prefers voting methods. She continued that "we call on our history and our culture, we just experience it, and say 'we've got to give everybody a voice.' So it's accepted, it's not discouraged, where I think in the UN circles it's discouraged to try to reach consensus."[29] As I have heard many Indigenous Caucus members say, "consensus does not mean unanimity," and sometimes in the end a consensus document means that discussions were held for long enough that opposing viewpoints were heard and compromises made, and on rare occasions a vote was taken.

I attended one Indigenous Caucus meeting in Geneva[30] at which the objective was to produce a single collective document to be presented to the UN member states. The caucus spent three full days and evenings (Monday through Wednesday) in discussions and negotiations and aimed to have a collective document drafted, agreed on, and presented to the states by Thursday morning. In this meeting, the chair of the Indigenous Caucus noted that the document to be agreed on had to be initiated by Indigenous peoples and presented to the states, not the other way around, and he therefore eliminated any circulating state-initiated drafts and encouraged the circulation of Indigenous-initiated drafts so that the caucus could examine all of the Indigenous texts. In an expression of the ideal of Indigenous collectivity and unity, the chair made sure to mention that several drafts circulating were not the creations of individual Indigenous organizations but the products of consultations and negotiations by multiple Indigenous organizations from several regions.

This Indigenous Caucus meeting opened with the selection of chairpersons. It was mentioned that it is a long-standing tradition of the Indigenous Caucus to elect co-chairs, one English speaking and one Spanish speaking, so as to avoid North American dominance, encourage flat and wide leadership, and reduce the potential for Global North–Global South conflict. At this meeting, no election was held; rather, the chairs were decided by consensus, acknowledged as an Indigenous Caucus tradition. A motion was heard to rename the English-speaking chair of the Indigenous Caucus. In another reflection of horizontal leadership style, the chair spoke, with great humility, about the efforts of so many other Indigenous peoples and acknowledged their commitment, completely deflecting any attention to himself or his personal accomplishments as chair. He was reseated as the chair by consensus in the room. The Spanish-speaking chair was likewise reseated, by consensus, later in the afternoon once a crucial mass of Spanish-speaking organizations was present in the room.

Over the course of the three days of Indigenous Caucus discussions, several points were repeatedly made, all of which testified to the importance and centrality of the horizontal leadership model that draws attention away from any individual or prominent group. Although one particular organization had brought forward several draft texts, it was emphasized repeatedly that they were not only from that organization but also had been seen, discussed, and brought forward by a group of Indigenous organizations in consultation with the prominent organization. It was also mentioned repeatedly in discussions that the thirty-year tradition of the Indigenous Caucus was to make decisions by consensus, even though doing so could be a long and difficult process. It was mentioned frequently that the purpose of Indigenous Caucus meetings is to bring Indigenous peoples together, not only to discuss issues, with the broadest possible Indigenous participation, but also to decide on global Indigenous collective actions and strategies. As the chair reminded everyone in the room, "our purpose is to agree on a text. We need to use our time effectively in order to deal with substantive issues of the text."[31]

Occasionally, in the Indigenous Caucus, a charge is made that a single, usually large, Northern/Western hemispheric organization is bringing forward a draft text that represents only its views. In such a case, the organization in question is quick to respond and presents evidence that the draft is actually the result of consultation with and consensus among a multitude of Indigenous organizations representing the Global North and Global South, North America, and elsewhere.

However strong the desire for consensus positions and drafts, the reality is that objectives differ among various Indigenous groups of the Global North and Global South, and sometimes the process of working out these differences creates the conditions for disunity and dissensus. In the Indigenous Caucus meeting that I observed in Geneva, Indigenous organizations from the Global North and Global South had vastly different notions of what the final text should contain. It took every bit of the three days of discussions and negotiations, along with some informal evening sessions, to arrive by Thursday morning at a consensus position, which ultimately represented a compromise position.

Centrality of Elders, Women, and Youth

Broad and open participation by Indigenous peoples, reflecting a bottom-up, grassroots nature, has also always been a core objective of the movement. Strong attention is also paid to balanced geographic inclusion among delegates. Achieving a mix of community-based people, tribal governments, and political organizations has also been a goal. As Les Malezer, the former Pacific Indigenous representative of the United Nations Permanent Forum on Indigenous Issues, writes, "through unity and determination" Indigenous peoples have been successful and strong at the United Nations because of their "open, inclusive, informal, unstructured assembly for delegations participating in United Nations and related forums."[32]

Elders and youth have always been included within the movement and often play a central role in meetings. Ever since the global Indigenous rights movement was born, at the first meeting of the International Indian Treaty Council, Elders, traditional leaders, and youth have been central to all meetings. Mohawk leader Kenneth Deer writes about the first entrance of Elders, youth, and traditional Indigenous leaders at the UN grounds in Geneva in the summer of 1977: "The presence of 'Red Indians' caused a stir in Geneva and the UN itself, and there was talk that the Indigenous representatives might not be allowed into the building. Undeterred, they walked through the gates in groups. UN staff watched from the windows as delegation after delegation in full regalia walked by their offices and entered the meeting room. These delegations were the ones that opened the doors of the UN to let other peoples follow."[33] Youth have also always been present in meetings of the global Indigenous rights movement, and they have met as a caucus ever since the inaugural meeting of the United Nations Permanent Forum on Indigenous Issues in 2002, and by 2006 they had an enhanced level of institutionalization at the United Nations as a formal caucus. The Youth Caucus is composed of Indigenous youth from various states, regions, and organizations who meet to discuss issues of particular interest to them. They present regular statements to the Permanent Forum.

Both the credentialing process and the UN speaking rules have presented huge challenges to the movement's model of open participation over the years, but the movement has successfully, and consistently, advocated for important alterations of UN rules to permit openness in both attending and speaking. During the days of the Working Group on Indigenous Populations (1982–2006), the UN record shows that Indigenous participants insisted on a change to normal UN rules that allowed only those with official UN non-governmental organization (NGO) credentials to attend and speak during Working Group meetings. Indigenous participants insisted that any Indigenous person or organization that could get to Geneva should be entitled to speak in the Working Group, and the UN rules were successfully changed in accordance with the demands of the Indigenous participants. In fact, the Working Group on Indigenous Populations had the most open participation rules that the United Nations has ever allowed.

Early activist movements that formed the roots of the global Indigenous rights movement, especially the American Indian Movement in the United States and the National Indian Brotherhood in Canada, were male dominated in both leadership and participation, often with a certain warrior ethos. This pattern began to shift at the first Treaty Conference in 1974 as the direct action approach to activism gave way to a more global diplomatic approach. This newer approach was grounded in traditional Indigenous ways, which included participation and leadership by Elders, youth, and community leaders, many of whom were women. Legal scholar Russel Barsh writes about the role of women in the early days of the global Indigenous Caucus: "At a closed-door session of the indigenous peoples' caucus nearly 30 years ago, a group of women from the North American prairies confronted the all-male delegation of Mi'kmaq from Atlantic Canada. 'Where are your *women*?' they demanded. The eldest Mi'kmaq in the delegation answered sheepishly, 'Who do you think *sent* us here?'"[34] As Barsh points out, the public face of gender and leadership varies greatly among Indigenous peoples from around the world, and he notes that Indigenous cultures vary widely in their expectations for the role of women in public, political discussions. Nevertheless, he notes, the role and status of women in Indigenous circles at the United Nations have always been a focus of discussion. In the 1980s, some of the leading delegations (from the Haudenosaunee Confederacy and the Mi'kmaq) were matriarchal societies, and thus these delegations were often strongly female. Sometimes delegations appeared to be entirely male, but in reality they were often directed, on a day-to-day basis, by a female leadership group at home.

Women have been central to the Indigenous Caucus meetings that I have attended in Geneva and New York as well as the UNPFII sessions and Indigenous organization meetings and community consultations that I have observed. Formal speakers include nearly equal proportions of men and women. At the IITC board meeting that I observed in 2007, only four of the thirteen board members were women, but their voices were disproportionately strong. When they spoke, the men listened. As Māori activist Hinewirangi Kohu stated, "it's good to have plenty of women on the IITC . . . , strong women, . . . And then the men, too, who can put up with me, I'm the worst. But, you know, I can't be ignored either, and they know it."[35] Andrea

Carmen (Yaqui) started working at the IITC as a student intern in 1976, joined the staff in 1983, and has served as the executive director since 1992.[36] She has a consistently strong and vocal presence in global Indigenous politics.

Of the IITC staff, including program consultants, legal representatives, and trainers, the vast majority are female. Many organizations that regularly participate in the Indigenous rights movement have been founded and headed by women, and Indigenous women often hold high leadership positions within UN Indigenous bodies. For example, the American Indian Law Alliance was founded and headed by Tonya Gonnella Frichner (Onondaga), who also served as an expert member of the UNPFII from 2008 to 2010. Na Koa Ikaika o Ka Lāhui Hawai'I, a Hawaiian sovereignty NGO, was founded by Mililani Trask, and Tebtebba, a Philippines-based international Indigenous advocacy organization, was founded and headed by Victoria Tauli-Corpuz (Kankanaey Igorot), also the chair of the UNPFII from 2005 to 2010 and appointed UN special rapporteur on the rights of Indigenous peoples in May 2014. Female presence and leadership, equal to and balanced with male leadership, have always been essential features of the global Indigenous rights movement and key to its collective and community focus—its deliberate anti-celebrity.

Conclusion

In his final remarks to the United Nations Permanent Forum on Indigenous Issues at the end of his term as United Nations special rapporteur on the rights of Indigenous peoples in May 2014, James Anaya highlighted three "animating characteristics" of the Indigenous rights movement that led to the collective achievements that the UN Declaration on the Rights of Indigenous Peoples represents, elements that will continue to lead to future successes for the movement.[37] First, Anaya noted how the Indigenous rights movement was able to work to enlighten and educate the world community on the "conditions, aspirations and contributions" of Indigenous peoples and to let the world know that Indigenous peoples are not simply historical figures of either savagery or romanticism but contemporary peoples and political actors with their own goals and objectives.

Second, Anaya described a particular strength of the movement, "principled pragmatism," the "tendency to be pragmatic and constructive in the search for solutions that are grounded in fundamental principles." Anaya saw this strength as the people's collective ability to find constructive solutions to thorny problems. He noted that, during his tenure as the UN special rapporteur, he had many opportunities to see how Indigenous peoples work in specific local contexts in the same way that the global movement functions, with a focus on being creative and "open to building common ground for peaceful coexistence and amicable relations."

And third, Anaya mentioned the movement's strength of optimism coupled with tenacity. Although Haudenosaunee Chief Deskaheh had not been successful in gaining access to the League of Nations when he travelled to address that body in Geneva in 1923, his optimism and tenacity carried forward to the 1970s and beyond as the Indigenous rights movement pushed for a UN declaration. And, Anaya noted, the same optimism and tenacity will continue to lead Indigenous peoples toward future imaginings of how Indigenous rights can be implemented.

All of these strengths—enlightenment, principled pragmatism, optimism, and tenacity—are collective, communal behaviours that stem from a grounding in transnational Indigenous ways of being. So, though some social movements and humanitarian causes around the world often enjoy tangible benefits from celebrity attention and publicity, the Indigenous rights movement stands in stark contrast to this global phenomenon, deliberately throwing off any hint of celebrity or the cult of individualism associated with it. The notion of celebrity itself is born from a focus on the individual as "special" and an ideal type somehow above and distinct from the group. The global Indigenous rights movement works in multiple ways to counter any notion of praise or focused attention on any particular individual or individual organization. Celebrity exists only because of a focus on the individual, and such an ontology is deeply embedded and heavily invested in a set of dominant power relations and hierarchical political and social structures. It is precisely these hegemonic power relations and structures that the global Indigenous rights movement pushes against in both its advocacy and its daily practice of a counter-paradigm based on Indigenous values and ways of being.

NOTES

1 Sheryl Lightfoot, *Global Indigenous Politics: A Subtle Revolution*, vol. 8, *Worlding beyond the West* (New York: Routledge, 2016).

2 Franke Wilmer, *The Indigenous Voice in World Politics: Since Time Immemorial* (Newbury Park, CA: SAGE, 1993), 128.

3 Chris Rojek, *Celebrity* (London: Reaktion, 2001), 143–79.

4 Graeme Turner, *Understanding Celebrity* (London: SAGE, 2013), 6–7.

5 Andreas Hepp, *Cultures of Mediatization* (Cambridge, UK: Polity, 2013).

6 Chris Rojek, *Fame Attack: The Inflation of Celebrity and Its Consequences* (New York: Bloomsbury Academic, 2012); Chris Rojek, "Celebrity," in *The Wiley Blackwell Encyclopedia of Consumption and Consumer Studies*, ed. Daniel Thomas Cook and J. Michael Ryan (West Sussex, UK: John Wiley and Sons, 2015), 1–3, https://doi:10.1002/9781118989463.wbeccs036 (accessed 19 September 2020).

7 Mark Wheeler, *Celebrity Politics* (Cambridge, UK: Polity, 2013).

8 Ronald Niezen, *The Origins of Indigenism: Human Rights and the Politics of Identity* (Berkeley: University of California Press, 2003).

9 Moana Jackson, interview by the author, Wellington, NZ, 11 March 2008.

10 Andrea Muehlenbach, "'Making Place' at the United Nations: Indigenous Cultural Politics at the U.N. Working Group on Indigenous Populations," *Cultural Anthropology: Journal of the Society for Cultural Anthropology* 16, no. 3 (2001): 415–48.

11 Paul Whitinui, "Indigenous Autoethnography: Exploring, Engaging, and Experiencing 'Self' as a Native Method of Inquiry," *Journal of Contemporary Ethnography* 43, no. 4 (2013): 456–87.

12 Victoria Tauli-Corpuz, comments at the Seventh Session of the United Nations Permanent Forum on Indigenous Issues, New York, 2008.

13 Bill Means, interview by the author, Minneapolis, 17 January 2008.

14 Anonymous Indigenous activist 6, interview by the author, 2007.

15 Ibid.

16 Claire Charters, personal communication with the author, 10 November 2007.

17 Tonya Gonnella Frichner, interview by the author, New York, 3 December 2011.

18 International Indian Treaty Council, Board of Directors Meeting, Mille Lacs, MN, 27 September 2007, author's notes.

19 International Indian Treaty Council, Declaration of Continuing Independence, Standing Rock Indian Country, June 1974.

20 Ibid.

21 Ibid.

22 International Indian Treaty Council, "Guiding Principles," https://www.iitc.org/about-iitc/guiding-principles/ (accessed 20 December 2017).

23 Means, interview, 17 January 2008.

24 Ibid.

25 Anonymous Indigenous activist 6, interview by the author, 2007.

26 NGO Committee on Human Rights, *Report of International NGO Conference on Discrimination against Indigenous Populations in the Americas—1977* (Geneva: United Nations, 1978).

27 Roxanne Dunbar-Ortiz, "The First Ten Years from Study to Working Group 1972–1982," in *Indigenous Peoples' Rights in International Law: Emergence and Application*, ed. Roxanne Dunbar-Ortiz, Dalee Sambo Dorough, Gudmundur Alfredsson, Lee Swepston, and Petter Wille (Kautokeino, Norway: Galdu, 2015), 42–87.

28 Anonymous Indigenous activist 1, interview by the author, 2007.

29 Anonymous Indigenous activist 17, interview by the author, 2010.

30 Date not disclosed to protect the anonymity of the participants.

31 Indigenous Caucus, Geneva, author's notes.

32 Les Malezer, "Dreamtime Discovery: New Reality and Hope," in *Realizing the UN Declaration on the Rights of Indigenous Peoples: Triumph, Hope, and Action*, ed. Jackie Hartley, Paul Joffe, and Jennifer Preston (Saskatoon: Purich, 2010), 29–46.

33 Kenneth Deer, "Reflections on the Development, Adoption, and Implementation of the UN Declaration on the Rights of Indigenous Peoples," in *Realizing the UN Declaration on the Rights of Indigenous Peoples: Triumph, Hope, and Action*, ed. Jackie Hartley, Paul Joffe, and Jennifer Preston (Saskatoon: Purich, 2010), 18–28.

34 Russel Barsh, "The Inner Struggle of Indigenous Peoples," in *Indigenous Peoples' Rights in International Law: Emergence and Application*, ed. Roxanne Dunbar-Ortiz, Dalee Sambo Dorough, Gudmundur Alfredsson, Lee Swepston, and Petter Wille (Kautokeino, Norway: Galdu, 2015), 88–95.

35 Hinewirangi Kohu, interview by the author, Mille Lacs, MN, 26 September 2007.

36 Andrea Carmen, interview by the author, Mille Lacs, MN, 26 September 2007.

37 James Anaya, "Address by the United Nations Special Rapporteur on the Rights of Indigenous Peoples to the United Nations Permanent Forum on Indigenous Issues," New York, 20 May 2014.

CHAPTER 11

Makings, Meanings, and Recognitions: The Stuff of Anishinaabe Stars

w. C. Sy

Seeing Through to Another Reality

In her essay for the installation exhibition *Godi'Nigoha': The Women's Mind*, Mohawk Deborah Doxtator-ban posits the problem of Euro–North American intellectual and physical impositions on the land with regard to their influences on Rotinonhsyonni women's mind.[1] In Rotinonhsyonni thought, land and mind are one; in Rotinonhsyonni creation, Sky Woman, who falls from the sky to the land, presumably *seeing through to the land*, is a central figure.[2] Doxtator examines several versions of her nation's creation story, illuminating a salient pattern: for Rotinonhsyonni, the world began with an "unsettled, restless mind searching for a solution to some sort of unresolved problem."[3] In the exhibit, she illuminates and mobilizes the "unsettled, restless mind" as a "catalyst for creative re-envisionings of how we perceive our intellectual connection to the world we live in now."[4] In doing so, Doxtator conceptualizes the artistic installations of four Rotinonhsyonni artists—Patricia Deadman, Kelly Greene, Shelley Niro, and Jolene Rickard—as creative responses to three problems: Euro–North American transformation of the natural world through patriarchal capitalist interest; interference in women's seeing through to the land; and reshaping of mind-land connections. The exhibit itself, with its deliberate focus on *women's mind* and *women's artistic responses to a problem*, intentionally intervenes in the ways in which Western intellectual traditions have transformed Rotinonhsyonni thought about women and the land.

Invoking both the idea of the unsettled mind and a way of seeing beyond the empirical and social, Mohawk political anthropologist Audra Simpson elucidates historical and political-economic capabilities, and culpabilities, of affect as it functions through contemporary forms of settler state governance. In "Reconciliation and Its Discontents: Settler Governance in an Age of Sorrow," Simpson explicates problematics with the residential school-driven reconciliation movement in Canada, rendering for her audience, "an emotional history of the present."[5] She locates these problematics with and within a present state governance that she argues maintains an enduring settler colonial politic through the employment of affect in its response to Indigenous refusal of dispossession of bodies, youth, land, and life. Drawing on political personas such as Barack Obama, Justin Trudeau, and Wab Kinew as well as comparative political events in Canada, Simpson provides methods for understanding that and how "publics" are constructed, produced, or performed in ways that create affect. This affect is mobilized for particular purposes, in particular ways vis-à-vis its marketability.

For Simpson, affect here, and its ability to legitimate and sustain dispossession, is generated through spectacle. Drawing in part on French post-structuralist Guy Debord, Simpson elaborates stating,

> Spectacles help to govern. Spectacles are the big thing that takes up all of your visual energy and doesn't tell you how it's produced. It's a perfect sort of object or product or commodity. There are people that are themselves like spectacles. . . . Spectacles also help to move sentiment, I think, in ways that can be quite forceful. But the key with spectacles is they themselves don't show you how they are produced so we don't ask . . . why are these things significant? Because they demand that we not ask after why they're significant. . . . [Spectacle] uses affect, it uses performance, it uses good feelings and it expects you to have those feelings. If you don't have those feelings, then you're bad news.[6]

She elucidates spectacles of skin, youth, savagery, repair, pain, and in the reconciliatory moment, contrition. For example, with reference to Obama and Trudeau, Simpson signifies that and how their phenotypical, age, and/or biographical particularities are made politically meaningful within socio-political contexts through affect. She details this in the following:

> This is where Obama, where [citizens] go after his biography and they're like "Oh but, he was born in Hawai'i; oh, but his mom is white; oh but, but, but, but." You know, they need him to be a certain way and that's to be a Black man. But he's a complicated Black man. And Trudeau is the perfect, handsome white man. He's a spectacle of sorts also and that's why him with the headdress on was "Whoa!" for some of us and for others it was like "Yea, man! He's wearing a headdress; he's got an Indian "name". . . . Why is this so electorally significant? Why is Trudeau so significant? I mean, I have a hard time getting away from his lineage . . . but he's also operating as this spectacle of benevolent, fresh-faced whiteness that's going to lead us out of something. But even his own biography suggests something pretty scary for us. His dad was the architect of the White Paper. So that's where I see spectacles and sentiment doing this kind of work. It's like the work of force that can't happen anymore because this is supposedly a democratic state that doesn't use violence to govern.[7]

Finally, Simpson highlights the marketability of reconciliation identifying it as a technique of capitalism. She accomplishes this through her reading of Wab Kinew, an Anishinaabe cultural persona-turned-political figure.[8] While running for a political party of the Canadian settler state in 2016, Kinew became embroiled in controversy arising from misogynist, homophobic, fatphobic, and classist attitudes he conveyed in public arenas prior to his aspirations for political office.[9] As a result, he embarked on a campaign to repair his image through apology and self-proclaimed accountability. This public situation is understood through spectacle and affect but is further explained as reflecting an embodied linkage between reconciliation and capitalism. Referring to reconciliatory spectacles, Simpson says,

> To me, [Wab Kinew is] a perfect neoliberal subject, and he's performing this aggressive capital accumulation within himself as he remakes himself to meet the market for sympathy and votes. This is the perfect embodiment of that process, and it's within the frame of reconciliation or conciliation that you see these performances of being sorry and then starting over anew. So, it holds hands with capitalism; it holds hands with the recognition process. They're all in it together. They are embodiments of that and spectacles of it that I think, tying it with the question of affect, that are doing this kind of work for us and producing a sense of what is virtuous and helping to define political behaviour and what is possible.[10]

Simpson's consideration of reconciliation in Canada disrupts spectacle by revealing that deeper forces are at play through the mobilization of affect vis-à-vis public personas. A form of critical activity, she wants listeners of the auditory testimonies of the Truth and Reconciliation Commission and viewers of the visual to "move away from event and into structure, logic; a making clear of things that may have not been linked in [our] minds" and to think about the spectacle of political personas such as Obama, Trudeau, and Kinew, and the way this creates a marketable affect that sustains the settler state.[11]

Where Doxtator renders artistic engagements to attend to the problematic of capitalist patriarchal interference in Rotinonhsyonni women's ability to see through to the land, and Simpson draws attention to how state processes and political personas are publicly performed in ways that sustain settler colonialism through manipulative affect, both invoke a critical method of "seeing beyond the seen."[12] In relation to the present project on Indigenous celebrity, this method resonates with my reflections on and varied experiences with what I consider to be contemporary formations of Indigenous celebrity. I see these formations as a paradox of positively generative and exciting possibility and a (re)product(ion) of colonial, capitalist, classist, and/or settler (hetero)patriarchal and (hetero)sexist influences and relationalities that circulate through networks of particular power.

As a witness of Indigenous celebrity formation during the wake and ripple effects of Idle No More (c. 2012–14), I champion Indigenous peoples who enter into and engage with a broad public with the goal of affirming and advancing Indigenous peoples' sovereignties. Although these publics are undoubtedly animated with Indigenous peoples and non-Indigenous allies who share the same goals, the public, because of the global and settler colonial structures that shape it, is already a place where settler colonialism operates tirelessly to maintain or reinvent itself, doing so by first denying and making invisible Indigenous peoples' sovereignties. Although the public might be a place that delivers accolades and generates social, material, and economic power for individual Indigenous people or groups who have some level of celebrity status, it can also be fickle, hostile, and dangerous.

My position as witness of Indigenous celebrity is a self-driven repositioning from that of the personal, intimate, and relational. My personal and painful relational experiences involved those whose aspirations for individual celebrity were stronger, from my perspective, than the commitment and desire to uphold and practise decolonial and Indigenous relational principles of community knowledge production, care, and accountability. These experiences have powerfully shaped my reflections on this subject and motivated me to identify and attend to what I see as a problematic of Indigenous celebrity. Learning from the relationally inside-out, I have seen, to some extent, the unseen of celebrity formation. That is, I have come to see Indigenous celebrity, or celebrities, and the social-economic landscape that these formations and personas arise from or are embedded within, as products of colonial, capitalist, and/or (hetero)patriarchal and (hetero)sexist influences and relationalities. Where Doxtator invokes the metaphor and practice of seeing (through to) the land beyond the interferences, and Simpson prompts a critical reading of public political processes and personas, I consider a practice of seeing (through to) the social landscape and production of celebrity formations. Like Sky Woman, I am moved to find a solution to a problem that eases my mind. I am motivated by discontent to consider the ways that Indigenous celebrity formations can entrench or reproduce settler colonial hierarchies and relations of extraction and exploitation. From this location, I want to eschew the expected: that is, to celebrate Indigenous celebrity in settler public spaces as though it is a great arrival, an outcome of a transforming and decolonizing settler political, social, and historical context, as though Indigenous celebrity has nothing to do with individual aspirations for status built on stepping on or taking from others. What I want to do is suspend a celebration of Indigenous celebrity and offer a critique without being marked or diminished to a "crab in a bucket." I want to understand the why of my unsettled mind and give testimony to my personal wounds from unknowing entanglements with those wanting to be celebrities.

Yet I am not convinced that entering this subject through discussion of its problematic or by giving testimony is the best way to resolve it. By "the best way," I mean the way that generates opportunity to recreate Indigenous life worlds according to Indigenous axiologies and epistemologies. When I think about disclosing intimate, lived knowledge of the reproduction of exploitative power dynamics in Indigenous relationalities as a hopeful method of preventing them elsewhere, I weigh the plausibility of generative potential against other possible methods. I ponder a world where unsettled minds and discontented hearts about Indigenous celebrity might not exist because they don't need to, where celebrity doesn't nurture itself on the non-consenting use or exploitation of people's labour or the silencing of those who voice their refusal or lack of consent. I imagine a world that generates itself through mutually reciprocal, collaborative, open, consensual, and accountable relationships and, in a capitalist system, where benefits are equitable.[13]

I deny utopian visions of this generative world and think instead of worlds where exploitative behaviours and patterns are widely recognized and accepted as *existing* such that activation against them is the norm. I envision a world where windigoism is remembered as being a part of the complexities of being human and a social reality in our communities; and importantly, where there are mechanisms, social processes, and will to prevent, stop, or reconcile extractive, exploitive behaviour and relations. Indigenous oral histories and narratives abound about those beings who are incessantly hungry and, in this state, feed on others. In Anishinaabeg cultural contexts, these beings are known as windigos, their power so great that some people in some communities do not speak this name. For the less naive among us, windigo and windigo nature among Anishinaabeg is neither novel nor unique. We ought not be surprised when it becomes evident that windigoism is occurring; we must not be obtuse to the fact that these dynamics do occur, or, under capitalism, consider them natural. And yet, they do occur and with little community will to intervene.

I have heard that this feeding behaviour is grounded in a kind of ceremony or spiritual connection—that the windigo, who cannot help itself, feeds only on select beings that can sustain it. Elsewhere, in conversation about Anishinaabeg womxn's work at the sugar bush, Amy McCoy, an Ojibway mother and cultural educator from the Sault Tribe in Sault Ste. Marie, Michigan, shared what she has been taught about windigo. She stated that "people talk about windigo in different ways" and that some say that "windigo is inside of us . . . and it preys on when we take the easy way, or we think that life is so easy and we don't have to work."[14] Although she does not believe that "we all have windigo spirit inside of us," she does believe that "we can be taken by that spirit" and that "we have a choice of whether we feed him or not."[15] Others, such as Gidigaa Migisi Doug Williams, nozhe odoodem, a Mississauga Elder and educator from the Curve Lake First Nation, note that nearing the end of winter, when Anishinaabe lived off the land and nutritional food was scarce in some situations, womxn occasionally exhibited behaviour that was misunderstood as windigoism but was actually caused by mineral deficiency.[16]

I'm unsure whether the "hunger feeding" that occurs in contemporary Indigenous-settler society is the same as the windigoism experienced in pre-capitalist, land-based societies.[17] It seems that the windigoism that arises from each way of living might be similar yet different; although hunger and feeding exists in each kind of society, each kind of society produces *different kinds* of extreme forms of hunger and feeding. For instance, where windigoism in a pre-capitalist, land-based society is considered a spirit that takes over a person who then consumes others, which, because it is detrimental to the well-being of community, is thus attended to by community members, in a globalized, settler colonial, capitalist society windigoism may be different.[18] It may be considered a spirit of excessive consumption that is criticized and rejected by some as unacceptable while simultaneously being encouraged and reinforced by others who think that the ability to vastly consume and grow is admirable as it signifies success. Two extreme kinds of hunger arise from and exist in different locations within global, settler colonial, capitalist, hierarchical structures: those whose bodies are literally starving from a lack of nutritional sustenance and those whose well-nourished, cared-for bodies hunger for various forms of social and economic capital.

In these historical worlds where the spirit of windigo exists and acts, there are also structures, mechanisms, and the will to deal effectively with such behaviours. In imagining worlds that differ from the present one, I ask "how did Indigenous peoples of the past know, or practise, celebrity?" Thinking about my own nation, I wonder "how did old-time Anishinaabeg know, or practise, celebrity?" Did celebrities emerge as the result of valiant acts? I wonder whether old-time Anishinaabeg created celebrities among themselves and, if so, for what purpose. Did celebrity ever become out of control? Did champions of Anishinaabeg celebrity ever unintentionally create a problem personality or, worse, a windigo through their own needs for celebrity? What drives Anishinaabeg to want, need, create, or protect celebrity?

Imagining how old-time Anishinaabeg would have known or practised celebrity is one method for engaging a problematic of Indigenous celebrity as it exists now. This approach resonates at a higher vibration in the present context and lurches forward in anticipation of a different future. This is a future in which structures are not founded on power dynamics and hierarchies attached to exploitative progress, growth, development, and expansion but grounded in Indigenous values of moderation, sharing, and mutual reciprocity (i.e., balance) with and accountability to the natural and spiritual worlds. These worlds, as Vandana Shiva indicates, challenge our shrunken minds and leverage our endless creative and diverse potentialities toward communities that care for the natural world and each other.[19] Despite the constant structural state of war, space exploration, and violence, we can build and rebuild such communities. This approach resonates deeply with my desire to write from within my nation, clan, and name as well as my ongoing intellectual proclivities; as being Ojibway, as belonging to makwa odoodem (Bear Clan); as waaseyaa'sin (a kind of glowing rock); and as a person who understands the world both through the spiritual and ceremonial as well as Anishinaabe material feminist interests.[20]

The following, then, is an engagement with Anishinaabe knowledges and imaginative interpretation of the *how* of old-time Anishinaabeg ways of being in order to invoke Anishinaabeg meanings, makings, and recognitions of celebrity. I consider celebrity through Anishinaabeg naming and clan systems, through Anishinaabe ancestral thought and kinship, and through value systems of leadership. Set out in the first person, these knowledges and imaginative considerations are offered as an alternative to the dominant formations of Indigenous celebrity and celebrity production through middle-class-oriented media and other publics in Canada. Although they are also offered as a framework for reading and interpreting contemporary celebrity from within Anishinaabeg thought, values, and epistemology, regardless of whether those celebrities are Indigenous or non-Indigenous, Anishinaabeg or non-Anishinaabeg, the potentiality of Indigenous knowledges and interpretations is already and always activatable from within one's own Indigenous nation.

Naming: Each of Us Is Star Stuff

Walking across campus on a brooding and chilly autumn day, I'm overwhelmed with the memory of the dream that came to me during the fast for my name—the memory of the dream itself, the emotions associated with it upon waking, and the emotions upon sharing the dream when my friend and Elder who "put me out" came to get me at my lodge in the forest. He said, "That's it. That's your name. Now we'll have to figure out how to turn this story into a name in the language." Being one of many born into a world distanced from my Anishinaabeg practices, I was exhilarated and relieved. When I first learned that we have practices unique to us as Anishinaabeg that keep us connected to spirit, to the natural world, and to each other through naming, I felt instant joy, quickly followed by longing and grief. I was overwhelmed with gratitude for finally coming into this knowledge; I was desperate to have my name as soon as possible; and I mourned the loss of not knowing or practising this my whole life. I learned that my name was there, coming to me, yet the journey of us arriving to each other didn't occur until about twenty years later after much trust in the process, ceremonial discipline, and spiritual endurance.

I think about the people who were my helpers in that ceremony. I think about the "coming back" part of it. I'm filled with the memories and the feelings. I think of the long, precarious, and patiently made trails that got me to that moment. Still walking, I think about some of the people out in the world whom I know by their Anishinaabe names: spirit of the young female bear, spotted eagle, rock woman, northern lights woman, warm southern winds woman, little oak, walking earth woman, little cloud, returning flame, black bird woman, sun shining out woman, still water woman, grandmother helper woman, strong heart, star woman, water woman, walks on hard crusted snow, and coming light woman.[21]

I imagine all of these Anishinaabeg out there in the universe. I imagine each of the humans whom I know who belong to these names, names that come from spirit, names that came to them in various ways. I imagine them as a map of points out in a universe, as stars. anang. anangwan. Starworld. I am no longer walking alone across a university campus on a dreary day but moving through a universe of Anishinaabeg stars, a constellation tethered to something grander than each of us alone and all of us together. In this world, regardless of relationships with each other, individually we are a part of the Anishinaabeg world, as a collective.

Burdened by the power and problematic of contemporary formations of Anishinaabeg celebrity in a larger human world built for "getting more" and fuelled by human complexities such as greed, jealousy, unhealthy competition, or the feeling of not having enough or being enough, I think that naming offers some insight into the *how* of Anishinaabeg celebrity. Naming, and names, manifest individuals whose spirit and sacredness are recognized through some kind of ceremonial process. Individuals are divine manifestations of creation, spirit, and the universe; individuals, through their names, will *always* be connected to creation, spirit, and the universe; by ceremonially taking care of their names, they will *always* have a process to tap into this sacredness, thereby activating its power in this physical world. In this way, individuals are celebrities in their own right, being part and parcel of creation in all of its vastness and a social network of humans who recognize and honour this. In this world, no *one* is a celebrity, but every*one*'s spirit is recognized and celebrated—this is the gift of individual, albeit interdependent, being. In this world, Anishinaabeg know that we are part of a whole and that our significance, reflected in part through our names, binds us to spirit and is enacted as a responsibility intended to serve the whole.

What a beautiful vision on a dull day: Anishinaabe people lighting up the universe with the essence of who we are and this essence encapsulated through our names. All people are recognized deeply for their highly nuanced relationality with the spiritual, natural, and supernatural worlds and for being integral parts of infinite creation. We are recognized with awe, humility, and the occasional good-natured tease intended to keep us humble.

Ododemiwin (Clan System): It Takes Many Rock Stars to Govern

Sitting at the top of a mountain in Lekwungen territory called P'KALS, I'm immersed in thoughts about my n'odoodem, my clan and clan business.[22] When I learned who my clan was, it was ceremonied in much the same way that my name was. In this case, I had questions about the methods for knowing our clans, so I sought counsel from an additional person deeply practised in Anishinaabe ceremony and knowledge. In my uncertainty about and desire for a method that was meaningful, she replied, "Well, just fast for it. Do a four-day fast." Several years and two fasts later, I returned to tell her what had happened and who my clan was. She told me what we would do, and then we did it. In a makwa odoodem gathering, I was brought into my family. We feasted, and I was told how to care for my clan. I was told to feast it every season, and she told me that I could not partner with another from this clan—we are direct relatives. She also told me to remember that this holds true even when I move out of our territory. She said, with a twinkle in her eye, "No Bear Clan over there where you are moving to either!" We laughed.

Here on this mountain, I imagine what life may have been like for the Lekwungen families whose lands I now live in and whose mountain I feast my clan on. And I imagine our own Anishinaabeg history. Our governance. How it used to be. How it *maybe* used to be. I recall attending an Anishinaabe gathering several years back and sitting in a big open-air tent with many others. It was a beautifully sunny summer day by the water in Anishinaabe country. Up front were two Anishinaabeg men who were the speakers for that particular part of the gathering. I recall those men emphasizing the clans that they belonged to while they were up front talking to the rest of us. I recall them bantering back and forth with each other in a jovial way. They were jokingly jabbing each other about how their own clan was better than the other's clan. In doing so, they were calling on the responsibilities that their respective clans had to the whole, how their own clan responsibilities were more vital to the whole than the other's clan responsibilities, and how they excelled at carrying out those responsibilities. The space of that moment, from my experience of it, was filled with very good, fun-loving energy.

These men, putting their clans up front, were leaders of that event. They were without a doubt "the stars of the show." And, in that moment, we collectively witnessed a jostling for power through the use of humour. Was there any element of truth to the jostling that we witnessed, or were they performing the humanness that exists among Anishinaabeg? Was it a bit of both? Sitting on P'KALS, I also wondered why, when we are told by some that clans move through the male line but are governed by women, these men were the hosts of the gathering. Was their prominence about gender and privilege or some specific responsibility arising from their clans and/or the particular relationality between clans? Or was this an effect of settler (hetero)patriarchy in our communities? Whatever the answer, in that space, those men, in relation to each other, conveyed important aspects of our humanity to reflect on: that humans have ego, that there is jostling for "the best" among Anishinaabeg, and that there can be a struggle in negotiating power. The strategy that they employed to convey these aspects of humanness was humour and at times awkwardness.

I go further back in history to a time that I can only imagine, and I do so based on what I've learned in the now. There is a hearty fire of oranges, reds, and yellows whose glow lights up the dark interior of a lodge. I see an array of our elder relatives sitting around that fire discussing something of importance to the entire group. Maybe it is a problem; maybe it is a discussion about what the past season has brought for the broader communities in their various locations; maybe it's a discussion of the future. The fire casts the images of our elder relatives in a warm, flickering glow, each flyer, animal, swimmer, and "little spirit" insect representing a perspective or concern related to the issue that they are discussing. They appear to be shapeshifters, part elder relative, part human elder. Behind them are members of their particular "family." There is a process that has occurred in order to determine who sits at that fire and who is responsible for carrying forth the perspectives of their[23] group, perspectives aligned with the responsibilities and gifts associated with that group. They are organized by what we now know as odoodem.

I think of how we are dominantly organized through settler colonial structures and, because of the power of these structures, we organize ourselves consciously and subconsciously today by gender, class, race, last name, sexuality, ability, religion or spiritual practice, age, or family name and formation (i.e., heterosexual, nuclear, marital families). Our human-centric-ness has become deeply embedded. This is evident from the categories that we utilize, human constructions whose boundaries and potentialities are also defined by humans. Instead of looking to our Elders (e.g., animals, flyers, swimmers, insects), our supernatural ones (those who have been here much longer and powerfully animate our worlds in unseen ways), and the knowledges that arise from our own personal ceremonial practices and sacred knowledges, we have become insular; we have become our own teachers; we have become human-centric. I think of clans. I think of old-time Anishinaabeg: we would have been looking constantly to the natural, supernatural, and spiritual worlds for lessons, guidance, and knowledge on how to be. Looking at each other through the clans that we belong to, we would be constantly cognizant of the natural world, of difference, and of the significance that each brings to the greater whole. In our dislikes of and disagreements with each other, we would recognize our interdependence and, except for the most extreme situations, persist in living well together.

For this feasting ceremony at P'KALS, I stay with imagination. Contemporary structures and categories are depressing, flat, and finite. I think of all those who attest to the need for a turn to the spirit, to our Indigenous epistemologies, to our creativity. I go out further to the warm glow of a hearty fire and to each of the clans sitting around it. I see each of them speaking to a matter at hand in an orderly fashion. Each knows that the voice, thinking, and interests being conveyed are not pre-eminent in this place, this community. They all know that their voices, thoughts, and interests are actually embodied in those behind them, those to whom they belong and are responsible. They know that they are mere carriers of their families' contribution and wisdom. In that process, they have their turn to say their personal piece, to articulate their personal interests and agendas. Their words at this fire convey an agreed upon collective message. The others at the fire know this. There is trust, dignity, and commitment to the whole. If a shared agreement cannot be made among the groups, then the final decision rests not with one sole authority but two clans whose discussions are also transparent. This is a gathering of people. All must contribute their best in order for the whole to do well. Here, by necessity, everyone is a star.

Elder Brother: The Last-Born Son Crosses Over from Oral to Print and Becomes Famous

There's this being in Anishinaabeg life worlds who is part spirit, part human. He goes by a name that, for some, can only be said in the winter. For this context, I'll refer to him as Elder Brother. He's known in Anishinaabeg circles in many ways: as a teacher, a trickster, a researcher, a helper, a shape-shifter. He's mostly known as someone who first helped to name the natural world that Anishinaabeg live in and then as someone who helped Anishinaabeg to survive in that world. His pedagogical approach with Anishinaabeg is typified by outrageous, perverse, "bad," humorous, flawed, or trickster-like, shape-shifting behaviour. Although he was the last of four sons born to Winonah (the eternal nurturer) and Epingishmok (the spirit of the west), he's uplifted by many Anishinaabeg as the first, and seemingly most important, of our Anishinaabeg relatives. This may be said of settlers too who seem to be very familiar with Indigenous tricksters and their purpose but not so familiar with the vast ancestry through which Indigenous nations descend and are in relation to. An exception to this making of Elder Brother as a singular superstar can be found in Basil Johnston-ban's retelling of the stories of all four brothers: Maudjee-kawiss, Pukawiss, Cheeby-aub-oozoo, and Elder Brother, in that order.[24] However, even with this attention and detail paid to the significance of his older brothers to Anishinaabeg history, Johnston gives more than double the amount of space to Elder Brother's story.

Stories of Elder Brother's adventures that unfolded on behalf of Anishinaabeg well-being circulated orally. Today his presence persists in published English texts, a relatively recent mode of documenting and disseminating knowledges in Anishinaabeg worlds. Given that it was the first explorers, traders, missionaries, and colonists who documented life in written English, Elder Brother crossed over from oral worlds into texts, which eventually evolved into public texts, and, from what I can tell, became famous. It's these settler publications that seem to isolate and commemorate Elder Brother as a pre-eminent being among Anishinaabeg. It's hard to know the contexts that shaped this construction of one Anishinaabeg being as pre-eminent among many.

Considering that there might be particular contexts that shape this construction opens up myriad questions. Were Elder Brother stories the most popular ones that Anishinaabeg told? Or were these the stories that Anishinaabeg predominantly told when settlers were around? Presumably, in order for settlers to be exposed to these stories, the contexts in which they were told likely were generated through relationalities of familiarity and perhaps some degree of trust. Perhaps, settlers became family or kin, and they disseminated these stories amongst their circles that extend beyond

Anishinaabeg home fires. How *did* Elder Brother stories emerge and circulate? Were other stories told? What effect did settler publishing of Elder Brother stories have on generating a market for them? Is the popularization of Elder Brother through print a true reflection of his real work with and for Anishinaabeg? And what is the effect of the popularization of Elder Brother through published texts on Anishinaabeg psyche? Do we elevate this idea of him as a celebrity ancestor because so much knowledge of our history has been fragmented, destroyed, erased, or eroded? Do we think that we need one predominant hero who can guide us home?

And is Elder Brother operating here? In the moment of this chapter? Or in the contemporary moment of Indigenous celebrity? Is his spirit operating as trickster or researcher or helper? Is revealing the unsettled, restless mind and discontent a mere reflection of pitiful human concern for things not really of importance? What kinds of things did old-time Anishinaabeg concern themselves with? What kinds of things will future Anishinaabeg concern themselves with? How did we, or how will we, find resolutions? How did we, or how will we, think deeply about the things that concern us? How did we, and how will we, see through to ourselves?

Ogichidaa: Stepping into the Light

Whenever I think of ogichidaa, I think of Indigenous individuals or groups of people who step out into a difficult situation for their people. They step out into a situation without knowing if there will be any negative consequence or positive outcome. They step into the situation with deliberation and with intention; forthwith and unyielding until it is time to return to their home fires again. The whole process of carrying out responsibilities in ogichidaa ways is bound to spirit and made manifest in ceremonial processes. Ogichidaa is tied to a reciprocal relationship with spirit in the act from beginning to end. To varying degrees, people will know that these spiritual responsibilities are being carried out and honoured.

When I think of ogichidaa, I think of someone who makes a personal sacrifice for their people; someone who pushes themselves to step up to a new reality, or through to a new reality, in order to support the people. Those who make sacrifices are surrounded by relations who inevitably, in some way, must likely sacrifice something too. When someone you know steps forth into a situation in all of the meanings of ogichidaa, it means that to some degree the ones whom they are directly responsible for or bound up in relationship with step forth too. Or at least they might bear some weight of ogichidaa practice.

I've not heard about or witnessed ogichidaa enacted for personal glory or gain. Being in an ogichidaa way might be cast as odd behaviour, queer behaviour, unpopular behaviour, or against the status quo. Not all Anishinaabeg might agree with it and it is often, in the historical context we are in, set against the violence of settler colonialism. Some might chastise it or argue that it is showboating; ironically, it can be considered an attempt to become a celebrity. In a contemporary context, settlers might do so too.[25] I'm unsure how, in a contemporary setting with social media and news, and a technological, capitalist world that thrives on isolation and individualism, ogichidaa and celebrity seeking might be discerned. Presumably, historically, a kind of relationality would have yielded some level of legitimacy for those engaged in ogichidaa processes. This still happens today. Yet, in the present capitalist context, there is a market for celebrity, and as such it can be hard to discern who is legitimately speaking to ogichidaa practice and who is supporting a brand or self-interest. In a capitalist society, some argue that discerning the genuineness or authenticity of relationalities from those that are capitalist is not the issue; rather, focusing on the function of the particular relationality within a given socio-political or socio-economic context is key.[26]

When I think of ogichidaa, I think of the quiet people. The ones who don't want to be in the spotlight but are called on by the community to do something that they don't necessarily want to do or don't even consider themselves skilled enough to do. However, in their case, someone in their communities sees that they have what is needed for the task at hand and requests that they step up and step out. Ogichidaa courageously respond to the needs of their community when called upon to do so.[27] I think too of communities that look out for their ogichidaa. The only glory in practising ogichidaa responsibilities is being bound to your community, a community that looks out for you as you step out and take the risks that you were summoned to take for community members, for ancestors, and for the future.

Anybody can be ogichidaa. In fact, I think that, at least sometime in each of our lives, we must embody this and enact it, particularly when called upon. As Puyallup Elder Ramone Bennett stated to a much younger group of people at a gathering in Seattle at the height of Idle No More,

> we were able to re-establish ourselves because it was our turn. It was our turn then, back in the '60s. Now it's your turn. Now this lady that's fasting, it's her turn. She's doing what any of us would do. She's doing what we have to do. You need to shout, because it's working. It's your turn. . . . It's their turn. . . . Keep shouting. Keep fighting. If all you have is your body, put it there. Your ancestors did. They fought for every right you enjoy. . . . And you know what? Your great-, great-, great-grandchildren will do the same thing.[28]

This is not the stuff of one person or one hero who represents one nation over a period of time or through all time. Ogichidaa is the stuff of every Anishinaabeg, every person, stepping out at least once in their lifetime to do something for their people, something that is difficult and might come with a cost. We must not think that being ogichidaa means individuals or groups of individuals who are flawless or without fault or that they will consistently and infinitely act in ways that are best for their communities. Anishinaabeg are complex beings whose lives are in constant flux with the life forces that shape us. Ogichidaa might step forth for the people in one context and do well at that, and on another occasion they might be engaged in activities that are self-serving or even transgress Anishinaabeg values, laws, and ways of being.[29] When I think of ogichidaa, I think of so many people. I think of the present context of global and settler colonial violence and the echoes of its historical processes. I think about how, for many of our people, just waking up and being engaged with the life force, in many ways, is being ogichidaa.

Starry Eyed from Now On

Being present with the potential creative and theoretical space opened up through the unsettled mind and discontent, Doxtator and Simpson provide Indigenous peoples tools for negotiating realities created by global, settler colonial desires. Where Doxtator draws on Rotinonhsyonni traditional narrative and thought to query how the mind and artistic endeavour might prompt seeing through the industrial, capitalist, and patriarchal realities reshaping Indigenous lands, waters, and the women's mind. Simpson articulates a complex and insightful critical analytical approach to reading an instantiation of contemporary settler governance and the personas that animate it. In doing so, she compels seeing beyond images, sound bites, and the rhetoric presented to us through public performances. Drawn by how Doxtator and Simpson unapologetically open up their engagements with the problematics of different settler colonial processes by locating their projects as matters of the mind and heart, I attend here to the problematic of Indigenous celebrity. In strategizing an approach that attends to resolving these problems and generates a method for critical engagement with contemporary formations of Indigenous celebrity, I embark on a creative endeavour utilizing Indigenous knowledges from within Anishinaabeg lifeways and the imaginative.

Reflecting on Anishinaabe epistemologies of naming and governance, the work of an ancestral helper, and certain individual ways of being yields a way of knowing celebrity through Anishinaabeg eyes. In the absence of a framework or guideposts through which to navigate what is presented to or performed for us in public spaces that are either settler spaces or highly mediated by settler influences, it is easy to be seduced into believing or feeling what we see or hear. My imaginative excursions into Anishinaabeg names, odoodemiwin, Elder Brother's crossover, and ogichidaa through starry-eyed lenses offer a method to navigate the complexities of Indigenous celebrity. This method creates a background against which to consider what celebrity might have looked like historically. It provides a constellatory lens through which to consider Indigenous celebrity today. Having the structural, epistemological, and cultural tools or methods to navigate what we are being presented with in public is one way to empower our readings, interpretations, and engagements with celebrity.

NOTES

1 Deborah Doxtator, "Godi'Nigoha': The Women's Mind and Seeing Through to the Land," in *Godi'Nigoha: The Women's Mind*, by The Woodland Cultural Centre's curators Deborah Doxtator and Lynn Ann Hill (Brantford, ON: Woodland Cultural Centre, 1997), 29–41. Rotinonhsyonni is the original name of the group of Indigenous peoples more commonly known as Haudenosaunee, Six Nations, or, from a historical French perspective, Iroquois. Skahenndoweneh Swamp, personal communication with the author, January 2010.

2 Tom Hill, "Preface and Acknowledgements," in *Godi'Nigoha: The Women's Mind*, by Deborah Doxtator and Lynn Ann Hill (Brantford, ON: Woodland Cultural Centre, 1997), 6.

3 Doxtator, "Godi'Nigoha,'" 29.

4 Ibid.

5 Audra Simpson, "Reconciliation and Its Discontents: Settler Governance in an Age of Sorrow," public lecture, University of Saskatchewan, 22 March 2016, https://www.youtube.com/watch?v=vGl9HkzQsGg (accessed 21 September 2017).

6 Ibid., 1:09–1:11.

7 Ibid., 6:46–9:40; 1:10.

8 Ibid., 1:16.

9 CBC News, "NDP's Wab Kinew responds to Twitter controversy: 'I've been an open book,'" 11 March 2016, https://www.cbc.ca/news/canada/manitoba/manitoba-liberals-wab-kinew-misogynistic-comments-1.3487073 (accessed 20 November 2020).

10 Ibid., 1:17.

11 Ibid., 55:10.

12 James Dumont, an Anishinaabe ceremonialist and educator, first introduced me to the idea of "the seen and the unseen" as a particular way for Anishinaabe to see the physical and spiritual worlds. James Dumont, personal communication with the author, 1995–96.

13 I write on reciprocity and mutual reciprocity in w. C. Sy, "Relationship with Land in Anishinaabeg Womxn's Historical Research," in *Reshaping Women's History: Voices of Nontraditional Historians,* ed., Julie Gallagher and Barbara Winslow (Chicago: University of Illinois Press, 2018).

14 Amy McCoy, personal communication with the author, 5 August 2014. Permission to include these insights confirmed.

15 Ibid.; personal communication with the author, 2 July 2019.

16 Gidigaa Migisi Doug Williams, personal communication with the author, 12 June 2014. Further, Gidigaa Migisi discusses how namebin, the sucker, harvested in the early spring, was a coming-out-of-winter medicine that a woman might have needed to restore nutritional and mineral deficiencies. Permission to include these insights confirmed 27 September 2020.

17 I extend gratitude to Maya Chacaby, Anishinaabe educator and cultural practitioner, for her thinking that we need to consider the context in which we are applying a consideration of Anishinaabe values, stories, and philosophies. She reminds that Anishinaabe ways that arise from land-based times will not fluidly translate into capitalist contexts.

18 For a contemporary engagement with windigoism through an indigenous feminist legal analysis, see Val Napolean et. al, *Mikomosis and the Wetiko* (Victoria: Indigenous Law Research Unit, 2013).

19 Vandana Shiva, *Growth=Poverty*, Festival of Dangerous Ideas 2013, 10 November 2013, https://www.youtube.com/watch?v=7M3WJQbnHKc&t=2724s (accessed 27 October 2017).

20 Dian Million, "Spirit and Matter: Resurgence as Rising and (Re)Creation as Ethos," panel 4 presentation, Grounding Resurgence, Reconciliation in a Time of Resurgence, University of Victoria, 18 March 2017, https://www.uvic.ca/interdisciplinary/indigenousnationhood/workshops/irar/index.php (accessed 27 October 2017). In this talk, Million asserted a need for resurgence grounded in and fuelled by spirit and the epistemologies specific to Indigenous nations. She provided examples to illustrate her meaning that included writing and practising from our clan orientations. Million also asserted that a focus on this approach should take priority over a focus on structural and social locations. Her assertions resonated strongly with my own orientations, but my position is that Indigenous peoples must recognize, negotiate, mitigate, and try to transform the structural powers that place us and keep us confined within settler-constructed social locations that have detrimental material, economic, and subsistence impacts on our corporeal well-being.

21 I've written the names here in English out of recognition of the personal nature, privacy, spiritual power, and intimacy of these names when they are written or spoken in Anishinaabemowin.

22 Lekwungen educator, Cheryl Bryce, shared this information during a decolonial bus tour of Victoria, British Columbia organized for faculty at the University of Victoria. We were at Cadboro Bay and she was discussing the mountain that is popularly known as Mt. Tolmie, 4 November 2017. Lekwungen artist, Bradley Dick, spells the Lekwungen name for this mountain as P'KALS.

23 I utilize "their" here, and later in the chapter, to disrupt the gender binary conveyed by his or her. This is in line with my efforts to make space for gender diversity in history, and in this case, historical imaginings.

24 Basil Johnston, *The Manitous: The Spiritual World of the Ojibway* (St. Paul: Minnesota Historical Society Press, 2001), 17–95.

25 In this case, I think of Mushkego Chief Theresa Spence, who fasted between December 2012 and January 2013 in Ottawa to protest the dishonour of the Crown in its treaty responsibilities for her people. I recall the wide range of attitudes conveyed about her actions from both Indigenous and non-Indigenous peoples.

26 Nicole Constable, "The Commodification of Intimacy: Marriage, Sex, and Reproductive Labour," *Annual Review of Anthropology* 38 (2009): 54–56.

27 In this case, I think of Omàmìwinini historian Paula Sherman and her leadership for her Algonquin community, Ardoch Algonquin First Nation, during their land protection against uranium mining.

28 Ramona Bennett, *Idle No More* [video], dir. Dave Wilson, 2 January 2013, https://www.youtube.com/watch?v=ksESR2BVlqY (accessed 1 November 2017).

29 I'm thinking here of Ojibwe leader and business person Phil Fontaine, who was one of the first people to publicly speak about the residential school abuses he and so many other children endured, leading the way for a public inquiry which ultimately resulted in the Truth and Reconciliation Commission. Fontaine has also been publicly criticized and shamed for his role as a consultant with resource development companies in Canada.

Acknowledgements

In the fall of 2016, the co-editors of this book, along with Dr. Zoe S. Todd from Carleton University, engaged in a series of conversations with one another over a number of months on the matter of Indigenous relationships to celebrity and fame, a conversation that intensified in light of the questions raised regarding Joseph Boyden's self-identification as Indigenous. This led to the development of the book project and the selection of the thoughtful and engaging chapters contained herein. The editors would like to extend our gratitude to Dr. Todd for her contributions to our thinking and early work on this project.

We are also grateful to have had the support of a group of wonderful colleagues and friends during the early development of this project—Chris Andersen, Adam Gaudry, Chelsea Vowel, and Darren O'Toole. We would also like to extend our gratitude to the staff and faculty of the Department of Sociology at the University of Toronto Mississauga; the School of Indigenous and Canadian Studies at Carleton University; and the Department of Indigenous Studies at the University of Saskatchewan.

We are deeply grateful as well to our families and friends. Jennifer especially wishes to acknowledge the supportive contributions and caretaking of Sam Adese, Grams, KB Harwood, Malissa Phung, and Geraldine King. She would also like to extend special acknowledgement to early childhood educators J.A., Z.C., and F.L.

We would also like to acknowledge the authors who have contributed chapters for the book. We have greatly appreciated reading your thoughtful, engaging chapters, and working with you over the past few years. And we would like to extend our deep appreciation to Jill McConkey and the team at University of Manitoba Press; Jill has been a kind, generous, and supportive editor and publisher. Thank you.

Selected Bibliography

Abbattista, Guido. "Humans on Display: Reflecting on National Identity and the Enduring Practice of Living Human Exhibitions." In *Moving Bodies Displaying Nations: National Cultures, Race and Gender in World Expositions: Nineteenth to Twenty-First Century*, edited by Guido Abbattista, 241–71. Trieste, EUT Edizioni Università di Trieste, 2014.

Abbey, Sue. "Noonuccal, Oodgeroo (1920–1993)." In *Australian Dictionary of Biography*. Canberra: National Centre of Biography, Australian National University, 2017. http://adb.anu.edu.au/biography/noonuccal-oodgeroo-18057/text29634 (accessed 8 January 2018).

"Aboriginal Mission Boy Won Fame as World Class Tenor." *Daily Mirror* [Sydney?], 11 August 1976, 70. Cutting held in National Library of Australia, Canberra, Biographical Cuttings on Harold Blair, Opera Singer, Containing One or More Cuttings from Newspapers or Journals.

Aboriginal Welfare: Initial Conference of Commonwealth and State Aboriginal Authorities Held at Canberra, 21st to 23rd April, 1937. Canberra: Commonwealth Government Printer, 1937.

Adorno, Theodor, and Max Horkheimer. "The Culture Industry: Enlightenment as Mass Deception." In *Dialectic of Enlightenment*, trans. John Cumming, 121–67. New York: Herder and Herder, 1972.

Agoramoorthy, Govindasamy, and Chandrakasan Sivaperuman. "Tourism, Tribes and Tribulations in Andaman Islands." *Current Science* 106, no. 2 (2014): 141.

Alfred, Gerald R., and Wilbert H. Ahern. *Heeding the Voices of Our Ancestors: Kahnawake Mohawk Politics and the Rise of Native Nationalism*. Toronto: Oxford University Press, 1995.

Allan, Chris. "Baby by-the-Falling-Waters Joins the Fight." *Gazette* [Montreal], 23 February 1971, n. pag. Collection of kahntinetha Horn.

Allen, Kim, and Heather Mendick. "Young People's Uses of Celebrity: Class, Gender and 'Improper' Celebrity." *Discourse: Studies in the Cultural Politics of Education* 34, no. 1 (2013): 77–93.

Ambrosio, Antonino. *A Heartbeat and a Guitar: Johnny Cash and the Making of* Bitter Tears. New York: Nation Books, 2009.

Anae, Melani, Eve Coxon, Diane Mara, Tanya Wendt-Samu, and Christine Finau. *Pasifika Education Research Guidelines*. Auckland: Auckland Uniservices, University of Auckland, 2001.

Anaya, James. "Address by the United Nations Special Rapporteur on the Rights of Indigenous Peoples to the United Nations Permanent Forum on Indigenous Issues." New York, 20 May 2014.

Anderson, Clare. "Colonization, Kidnap and Confinement in the Andamans Penal Colony, 1771–1864." *Journal of Historical Geography* 37, no. 1 (2011): 68–81.

———. "The Politics of Convict Space: Indian Penal Settlements and the Andaman Islands." In *Isolation: Places and Practices of Exclusion*, edited by Carolyn Strange and Alison Bashford, 40–55. New York: Routledge, Taylor and Francis, 2003.

Andrew-Gee, Eric. "The Making of Joseph Boyden." *Globe and Mail*, 4 August 2017. https://www.theglobeandmail.com/arts/books-and-media/joseph-boyden/article35881215/ (accessed 15 January 2020).

Andrews, Shirley. "The Australian Aborigines: A Summary of Their Situation in All States in 1962." State Library of Victoria, Council for Aboriginal Rights (Vic.), Papers, Box 3/4, MS 12913. http://indigenousrights.net.au/resources/documents/the_australian_aborigines_a_summary_of_their_situation_in_all_states_in_1962 (accessed 14 December 2017).

Atkin, Charles, and Martin Block. "Effectiveness of Celebrity Endorsers." *Journal of Advertising Research* 23, no. 1 (1983): 57–61.

Attwood, Bain. *Rights for Aborigines*. Crows Nest, Australia: Allen and Unwin, 2003.

Australian Bureau of Statistics. *Counting: Persons, Place of Usual Residence*. Canberra: Australian Bureau of Statistics, 2016.

Australian Human Rights Commission. "Track the History Timeline: The Stolen Generations." https://www.humanrights.gov.au/track-history-timeline-stolen-generations (accessed 11 January 2018).

baird, jessie little doe. "Wampanoag: How Did This Happen to My Language?" In *Bringing Our Languages Home: Language Revitalization for Families*, edited by Leanne Hinton, 19–32. Berkeley, CA: Heyday Books, 2013.

Baldwin, Daryl, Karen Baldwin, Jessie Baldwin, and Jarrid Baldwin. "Myaamiaataweenki oowaaha: 'Miami spoken here.'" In *Bringing Our Languages Home: Language Revitalization for Families*, edited by Leanne Hinton, 3–18. Berkeley, CA: Heyday Books, 2013.

Barrera, Jorge. "Author Joseph Boyden's Shape-Shifting Indigenous Identity." APTN News, 23 December 2016. https://aptnnews.ca/2016/12/23/author-joseph-boydens-shape-shifting-indigenous-identity (accessed 21 February 2019).

———. "Similarities between Joseph Boyden Story and Ojibway Healer's Published Work Trigger Questions." APTN News, 22 February 2017. https://aptnnews.ca/2017/02/22/similarities-between-joseph-boyden-story-and-ojibway-healers-published-work-trigger-questions (accessed 21 February 2018).

Barsh, Russel. "The Inner Struggle of Indigenous Peoples." In *Indigenous Peoples' Rights in International Law: Emergence and Application*, edited by Roxanne Dunbar-Ortiz, Dalee Sambo Dorough, Gudmundur Alfredsson, Lee Swepston, and Petter Wille, 88–95. Kautokeino, Norway: Galdu, 2015.

Battiste, Marie. "Micmac Literacy and Cognitive Assimilation." In *Indian Education in Canada: The Legacy*, edited by Jean Barman, Yvonne Hébert, and Don McCaskill, 23–44. Vancouver: UBC Press, 1986.

———. "Micmac Literacy and Cognitive Assimilation: A Paper Presented to the Mokakit Indian Education Research Association 1984 International Conference London, Ontario." 26 July 1984. https://files.eric.ed.gov/fulltext/ED267957.pdf (accessed 29 November 2017).

Baviskar, Amita. "Adivasi Encounters with Hindu Nationalism in MP." *Economic and Political Weekly*, 26 November–2 December 2005, 5105–13.

Bederman, Gail. *Manliness and Civilization: A Cultural History of Gender and Race in the United States, 1880–1917*. Chicago: University of Chicago Press, 1995.

Bell, Betty Louise. "Pocahontas: 'Little Mischief' and the 'Dirty Men.'" *Studies in American Indian Literatures* 6, no. 1 (1994): 63–70.

Bennett, Ramona. *Idle No More* [video]. Directed by Dave Wilson. 2 January 2013. https://www.youtube.com/watch?v=ksESR2BvlqY (15 October 2020)

Benton-Banai, Edward. *The Mishomis Book: The Voice of the Ojibway*. Minneapolis: University of Minnesota Press, 1988.

Bergin, Paul. "Maori Sport and Cultural Identity in Australia." *Australian Journal of Anthropology* 13, no. 3 (2002): 257–69.

Besnier, Niko. "The Athlete's Body and the Global Condition: Tongan Rugby Players in Japan." *American Ethnologist* 39, no. 3 (2012): 491–510.

———. "Sports Mobilities across Borders: Postcolonial Perspectives." *International Journal of the History of Sport* 32, no. 7 (2015): 849–61.

Besnier, Niko, and Margaret Jolly. "Afterword: Shape-Shifting Mana: Travels in Space and Time." In *New Mana: Transformations of a Classic Concept in Pacific Languages and Cultures*, edited by Matt Tomlinson and Ty P. Kawika Tengan, 349–68. Canberra: ANU Press, 2016.

Beynon, John. *Masculinities and Culture*. London: Open University Press, 2002.

Bhabha, Homi. *The Location of Culture*. London: Routledge, 1994.

———. "Of Mimicry and Man: The Ambivalence of Colonial Discourse." *October* 28 (1984): 125–33.

Bhaumik, Subir. "Tsunami Folklore 'Saved Islanders.'" BBC News, 20 January 2005. http://news.bbc.co.uk/2/hi/south_asia/4181855.stm.

Bijoy, C.R. "The Adivasis of India: A History of Discrimination, Conflict, and Resistance." *PUCL Bulletin* 1 no. 1 (2003): 54–61.

Billy Jack. Directed by Tom Laughlin. Performed by Tom Laughlin. National Student Film Corporation/Warner Brothers, 1971.

Bishop, Catherine, and Richard White. "Explorer Memory and Aboriginal Celebrity." In *Indigenous Intermediaries: New Perspectives on Exploration Archives*, edited by Shino Konishi, Maria Nugent, and Tiffany Shellam, 31–66. Canberra: ANU Press, 2015.

Bodo, Peter. *The Courts of Babylon: Tales of Greed and Glory in a Harsh New World of Professional Tennis*. New York: Scribner, 1995.

Bolen, Michael. "Justin Trudeau Defeats Patrick Brazeau in Charity Boxing Fight." *Huffington Post*, 31 March 2012. https://www.huffingtonpost.ca/2021/03/31/trudeau-brazeau-boxing-justin-patrick_n_1394122.html (accessed 13 September 2020).

Boorstin, Daniel J. *The Image: A Guide to Pseudo-Events in America*. 1961; reprinted New York: Vintage, 2012.

Borell, P.J. "He iti hoki te mokoroa: Maori Contributions to the Sport of Rugby League." MA thesis, University of Canterbury, 2012.

Bourke, Joanna. *Dismembering the Male: Men's Bodies, Britain and the Great War*. London: Reaktion, 1996.

Bourrie, Mark. "From the Archives: The Rise and Fall of Patrick Brazeau." *Ottawa Magazine*, 29 October 2015. https://ottawamagazine.com/people-and-places/from-the-archives-the-rise-fall-of-patrick-brazeau (accessed 13 September 2020).

Boyden, Joseph. "First Came Truth. Now Comes the Hard Part." *Maclean's*, 25 June 2015. https://www.macleans.ca/news/canada/first-came-truth-now-comes-the-hard-part/ (accessed 15 January 2020).

———. "My Name Is Joseph Boyden." *Maclean's*, 2 August 2017. https://www.macleans.ca/news/canada/my-name-is-joseph-boyden/ (accessed 9 January 2019).

Brading, D.A. *The First America: The Spanish Monarchy, Creole Patriots and the Liberal State 1492–1867*. Reprint ed. Cambridge, UK: Cambridge University Press, 1993.

Brockington, Dan. *Celebrity Advocacy and International Development*. London: Routledge, 2014.

Broome, Richard. *Aboriginal Australians: Black Responses to White Dominance 1788–2001*. 3rd ed. Crows Nest, Australia: Allen and Unwin, 2002.

Brown, David. "Pierre Bourdieu's 'Masculine Domination' Thesis and the Gendered Body in Sport and Physical Culture." *Sociology of Sport Journal* 23, no. 2 (2006): 162–88.

Brown, Toyacoya. "The Sights and Sounds from the Mni Wiconi Benefit Concert." PowWows.com—Native American Pow Wows, 24 January 2017. http://www.powwows.com/sights-sounds-mni-wiconi-benefit-concert/ (accessed 6 March 2019).

Bruce, Toni, and Christopher Hallinan. "The Quest for Australian Identity." *Sport Stars: The Cultural Politics of Sporting Celebrity* 2, no. 3 (2001): 257–73.

Buchan, Bruce. "Traffick of Empire: Trade, Treaty and *Terra Nullius* in Australia and North America, 1750–1800." *History Compass* 5, no. 2 (2007): 386–405.

Buchbinder, David. *Performance Anxieties: Re-Producing Masculinity*. St Leonards, Australia: Allen and Unwin, 1998.

Budd, Michael. *The Sculpture Machine: Physical Culture and Body Politics in the Age of Empire*. London: Palgrave Macmillan, 1997.

Bunge, Robert. "Language: The Psyche of a People." In *Our Languages, Our Survival*, edited by Freda Ahenakew and Shirley Fredeen, 13–20. Vermillion: University of South Dakota, 1987.

Butunyi, Cosmus. "Bono: Celebrity Is a Currency to Be Used to Bring about Change." *The East African*. 12 April 2010. http://www.theeastafrican.co.ke/magazine/Bono-Celebrity-is-a-currency-to-be-used-to-bring-about-change/434746-897132-idv6dj/index.html (accessed 28 October 2017).

Canada. Royal Commission on Aboriginal Peoples. *Gathering Strength*. Vol. 3 of *Report of the Royal Commission on Aboriginal Peoples*. Ottawa: Canada Communications Group, 1996.

Carmen, Andrea. Interview by the author. Mille Lacs, MN, 26 September 2007.

Cashmore, Ellis. *Beyond Black: Celebrity and Race in Obama's America*. London: A&C Black, 2012.

"Cathy Freeman." Australian Institute of Aboriginal and Torres Strait Islander Studies (AIATSIS). 22 May 2017. https://aiatsis.gov.au/explore/articles/cathy-freeman(accessed 15 January 2020).

Cawley, Evonne Goolagong, and Phil Jarratt. *Home! The Evonne Goolagong Story*. East Roseville, Australia: Simon and Schuster, 1993.

CBC News. "Patrick Brazeau: Harper's Strategic Aboriginal Appointment." CBC News, 13 February 2013. https://www.cbc.ca/news/canada/patrick-brazeau-harper-s-strategic-aboriginal-appointment-1.1411015 (accessed 13 September 2020).

Chakravarti, Uma. "Conceptualising Brahmanical Patriarchy in Early India: Gender, Caste, Class and State." *Economic and Political Weekly*, 3 April 1993, 579–85.

Charters, Claire. Personal communication with the author. 10 November 2007.

Clare, Anthony. *On Men: Masculinity in Crisis*. London: Chatto and Windus, 2000.

Clark, Jennifer. *Aborigines and Activism: Race, Aborigines and the Coming of the Sixties to Australia*. Crawley: University of Western Australia Press, 2008.

Clarke, Robert G.H. *Celebrity Colonialism: Fame, Power and Representation in Colonial and Postcolonial Cultures*. Newcastle upon Tyne, UK: Cambridge Scholars Publishing, 2009.

Clune, Frank. "Albert Namatjira: Aboriginal Artist." *Trans-Air* 7, no. 11 (1956): n. pag. Cutting held in National Library of Australia, Canberra, Biographical Cuttings on Albert Namatjira, Artist, Containing One or More Cuttings from Newspapers or Journals.

CNN. "Actor on Native American Roles: 'They Like Us in the. . . .'" YouTube, 9 May 2017. https://www.youtube.com/watch?v=rBrFBxaFz-o (accessed 7 March 2019).

Codrington, Robert H. *The Melanesians: Studies in Their Anthropology and Folk-Lore*. 1891; reprinted New Haven, CT: Human Relations Area Files Press, 1957.

Coffey, John, and Bernie Wood, eds. *100 Years: Maori Rugby League 1908–2008*. Wellington, NZ: Huia Publishers, 2008.

Collins, Felicity. "The Ethical Violence of Celebrity Chat: Russell Crowe and David Gulpilil." *Social Semiotics* 18, no. 2 (2008): 191–204.

Connell, Raewyn. *Masculinities*. 2nd ed. Berkeley: University of California Press, 2005.

Cooper, James Fenimore. *The Last of the Mohicans*. London: Ward, Lock, 1888.

Coulthard, Glen S. "Subjects of Empire: Indigenous Peoples and the 'Politics of Recognition' in Canada." *Contemporary Political Theory* 6, no. 4 (2007): 437–60.

Counihan, Noel. "The Tragedy of Albert Namatjira." *Tribune* [Sydney], 1 April 1959, 6.

Courchene, Darren. "Language as the Root of Ojibwe Knowledge." *Geez Magazine*, Fall 2015. http://www.academia.edu/30414319/Language_as_the_root_of_Ojibwe_knowledge (accessed 20 October 2018).

Craft, Aimee. "Anishinaabe Nibi Inaakonigewin Report: Reflecting the Water Laws Research Gathering Conducted with Anishinaabe Elders." 2014. http://create- h2o.ca/pages/annual_conference/presentations/2014/ANI_Gathering_Report_June24.pdf (accessed on 28 November 2017).

Cupples, Julie, and Kevin Glynn. "The Celebritization of Indigenous Activism: Tame Iti as Media Figure." *International Journal of Cultural Studies* 22, no. 6 (2019): 770–87.

Darby, Paul. "The New Scramble for Africa: The African Football Labour Migration to Europe." *European Sports History Review* 3 (2001): 217–44.

Dasgupta, Jayant. *Japanese in Andaman and Nicobar Islands: Red Sun over Black Water*. New York: Berghahn Books, 2002.

Das Gupta, Sanjukta, and Raj Sekhar Basu. *Narratives from the Margins: Aspects of Adivasi History in India*. New Delhi: Primus Books, 2012.

Dawes, Kwame. "Re-Appropriating Cultural Appropriation." In *Borrowed Power: Essays on Cultural Appropriation*, edited by Bruce H. Ziff and Pratima V. Rao, 109–21. New Brunswick, NJ: Rutgers University Press, 1997.

"Deadline Arrives for Dakota Access Protesters to Leave." MSNBC, 22 February 2017. https://www.msnbc.com/msnbc-news/watch/deadline-arrives-for-dakota-access-protesters-to-leave-882700867856 (accessed 7 March 2019).

Debord, Guy. *Society of the Spectacle*. New York: Zone Books, 1967.

Deer, Kenneth. "Reflections on the Development, Adoption, and Implementation of the UN Declaration on the Rights of Indigenous Peoples." In *Realizing the UN Declaration on the Rights of Indigenous Peoples: Triumph, Hope, and Action*, edited by Jackie Hartley, Paul Joffe, and Jennifer Preston, 18–28. Saskatoon: Purich, 2010.

De Korne, Haley. "The Multilingual Realities of Language Reclamation: Working with Language Contact, Diversity, and Change in Endangered Language Education." *Language Documentation and Description* 14 (2016): 111–35.

de Las Casas, Bartolomé. *The Devastation of the Indies: A Brief Account*. 1552. Baltimore, MD: Johns Hopkins University Press, 1992.

Deloria, Philip J. *Playing Indian*. New Haven, CT: Yale University Press, 1998.

Deshmane, Akshay. "10 Lakh Adivasis Face Eviction from Their Land: It All Hinges on One SC Order." *HuffPost India*, 3 July 2019, sec. "News." https://www.huffingtonpost.in/entry/modi-govt-tribal-rights-forests-supreme-coure_in_5d1c4b46e4b03d6116443090 (accessed 5 March 2020).

Dewey, Robert F. "Embracing Rugby and Negotiating Inequalities in the Pacific Islands." Paper presented at the Traditional Knowledge Conference 2008: Te Tatau Pounamu—The Greenstone Door, Knowledge Exchange Programme, Auckland, 2010.

———. "Pacific Islands Rugby Alliance (PIRA): Rugby in 'Our Sea of Islands.'" *International Journal of the History of Sport* 31, no. 11 (2014): 1406–20.

Diaz, Vicente. "Tackling Pacific Hegemonic Formations on the American Gridiron." *Amerasia Journal* 37, no. 3 (2011): 90–113.

DiEmanuele, Elizabeth. "Moving towards 'Pow Wow–Step': Constructions of 'the Indian' and A Tribe Called Red's Mobilization of Art as Resistance." MA thesis, McMaster University, 2015.

Docker, Edward W. *The Blackbirders: A Brutal Story of the Kanaka Slave-Trade*. Sydney: Angus and Robertson, 1981.

Doxtator, Deborah. "Godi'Nigoha': The Women's Mind and Seeing Through to the Land." In *Godi'Nigoha: The Women's Mind*, by The Woodland Cultural Educational Centre's curators Deborah Doxtator and Lynn Ann Hill, 29–41. Brantford, ON: Woodland Cultural Educational Centre, 1997.

Drake, Philip, and Andy Miah. "The Cultural Politics of Celebrity." *Cultural Politics: An International Journal* 6, no. 1 (2010): 49–64.

Driessens, Olivier. "The Celebritization of Society and Culture: Understanding the Structural Dynamics of Celebrity Culture." *International Journal of Cultural Studies* 16, no. 6 (2013): 641–57.

Dunbar-Ortiz, Roxanne. "The First Ten Years from Study to Working Group 1972–1982." In *Indigenous Peoples' Rights in International Law: Emergence and Application*, edited by Roxanne Dunbar-Ortiz, Dalee Sambo Dorough, Gudmundur Alfredsson, Lee Swepston, and Petter Wille, 42–87. Kautokeino, Norway: Galdu, 2015.

Duncan, Alan T. "Blair, Harold (1924–1976)." In *Australian Dictionary of Biography*. Canberra: National Centre of Biography, Australian National University, 1993. http://adb.anu.edu.au/biography/blair-harold-9520/text16761 (accessed 12 January 2018).

Durie, Mason H. *Te Mana. Te Kāwanatanga: The Politics of Māori Self-Determination*. Auckland: Oxford University Press, 1988.

Duvall, Deborah L. *Tahlequah and the Cherokee Nation*. Charleston, SC: Arcadia Publishing, 2000.

Duvall, Spring-Serenity, and Nicole Heckemeyer. "#BlackLivesMatter: Black Celebrity Hashtag Activism and the Discursive Formation of a Social Movement." *Celebrity Studies* 9, no. 3 (2018): 391–408.

Dyer, Richard. *Heavenly Bodies: Film Stars and Society*. London: Routledge, 2011.

Dyrenfurth, Nick. *Mateship: A Very Australian History*. Melbourne: Scribe Publications, 2015.

Edison Manufacturing Company. *Sioux Ghost Dance*. 1894. www.loc.gov/item/00694139/ (accessed 13 September 2020).

Edwards, Stassa. "When Criticism Becomes Persecution." *Jezebel*, 10 January 2017. https://jezebel.com/when-criticism-becomes-persecution-1790803651 (accessed 21 February 2019).

Edwards, Tim. *Cultures of Masculinity*. New York: Routledge, 2006.

Equality Labs. "Why Do We Say No to Holi? A Guide to Challenge Casteism." *Medium.com* (blog), 2 March 2020. https://medium.com/@EqualityLabs/why-do-we-say-no-to-holi-a-guide-to-challenge-casteism-ad592d0735cb (accessed 5 March 2020).

Erueti, Bevan, and Farah R. Palmer. "Te Whariki Tuakiri (the Identity Mat): Māori Elite Athletes and the Expression of Ethno-Cultural Identity in Global Sport." *Sport in Society* 17, no. 8 (2013): 1061–75.

Fagan, Sean. *The Rugby Rebellion: Pioneers of Rugby League*. Kellyville, Australia: RL1908, 2007.

Fairbairn-Dunlop, Tagaloatele Peggy. "Reconnecting to Our Sea of Islands: Pacific Studies in the Next Decade." *AlterNative: An International Journal of Indigenous Peoples* 4, no. 1 (2008): 45–56.

Falcous, Mark. "Rugby League in the National Imaginary of New Zealand Aotearoa." *Sport in History* 27, no. 3 (2007): 423–46.

"Fame Was Death to Aboriginal Artist." *Daily Mirror* [Sydney?], 24 July 1967, 28. Cutting held in National Library of Australia, Canberra, Biographical Cuttings on Albert Namatjira, Artist, Containing One or More Cuttings from Newspapers or Journals.

Fardon, Don. (*The Lament of the Cherokee Reservation Indian) Indian Reservation* [vinyl]. Pye Records, 1968.

Farnell, Brenda. *Do You See What I Mean? Plains Indian Sign Talk and the Embodiment of Action*. Austin: University of Texas Press, 1995.

Farrelly, Trisia, and Unaisi Nabobo Baba. "Talanoa as Empathic Apprenticeship." *Asia Pacific Viewpoint* 55, no. 3 (2014): 319–30.

Ferris, Kerry O. "The Next Big Thing: Local Celebrity." *Society* 47, no. 5 (2010): 392–95.

———. "The Sociology of Celebrity." *Sociology Compass* 1, no. 1 (2007): 371–84.

Flags of Our Fathers. Directed by Clint Eastwood. Produced by Robert Lorenz and Steven Spielberg. Paramount Pictures, 2006.

Foley, Gary. "Black Power in Redfern 1968–1972." The Koori History Website. Updated 5 October 2001. http://www.kooriweb.org/foley/essays/essay_1.html (accessed 19 May 2008).

Foucault, Michel. *The History of Sexuality: Volume 1, An Introduction*. Translated by Robert Hurley. New York: Pantheon, 1978.

———. *Power/Knowledge: Selected Interviews and Other Writings, 1972–1977.* Edited by Colin Gordon. Brighton, UK: Harvester Press, 1980.

Francis, Daniel. *The Imaginary Indian: The Image of the Indian in Canadian Culture.* 1992; reprinted Vancouver: Arsenal Pulp Press, 2004.

Frichner, Tonya Gonnella. Interview by the author. New York, 3 December 2011.

Fry, Greg. "Framing the Islands: Knowledge and Power in Changing Australian Images of the South Pacific." *Contemporary Pacific* 9, no. 2 (1997): 305–44.

Gangopadhyay, Sunil. *Sabuj Dwiper Raja.* Kalakātā: Ananda Publishers, 2014.

Geniusz, Mary Siisip. *Plants Have So Much to Give Us, All We Have to Do Is Ask: Anishinaabe Botanical Teachings.* Minneapolis: University of Minnesota Press, 2015.

Giacona, Christina. *The Indigenous of Turtle Island: Native American Music in North America.* Dubuque, IA: Kendall Hunt Publishing, 2018.

Goldberg, David Theo. *Racist Culture: Philosophy and the Politics of Meaning.* Oxford: Blackwell, 1993.

Goodheart, Adam. "The Last Island of the Savages." *American Scholar* 69, no. 4 (2000): 13–44.

Government of India. "Constitution of India, National Portal of India." https://www.india.gov.in/my-government/constitution-india (accessed 5 March 2020).

Gowen, Annie. "'He Lost His Mind': Slain Missionary John Allen Chau Planned for Years to Convert Remote Tribe." *Washington Post*, 27 November 2018. https://www.washingtonpost.com/national/he-lost-his-mind-slain-missionary-john-allen- chau-planned-for-years-to-convert-remote-tribe/2018/11/27/eb13d7ad-4685-4748-951b- 790d671f655d_story.html (accessed 5 March 2020).

Grant, Stan. "How Rugby League Player Dean Widders Stared Racism in the Face and Won." *Guardian*, 22 January 2016. https://www.theguardian.com/australia-news/2016/jan/22/how-rugby-league-player-dean-widders-stared-racism-in-the-face-and-won (accessed 6 May 2016).

Green, Rayna D. "The Pocahontas Perplex: The Image of Indian Women in American Culture." *Massachusetts Review* 16, no. 4 (1975): 698–714.

Greene, Graham. "Has Anyone Noticed the Evil Being Done by the Money Grubbing Bastards at Standing Rock. . . . It's Just Deplorable. So Much for Police Protection." Twitter. 16 September 2016. https://twitter.com/rafeolla/status/776924873809592320?lang=en (accessed 6 March 2019).

Haebich, Anna. *Broken Circles: Fragmenting Indigenous Families 1800–2000.* Fremantle, Australia: Fremantle Arts Centre Press, 2000.

———. "Imagining Assimilation." *Australian Historical Studies* 33, no. 118 (2002): 61–70.

———. *Spinning the Dream: Assimilation in Australia 1950–1970.* North Fremantle, Australia: Fremantle Press, 2008.

Hamer, Paul. "One in Six? The Rapid Growth of the Maori Population in Australia." *New Zealand Population Review* 33, no. 1 (2008): 153–76.

———. "'Unsophisticated and Unsuited': Australian Barriers to Pacific Islander Immigration from New Zealand." *Political Science* 66, no. 2 (2014): 93–118.

"Harold Blair: Cane-Cutter to Top Tenor." *Age* [Melbourne], 22 May 1976, 2. Cutting held in National Library of Australia, Canberra, Biographical Cuttings on Harold Blair, Opera Singer, Containing One or More Cuttings from Newspapers or Journals.

Hau'ofa, Epeli. "Our Sea of Islands," in *A New Oceania: Rediscovering Our Sea of Islands*, ed. Eric Waddell, Vijay Naidu, and Epeli Hau'ofa, 2–16. Suva, Fiji: School of Social and Economic Development, University of the South Pacific, 1993.

Hawkes, Gina, David Pollock, Barry Judd, Peter Phipps, and Elinor Assoulin. "Ngapartji Ngapartji: Finding Ethical Approaches to Research Involving Indigenous Peoples, Australian Perspectives." *Ab-Original: Journal of Indigenous Studies and First Nations and First Peoples' Cultures* 1, no. 1 (2017): 17–41.

Haynes, John. *All Blacks to All Golds*. West Yorkshire: League Publications League Publications, 2007.

Heizer, Robert F., and Theodora Kroeber, eds. *Ishi the Last Yahi: A Documentary History*. Berkeley: University of California Press, 1979.

Hepp, Andreas. *Cultures of Mediatization*. Cambridge, UK: Polity, 2013.

Heppler, Jason. "Framing Red Power: The American Indian Movement, the Trail of Broken Treaties, and the Politics of Media." MA thesis, University of Nebraska Lincoln, 2009.

Hilburn, Robert. *Johnny Cash: The Life*. New York: Little, Brown, 2013.

Hill, Jane H. "'Expert Rhetorics' in Advocacy for Endangered Languages: Who Is Listening and What Do They Hear?" *Journal of Linguistic Anthropology* 12, no. 2 (2002): 119–33.

Hill, Tom. "Preface and Acknowledgements." In *Godi'Nigoha: The Women's Mind*, by Deborah Doxtator and Lynn Ann Hill, 29–41. Brantford, ON: Woodland Cultural Educational Centre, 1997.

Hodge, Bob. "Poetry and Politics in Oodgeroo: Transcending the Difference." *Australian Literary Studies* 16, no. 4 (1994): 63–76.

Hokowhitu, Brendan. "Foucault, Genealogy, Sport and Indigeneity." In *Examining Sport Histories: Power, Paradigms, and Reflexivity*, edited by Richard Pringle and Murray Phillips, 225– 48. Morgantown, WV: FiT Publishing, 2013.

———. "Tackling Maori Masculinity: A Colonial Genealogy of Savagery and Sport." *Contemporary Pacific* 16, no. 2 (2004): 259–84.

———. "Taxonomies of Indigeneity: Indigenous Heterosexual Patriarchal Masculinity." In *Indigenous Men and Masculinities: Identities, Legacies, Regeneration*, edited by Robert Alexander Innes and Kim Anderson, 80–95. Winnipeg: University of Manitoba Press, 2015.

Hopper, Tristan. "Rivals Justin Trudeau and Senator Patrick Brazeau Facing Off in Charity Boxing Bout." *National Post*, 18 January 2012. https://nationalpost.com/news/canada/rivals-justin-trudeau-and-senator-patrick-brazeau-facing-off-in-charity-boxing-bout (accessed 13 September 2020).

Horn, kahntinetha. "Experiences with the Seaway Construction." Class lecture, Indigenous Politics and Resurgence, Carleton University, 5 October 2017.

Horn-Miller, Kahente. "From Paintings to Power: The Meaning of the Mohawk Warrior Flag Twenty Years after Oka." *Socialist Studies: Journal of the Society for Socialist Studies* 6, no. 1 (2010): 96–124.

———. "Ma Takes on the *Toronto Telegram*." *Coffee with My Ma*. Podcast audio, 16 April 2018. https://www.stitcher.com/podcast/coffee-with-my-ma/e/55615698 (accessed 30 November 2019).

———. "A Symbol of Indigenous Unification and Impetus to Assertion of Identity and Rights Commencing in the Kanienkehaka Community of Kahnawake." MA thesis, Concordia University, 2003.

Horton, Peter. "Pacific Islanders in Global Rugby: The Changing Currents of Sports Migration." *International Journal of the History of Sport* 29, no. 17 (2012): 2388–404.

———. "Pacific Islanders in Professional Rugby Football: Bodies, Minds and Cultural Continuities." *Asia Pacific Journal of Sport and Social Science* 3, no. 3 (2014): 222–35.

Huffington Post Canada. "Patrick Brazeau Suggests Theresa Spence Gained Weight during Protest." *Huffington Post Canada*, 31 January 2013. https://www.huffingtonpost.ca/2013/01/31/patrick-brazeau-theresa-spence_n_2589799.html (accessed 13 September 2020).

Idle No More. http://www.idlenomore.ca (accessed 1 June 2020).

Ilaiah, Kancha. *Post-Hindu India: A Discourse in Dalit-Bahujan, Socio-Spiritual and Scientific Revolution*. Thousand Oaks, CA: SAGE, 2009.

Imam, Abu. "Sir Alexander Cunningham (1814–1893): The First Phase of Indian Archaeology." *Journal of the Royal Asiatic Society of Great Britain and Ireland* 3–4 (1963): 194–207.

India Parliament House of the People and India Parliament Lok Sabha. *Lok Sabha Debates*. Lok Sabha Secretariat, 1995.

Indian Express. "French Filmmakers Shoot Jarawa Tribe, Booked." *Indian Express*, 25 October 2014. http://indianexpress.com/article/india/india-others/french-filmmakers-shoot-jarawa-tribe-booked/ (accessed 5 March 2020).

Innes, Robert Alexander, and Kim Anderson, eds. *Indigenous Men and Masculinities: Legacies, Identities, Regeneration*. Winnipeg: University of Manitoba Press, 2015.

International Indian Treaty Council. Declaration of Continuing Independence. Standing Rock Indian Country, June 1974.

———. "Guiding Principles." https://www.iitc.org/about-iitc/guiding-principles/ (accessed 20 December 2017).

"I Ran Away from Games Fame, Says Cathy Freeman." *West Australian* [Perth?], 19 May 2017. https://thewest.com.au/sport/i-ran-away-from-my-icon-status-says-cathy-freeman-ng-b88481683z (accessed 15 January 2020).

Irvine, Judith T., and Susan Gal. "Language Ideology and Linguistic Differentiation." In *Regimes of Language: Ideologies, Polities, and Identities*, edited by Paul V. Kroskrity, 35–83. Santa Fe: School of American Research Press, 2000.

Ishi, and Bernie Krause. *Ishi: The Last Yahi*. San Francisco, CA: Wild Sanctuary, 1992.

Jackson, Moana. Interview by the author. Wellington, NZ, 11 March 2008.

Jackson, Sarah J. *Black Celebrity, Racial Politics, and the Press: Framing Dissent*. New York: Routledge, 2014.

Jaoul, Nicolas. "Beyond Citizenship: Adivasi and Dalit Political Pathways in India." *Focaal* 76 (2016): 3–14.

Johari, Aarefa. "Dalits, Adivasis, Muslims Targeted in at Least Five Incidents since BJP Won the Election." *Scroll.In*. 27 May 2019. https://scroll.in/article/924841/dalits-adivasis-muslims-targeted-in-at-least-five-incidents-since-bjp-won-the-election (accessed 5 March 2020).

Johnston, Basil. *The Manitous: The Spiritual World of the Ojibway*. St. Paul: Minnesota Historical Society Press, 2001.

Jones, Max. "What Should Historians Do with Heroes? Reflections on Nineteenth- and Twentieth-Century Britain." *History Compass* 5, no. 2 (2007): 439–54.

Jones, Michael E. "Celebrity Endorsements: A Case for Alarm and Concern for the Future." *New England Law Review* 15, no. 3 (1979): 521–44.

Justice League. Directed by Zack Snyder. Performed by Gal Gadot, Ben Affleck, and Jason Momoa. DC Films/Warner Brothers Pictures, 2017.

Ka'ili, Tevita O. "Tauhi va: Nurturing Tongan Sociospatial Ties in Maui and Beyond." *Contemporary Pacific* 17, no. 1 (2005): 83–114.

Kambhampaty, Anna Purna, Madeleine Carlisle, and Melissa Chan. "Justin Trudeau Wore Brownface at 2001 'Arabian Nights' Party while He Taught at a Private School." *Time*, 18 September 2019. https://time.com/5680759/justin-trudeau-brownface-photo/ (13 September 2020).

Kamins, M.A. "Celebrity and Noncelebrity Advertising in a Two-Sided Context." *Journal of Advertising Research* 29, no. 3 (1989): 34–42.

Kearney, Judith, and Matthew Glen. "The Effects of Citizenship and Ethnicity on the Education Pathways of Pacific Youth in Australia." *Education, Citizenship and Social Justice* 12, no. 3 (2017): 1–13.

Keeshig [Tobias], Lenore. "Stop Stealing Native Stories." *Globe and Mail*, 26 January 1990, A7.

Kell, Peter. *Good Sports: Australian Sport and the Myth of the Fair Go.* Annandale, NSW: Pluto Press, 2000.

Kerin, Rani. "Charles Duguid and Aboriginal Assimilation in Adelaide, 1950–1960: The Nebulous 'Assimilation' Goal." *History Australia* 2, no. 3 (2005): 85.1–85.17.

Kidwell, Clara Sue. "What Would Pocahontas Think Now? Women and Cultural Persistence." *Native American Literatures* 17, no. 1 (1994): 149–59.

King, Kendall A., and Mary Hermes. "Why Is This So Hard? Ideologies of Endangerment, Passive Language Learning Approaches, and Ojibwe in the United States." *Journal of Language, Identity and Education* 13, no. 4 (2014): 268–82.

Kleinert, Sylvia. "The Critical Reaction to the Hermannsburg School." In *The Heritage of Namatjira: The Watercolourists of Central Australia*, edited by Jane Hardy, J.V.S. Megaw, and M. Ruth Megaw, 217–47. Port Melbourne: William Heinemann Australia, 1992.

———. "Namatjira, Albert (Elea) (1902–1959)." In *Australian Dictionary of Biography*. Canberra: National Centre of Biography, Australian National University, 2000. http://adb.anu.edu.au/biography/namatjira-albert-elea-11217/text19999 (accessed 4 January 2018).

Kohu, Hinewirangi. Interview by the author. Mille Lacs, MN, 26 September 2007.

Kroeber, Theodora. *Ishi in Two Worlds: A Biography of the Last Wild Indian in North America.* Berkeley: University of California Press, 1976.

Kroeber, Theodora, and Ruth Robbins. *Ishi, Last of His Tribe*. Berkeley, CA: Parnassus Press, 1964.

Kroskrity, Paul V., ed. *Telling Stories in the Face of Danger: Language Renewal in Native American Communities*. Norman: University of Oklahoma Press, 2012.

Lahiri, Nayanjot. "Archaeology and Identity in Colonial India." *Antiquity* 74, no. 285 (2000): 687–92.

Lake, Randall A. "Enacting Red Power: The Consummatory Function in Native American Protest Rhetoric." *Quarterly Journal of Speech* 69 (1983): 127–42.

Lakisa, David, Daryl Adair, and Tracy Taylor. "Pasifika Diaspora and the Changing Face of Australian Rugby League." *Contemporary Pacific* 26, no. 2 (2014): 347–67.

Lal, Brij V., and Kate Fortune, eds. *The Pacific Islands: An Encyclopedia, Vol. 1*. Honolulu: University of Hawaii Press, 2000.

Lalmalsawma, David. "India Speaks 780 Languages, 220 Lost in Last 50 Years—Survey." *Reuters Blogs*. 7 September 2013. http://blogs.reuters.com/india/2013/09/07/india-speaks-780-languages-220-lost-in-last-50-years-survey/ (accessed 13 September 2020).

LaRocque, Emma. *When the Other Is Me: Native Resistance Discourse, 1850–1990*. Winnipeg: University of Manitoba Press, 2011.

"Last 2 Speakers of Dying Language Won't Speak to Each Other." *Huffington Post*, 14 April 2010. https://www.huffpost.com/entry/ayapaneco-dying-languages_n_849319?guccounter=1&-guce_referrer=aHR0cHM6Ly93d3cuZ29vZ2xlLmNvbS8&guce_referrer_sig=AQAAA-I1clg8ImhsQ993zH3bQfcyXUDx7SiVcsskiAl3SMXVGESYad8lNxujSubL4iDFTWNX-A5Uy5e_-FWjfvTOdmCxMLofFSieocq5HxKhAlxJBwsE5oqWSQBkz6SkV3JgzlsNSe6sFq1-RaXQUiFtduEW5Osdc8ml77qJ8IDu_AXezLL (accessed 14 July 2014).

Lee, Helen, and Steve Francis. *Migration and Transnationalism: Pacific Perspectives*. Canberra: Australian National University E Press, 2009.

Leon, Melissa. "Jason Momoa on Speaking Out for NoDAPL: 'I Don't Mind Standing Up for What I Believe In.'" *Daily Beast*. 4 February 2017. https://www.thedailybeast.com/jason-momoa-on-speaking-out-for-nodapl-i-dont-mind-standing-up-for-what-i-believe-in (accessed 7 March 2019).

Leonard, Wesley Y. "Challenging 'Extinction' through Modern Miami Language Practices." *American Indian Culture and Research Journal* 35, no. 2 (2011): 135–60.

———. "Producing Language Reclamation by Decolonizing 'Language.'" *Language Documentation and Description* 14 (2016).

———. "When Is an 'Extinct Language' Not Extinct? Miami, a Formerly Sleeping Language." In *Sustaining Linguistic Diversity: Endangered and Minority Languages and Language Varieties*, edited by Kendall A. King, Natalie Schilling-Estes, Lyn Fogle, Jia Jackie Lou, and Barbara Soukup, 23–33. Washington, DC: Georgetown University Press, 2008.

Leonard, Wesley Y., and Erin Haynes. "Making 'Collaboration' Collaborative: An Examination of Perspectives that Frame Linguistic Field Research." *Language Documentation and Conservation* 4 (2010): 268–93.

Leslie, Larry Z. *Celebrity in the 21st Century: A Reference Handbook*. Santa Barbara, CA: ABC-CLIO, 2011.

Lester, Gary. *The Story of Australian Rugby League*. Sydney: Lester Townsend Publishing, 1988.

Levin, Jennifer. "A Benefit for Protectors: Stand and Rock." *Santa Fe New Mexican*, 29 December 2016. https://www.santafenewmexican.com/pasatiempo/music/in_concert/a-benefit-for-protectors-stand-and-rock/article_eae4dba0-1880-5323-af5a-2023917dd710.html (accessed 7 March 2019).

Lewis, Daniel. "Civoniceva Urges NRL to Educate Racist Minority." *Brisbane Times*, 8 March 2011. https://www.brisbanetimes.com.au/sport/nrl/civoniceva-urges-nrl-to-educate-racistminority-20110308-1bmn4.html (27 March 2011).

Lightfoot, Sheryl. *Global Indigenous Politics: A Subtle Revolution*. Vol. 8, *Worlding beyond the West*. New York: Routledge, 2016.

Lilomaiava-Doktor, Saili. "Beyond Migration: Samoan Population Movement (Malaga) and the Geography of Social Space (Va)." *Contemporary Pacific* 21, no. 1 (2009): 1–32.

Little Bear, Leroy. "Jagged Worldviews Colliding." In *Reclaiming Indigenous Voice and Vision*, edited by Marie Battiste, 77–85. Vancouver: UBC Press, 2000.

Lockwood, Douglas. "Rise and Fall of a Great Aborigine." *Advertiser*, 2 August 1958, n. pag. Cutting held in National Library of Australia, Canberra, Biographical Cuttings on Albert Namatjira, Artist, Containing One or More Cuttings from Newspapers or Journals.

———. "The Tragedy of Albert Namatjira." *Herald*, 2 August 1958, n. pag. Cutting held in National Library of Australia, Canberra, Biographical Cuttings on Albert Namatjira, Artist, Containing One or More Cuttings from Newspapers or Journals.

Luger, Chelsey. "From the Black Eyed Peas to N7: Nike and Taboo Form Unique Collaboration." Indian Country Media Network. 28 September 2016. https://indiancountrymedianetwork.com/culture/health-wellness/from-the-black-eyed-peas-to-n7-nike-and-taboo-form-unique-collaboration (accessed 6 March 2019).

Lukaniec, Megan. "From Archives to Adult and Child Language Learning: Reconstructing and Revitalizing Wendat (Iroquoian)." Paper presented at the 89th Annual Meeting of the Linguistic Society of America, Portland, Oregon, 2015.

Lyndall, Ryan. "Truganini (Trukanini)." In *The Oxford Companion to Australian History*, edited by Graeme Davison, John Hirst, and Stuart Macintyre, 651–52. Melbourne: Oxford University Press, 1998.

Macintyre, Stuart. *A Concise History of Australia*. 2nd ed. Port Melbourne: Cambridge University Press, 2004.

Macpherson, Cluny, Paul Spoonley, and Melani Anae. *Tangata O Te Moana Nui: The Evolving Identities of Pacific Peoples in Aotearoa/New Zealand*. Palmerston North, NZ: Dunmore Press, 2001.

Magee, Jonathan, and John Sugden. "'The World at Their Feet': Professional Football and International Labor Migration." *Journal of Sport and Social Issues* 26, no. 4 (2002): 421–37.

Magubane, Zine. "The (Product) Red Man's Burden: Charity, Celebrity, and the Contradictions of Coevalness." *Journal of Pan African Studies* 2, no. 6 (2008): 1–25.

Maguire, Joseph, and Mark Falcous, eds. *Sport and Migration: Borders, Boundaries and Crossings*. Oxon, UK: Routledge, 2011.

Malezer, Les. "Dreamtime Discovery: New Reality and Hope." In *Realizing the UN Declaration on the Rights of Indigenous Peoples: Triumph, Hope, and Action*, edited by Jackie Hartley, Paul Joffe, and Jennifer Preston, 29–46. Saskatoon: Purich, 2010.

Marcus, Sharon. *The Drama of Celebrity*. Princeton, NJ: Princeton University Press, 2019.

Marlow, Karina. "15 Years On, Cathy Freeman's Olympic Gold Still a Potent Symbol of Reconciliation." National Indigenous Television (NITV), 25 September 2015. https://www.sbs.com.au/nitv/article/2015/09/25/15-years-cathy-freemans-olympic-gold-still-potent-symbol-reconciliation (accessed 15 January 2020).

Marsters, C.P.E. "Young Pacific Male Athletes and Positive Mental Wellbeing." Master of Public Health thesis, University of Auckland, 2017.

"Marvel Becoming." Facebook. 31 August 2017. https://www.facebook.com/MarvelBecoming/videos/10155561865232488/?eid=ARAavWgf3AB3JseoITAbsy4wLQIMiCpvO-uEDGRo1IW3dU5P-m6VuouosCB9gOi17w-C21A51GNtFA9GK (accessed 7 March 2019).

Marvel Entertainment. *Taboo of Black Eyed Peas Becomes Red Wolf—Marvel Becoming*. YouTube. 24 July 2017. https://www.youtube.com/watch?v=LLHVtsIqdeA (accessed 6 March 2019).

Marwick, Alice E. *Status Update: Celebrity, Publicity, and Branding in the Social Media Age*. New Haven, CT: Yale University Press, 2013.

Marwick, Alice E., and Danah Boyd. "I Tweet Honestly, I Tweet Passionately: Twitter Users, Context Collapse, and the Imagined Audience." *New Media and Society* 13, no. 1 (2010): 114–33.

Mascord, Steve. "Discord: Pronouncing Polynesian Players' Names Correctly Not Just a Matter of Sticks and Stones." *Sydney Morning Herald*, 31 August 2017. http://www.smh.com.au/rugby-league/discord-its-not-just-sticks-and-stones-20170830-gy7lyi.html (accessed 3 September 2017).

Maynard, John. "Vision, Voice and Influence: The Rise of the Australian Aboriginal Progressive Association." *Australian Historical Studies* 34, no. 121 (2003): 91–105.

Mays, Kyle. "Indigenous Dreamin': How Indigenous Hip Hop Rejects the Colonial Politics of Authenticity and Recognition." Presentation at Decolonization in Comparative Context, Amherst College, Amherst, MA, 27 October 2017.

Mazer, Sharon. "Donald Trump Shoots the Match." *TDR: The Drama Review* 62, no. 2 (2018): 175–200.

Mbembe, Achille. "Necropolitics," *Public Culture* 15, no. 1 (2003): 11–40.

McBride, Michael. "Resource Extraction and American Indians: The Invisible History of America." *National Geographic Blog*. 14 December 2017. https://blog.nationalgeographic.org/2017/04/28/resource-extraction-and-american-indians-the-invisible-history-of-america/ (accessed 7 March 2019).

McCallum, Mary Jane. *Indigenous Women, Work, and History, 1940–1980*. Winnipeg: University of Manitoba Press, 2013.

McCardle, Bennett. "Kahn-Tineta Horn." In *Canadian Encyclopedia*. 4 February 2008. Updated by Michelle Filice, 25 January 2016. http://www.thecanadianencyclopedia.ca/en/article/kahn-tineta-horn/ (accessed 18 November 2017).

McClintock, Herbert. "Homage to Namatjira." *Tribune* [Sydney], 19 August 1959, 6.

McGrath, Ann. "A National Story." In *Contested Ground: Australian Aborigines under the British Crown*, edited by Ann McGrath, 1–54. St Leonards, Australia: Allen and Unwin, 1995.

McCracken, Grant. "Who Is the Celebrity Endorser? Cultural Foundations of the Endorsement Process." *Journal of Consumer Research* 16, no. 3 (1989): 310–21.

McCurdy, Patrick. "Conceptualizing Celebrity Activists: The Case of Tamsin Omond." *Celebrity Studies* 4 (2013): 311–24.

McDonald, Brent. "Developing 'Home-Grown' Talent: Pacific Island Rugby Labour and the Victorian Rugby Union." *International Journal of the History of Sport* 31, no. 11 (2014): 1332–44.

McDonald, Brent, and Lena Rodriguez. "'It's Our Meal Ticket': Pacific Bodies, Labour and Mobility in Australia." *Asia Pacific Journal of Sport and Social Science* 3, no. 3 (2014): 236–49.

McGavin, Kristen. "Being 'Nesian': Pacific Islander Identity in Australia." *Contemporary Pacific* 26, no. 1 (2014): 126–54.

McGrath, Barbara Burns, and Tevita O. Ka'ili. "Creating Project Talanoa: A Culturally Based Community Health Program for U.S. Pacific Islander Adolescents." *Public Health Nursing* 27, no. 1 (2010): 17–24.

McGregor, Russell. "Assimilationists Contest Assimilation: T.G.H. Strehlow and A.P. Elkin on Aboriginal Policy." *Journal of Australian Studies* 75 (2002): 43–50.

———. "'Breed Out the Colour': Or the Importance of Being White." *Australian Historical Studies* 33, no. 120 (2002): 287–90.

———. *Imagined Destinies: Aboriginal Australians and the Doomed Race Theory, 1880–1939*. Carlton South, Australia: Melbourne University Press, 1997.

McNally, Michael. *Honoring Elders: Aging, Authority, and Ojibwe Religion*. New York: Columbia University Press, 2009.

Means, Bill. Interview by the author. Minneapolis, 17 January 2008.

Means, Russell, and Bayard Johnson. *If You've Forgotten the Names of the Clouds, You've Lost Your Way: An Introduction to American Indian Thought and Philosophy*. Porcupine, SD: Treaty Publications, 2012.

Meek, Barbra A. "And the Injun Goes 'How!' Representations of American Indian English in White Public Space." *Language in Society* 35, no. 1 (2006): 93–128.

———. "Failing American Indian Languages." *American Indian Culture and Research Journal* 35, no. 2 (2011): 43–60.

———. *We Are Our Language: An Ethnography of Language Revitalization in a Northern Athabaskan Community*. Tucson: University of Arizona Press, 2010.

Merriam-Webster. https://www.merriam-webster.com/dictionary/celebrity (accessed 5 August 2020).

Meyers, Erin. "'Can You Handle My Truth?' Authenticity and the Celebrity Star Image." *Journal of Popular Culture* 42, no. 5 (2009): 890–907.

Miller, Karl Hagstrom. *Segregating Sound: Inventing Folk and Pop Music in the Age of Jim Crow*. Refiguring American Music. Durham, NC: Duke University Press, 2010.

Miller, Lantz Fleming. "Rights of Self-Delimiting Peoples: Protecting Those Who Want No Part of Us." *Human Rights Review* 14, no. 1 (2013): 31–51.

Million, Dian. "Spirit and Matter: Resurgence as Rising and (Re)Creation as Ethos." Panel Presentation, Grounding Resurgence, Reconciliation in a time of Resurgence, University of Victoria, 18 March 2017.

Misra, Neelesh. "Stone Age Cultures Survive Tsunami Waves." NBC News, 4 January 2005. http://www.nbcnews.com/id/6786476/ns/world_news-tsunami_a_year_later/t/stone-age-cultures-survive-tsunami-waves/ (accessed 5 March 2020).

Mitchell, Michael Kanentakeron, dir. *You Are on Indian Land*. National Film Board of Canada, 1969.

Mohawks in Beehives + Other Work. Mercer Union: A Centre for Contemporary Art. http://www.mercerunion.org/exhibitions/mohawks-in-beehives-other-work/ (accessed 18 November 2017).

Molnar, Gyozo, and Yoko Kanemasu. "Playing on the Global Periphery: Social Scientific Explorations of Rugby in the Pacific Islands." *Asia Pacific Journal of Sport and Social Science* 3, no. 3 (2014): 175–85.

Mooney, Christopher, and John Ramsland. "Growing Up and Breaking Away from the Mission: The Formative Years of Aboriginal Celebrities of the 1950s." *ISAA Review* 6, no. 1 (2007): 6–15.

Moore, T. Inglis. "Aboriginal Poet: Technique Has Matured." *Canberra Times*, 17 December 1966, 13.

Moran, Anthony. "White Australia, Settler Nationalism and Aboriginal Assimilation." *Australian Journal of Politics and History* 51, no. 2 (2005): 168–93.

Morgan, Cecilia. *Travellers through Empire: Indigenous Voyages from Early Canada*. Montreal and Kingston: McGill-Queen's University Press, 2017.

Morin, Brandi. "Standing Rock Music Video Hip-Hop Artists Take Home MTV VMA." CBC News, 28 August 2017. https://www.cbc.ca/news/indigenous/standing-rock-music-video-hip-hop-artists-take-home-mtv-vma-1.4265830 (accessed 7 March 2019).

Muehlenbach, Andrea. "'Making Place' at the United Nations: Indigenous Cultural Politics at the U.N. Working Group on Indigenous Populations." *Cultural Anthropology: Journal of the Society for Cultural Anthropology* 16, no. 3 (2001): 415–48.

Muehlmann, Shaylih. "Von Humboldt's Parrot and the Countdown of Last Speakers in the Colorado Delta." *Language and Communication* 32, no. 2 (2012): 160–68.

Mulvey, Laura. "Visual Pleasure and Narrative Cinema." *Screen* 16, no. 3 (1975): 6–18.

Mumm, Gregory, and Donna O'Connor. "The Motivational Profile of Professional Male Fijian Rugby Players and Their Perceptions of Coaches' and Managers' Cultural Awareness." *Asia Pacific Journal of Sport and Social Science* 3, no. 3 (2014): 202–21.

Murphy, Tab, Tom Berenger, and Barbara Hershey. 1995. *Last of the Dogmen*. [S.l.]: Veronica.

Murray, Steve. "No One Said There Would Be Blood: Steve Murray at the Justin Trudeau Boxing Match." *National Post*, 2 April, 2012. https://nationalpost.com/news/canada/no-one-said-there-would-be-blood-steve-murray-at-the-justin-trudeau-boxing-match (accessed 13 September 2020).

Nabobo-Baba, Unaisi. "Decolonising Framings in Pacific Research: Indigenous FijianVanua Research Framework as an Organic Response." *AlterNative: An International Journal of Indigenous Peoples* 4, no. 2 (2008): 140–54.

National Post. "Tory Senator Apologizes for Calling Reporter a Bitch after Report on Poor Attendance Record." *National Post*, 27 June 2013. https://nationalpost.com/news/canada/patrick-brazeau-jennifer-ditchburn (accessed 13 September 2020).

National Rugby League Game Development, *Pasifika Participation Data.* Sydney: National Rugby League, LeagueNet, 2017.

NGO Committee on Human Rights. *Report of International NGO Conference on Discrimination against Indigenous Populations in the Americas—1977.* Geneva: United Nations, 1978.

Niezen, Ronald. *The Origins of Indigenism: Human Rights and the Politics of Identity*. Berkeley: University of California Press, 2003.

Nuwer, Rachel. "Languages: Why we must save dying tongues." BBC Future. 5 June 2014 https://www.bbc.com/future/article/20140606-why-we-must-save-dying-languages (accessed 12 August 2015).

O'Brien, Jean M. *Firsting and Lasting: Writing Indians Out of Existence in New England*. Minneapolis: University of Minnesota Press, 2010.

Ohanian, Roobina. "Construction and Validation of a Scale to Measure Celebrity Endorsers' Perceived Expertise, Trustworthiness, and Attractiveness." *Journal of Advertising* 19, no. 3 (1990): 39–52.

———. "The Impact of Celebrity Spokespersons' Perceived Image on Consumers' Intention to Purchase." *Journal of Advertising Research* 31, no. 1 (1991): 46–54.

Osmond, Gary. "The Nimble Savage: Press Constructions of Pacific Islander Swimmers in Early Twentieth-Century Australia." *Media International Australia* 157 (2015): 133–43.

Otsuka, Setsuo. "Talanoa Research: Culturally Appropriate Research Design in Fiji." Paper presented at the International Education Research Conference, Melbourne, 2005.

Ottawa Citizen. "Patrick Brazeau's Two-Year Downward Spiral." *Ottawa Citizen*, 20 May 2014. https://ottawacitizen.com/news/local-news/brazeaus-two-year-downward-spiral (accessed 27 November 2017).

"The *Ottawa Journal* from Ottawa, Ontario, Canada Page 8." 8 May 1968. Newspapers.com. https://www.newspapers.com/newspage/44459699/ (accessed 27 November 2017).

Otunuku, Mo'ale. "How Can Talanoa Be Used Effectively as an Indigenous Research Methodology with Tongan People?" *Pacific-Asian Education* 23, no. 2 (2011): 43–52.

Palanichamy, Malliya Gounder, et al. "Comment on 'Reconstructing the Origin of Andaman Islanders.'" *Science* 311, no. 5760 (2006): 470.

Palmer, Farah, and T.M. Masters. "Maori Feminism and Sport Leadership: Exploring Māori Women's Experiences." *Sport Management Review* 13, no. 4 (2010): 331–44.

Panapa, Lameko, and Murray Phillips. "Ethnic Persistence: Towards Understanding the Lived Experiences of Pacific Island Athletes in the National Rugby League." *International Journal of the History of Sport* 31, no. 11 (2014): 1374–88.

Pandya, Vishvajit. "Contacts, Images and Imagination: The Impact of a Road in the Jarwa Reserve Forest, Andaman Islands." *Bijdragen Tot de Taal-, Land-En Volkenkunde* 158, no. 4 (2002): 799–820.

Paul Revere and The Raiders. *Indian Reservation (The Lament of the Cherokee Reservation Indian)* [vinyl]. Columbia, 1971.

Pearson, Joseph, and Clay Wilson. "Nigel Vagana Says Ignorance Is No Excuse after Matty Johns Show Is Accused of Casual Racism." Stuff. 26 August 2017. https://www.stuff.co.nz/sport/league/96183528/nigel-vagana-says-ignorance-is-no-excuse-after-matty-johns-show-isaccused-of-casual-racism (accessed 31 August 2017).

Pegoraro, Rob. "The 'No Nukes' Concert, with Bonnie Raitt." *Washington Post*, 27 September 1997. https://www.washingtonpost.com/archive/lifestyle/1997/09/27/the-no-nukes-concert-with-bonnie-raitt/0d0f8d8a-e4e5-4a39-a44f-a4039715052f/?noredirect=on&utm_term=.5e51531ed8ab (accessed 7 March 2019).

Perley, Bernard C. "Zombie Linguistics: Experts, Endangered Languages and the Curse of Undead Voices." *Anthropological Forum* 22, no. 2 (2012): 133–49.

Petersen, David. *Ishi: The Last of His People*. Picture-Story Biographies. Chicago: Children's Press, 1991.

Phillips, Stephanie. "The Kahnawake Mohawk and the St. Lawrence Seaway." PhD Diss. Montréal: McGill University, 2000.

Popoola, Rosemary, Matthew Egharevba, and Oluyemi Oyenike Fayomi. "Celebrity Advocacy and Women's Rights in Nigeria." *Journal of Asian and African Studies* 56, no. 1 (2020): 1–16.

Press Information Bureau. Ministry of Tribal Affairs. Government of India. "Punishment for Exploitation of Tribals in Andaman and Nicobar Islands." 30 November 2012. https://pib.gov.in/newsite/PrintRelease.aspx?relid=89726 (accessed 5 March 2020).

Puletua, Frank. "Chocolate Soldier: The Emergence of Pacific Players in the NRL." 15th Annual Tom Brock Lecture. Sydney: Tom Brock Bequest Committee and the Australian Society for Sports History, 2014.

Pulotu-Endemann, Fuimaono K., et al. *Seitapu Pacific Mental Health and Addiction Clinical and Cultural Competencies Framework*. Auckland: Te Pou, 2007.

Rainwater, Marvin. *The Pale Faced Indian*[vinyl]. MGM Records, 1959.

Ramsland, John, and Christopher Mooney. *Remembering Aboriginal Heroes: Struggle, Identity and the Media*. Melbourne: Brolga Publishing, 2006.

Rao, V. Srinivasa. *Adivasi Rights and Exclusion in India*. New York: Routledge, 2018.

Ratley, Neil, and Shane de Barra. "Former Queensland State of Origin Star Billy Moore under Fire over 'Coconut' Remark." *Sydney Morning Herald*, 30 July 2015. https://www.smh.com.au/sport/nrl/former-queensland-state-of-origin-star-billy-moore-under-fireover-coconut-remark-20150730-gioa9l.html (accessed 1 August 2015).

Ravulo, Jioji. *Pacific Communities in Australia*. Sydney: University of Western Sydney, 2015.

Raymond, Emilie. *Stars for Freedom: Hollywood, Black Celebrities, and the Civil Rights Movement*. Seattle: University of Washington Press, 2015.

Red Bow, Buddy. *Indian Reservation* [vinyl]. Native Spirit, 1981.

Reddy, Sunita. "Mega Tourism in Andaman and Nicobar Islands: Some Concerns." *Journal of Human Ecology* 21, no. 3 (2007): 231–39.

Redmond, Sean, and Su Holmes. "Introduction." In *Stardom and Celebrity: A Reader*, edited by Sean Redmond and Su Holmes, 13–16. Los Angeles: SAGE, 2007.

Reel Injun. Directed by Neil Diamond, Catherine Bainbridge, Jeremiah Hayes, Christina Fon, and Linda Ludwick. Lorber Films, 2010.

Rickett, Oscar. "An Interview with a Member of a Human Safari Tribe." *Vice*, 18 February 2013. https://www.vice.com/en_au/article/bnykw5/everyone-needs-to-stop-exploiting- the-jara-wa-tribe (accessed 5 March 2020).

Rise on Fire. *A Missionary Dies for the Gospel—John Allen Chau*. 2018. https://www.youtube.com/watch?v=DMhCPfA4RTk (accessed 5 March 2020).

Ritchie, Dean. "Warriors' Culture Slammed as Club Sinks to 'Soul-Destroying' Nine-Game Losing Streak." *Daily Telegraph*, 6 March 2016. https://www.dailytelegraph.com.au/sport/nrl/warriors-culture-slammed-as-club-sinks-to-souldestroying-ninegame-losingstreak/news-story/daf5a011898cdcbfb67b285c9c292014 (accessed 7 March 2016).

Rivenburgh, Nancy K. "Media Framing of Complex Issues: The Case of Endangered Languages." *Public Understanding of Science* 22, no. 6 (2013): 704–17.

Roberts, Pamela, and Jed Riffe. *Ishi: The Last Yahi*. Directed by Rattlesnake Productions. Berkeley Media, 1993.

Robertson, Carmen. "'Indian Princess/Indian Squaw': Representations of Indigenous Women in Canada's Printed Press." In *Culture and Power: Identity and Identification*, edited by Angel Mateos-Aparicio Martin-Albo and Eduardo de Gregorio-Godeo, 129–45. Newcastle upon Tyne, UK: Cambridge Scholars, 2013.

Rojek, Chris. "Celebrity." In *Wiley-Blackwell Encyclopedia of Consumption and Consumer Studies*, edited by Daniel Thomas Cook and J. Michael Ryan, 1–3. New York: Wiley-Blackwell, 2015.

———. *Celebrity*. London: Reaktion Books, 2001.

———. "Celebrity and Celetoid." In *The Blackwell Encyclopedia of Sociology*. 15 February 2007. https://doi.org/10.1002/9781405165518.wbeosc013 (accessed 23 June 2017).

———. *Fame Attack: The Inflation of Celebrity and Its Consequences*. New York: Bloomsbury Academic, 2012.

Romancito, M. Elwell. "Two Taos Concerts Set to Benefit Standing Rock." *Taos News*, 28 November 2016. https://taosnews.com/stories/two-taos-concerts-set-to-benefit-standing-rock,20177 (accessed 7 March 2019).

"A Rose from the Dust." *Daily Mirror*, 10 December 1984, 32. Cutting held in National Library of Australia, Canberra, Biographical Cuttings on Lionel Rose, Boxing Champion, Containing One or More Cuttings from Newspapers or Journals.

Rose, Samantha, Max Quanchi, and Clive Moore. *A National Strategy for the Study of the Pacific*. Brisbane: Australian Association for the Advancement of Pacific Studies, 2009.

Rosenbaum, Cary. "Wes Studi Shares #NoDAPL Experience with the Traveling NDN." *Tribal Tribune*, 21 October 2016. http://www.tribaltribune.com/opinion/article_bc3f91f4-955a-11e6-86f2-fb-306f47a8dc.html (accessed 6 March 2019).

Rowe, David. "Rugby League in Australia: The Super League Saga." *Journal of Sport and Social Issues* 21, no. 2 (1997): 221–26.

Rowe, Gordon. *Sketches of Outstanding Aborigines*. [Adelaide?]: [Aborigines' Friends' Association?], [1956?].

Rowse, Tim. "Contesting Assimilation." In *Contesting Assimilation*, edited by Tim Rowse, 1–24. Perth: API Network, 2005.

Ryan, Greg. *The Changing Face of Rugby: The Union Game and Professionalism since 1995*. Newcastle, UK: Cambridge Scholars Publishing, 2008.

Safi, Michael, and Denis Giles. "India Has No Plans to Recover Body of US Missionary Killed by Tribe." *Guardian*, 28 November 2018, sec. "World News." https://www.theguardian.com/world/2018/nov/28/india-body-john-allen-chau- missionary-killed-by-sentinelese-tribe (accessed 5 March 2020).

Saini, Ajay. "The Lesson from This Missionary's Death? Leave the Sentinelese Alone." *Guardian*, 27 November 2018, sec. "Opinion." https://www.theguardian.com/commentisfree/2018/nov/27/missionary-death-sentinelese- andaman-islands (accessed 5 March 2020).

Salazar, Noel B. "Imagineering Otherness: Anthropological Legacies in Contemporary Tourism." *Anthropological Quarterly* 86, no. 3 (2013): 669–96.

Samu, Kathleen S., and Tamasailau Suaalii-Sauni. "Exploring the 'Cultural' in Cultural Competencies in Pacific Mental Health." *Pacific Health Dialog* 15, no. 1 (2009): 120–30.

Sanchez, John, and Mary E. Stuckey. "The Rhetoric of American Indian Activism in the 1960s and 1970s." *Communication Quarterly* 48, no. 2 (2000): 120–36.

Sarkar, Sonia. "India's Marginalised Minorities Unite against Hindu Nationalism." *South China Morning Post* [Hong Kong], 23 February 2020, sec. "This Week in Asia." https://www.scmp.com/week-asia/politics/article/3051781/marginalised-under-modi-how-indias-minorities-are-starting-stand (accessed 5 March 2020).

Saul, John Ralston. *A Fair Country: Telling Truths about Canada*. Abingdon: Penguin Canada, 2009.

Schaaf, Matani. "Elite Pacific Male Rugby Players' Perceptions and Experiences of Professional Rugby." *Journal of Thematic Dialogue* 7 (2006): 41–54.

Sen, Asoka Kumar. *Indigeneity, Landscape and History: Adivasi Self-Fashioning in India*. New Delhi: Routledge India, 2017.

Sen, Satadru. "Savage Bodies, Civilized Pleasures: MV Portman and the Andamanese." *American Ethnologist* 36, no. 2 (2009): 364–79.

Senft, Theresa M. *Camgirls: Celebrity and Community in the Age of Social Networks*. New York: Peter Lang, 2008.

———. "Microcelebrity and the Branded Self." In *A Companion to New Media Dynamics*, edited by John Hartley, Jean Burgess, and Axel Bruns, 346–55. New York: Wiley-Blackwell, 2013.

Seven Generations Education Institute. "Mino-Bimaadiziwin, Principles." http://www.7generations.org/?page_id=104 (accessed 29 November 2017).

———. "The Seven Grandfather Teachings, The Seven Teachings." http://www.7generations.org/?page_id=2396 (accessed 29 November 2017).

Shenandoah and Bucher Making Bitter Tears—Sacred Ground. YouTube. 24 January 2009. https://www.youtube.com/watch?v=Tmij0O-T7JU (accessed 25 October 2016).

Shiu, Roannie Ng. "Sports Diplomacy in the Pacific: Developing Pacific Rugby League Elite Athletes for Diplomacy and Development." In *State, Society and Governance in Melanesia*. Canberra: Australian National University, 2016.

Shiva, Vandana. *Growth=Poverty*. Festival of Dangerous Ideas 2013. 10 November 2013. https://www.youtube.com/watch?v=7M3WJQbnHKc&t=2724s (accessed 5 March 2020).

Shoemaker, Adam. *Black Words White Page: Aboriginal Literature, 1929–1988*. 3rd ed. Canberra: ANU E Press, 2004.

Silko, Leslie Marmon. *Ceremony*. New York: Penguin Books, 1977.

Simpson, Audra. *Mohawk Interruptus: Political Life across the Borders of Settler States*. Durham, NC: Duke University Press, 2014.

———. "On Ethnographic Refusal: Indigeneity, 'Voice' and Colonial Citizenship." *Junctures: The Journal for Thematic Dialogue* 9 (2007): 67–80.

———. "Reconciliation and Its Discontents: Settler Governance in an Age of Sorrow." Public lecture, University of Saskatchewan, 22 March 2016. https://www.youtube.com/watch?v=vGl9HkzQsGg.

Simpson, Katie. "Trudeau 'Regrets' Comments in *Rolling Stone* about Senator Patrick Brazeau." CBC News, 1 August 2017. https://www.cbc.ca/news/politics/trudeau-regrets-rolling-stone-comments-brazeau-1.4230498.

Simpson, Leanne Betasamosake. *As We Have Always Done: Indigenous Freedom through Radical Resistance*. Minneapolis: University of Minnesota Press, 2017.

———. *Dancing on Our Turtle's Back: Stories of Nishnaabeg Re-Creation, Resurgence and a New Emergence*. Winnipeg: Arbeiter Ring Publications, 2011.

Skene, Patrick. "The Forgotten Story of Olsen Filipaina, the Polynesian Who Tamed Wally Lewis." *Guardian*, 30 April 2015. http://www.theguardian.com/sport/blog/2015/apr/30/the-forgotten-story-of-olsen-filipaina (accessed 30 April 2015).

Smith, Linda Tuhiwai. *Decolonizing Methodologies: Research and Indigenous Peoples*. 2nd ed. London: Zed Books, 2012.

Smoke Signals. Directed by Sherman Alexie. Produced by Sherman Alexie, Chris Eyre, Scott Rosenfelt, and Larry Estes. Performed by Adam Beach, Evan Adams, Irene Bedard, Gary Farmer, and Tantoo Cardinal. Miramax Films, 1998.

Soundararajan, Thenmozhi. "Twitter's Caste Problem." *New York Times*, 3 December 2018, sec. "Opinion." https://www.nytimes.com/2018/12/03/opinion/twitter-india-caste-trolls.html (accessed 5 March 2020).

Spencer, Paul. "Native Americans Are Resisting the Dakota Pipeline with Tech and Media Savvy." Motherboard. 29 October 2016. https://motherboard.vice.com/en_us/article/78kmw4/tech-behind-the-dakota-access-pipeline-protests (accessed 7 March 2019).

Spielmann, Roger. *"You're So Fat!" Exploring Ojibwe Discourse*. Toronto: University of Toronto Press, 1998.

Starn, Orin. *Ishi's Brain: In Search of America's Last "Wild" Indian*. New York: Norton, 2004.

Stevenson, Andrew. "Polys Put the Mettle On." *Sydney Morning Herald*, 28 February 2009. https://www.smh.com.au/sport/nrl/polys-put-the-mettle-on-20090228-gdte5i.html (accessed 27 April 2013).

Stewart-Withers, Rochelle, Koli Sewabu, and Sam Richardson. "Talanoa: A Contemporary Qualitative Methodology for Sport Management." *Sport Management Review* 20, no.1 (2017): 55–68.

Stronach, Megan, and Daryl Adair. "Dadirri: Using a Philosophical Approach to Research to Build Trust between a Non-Indigenous Researcher and Indigenous Participants." *Cosmopolitan Civil Societies: An Interdisciplinary Journal* 6, no. 2 (2014), 117–34.

Studi, Wes. "I'm on My Way to Standing Rock Today. I'll Be There as Long as I Can to Help with the Movement!" Twitter. 3 October 2016. https://twitter.com/wesleystudi/status/782951231031390208?lang=en (accessed 6 March 2019).

Suaalii-Sauni, Tamasailau, and Saunimaa M. Fulu Aiolupotea. "Decolonising Pacific Research, Building Pacific Research Communities and Developing Pacific Research Tools: The Case of the Talanoa and the Faafaletui in Samoa." *Asia Pacific Viewpoint* 55, no. 3 (2014): 331–44.

Suicide Squad. Directed by David Ayer. Performed by Will Smith, Jared Leto, and Margo Robie. Warner Brothers Home Entertainment, 2016.

Suslak, Daniel F. "Ayapan Echoes: Linguistic Persistence and Loss in Tabasco, Mexico." *American Anthropologist* 113, no. 4 (2011): 569–81.

Switzer, Maurice. "Opinion: Indigenous Cultural Police and Joseph Boyden." *Anishinabek News*, 5 September 2018. http://anishinabeknews.ca/2018/09/05/opinion-indigenous-cultural-police-and-joseph-boyden (accessed 21 February 2019).

Taboo. *Stand Up/Stand N Rock #NoDAPL (Official Video)*. YouTube. 4 December 2016. https://www.youtube.com/watch?v=Onyk7guvHK8 (accessed 7 March 2019).

"Taboo from Black Eyed Peas Speaks Out for Indigenous Rights." MSNBC. 10 March 2017. https://www.msnbc.com/msnbc-news/watch/taboo-from-black-eyed-peas-speaks-out-for-indigenous-rights-894974531542 (accessed 7 March 2019).

Tarbell, Reaghan, dir. *Little Caughnawaga: To Brooklyn and Back*. National Film Board of Canada, 2008.

Tauli-Corpuz, Victoria. Comments at the Seventh Session of the United Nations Permanent Forum on Indigenous Issues, New York, 2008.

Teaiwa, Katerina. "Niu Mana, Sport, Media and the Australian Diaspora." In *New Mana: Transformations of a Classic Concept in Pacific Languages and Cultures*, edited by Matt Tomlinson and Ty P. Kawika Tengan, 107–30. Acton, Australia: ANU Press, 2016.

———. "On Analogies: Rethinking the Pacific in a Global Context." *Contemporary Pacific* 18, no. 1 (2006): 71–87.

———. "Reframing Oceania: Lessons from Pacific Studies." In *Framing the Global: Entry Points for Research*, edited by Hilary E. Kahn, 67–96. Bloomington: Indiana University Press, 2014.

Tengan, Ty P. Kawika, and Jesse M. Markham. "Performing Polynesian Masculinities in American Football: From 'Rainbows' to Warriors." *International Journal of the History of Sport* 26, no. 16 (2009): 2412–31.

Thaman, Konai H. "Decolonizing Pacific Studies: Indigenous Perspectives, Knowledge, and Wisdom in Higher Education." *Contemporary Pacific* 15, no. 1 (2003): 1–17.

Than, Ker, and Chris Rainier. "See and Hear Last Speakers of Dying Languages." *National Geographic*, 18 February 2012. http://news.nationalgeographic.com/news/2012/02/pictures/120217-talking-dictionaries-vanishing-languages-science-hear-audio/ (accessed 27 January 2016).

Thapar, Romila. "They Peddle Myths and Call It History." *New York Times*, 17 May 2019, sec. "Opinion." https://www.nytimes.com/2019/05/17/opinion/india-elections-modi-history.html (accessed 5 March 2020).

Thomas, Cora. "From 'Australian Aborigines' to 'White Australians.'" *Australian Aboriginal Studies* 1 (2001): 22–23.

Thomas, Daniel. "Albert Namatjira and the Worlds of Art: A Re-Evaluation." In *Albert Namatjira: The Life and Work of an Australian Painter*, edited by Nadine Amadio, Anne Blackwell, Jonah Jones, and Daniel Thomas, 21–26. South Melbourne, Australia: Macmillan, 1986.

Thomas, Laurie. "Namatjira: Tragic Symbol of a Lost People." *Woman's Day with Woman*, 27 October 1958, n. pag. Cutting held in National Library of Australia, Canberra, Biographical Cuttings on Albert Namatjira, Artist, Containing One or More Cuttings from Newspapers or Journals.

Thomas, Sonja. "The Women's Wall in Kerala, India, and Brahmanical Patriarchy." *Feminist Studies* 45, no. 1 (2019): 253–261.

Thurman, Judith. "A Loss for Words: Can a Dying Language Be Saved?" *New Yorker*, 30 March 2015. http://www.newyorker.com/magazine/2015/03/30/a-loss-for-words (accessed 16 February 2016).

Tomlinson, Matt, and Ty P. Kawika Tengan, eds. *New Mana: Transformations of a Classic Concept in Pacific Languages and Cultures.* Canberra: ANU Press, 2016.

Turner, Graeme. "The Mass Production of Celebrity: 'Celetoids,' Reality TV and the 'Demotic Turn.'" *International Journal of Cultural Studies* 9, no. 2 (2006): 153–65.

———. *Understanding Celebrity.* London: SAGE, 2013.

Turner, Graeme, Frances Bonner, and P. David Marshall. *Fame Games: The Production of Celebrity in Australia.* Cambridge, UK: Cambridge University Press, 2000.

"Two Years till Wimbledon?" *Dawn* 17, no. 3 (1968): 1.

UNESCO Ad Hoc Expert Group on Endangered Languages. "Language Vitality and Endangerment." 2003.

Uperesa, Fa'anofo L., and Tom Mountjoy. "Global Sport in the Pacific: A Brief Overview." *Contemporary Pacific* 26, no. 2 (2014): 263–79.

Vaioleti, Timote M. "Talanoa Research Methodology: A Developing Position on Pacific Research." *Waikato Journal of Education* 12, no. 1 (2006): 21–34.

Valiotis, Chris. "Suburban Footballers of Pacific Islander Ancestry: The Changing Face of Rugby League in Greater Western Sydney." In *Centenary Reflections: 100 Years of Rugby League in Australia*, edited by Andrew Moore and Andy Carr, 141–56. Melbourne: Australian Society for Sports History, 2008.

van Gastel, Ada. "Van Der Donck's Description of the Indians: Additions and Corrections." *William and Mary Quarterly* 47, no. 3 (1990): 411–21.

Van Toorn, Penny. "Indigenous Texts and Narratives." In *The Cambridge Companion to Australian Literature*, edited by Elizabeth Webby, 19–49. Cambridge, UK: Cambridge University Press, 2000.

Waghule, Pradnya. "Reading Caste in Holi: The Burning of Holika, a Bahujan Woman." *Feminism in India*, 12 March 2017. https://feminisminindia.com/2017/03/13/caste-holi-burning-holika-bahujan/ (accessed 5 March 2020).

Waterhouse, Richard. "Australian Legends: Representations of the Bush, 1813–1913." *Australian Historical Studies* 31, no. 115 (2000): 201–21.

Weaver, Andrew J. "The Role of Actors' Race in White Audiences' Selective Exposure to Movies." *Journal of Communication* 61, no. 2 (2011): 369–85.

Weiss, Jeffrey. "Celebs Line Up to Oppose a Pipeline across Rural West Texas Landscape." *Dallas News*, 10 June 2016. https://www.dallasnews.com/business/energy/2016/06/10/celebs-line-oppose-pipeline-across-rural-west-texasnbsplandscape (accessed 7 March 2019).

Wheeler, Mark. *Celebrity Politics.* Cambridge, UK: Polity, 2013.

White Wolf. "From Standing Rock to Washington: Actor Wes Studi Is Everywhere as a Water Protector." *White Wolf Pack*, March 2017. http://www.whitewolfpack.com/2017/03/from-standing-rock-to-washington-actor.html (accessed 7 March 2019).

Whitinui, Paul. "Indigenous Autoethnography: Exploring, Engaging, and Experiencing 'Self' as a Native Method of Inquiry." *Journal of Contemporary Ethnography* 43, no. 4 (2013): 456–87.

Wickline, Dan. "Taboo of the Black Eyed Peas Becomes Marvel's Red Wolf." Bleeding Cool News and Rumors. 24 July 2017. https://www.bleedingcool.com/2017/07/24/taboo-black-eyed-peas-marvels-red-wolf/ (accessed 6 March 2019).

Willard, Tim. "The Big Difference between the Celebrity Leader and the Devoted Leader." *Church Leaders*, 12 December 2014. https://churchleaders.com/pastors/pastor-articles/244313-big-difference-celebrity-leader-devoted-leader.html (accessed 5 March 2020).

Wilmer, Franke. *The Indigenous Voice in World Politics: Since Time Immemorial.* Newbury Park, CA: SAGE, 1993.

Windtalkers. Directed by John Woo. Performed by Adam Beach, Nicolas Cage, and Peter Stormare. Lion Rock Productions and Metro Goldwyn Mayer/MGM Distribution Company, 2002.

Wissot, Lauren. "Sterlin Harjo on the Dos and Don'ts of Filming in Indian Country." International Documentary Association. 18 October 2017. https://www.documentary.org/online-feature/sterlin-harjo-dos-and-donts-filming-indian-country (accessed 6 March 2019).

Wolff, Kristina. "Strategic Essentialism." In *Blackwell Encyclopedia of Sociology.* Online: John Wiley and Sons, 2007. https://doi.org/10.1002/9781405165518.wbeoss268 (accessed 5 March 2020).

Wolff, Kurt, and Orla Duane. *Country Music: The Rough Guide.* London: Rough Guides, 2000.

Wong, Jessica. "Joseph Boyden Sorry 'for Taking Too Much of the Airtime' on Indigenous Issues." CBC News, 11 January 2017. https://www.cbc.ca/news/entertainment/boyden-cbc-indigenous-roots-1.3931284 (accessed 15 January 2020).

Yadav, Sidharth. "Modi Must See Dalit-Adivasi Unity against CAA: Yogendra Yadav." *Hindu,* 28 January 2020, sec. "Other States." https://www.thehindu.com/news/national/other-states/modi-must-see-dalit-adivasi-unity-against-caa-yogendra-yadav/article30670311.ece (accessed 5 March 2020).

Yakabuski, Konrad. "Attacks on Joseph Boyden's Identity Should Set Off Alarm Bells." *Globe and Mail,* 29 December 2016. https://www.theglobeandmail.com/opinion/attacks-on-joseph-boydens-identity-should-set-off-alarm-bells/article33444228 (accessed 21 February 2019).

York, Lorraine. "Celebrity and the Cultivation of Indigenous Publics in Canada." In *Celebrity Cultures in Canada,* edited by Katja Lee and Lorraine York, 93–110. Waterloo, ON: Wilfrid Laurier University Press, 2016.

Young, James O., and Susan Haley. "'Nothing Comes from Nowhere': Reflections on Cultural Appropriation as the Representation of Other Cultures." In *The Ethics of Cultural Appropriation,* edited by James O. Young and Conrad G. Brunk, 268–89. Chichester, UK: Wiley-Blackwell, 2009.

Zakus, Dwight, and Peter Horton. "Pasifika in Australian Rugby: Emanant Cultural, Social and Economic Issues." *Sporting Traditions* 26, no. 2 (2009): 67–86.

Zehmisch, Philipp. "Between Mini-India and Sonar Bangla: The Memorialisation and Place-Making Practices of East Bengal Hindu Refugees in the Andaman Islands." In *Partition and the Practice of Memory,* edited by Churnjeet Mahn and Anne Murphy, 63–88. Cham, Switzerland: Springer, 2018.

Contributors

Daryl Adair is an Associate Professor of Sport Management at the University of Technology Sydney. He has interests in sport management, sport history, Olympic Games, ethnicity, and indigeneity of sport.

Jennifer Adese (Otipemisiwak/Métis) is a Canada Research Chair in Métis Women, Politics, and Community and an Associate Professor in the Department of Sociology at the University of Toronto Mississauga. Jennifer is co-editor (with Chris Andersen) of *A People and a Nation: New Directions in Contemporary Métis Studies* (UBC Press, 2021). Her work has appeared in *TOPIA*, *American Indian Quarterly*, *SAIL: Studies in American Indian Literatures*, *MediaTropes*, *Decolonization: Indigeneity, Education and Society* (*DIES*), *PUBLIC*, and appears in select edited anthologies on Indigenous art, representation, and resistance.

Kim Anderson is Cree/Metis and Associate Professor in Family Relations and Applied Nutrition at the University of Guelph. She is the author of many books, including *A Recognition of Being: Reconstructing Native Womanhood* (Canadian Scholars Press, revised edition, 2015), *Life Stages and Native Women: Memory, Teachings, and Story Medicine* (University of Manitoba

Press, 2011), and she co-edited with Robert Alexander Innes, *Indigenous Men and Masculinities: Legacies, Identities, Regeneration* (University of Manitoba Press, 2015).

Renée E. Mazinegiizhigoo-kwe Bédard is of Anishinaabeg (Ojibwe/ Nipissing/Omàmiwinini) and French-Canadian ancestry. She is a member of Okikendawt (Dokis First Nation). She holds a PhD from Trent University in Indigenous Studies. Currently, she is an Assistant Professor at Western University in the Faculty of Education. Her areas of publication include practices of Anishinaabeg motherhood and maternal philosophy and spirituality, along with environmental issues, women's rights, Indigenous Elders, Anishinaabeg artistic expressions, and Indigenous education.

Aadita Chaudhury is a PhD student at the Department of Science and Technology Studies at York University and a Graduate Associate at the York Centre for Asian Research. She holds a Master's degree in Environmental Studies from York University's Faculty of Environmental Studies, and a Bachelor of Applied Science at University of Toronto's Department of Chemical Engineering and Applied Chemistry. Her research surrounds the anthropology and philosophy of biology and the ecological sciences, cartography, postcolonial and feminist studies of science and technology, and environmental and medical humanities.

Jenny L. Davis is a citizen of the Chickasaw Nation and an Associate Professor of Anthropology and American Indian Studies at the University of Illinois, Urbana-Champaign where she is the director of the American Indian Studies Program. She is the author of *Talking Indian: Identity and Language Revitalization in the Chickasaw Renaissance* (University of Arizona Press, 2019) and *Trickster Academy* (University of Arizona Press, forthcoming).

Karen Fox is a Research Fellow at the National Centre of Biography in the School of History at the Australian National University, and a Research Editor for the *Australian Dictionary of Biography*. A historian of Australia and New Zealand, she researches honours systems, fame and celebrity, and biography. She is the author of *Māori and Aboriginal Women in the Public Eye: Representing Difference, 1950–2000* (ANU Press, 2011).

Christina Giacona is a lecturer at the University of Oklahoma and currently teaches courses in Native American, World, and Popular Music. She has commissioned and premiered over fifty new works since founding the Los Angeles New Music Ensemble in 2007, and produced five albums. She performs as a clarinetist with the Fort Smith Symphony and has published a Native American Music textbook through Kendall Hunt Publishing. Her most current research focuses on the ways Native Americans are stereotyped in American popular music, and she recently completed a National Endowment for the Humanities fellowship for her research at the Library of Congress.

Jonathan G. Hill is of Southeastern Indigenous descent. He is a PhD candidate at the University of Massachusetts Amherst, where his doctoral research focuses on Indigenous musicians in Northeastern Oklahoma and their influences in the production of mainstream American music. Jonathan has spent nearly a decade working with Indigenous communities in the Northeastern United States and has worked as cultural programmer and liaison, lead teacher, and as a researcher and panelist in the revolving state-sponsored assessment, Discussions for and with Massachusetts Native Peoples.

Brendan Hokowhitu of Ngāti Pukenga is Professor of Indigenous Studies in the Faculty of Māori and Indigenous Studies at the University of Waikato. Currently, Brendan is the President Elect of the Native American and Indigenous Studies Association. His influential publications include over sixty peer-reviewed journal articles and book chapters that helped lead to the creation of Indigenous masculinities, and critical Indigenous sports studies as sub-fields. Recently he was the lead editor of the *Routledge Handbook of Critical Indigenous Studies* (2020).

Kahente Horn-Miller (Kahente means "she walks ahead") (Kanien:keha'ka/Mohawk) is the Assistant Vice-President (Indigenous Initiatives), and Associate Professor in the School of Indigenous and Canadian Studies at Carleton University. The mother of four daughters, she is an active member of her community and a figurative bridge builder as she continues to research and write on issues that are relevant to her work and academic interests, such as Indigenous methodologies, Indigenous women, identity politics, colonization, Indigenous governance, and consensus-based decision making for her community and the wider society.

Robert Alexander Innes is a member of Cowessess First Nation and an Associate Professor in the Department of Indigenous Studies at the University of Saskatchewan. He is the author of *Elder Brother and the Law of the People: Cowessess First Nation and Contemporary Kinship* (2013) and is the co-editor, along with Kim Anderson, of *Indigenous Men and Masculinities: Legacies, Identities, Regeneration* (2015), both with the University of Manitoba Press.

David Lakisa is a PhD candidate at the University of Technology Sydney currently researching for his thesis, "Managing Pasifika in the National Rugby League." He has worked as the Pacific Islander coaching and development officer for the New South Wales Rugby League.

Sheryl Lightfoot is Anishinaabe, a citizen of the Lake Superior Band of Ojibwe, enrolled at the Keweenaw Bay Indian Community in Baraga, Michigan. She is a Canada Research Chair in Global Indigenous Rights and Politics and Associate Professor in First Nations and Indigenous Studies and Political Science at the University of British Columbia, where she also serves as Senior Adviser to the President on Indigenous Affairs. Widely published in numerous journals and books, her first book, *Global Indigenous Politics: A Subtle Revolution*, was published in 2016 by Routledge Press.

Virginia McLaurin earned a Master's Degree in Anthropology and a Graduate Certificate in Native American and Indigenous Studies from the University of Massachusetts Amherst where she is currently completing her PhD. Her research focuses on Indigenous representation in mainstream and independent media.

w. C. Sy is an Assistant Professor in Gender Studies at University of Victoria. Her work has appeared in *Keetsahnak, Our Missing and Murdered Indigenous Sisters* (University of Alberta Press, 2018), edited by Kim Anderson, Maria Campbell, and Christi Belcourt; *Reshaping Women's*

History: Voices of Nontraditional Women Historians (University of Illinois Press, 2018), edited by Julie Gallagher and Barbara Winslow; and, *Unsettling Activisms: Critical Interventions on Aging, Gender, and Social Change* (Canadian Scholars Press, 2018), edited by May Chazan, Melissa Baldwin, and Patricia Evans. Her poetry appears in *Contemporary Verse 2* and *The New Quarterly*; and, in *Gush: Menstrual Manifestos for our Times* (Frontenac House, 2018), edited by Rosanna Deerchild, Ariel Gordon, and Tanis MacDonald.

Tracy Taylor is the Dean for the Murdoch Business School in Perth, Australia. Her research covers people management, executive leadership development, cultural diversity, and volunteer management.

Katerina Teaiwa is an Associate Professor in the School of Culture, History, and Language at the Australian National University. Her research areas look at Pacific studies, history, and performing arts.

Index

J

K

L

M

N

O

P

R

S